THE ULTIMATE EU TEST BOOK

THE ULTIMATE EU TEST BOOK

by

András Baneth and Gyula Cserey

JOHN HARPER
PUBLISHING

Published by John Harper Publishing
27 Palace Gates Road
London N22 7BW, United Kingdom.

www.johnharperpublishing.co.uk

ISBN 0–9543811–9–X

Typeset in 9 & 10/11pt Palatino

Printed and Bound in Great Britain by Biddles Ltd.

First published in 2005;
second impression 2005

TABLE OF CONTENTS

QUESTIONS

ANSWERS

ABOUT THE AUTHORS

András Baneth is a lawyer working for the Court of Justice of the European Communities in Luxembourg. He holds an M.A. in law and political sciences from Szeged University, Hungary, and the degree of Master of European Public Administration from the College of Europe, Brugge, Belgium. He has previously participated in several academic and traineeship programmes in the USA, France, Spain and Hungary, and also worked for the Hungarian Parliament. He is the author of several articles and a frequent guest lecturer at academic seminars.

Gyula Cserey is a lawyer working for the European Commission in Brussels. He holds an M.A. in law and political sciences from the Pázmány Péter Catholic University, Hungary. He has taken part in various academic programmes and projects in the USA and Hungary, and also worked for a leading international law firm and the European Parliament. He is the author of numerous academic articles and a frequent contributor to leading periodicals.

The text was proof read by Jacqueline Keresztény.

FOREWORD

EU headquarters in Brussels, Luxembourg and Strasbourg are not only important institutions for Europe and the outside world, but they are also attractive working places for many. High professional standards, meaningful jobs and relatively good salaries explain the keen competition for vacant places in the various offices. Above all, young people are motivated to spend some time with an EU institution to obtain experience.

The entry procedure is based on high requirements of the applicants. They should know many important details about the structure, history and functioning of the sophisticated integration machinery. The present test book can be of great help offering a systematic preparation for the entry exam. The authors passed this exam with success and collected the multifold experience of others, too. By discovering the answers to all the questions an applicant can be well prepared for it over a short period.

Working with the EU is a useful exercise for all those who are interested in politics, business and law in Europe but can offer a rich experience for many others dealing with any particular field of governance, regulation or control. Integration rules and events are present in the every day life of our Continent. The present test book also may be useful for persons who are not directly interested in using it to obtain a job, but who might wish to test their knowledge of European issues. Therefore, this volume is an excellent tool for achieving any of these goals.

Prof. Dr. Péter Balázs
Former Member of the European Commission

INTRODUCTION

The purpose of the book

This volume was written specifically as a practical guide to enable the reader to test their knowledge of the European Union (EU). In addition to testing familiarity with the historical growth of the EU, its institutions and policies, the questions aim at highlighting recent trends and developments. *The Ultimate EU Test Book* is intended to help students and professionals alike in any discipline, who wish to test their understanding of EU developments. Furthermore, this book has the clear and practical objective of facilitating preparation for the recruitment exams organised on a regular basis by the European Personnel Selection Office (EPSO).

How the book is organised

The *Ultimate EU Test Book* is divided into three parts:
The first part of the book gives information on recruitment into the EU institutions. This part contains a set of "have to knows" and "nice to knows" based on the experience of the authors. It also presents topic hints for an essay and a collection of recommended websites. When choosing the essay subjects, the authors relied upon their personal experience and current events that may serve as a good resource for essay topics.

The second and third parts contain, respectively, the questions and answers for tests that are designed to help the user prepare to answer multiple choice tests and verbal and numerical reasoning tests under time-pressure and challenging wording. These materials introduce the user to the kinds of questions to be answered when taking EU knowledge tests (including EPSO tests), and include hints for responding to the different kinds of questions. Even though the questions are principally aimed at those taking part in a recruitment procedure, they can efficiently and powerfully test anyone's knowledge of the European Union.

The answer keys contain a summary grid showing which answers are correct, followed by further explanation. These answer keys are not meant to replace traditional textbooks, but rather to assist in a quick recall of events, names and various important data while checking the answers. The layout of the answer keys lends itself to a smooth and fast check and it may also be helpful to successfully identify the essence of the given issue. Where we believe that further reading may be useful, we indicate the most relevant sources and other related websites to be consulted.

Practice – and keep up to date

As a general remark, *The Ultimate EU Test Book* is not meant to be a substitute for learning. Therefore, it may be of little use to someone with a limited knowledge on the relevant subject matters. Once again, its aim is to provide a thought-provoking tool for rehearsal and self-testing. We also recommend the reader to practice the sample tests several times. This is the best way to get ready for the real test.

Furthermore, this book is not meant to be the last word on certain points that are subject to different opinions among contemporary sources. Considering that European integration is a constantly evolving and developing process, there are issues such as the European Constitution on which leading contemporary experts disagree. Therefore when presenting such issues, we only consider the established facts or issues where a consensus had been reached; differing views are tackled on a limited scale only.

Despite our greatest efforts to be thorough and up-to-date to the fullest possible extent, some information may have become outdated since the manuscript was submitted. Therefore we strongly advise keeping track of the news and latest developments in the major EU policy areas.

The task that lies ahead of anyone seeking a better understanding of how the European Union works and wishes to test his or her knowledge is undoubtedly very challenging. We hope that *The Ultimate EU Test Book* will help guide the user safely down the road in this direction.

András Baneth and Gyula Cserey

Brussels and Luxembourg, October 2005

For updated information related to this book, visit our website
www.eu-testbook.com

While every effort has been made to reflect the character of questions set in the concours, the authors have no affiliation with the European Personnel Selection Office (EPSO) or any other EU or non-EU recruitment office or agency and all questions in this book have been independently compiled.

THE EUROPEAN UNION'S PERSONNEL SELECTION AND RECRUITMENT PROCESS

Introduction

There are always a huge number of applicants who attempt to pass the open competitions knowing that this is the only way to become a full-fledged official of the European Union. Generally speaking, planned open competitions can be found in a provisional timetable on the website of the European Personnel Selection Office (EPSO)[1] – with an approximate indication of the exam dates. When the actual announcement is made, it is usually published in the press. Competitions usually attract significant media attention and therefore those who follow news on a regular basis will certainly know this information.

Due to the exclusive nature of the competitions, EPSO cannot consider any applications or CVs that are submitted outside the framework of an official competition.

The Recruitment Procedure

The recruitment procedure takes roughly one year from the time of publication until the drawing up of the reserve list. If we also include the time of actual appointment to a certain position, this procedure may last a few months more. The course of the recruitment procedure and the most important have-to-knows are summarised below.

Publication of the open competition in the Official Journal of the European Union

The official notice of competition is published in the Official Journal of the European Union (OJ) and it is considered to be the only official source of information. "Official" means that in case of any dispute, misunderstanding or erroneous information the text contained in the OJ notice of competition is the only reference.

The OJ appears on a daily basis and has three different editions. Competition notices are published in the "C" series that deal with communications and other notices. The easiest and most convenient way to read the competition notice is to consult the OJ on-line which is free of charge.

The OJ gives the specific conditions and requirements for the given competition, along with an indication of the number of posts available and information concerning the competition itself: who may apply, which prerequisites are to be met, deadlines etc.

On-line applications

Application for the majority of open competitions is done on-line. This is not only more convenient for the applicants but helps EPSO sort out those who do not qualify to sit the exams due to their nationality, insufficient level of education or lack of any other compulsory precondition.

---

[1] http://www.europa.eu.int/epso

There are exceptions for persons with a disability which does not allow them to submit their application on-line.

Applications on paper

Apart from the on-line applications, there are some competitions that require a paper application. In such cases candidates should ask for a printed copy of the OJ that contains the notice of competition (those downloaded from the internet are generally not accepted) and the "optical reader" registration form that eventually will need to be sent by post. The optical reader form is a special paper that the EPSO will scan and process the information digitally. It is advisable therefore to write in legible capital letters in dark ink.

Expenses

As a rule, no contribution is made towards any travelling or subsistence expenses associated with the pre-selection and written test(s). However, there may be an entitlement to a flat-rate contribution to travelling and subsistence expenses (by car, train or airplane, depending on the distance) to attend an oral test. Notification is given of the applicable rates and the procedure to follow when an invitation to attend is issued.

Quota system

There is no national quota system for European civil servants, but the institutions aim to base their recruitment on a broad geographical balance among the different Member States.

Qualification and experience required to enter a competition

The general requirements to take part in a competition are:

- To be a citizen of a Member State (or a citizen of an accession country in the case of open competition organised for accession countries' nationals);
- To be entitled to full rights as a citizen;
- To have fulfilled any obligations imposed by laws on completing military service;
- To meet the required personal criteria for the duties involved.

Some competitions require a minimum amount of professional experience. Relevant professional experience is considered as of obtaining the diploma or certificate required for admission to a competition or the first position occupied there after. The application should state the exact dates of the start and finish of each period of employment, the position held and nature of duties. Copies of references from the current employer and previous employers should be enclosed demonstrating that the requisite level and length of professional experience has been attained.

With regard to languages, the general rule is that there must be a thorough knowledge of an official language of the European Union and a satisfactory knowledge of another one. English, French and German are particularly important working languages.

Sending in a completed file

There are two possible procedures at this stage:

- In competitions with pre-selection tests the best performing candidates are requested to submit a full application before being considered for invitation to the following stage of the competition;

- In competitions based on tests and/or qualifications without pre-selection tests, the candidates are requested to submit a full application before being considered for the first stage of the competition.

Applications must include:

- A completed and signed application form (the signature warranting that the standards of good character required of European institution officials have been met and that the information provided is complete and accurate);

- A numbered annex listing educational qualifications and where necessary, documents certifying professional experience and/or any other document requested;

- A copy of all the supporting documents listed in these numbered annexes.

In cases where a Curriculum Vitae is required, we recommend using the European CV format, available on the EPSO website.

Tests

The competition is split into two parts: written tests and oral test. The selection board, nominated by EPSO, makes the decision as to who is to be considered an eligible applicant for the written tests in accordance with the requirements outlined in the competition notice. Eligible candidates will receive from EPSO an invitation for the written tests and those candidates who successfully passed the written tests will receive an invitation for the oral test.

Marking the tests

Candidates should achieve a mark of at least 50% in each unit of the written test.

Technically, if the number of those who passed all written tests is greater than the number of those the EU planned to invite to the oral test, only the best candidates are invited. If we take an example: 5000 candidates apply for the open competition from Member State A, and the number of those to be invited to the oral test is 250. If, say, there are 322 applicants who got more than 50% on each part of the written test, EPSO will draw up a list based on their score and only the best 250 candidates will be invited to the oral test. If there are fewer than 250 candidates eligible for the oral test, all of them will be invited to attend. Further, the same mechanism applies to the drawing up of the reserve lists.

If the competition has pre-selection tests, applicants are entitled to be sent, on request and within a month of the date of notification of their results, a copy of their answers together with a list of the correct answers. After the written tests, they may obtain, on request and within a month of the date of notification of their results, a copy of their written paper as well as a copy of their personal evaluation sheet including the selection board's remarks on their written test(s). Candidates who give up during the tests will have none of their tests marked.

Reserve list

At the end of the competition, the selection board draws up a list of candidates it considers qualified for the vacant posts. However, being included on a reserve list does not guarantee eventual employment. The reserve list is published in the Official Journal.

Recruitment

Once placed on the reserve list, the candidates may be contacted at any time by one of the EU institutions that receive an electronic list of candidates (the "e-laureates"). Once chosen, candidates' names are withdrawn from this list. Candidates may also initiate contacts and try to "lobby" for an interview, bearing in mind that they have fulfilled the formal requirements needed for the given post. This lobbying has proved successful in previous cases.

It is important to know that there is a limited validity of the reserve list, which is generally one year, but it may be prolonged if need be.

Before being appointed to a post, candidates must undergo a compulsory medical examination designed to verify their capability to perform duties associated with their positions.

Probation period

Successful candidates are initially recruited as probationer officials. Their appointment is not made permanent until they successfully complete the probation period, which is nine months.

The Admission Tests

The Written Tests

The nature of written tests varies from one competition to another; always consult the notice of competition. As a general rule, the written tests are held simultaneously for all applicants at all the designated test locations, which is usually Brussels and, if the open competition is related to enlargement, the capital (and possibly other big cities) of the given acceding country or countries. Since this is a competition, no exceptions to this rule are permitted and no applicants may sit any of the tests at a different date or at a different place.

Format, length, subject

Generalist competitions normally have five written parts, to be completed in one day with a lunch break included:

- General knowledge of European integration issues (Multiple Choice Questions, MCQ)
- Specific knowledge of European integration issues (MCQ)
- Verbal and numerical reasoning (MCQ)
- Essay, choosing one from a number of topics
- Short summary of the essay in the candidate's mother tongue

All the tests in this book relate to the above structure of questions. A set of MCQs containing 50 questions is usually to be completed within 40 minutes. That leaves less than one minute per question, so it is vital to be fast and efficient.

Linguistic competitions (translators and lawyer-linguists) generally do not have the above tests. Candidates are required to do two translations from two foreign languages into their mother tongues without the help of a dictionary and within a limited amount of time. At the oral exam, however, their knowledge of European integration is thoroughly tested.

Recent essay questions have included issues such as enlargement of the EU; the unemployment problem in the EU; multilingualism in the EU institutions; the Inter-Governmental Conference, etc., but it is not possible to anticipate subject matter for tests. The essay questions can be either very specific or rather general.[2] It may be wise to think of this part of the test as a "beginner's guide", rather than an academic work of art.

If applying as a specialist, expect a choice of specialist questions. One essay question might be

---

[2] Courtesy of www.euro-staff.gov.uk

compulsory and last for up to three-and-a-half-hours. Many competitions include a case study, which consists of factual documentation about a case or issue relating to an EU project or policy. Institutions other than the Commission may decide to set a précis or essay type question rather than case studies. Usually, however, there is a dossier test.

Examples of previous dossier tests have been:

- An old Official Journal, setting out the case for a particular piece of legislation. This has usually had some connection – though occasionally indirect – with the field of the competition. The final conclusions of this OJ may have been removed and the challenge would be to work this out based on the text provided.

- Candidates are often asked to prepare an executive summary, a briefing note or even a speech for a senior official in the Commission based on the information they are given in the dossier.

Purpose of the written tests

The written tests are designed to test the candidates' knowledge of the chosen field, their comprehension skills and ability to analyse and summarise. Also, the written tests check the candidates' drafting ability in a main language and in a second language.

There are a number of questions that require a summary of the documents and analysis of the advantages and disadvantages of the policy concerned. All questions normally must be answered in 3 to 4 hours. The documentation provided and the questions asked are structured differently for specialist and generalist options.

Although this part of the test is essentially about analytical skills and the ability to interpret given information, past candidates have commented that sound knowledge of the EU institutional structure and decision-making process was assumed. The language element of this paper will most likely be based on a subject related to the field of the competition.

How to prepare

Preparing for the EPSO written tests is far from being an easy exercise and experience has shown that most test takers had some sort of apprehension as they prepared. The way of preparing for the tests is really an individual choice. Some candidates may find that by simply looking at the tests' objectives and preparing on their own they feel confident they can take the tests. Other people may want to read text books, take web-based training, or actually go through instructor-led preparatory classes offered by a training centre. Whatever method you choose, know that *timing* is the linchpin. As you prepare for your test, you want to make sure that you start soon enough. Knowing when to begin your preparation process is critical to having enough time to prepare, without feeling rushed.

The first thing that you must remember is that tests are not written with the intention of catching you out. In fact the tests are only meant to test your knowledge of the European Union and assess whether you have a concise understanding of the field you chose. Experience has shown that the tests were written carefully, in order to ensure that they test the applicants' understanding of only those concepts covered as part of the chosen field. Therefore in theory, if you prepare for your tests properly by thorough revision of the topics in your competition (e.g. historical events of the EU, its institutions and policies, recent trends and developments) you should not encounter any problems during the tests. The ideal way is that you want to make sure that your preparation is part of your daily routine.

As far as the multiple choice questions are concerned, the best way of preparing is to practice in the same format that they will be examined in EPSO tests. This book has the clear and practical objective to facilitate your preparation in this way. As regards the essay/case study, you may expect topics that directly or indirectly relate to your chosen field. Therefore, prepare to be able to show an understanding of the basic issues raised by the questions, but also broader issues related to them; to refer to the basic laws, policies, judicial practice in the area and also to additional facts; show analytical skills including ability to synthesise material, present evidence and argue effectively, but also be able to qualify arguments and defend or attack established positions.

There are many resources that you can use as you begin the test preparation process. First of all, read the Treaties and other pieces of legislation, as well as other instruments (e.g. Presidency Conclusions, judgements of the Community Courts, EUROSTAT data) and policy papers that may be relevant to your chosen field. You will find much information online at the official websites of the different EU institutions. These websites inform you of the latest developments and emerging trends in the relevant areas. Apart from traditional text books and professional literature, you may want to visit on a regular basis web portals dedicated to EU affairs and subscribe to their newsletters (please refer to our recommendations of useful links). These keep you up-to-date with all the most important activities of the EU.

Tips

Regardless of your previous experiences with tests, below you will find some hints that may be helpful when taking the EPSO written tests:

- *Take time to read the questions and all other material provided.* If there is more than one question, check how many marks are allocated for each question. Allocate your time accordingly, and tackle the questions that give you the most marks first. You are sometimes given the choice of picking one subject from two or three questions. Invigilators remark that candidates often change their minds halfway through the competition, abandon their work and start on a different subject. This is not a good idea – be careful, indeed take your time, in making your initial choice and then stick to it. Decide how long you should spend on each paper, including time for planning. Try to keep to this schedule.

- *Be focused.* Examiners look for signs of planning – an opening, setting out the questions for consideration, a reasoned list of the arguments pro and con, a summary of the main arguments you wish to deploy and finally your conclusions. Some candidates put the conclusions at the beginning and then justify them. For the essay a clear conclusion is crucial: examiners often use it as the basis of their assessment. Ensure you demonstrate adequately how the conclusion has been arrived at. Avoid buzz phrases in place of logical thought. Demonstrate a breadth of knowledge.

- *Write neatly and legibly.* The examiners will not wish to toil through a wordy or illegible script. If your work is concise, well organised and tidy it will help you to make a favourable impression on the examiners and might earn extra marks.

- *Make your paper visual and clear.* Write short paragraphs, clear numbered headings, lots of white space on the page. All this makes the examiner want to read it. Try and restrict the number of sections to two or three.

- *Be creative* and try to find an interesting and memorable way of writing things and structuring your essay that sets you apart from others. Nonetheless, be factual, not philosophical; you are being recruited to develop and implement policy. Try not to lambaste the policy of the institution that you are trying to join: the person who marks your paper may have developed it.

The Oral Test

Candidates must pass the written tests to be eligible for the oral. The oral test is the very last stage of the competition. Whoever successfully completes the oral test will be shortlisted for an interview to be organised by one of the EU institutions at a later stage. It must be stressed therefore that passing the oral test is vital in order to succeed.

Face-to-face with EU staff

If all goes well, the oral test is the first occasion for candidates to meet officials[3] representing different institutions of the EU, whose decision will substantially influence the outcome of the selection procedure.

The oral test is administered by a Board consisting of approximately 2-5 members who are experts in their field. Information concerning the names of the Board members will be released on the EPSO website well in advance of the oral test. As a rule, the information does not indicate the specific institutions the members of the Board work in. Nevertheless, candidates are free to browse the internet to search for such information so that they can get some idea of the Board members' professional background. Candidates are forbidden to contact members of the Board about the competition.[4]

Purpose of the oral test

The format is often confused with an interview, which it is not. It is an examination and therefore does not lead directly to a job offer. The purpose of the oral module is to make sure that the candidate has excellent knowledge and comprehension of a broad range of issues and terms in the chosen field (e.g. European Public Administration, Law, Audit/Financial Management), and possesses communication and presentation skills necessary to convey his or her meaning. Moreover, a practical objective of the oral test is for the examiners to judge whether the candidate is ready to work for an EU institution and would fit in with the team.

The oral test does not provide an opportunity to "defend" statements or positions developed in the written essay. The rating in the oral examination will be combined with scores from the written tests before the final results are received. Passing the oral test is only a part of the qualifying procedure and does not therefore stand alone as a qualification.

Procedure of the oral test

The oral test is flexible with regard to timing. However, overall each candidate will be given approximately the same amount of time (about 45 minutes).

On entering the examination room, you will see the Board members sitting at a conference table with your CV in front of them. They will ask you to take a seat opposite them and they will introduce themselves. To ensure uniformity of testing, the Chairperson of the Board will make a few opening remarks about the purpose and the procedure of the oral test. You will always be given the opportunity to ask for further clarification if you feel that some relevant details remain unclear. Apart from administering the test, the Chairperson of the Board is responsible for setting the appropriate tone and impartial atmosphere so that you have a fair opportunity to demonstrate your qualities.

As a rule, your examiners will speak in the language that you have selected as the first lan-

---

[3] The slang word "Eurocrat", derived from "European Bureaucrat", is particularly favoured by people not in favour of the European Union. Therefore it is wise to avoid using this term.

[4] Only candidates exercising the rights of appeal available to them may (through the Director of EPSO) contact the Board in writing and in accordance with the procedures specified in each notice of competition.

guage. Be aware, however, that questions may be put to you in any other languages specified in your CV. It is unlikely that the examiners will speak to you in your mother tongue. If it should happen and you are in no doubt that the examiner is a non-native speaker, ensure that you react naturally and answer distinctly and clearly, so that the examiner may best understand your answer. Should you feel that you need to further clarify matters, take care not to patronise the examiner and that your body language is also entirely respectful.

The oral test will be in the form of discussion, question and answer. The examiners will rotate the questions in turn. Sometimes one examiner will ask an entire set of questions in a row, whilst on other occasions other examiners will interject questions. Your examiners are instructed to listen carefully; they will not argue, agree or encourage you. It follows therefore that you will be doing most of the talking. Your examiners may take notes while you are talking.

At the end of the oral test, you are expected to leave the examination room so that the Board may discuss the test. Your Chairperson will inform you that no feedback will be provided until the end of the whole competition cycle. Experience has shown that marking is a lengthy process and it could be several weeks or months before you are contacted.

How to prepare

Similar principles apply to preparing for the oral test as for the written tests. Your primary objective is the same: to organise your ideas, convey them clearly and supported as for the written tests with convincing reasoning. However, there are some clear differences to keep in mind. The most important is the purpose of the oral test. It is, of necessity, a fast moving exercise, and you do not have a lot of time for prolonged reflection. Therefore, you need to maintain a questioning and reflective approach throughout the whole oral test. Your examiners will also take the opportunity to evaluate your behavioural and emotional reactions. Keeping these points in mind will help you in both preparing and performing.

Be prepared throughout the entire oral test to receive questions relevant to any statements you have included in your CV. So make sure you set out your CV carefully and aim to communicate your strengths and achievements as clearly as possible to the examiners. It may sound obvious, but it is important that you scan through your CV once again before you enter the examining room in order to refresh your memory as to what you have written in it.

You have no way of preparing set responses, although it is always wise to try to anticipate questions that might arise. In the majority of cases the first question, for example, is something similar to the following: *Would you please introduce yourself in a few words and present your reasons for wanting to work in one of the institutions of the European Union?* As was said earlier, your motivation is being tested too. You need to appear articulate and credible when talking about what sparked your interest in applying for the competition.

Tips

This guide is not meant to be a gateway to unlocking your strengths and weaknesses as an oral test-taker. However, based on candidates' experience with previous EPSO tests, we can offer some practical hints that may be useful in preparing and taking the oral test.

- First, make sure you stick to the question. Always answer exactly the question asked without moving away from the main subject. Then, proceed immediately to explain, develop, and give evidence in support of your statements. Take care to support any and all generalisations with concrete evidence, relevant facts, and specific details that will convince your examiners that your answer is valid. Do not use abbreviations, acronyms or slang.

- Do not panic if your initial feeling is that you cannot answer a question adequately. Relax and pause for thought before you answer. Other examiners may interject questions or try to rephrase a question if they think you may have misunderstood. If you feel you are getting confused by having to respond to too many questions, you may ask your Chairperson whether you may take your time to reflect before giving a hasty response. Also, do not be afraid to ask the Board Member to rephrase the question.

• You are free to take scrap paper into the examination so you can take notes and summarise the questions you are being asked. Do not take prepared notes or other written materials into the oral examination.

• Be aware that some of the Board Members may wish to probe the limits of your knowledge; expect to encounter questions that you cannot answer fully.

• When the Board tells you the oral test is over and asks you if there is anything you would like to ask or add, never say "No". This is an opportunity to bring up additional information that would be relevant to your qualification.

• Leave the examination room with a positive attitude about yourself and your performance.

HINTS FOR ESSAY TOPICS

The aim of this section is to give a snapshot of possible essay topics that have been or could be asked at the EU recruitment exam, the *concours*. This is by no means exhaustive, therefore keeping track of current events and being up-to-date is essential.

Growth and employment in the light of the re-launched Lisbon Strategy.

Trends in current State aid policy and the effects of State aid on the Internal Market.

European external action pursuant to the Constitutional Treaty.

Briefing note for a study on enlargement and European enterprises + public procurement notice.

European enlargement – when and where should it end? Argue for or against.

The European neighbourhood policy – achievements and challenges to face.

Achievements of the single European market and the obstacles that still exist.

Democratic deficit, political crisis, challenged integration? – Analyse the French and Dutch referendums on the Constitutional Treaty.

European integration from the Treaties' point of view – ever closer, ever deeper?

Integrated Guidelines 2005 - 2008.

Demographic trends in the EU25 and their effect on how society is organised and social policy.

The 2007-2013 financial perspective – approach it from political, financial, or "competitiveness" perspective.

Asylum policy reconsidered – or fortress Europe? Argue for or against.

Regional policy in the EU25 – current situation and challenges ahead.

Development policy and the EU's role in the third world. Are the current efforts enough?

EU integration compared with other attempts or experiments to unify the continent.

Transatlantic links after Sept 11 and the Iraq war.

Subsidiarity, regionalism and federalism – trends in this decade.

The future of the Franco-German alliance as the motor of integration.

Social inclusion in the new Member States and future enlargement.

RECOMMENDED WEBSITES

Europa: http://europa.eu.int/index_en.htm

ScadPlus: http://europa.eu.int/scadplus/scad_en.htm

European Parliament Fact Sheets: http://www.europarl.eu.int/factsheets/default_en.htm

Court of Justice: http://www.curia.eu.int/en/transitpage.htm

Council of the European Union: http://ue.eu.int

European Court of Auditors: http://www.eca.eu.int

European Environment Agency glossary: http://glossary.eea.eu.int/EEAGlossary

Eur-lex: http://europa.eu.int/eur-lex/en/index.html

Treaties: http://europa.eu.int/eur-lex/lex/en/treaties/index.htm

European Convention: http://european-convention.eu.int

Full text of the Constitutional Treaty: http://europa.eu.int/constitution/download/print_en.pdf

European Personnel Selection Office: http://europa.eu.int/epso/index_en.htm

EU Phone book: http://www.europa.eu.int/idea/en/index.htm

Staff Regulations: http://europa.eu.int/comm/reform/index_en.htm

Citizen's Europe: http://europa.eu.int/youreurope/nav/en/citizens/home.html

Multilingual terminology: http://europa.eu.int/eurodicautom/Controller

EU ABC: http://www.euabc.com/

Euro-Know: http://www.euro-know.org/dictionary/

Wikipedia: http://www.wikipedia.org

Euractiv: http://www.euractiv.com

EU Observer: http://www.euobserver.com

EU Politix: http://www.eupolitix.com

For updated information relating to this book, visit www.eu-testbook.com

EUROPEAN INTEGRATION:
HISTORY, ENLARGEMENTS

75 QUESTIONS – ANSWERS PAGE 185

1. In which year was the North Atlantic Treaty Organisation (NATO) founded?

A. 1947

B. 1948

C. 1949

D. 1950

2. Which of the following countries are members of NATO but not members of the European Union?

A. Norway, Iceland, Turkey

B. Norway, Turkey, Hungary

C. Iceland, Greece, France

D. USA, Latvia, Cyprus

3. Who was Paul-Henri Spaak?

A. First President of the European Parliament

B. First President of the Council of Europe's Parliamentary Assembly

C. Vice-President of the Organisation for European Economic Co-operation (OEEC)

D. Dutch foreign minister

4. What was the so-called Pléven plan about?

A. The Coal and Steel Community

B. Military cooperation with NATO

C. Enhanced cooperation between Germany and France

D. Establishing a European Defence Community

5. The Treaty establishing the European Coal and Steel Community (ECSC) is also known as the ....

A. Treaty of Versailles

B. Brussels Treaty

C. Treaty of Paris

D. Luxembourg Treaty

6.   What was the Werner plan about?

A.   Creating a monetary union

B.   Harmonising the legislation on the common market

C.   Coordinating the Member States' taxation policy

D.   Compromise about the Council's decision making powers

7.   What was the Single European Act (SEA) aiming at?

A.   Establishing the free movement of persons

B.   Replacing the Treaty of Rome with new provisions

C.   Creating the Single Market

D.   Opening the way to the accession of new Member States

8.   In which year did Greece sign its Association Agreement with the European Community and in which year did it become member?

A.   1961, 1981

B.   1965, 1979

C.   1965, 1981

D.   1961, 1979

9.   What was the name of the agreement between Germany and France in 1963 that established closer ties between these two countries?

A.   Maastricht Agreement

B.   Berlin Convention

C.   De Gaulle Report

D.   Elysée Treaty

10.   Who was Altiero Spinelli?

A.   First President of the High Authority

B.   European federalist and Member of the European Commission

C.   Euro-sceptic Italian Prime Minister

D.   Secretary General of NATO

11.   Which countries joined the EC in 1973?

A.   Sweden, Ireland, Finland

B.   Denmark, Spain, Portugal

C.   United Kingdom, Ireland, Denmark

D.   United Kingdom, Spain, Portugal

12.   When was the Treaty of Rome signed?

A.   1 January 1958

B.   9 May 1950

C.   15 February 1951

D.   25 March 1957

13.   In which year was the Association Agreement with Turkey signed?

A.   1959

B.   1963

C.   1987

D.   1999

14.   Who was the first President of the European Commission of the European Economic Community (EEC)?

A.   Walter Hallstein

B.   Louis Armand

C. Christian Fouchet

D. Jean Rey

15. In which country was the Yaoundé Convention signed and when?

A. Gabon, 1965

B. Republic of Congo, 1963

C. Nigeria, 1965

D. Cameroon, 1963

16. What was the Merger Treaty of 1967?

A. A Treaty that provided for a single Commission and a single Council

B. A Treaty on company mergers and acquisitions in the Internal Market

C. A Treaty on merging the Euratom and the Council

D. A Treaty that provided for the creation of Trans-European companies

17. Who was not President of the European Commission?

A. Sicco Mansholt

B. Francois-Xavier Ortoli

C. Giscard d'Estaing

D. Franco Maria Malfatti

18. What did the Luxembourg Compromise touch upon?

A. Closer cooperation between the so-called Benelux countries

B. Decision making in the Council

C. Agreement concerning agricultural issues

D. Reinforcing the German-French tandem

19. In which year was the European Monetary System (EMS) introduced?

A. 1975

B. 1976

C. 1979

D. 1982

20. When was the European Parliament elected for the first time by direct universal suffrage and how long does a parliamentary term last?

A. 1964, 5 years

B. 1974, 4 years

C. 1979, 5 years

D. 1984, 4 years

21. What was the Checchini report about in 1988?

A. Progress report on achieving the Single Market

B. Reform of the Common Agricultural and Fisheries Policy

C. Recommendations on reform of the Structural Funds in Spain and Portugal

D. Advantages of the common market and costs of "non-Europe"

22. Which President of the European Commission served two terms?

A. Jacques Delors

B. Jacques Santer

C. Romano Prodi

D.   Walter Hallstein

D.   Austria, United Kingdom

23. **Which country was the 10th to join the European Communities?**

A.   Spain

B.   Portugal

C.   Greece

D.   Denmark

24. **Who was the French President when the Single European Act entered into force?**

A.   Valéry Giscard d'Estaing

B.   François Mitterand

C.   Charles de Gaulle

D.   Georges Pompidou

25. **Which countries were the most northern and eastern members of the European Community in 1985 (not considering outer islands and overseas territories)?**

A.   Ireland, Italy

B.   Denmark, Cyprus

C.   Sweden, Greece

D.   United Kingdom, Greece

26. **Which countries were not founding members of the European Free Trade Association (EFTA)?**

A.   Switzerland, Sweden

B.   Ireland, Finland

C.   Norway, Portugal

27. **How many Member States did the Council of Europe have when the first European Council was held?**

A.   18

B.   10

C.   24

D.   6

28. **Where is the European Court of Human Rights located?**

A.   Brussels

B.   Luxembourg

C.   The Hague

D.   Strasbourg

29. **In which year was the Maastricht Treaty agreed upon, which year was it signed and which year did it come into force?**

A.   1990, 1991, 1992

B.   1990, 1992, 1993

C.   1991, 1992, 1993

D.   1991, 1993, 1994

30. **In which country was the Schengen Agreement signed in 1985?**

A.   Germany

B.   Luxembourg

C.   The Netherlands

D.   Austria

31. 1990 was the European year of ....

A. Tourism

B. Cinema and television

C. Music

D. Nutrition and health

32. Which cities were the Cultural Capitals of Europe in 2002?

A. Riga (Latvia) and Porto (Portugal)

B. Bruges (Belgium) and Salamanca (Spain)

C. Stockholm (Sweden) and Patras (Greece)

D. Graz (Austria) and Copenhagen (Denmark)

33. When did Lithuania and Estonia submit applications to join the EU?

A. 1994

B. 1996

C. 1995

D. 1997

34. Which one of the following conditions were not among the Copenhagen criteria?

A. Stability of institutions and respect for and protection of minorities

B. Existence of a functioning market economy and the ability to cope with competitive pressure and market forces within the Union

C. Ability to take on the obligations of membership

D. Acceptance of the acquis communautaire without derogations

35. When did the Berlin wall collapse and when was Germany officially reunited?

A. 14 March 1988 / 1 September 1990

B. 20 October 1988 / 28 April 1989

C. 7 February 1990 / 14 April 1991

D. 9 November 1989 / 3 October 1990

36. Which of the following was not considered as a Community aid for the Central and Eastern European Countries in the context of Eastern enlargement?

A. PHARE

B. ISPA

C. CARDS

D. SAPARD

37. Which of the following countries did not belong to the so-called "Luxembourg six"?

A. Slovenia

B. Slovakia

C. Czech Republic

D. Poland

38. When were the enlargement negotiations closed for the ten applicant countries and when was the Treaty of Accession signed with them?

A. December 2002 / April 2003

B. February 2002 / September 2003

C. May 2001 / November 2003

D. October 2002 / December 2003

39. What was the name of the conference that brought together countries aspiring to join the EU, convened on 12 March 1998?

A. Luxembourg European Council

B. Helsinki Enlargement Summit

C. Warsaw Meeting

D. European Conference

40. Which of the following elements was not included in Agenda 2000?

A. Transatlantic relations after enlargement

B. Reinforcement of the pre-accession strategy

C. The challenges of enlargement

D. The impact of enlargement on the EU as a whole

41. Which of the following countries does not have candidate status?

A. Bulgaria

B. Croatia

C. Turkey

D. Norway

42. In relation to enlargement, what is the so-called twinning?

A. Special cooperation between cities

B. Bilateral trade agreements

C. Secondment programme for experts

D. Cross-border cooperation programs

43. Which of the following countries has the smallest population?

A. Belgium

B. Bulgaria

C. Finland

D. Sweden

44. Approximately how many square km is Romania's territory?

A. 139,200

B. 237,500

C. 189,900

D. 204,600

45. Which of the following countries is not a neighbour of Croatia?

A. Bosnia and Herzegovina

B. Serbia and Montenegro

C. Slovenia

D. Albania

46. How many chapters was the acquis grouped into in the framework of accession negotiations?

A. 31

B. 18

C. 42

D. 27

47. **What percentage of French voters voted in favour of the Maastricht Treaty?**

A.　57.45%

B.　51.50%

C.　53.90%

D.　50.08%

48. **What is the CFCU?**

A.　Central Financing and Contracting Unit

B.　Co-Financing of Community and Union projects

C.　Closed Framework of Customs Units

D.　Counter Fraud and Cheating Unit

49. **When did the European Commission publish for the first time a so-called country (or progress) report on the candidate countries?**

A.　1997

B.　1995

C.　1998

D.　1999

50. **When did the referendum on EU accession take place in Poland and how many were in favour?**

A.　2-3 May 2003 / 72.1%

B.　10-11 September 2003 / 64.9%

C.　22-23 October 2003 / 58. 3%

D.　7-8 June 2003 / 77.5%

51. **According to the 2003 financial agreement, what percentage of direct income aid do farmers of the "new" Member States receive in 2005? (from EU budget and from national sources)**

A.　25% + 25%

B.　30% + 30%

C.　30% + 25%

D.　25% + 30%

52. **In relation to the EU's budget, who said the following: "I want my money back"?**

A.　Charles de Gaulle

B.　Margaret Thatcher

C.　Helmut Kohl

D.　Silvio Berlusconi

53. **What is an "opt-out"?**

A.　Permanent non-application of specific legal rules

B.　Annulment of Community legislation

C.　Stricter application of a Community law than foreseen by the legislator

D.　Temporary non-application of legal rules

54. **When and where was the Conference on Security and Co-operation in Europe (now known as: Organisation for Security and Co-operation in Europe) founded?**

A.　1990, Austria

B.　1982, Geneva

C.　1949, The Hague

D.　1975, Helsinki

55. What is the common name of an Accession Agreement that implies prospects for EU membership?

A.   Assistance Partnership

B.   Partnership Project

C.   Europe Agreement

D.   Cooperation Act

56. What is a safeguard clause?

A.   Special measures regarding nuclear power plants in the "new" Member States

B.   A way "new" Member States can ensure that they receive all EU funds they are entitled to

C.   Special voting rights in the Council in case of equality of votes

D.   A rapid reaction measure when "new" Member States fail to fulfil their obligations

57. To whom was the Charlemagne Prize given in 2005?

A.   Carlo Azeglio Ciampi

B.   Giscard d'Estaing

C.   Jacques Delors

D.   Pat Cox

58. What was the Fouchet plan about?

A.   Creating a customs union by 1979

B.   Proposal for a more intergovernmental political community

C.   Military and police cooperation between the Benelux countries and France

D.   Strategic partnership with North African countries

59. What is the name of the integration theory according to which government tasks are gradually and continuously transferred from the national to the supra-national level?

A.   Institutionalism

B.   Functionality

C.   Subsidiarity

D.   Integrationalism

60. What was the name of the solemn declaration that called for the creation of the European Union?

A.   Stuttgart Declaration

B.   Dublin Statement

C.   Bruges Speech

D.   Maastricht Declaration

61. When and where was it decided to establish a Convention to prepare a European Constitutional Treaty?

A.   2000, Brussels

B.   2000, Rome

C.   2001, Laeken

D.   2002, Paris

62. What do we celebrate on 9 May ("Europe Day")?

A.   The end of the Second World War in Europe

B.   The Treaty on European Union was signed that day

C.   The day of the Schuman Declaration

D.   The day when the Treaty of Rome entered into force

63. Which year was the agreement on the Western European Union (WEU) signed and where?

A. 1946, London

B. 1957, Paris

C. 1951, Berlin

D. 1948, Brussels

64. What was decided at the Messina Conference?

A. Creation of a customs union

B. A wider Mediterranean cooperation

C. Fisheries arrangements with North African countries

D. Defence cooperation between the Member States

65. When was the Treaty of Nice signed and when did it enter into force?

A. 11 December 2000 / 1 October 2002

B. 26 February 2001 / 1 February 2003

C. 18 March 2002 / 1 May 2003

D. 25 June 2001 / 10 April 2002

66. Which European Council decided that "the fundamental rights applicable at European Union level should be consolidated in a charter" and which one approved it eventually?

A. Maastricht, Tampere

B. Biarritz, Brussels

C. Cologne, Nice

D. Copenhagen, Rome

67. When was the second referendum in Ireland on the Treaty of Nice?

A. February 2002

B. December 2001

C. May 2002

D. October 2002

68. What was the Ioannina compromise about?

A. Environmental subsidies to "new" Member States

B. Exemption from the Maastricht convergence criteria

C. Council decision making and national veto

D. Contribution to the Community budget and structural benefits

69. Since when has Iceland been a member of the European Free Trade Association (EFTA) and of the European Economic Area (EEA)?

A. 1970, 1992

B. 1968, 1995

C. 1972, 1986

D. 1978, 1996

70. How many articles does the Treaty establishing the European Union and the Treaty on the European Community have, as amended by the Treaty of Nice?

A. 53, 314

B. 42, 451

C. 78, 299

D. 67, 343

71. **What did the Dublin Convention deal with and when was it signed?**

A.   Prevention of cybercrime, 1991

B.   Asylum and refugees, 1990

C.   Judicial and police cooperation, 1995

D.   Human rights protection, 1992

72. **The ECU and ERM were the two main components of the .... launched in ....**

A.   Euro, 1999

B.   ECU, 1981

C.   European Monetary System, 1979

D.   European Currency Account, 1986

73. **What was the name of the report that contained proposals for direct elections to the European Parliament and other integration proposals?**

A.   Dehaene Report

B.   White book on European Democracy

C.   The way ahead: Europe in 2000

D.   Tindemans Report

74. **Which abbreviation was used for the Soviet dominated "Common market" in Central and Eastern Europe, established in 1949 (and ended in 1991)?**

A.   Comecon

B.   Clecat

C.   Fedesov

D.   Stabex

75. **For which of the following Member States did it take 33 years to become a member from the initial signing of the Association Agreement?**

A.   Cyprus

B.   Greece

C.   Malta

D.   Portugal

INSTITUTIONS OF THE EUROPEAN UNION

COUNCIL OF THE EUROPEAN UNION
EUROPEAN COUNCIL
40 QUESTIONS – ANSWERS PAGE 200

1. Which of the following statements is correct? The Council of the European Union (or Council of Ministers) ....

A. Is a supranational body

B. Is the principal legislative body of the EU

C. Expresses the will of the EU's citizens

D. Ensures that the Community law is uniformly interpreted and implemented in the Member States

2. The Council ....

A. Has exclusive power to adopt the EU's budget

B. Is the guardian of the Treaties

C. Is the manager and executor of EU policies and of international trade relations

D. Coordinates the general economic policies of the Member States

3. Who was Justus Lipsius?

A. A Roman philosopher, author of "Think Global, Act European"

B. Father-in-law of Hugo Grotius

C. A Belgian classical philologist, humanist and legislator

D. An imaginary person who has been held to be the source of European justice and humanism

4. **Which of the following statements is false? The Council of Europe was established earlier than the ....**

A. European Council

B. OEEC

C. OECD

D. NATO

5. **The Nordic Council ....**

A. Operates within the framework of the Council of the European Union

B. Includes the Faeroe Islands

C. Uses Swedish, Danish, Finnish and Norwegian as official working languages

D. Has its headquarters in Gothenburg

6. **The Council of the EU is led by a Presidency ....**

A. That is rotated between the Member States every 6 months

B. That is rotated between the Member States every 18 months

C. That is rotated between the Member States in succession set out in the Maastricht Treaty

D. In the form of an 18-month duration three-state team presidency

7. **On 1 July 2006 the EU Presidency moves to ....**

A. Austria

B. Poland

C. Finland

D. Germany

8. **Who was the President of the European Council in the second half of 2003?**

A. Dermot Ahern

B. Bertie Ahern

C. Franco Frattini

D. Silvio Berlusconi

9. **Who is the president of the Council?**

A. The head of state of the Member State holding the Presidency of the Council

B. The head of government of the Member State holding the Presidency of the Council

C. The Foreign Minister of the Member State holding the Presidency of the Council

D. The High Representative for CFSP

10. **The .... European Council, held in June 2002, decided to reorganise the Council formations in order to achieve greater focus and efficiency.**

A. Lisbon

B. Nice

C. Gothenburg

D. Seville

11. **The Council meets in .... different configurations.**

A. 9

B. 15

C. 25

D. 27

12. GAERC brings together ....

A.   Foreign Ministers

B.   Ministers for Education and Culture

C.   Economics and Finance Ministers

D.   Ministers for Agriculture and Fisheries

13. The abbreviation ECOFIN stands for a Council formation composed of ....

A.   Justice Ministers

B.   Ministers for Education and Culture

C.   Economics and Finance Ministers

D.   Ministers for Agriculture and Fisheries

14. Which of the following statements is false? The Competitiveness Council ....

A.   Was created in 2004

B.   Was created through the merging of three previous configurations

C.   May bring together Research Ministers

D.   Covers Internal Market, Industry and Research

15. The Secretary-General of the Council ....

A.   Is Mr. Charlie McCreevy

B.   Participates in General Affairs and External Relations Council meetings

C.   Chairs European Council meetings

D.   Is appointed by the European Parliament

16. Which of the following statements is false?

A.   GAERC holds separate meetings on General Affairs and on External Relations respectively

B.   In the field of CFSP, the Political and Security Committee helps define policies by drawing up opinions for the Council

C.   The Secretary-General of the Council is Mr. Javier Solana

D.   At its sessions on General Affairs, the Council deals with, among other things, foreign trade and development cooperation

17. Which of the following statements is incorrect? The COREPER ....

A.   Is made up of the heads or deputy heads of missions from the Member States in Brussels

B.   Is an auxiliary body of the Council

C.   Has the power to take decisions that belong, under the Treaty, to the Council

D.   Is not an EU institution

18. COREPER II ....

A.   Meets on a weekly basis

B.   Coordinates the work of COREPER I

C.   Is assisted by the MERTENS Group

D.   Was set up in 1967 by Article 4 of the Merger Treaty

19. The ANTICI Group assists ....

A.   The General Secretariat of the Council

B.   COREPER I

C.   COREPER II

D.   Both bodies of COREPER

20. The so-called Committee 133 was set up in the area of ....

A. External action

B. Trade

C. Agriculture

D. Police and judicial cooperation in criminal matters

21. The so-called Article 36 Committee was set up in the area of ....

A. External action

B. Trade

C. Agriculture

D. Police and judicial cooperation in criminal matters

22. The total number of votes in the Council is .... and qualified majority is .... votes emanating from a majority of Member States.

A. 87, 62

B. 124, 88

C. 732, 549

D. 321, 232

23. What does the term "population filter" refer to in respect of the voting system in the Council?

A. The possibility for a Member State to request verification that the qualified majority represents at least 62% of the total EU population

B. The bigger and medium-sized Member States could join forces so that they could achieve the minimum number of votes needed

C. The previous weights between 2 and 29 have

been extended by the Treaty of Nice into a wider band between 3 and 29

D. The Member States no longer have a blocking option

24. Which of the following areas does not require a unanimous decision by the Council?

A. Social security arrangements for migrant workers

B. Measures necessary for the rapid introduction of the single currency

C. Deciding the order of the rotating Presidency

D. Issuing directives for the mutual recognition of diplomas

25. Which of the following areas requires a unanimous decision by the Council?

A. Measures for the approximation of the national provisions that have as their object the establishment and functioning of the internal market

B. Incentive measures designed to encourage cooperation between Member States in the field of employment

C. Measures relating to sea and air transport

D. Laying down principles and rules for the procedure of conferring implementation powers on the Commission

26. Which of the following statements is incorrect?

A. The Amsterdam Treaty introduced qualified majority voting with regard to "Community incentive measures" to combat discriminatory treatment on various grounds

B. Incentive measures coming under cultural

policy are subject to unanimous decision-making in the Council

C. The consultation procedure is often coupled with unanimous decision-making in the Council

D. The Constitutional Treaty aims at further extending the scope of the application of qualified majority voting in the Council

27. Authorisation to establish enhanced cooperation is granted by the Council acting ....

A. Unanimously on a proposal from the Commission and after consulting the European Parliament

B. By qualified majority on a proposal from the Commission and after consulting the European Parliament

C. Unanimously on a proposal from the Commission and after receiving the assent of the European Parliament

D. Unanimously on a proposal from the Commission and after obtaining the opinion of the European Parliament

28. In the case of the.... the Council cannot make a decision in the absence of the European Parliament's opinion.

A. Consultation procedure

B. Cooperation procedure

C. Assent procedure

D. Codecision procedure

29. The Council must obtain the European Parliament's assent when dealing with ....

A. Harmonisation of the denomination and technical specifications of euro coins

B. Taxation schemes

C. A serious breach of fundamental rights by a Member State

D. Harmonisation of the internal market

30. One type of the information procedure is carried out concerning ....

A. The broad economic policy guidelines

B. Matters with asylum aspects

C. Taxation

D. The adoption of the budget

31. As regards the annual budget of the European Union, the Council ....

A. Is the main budgetary authority

B. Prepares the preliminary draft budget

C. Prepares the draft budget

D. Has the last word on non-compulsory expenditures

32. The common position ....

A. Is a so-called "B" item in the Council's agenda

B. Is the result of the first reading in the Council of a proposal under the codecision procedure

C. Is passed by unanimity in the Council

D. Is not published in the Official Journal of the European Community

33. The Conciliation Committee ....

A. Is to reconcile the differences between the Council, the Parliament and the Commission

B. Is made up of 30 members

C.   Has a role in the third stage of the codecision procedure

D.   Is convened by the President of the Council and the President of the European Parliament

34. The Conciliation Committee has the task of reaching agreement on a joint text ....

A.   By a qualified majority of its members

B.   By a qualified majority of the members of the Council and by a majority of the representatives of the European Parliament

C.   Within 6 weeks after the second reading of the Council

D.   Within 6 weeks after the second reading of the European Parliament

35. The European Council was first recognised in the ....

A.   Treaty of Rome

B.   Single European Act

C.   Maastricht Treaty

D.   Amsterdam Treaty

36. The 2005 Spring European Summit was held in ....

A.   Amsterdam

B.   Luxembourg

C.   London

D.   Brussels

37. The Nice summit determined that once the EU has reached .... members, all summits would take place in Brussels.

A.   27

B.   20

C.   25

D.   18

38. Which of the following statements is correct? The European Council ....

A.   Ensures coordination of the general economic policies of the Member States

B.   Addresses economic, social and environmental issues at its December meeting

C.   Is not an institution of the EU

D.   Was first recognised in the Maastricht Treaty

39. The main tasks of .... are preparing and coordinating the work of the Council, giving detailed evaluations of the dossiers and suggesting options.

A.   COREPER

B.   ECOFIN

C.   The Political Committee

D.   The MERTENS Group

40. The "Troika" which represents the Union in external relations in the field of the common foreign and security policy currently consists of ....

A.   The Member State currently holding the Presidency of the Council, the Member State which held it for the preceding six months and the Member State which will hold it for the next six months

B.   The Member State currently holding the

Presidency of the Council, the High Representative for CFSP and the Commission President

C.   The President of the Council, the President of the European Council and the President of the European Commission

D.   The President of the European Council, the High Representative for CFSP and the Commissioner responsible for External Relations and the European Neighbourhood Policy

EUROPEAN PARLIAMENT
50 QUESTIONS – ANSWERS PAGE 206

1.   The current 2004 - 2009 legislature is the .... term of the directly elected European Parliament (EP).

A.   5th

B.   6th

C.   7th

D.   8th

2.   Members of the European Parliament have been elected by direct universal suffrage since ....

A.   1957

B.   1958

C.   1977

D.   1979

3.   The first European Parliament elected by direct universal suffrage brought together Members from .... Member States.

A.   6

B.   9

C.   10

D.   12

4.   Which Treaty inserted a provision into the EC Treaty stating that EP elections must be held in accordance with a uniform procedure in all Member States?

A.   Single European Act

B.   Brussels Treaty

C.   Maastricht Treaty

D.   Amsterdam Treaty

5.   Where is the seat of the European Parliament located?

A.   Luxembourg

B.   Strasbourg

C.   Brussels

D.   Brussels and Strasbourg

6.   The Amsterdam Treaty set the maximum number of MEPs at ....

A.   626

B.   700

C.   732

D.   750

7.   The Treaty of Nice set the maximum number of seats in the European Parliament at ....

A.   626

B.   700

C.   732

D.   750

8.   The term of office of the EP's President, Vice-Presidents and Quaestors is ....

A.   One year

B.   One and a half years with possible extension

C.   Two and a half years

D.   Five years

9.   Whom does the Bureau of the European Parliament comprise?

A.   President and 14 Vice-Presidents

B.   President, the 14 Vice-Presidents and Quaestors

C.   President, the 14 Vice-Presidents, the Quaestors and political group chairmen

D.   President and political group chairmen

10.   The European Parliament elects.... Quaestors.

A.   2

B.   3

C.   5

D.   7

11.   A Quorum exists when ....

A.   One third of the component Members of Parliament are present

B.   The majority of the component Members of Parliament are present

C.   Each political group is sufficiently represented

D.   At least thirty-seven Members are present

12.   A political group in the European Parliament needs to comprise Members elected in at least .... of the Member States.

A.   3

B.   5

C.   One third

D.   One fifth

13.   The minimum number of Members required to form a political group is ....

A.   19

B.   29

C.   39

D.   49

14.   Which political group is the fourth largest in the European Parliament?

A.   Confederal Group of the European United Left – Nordic Green Left

B.   Group of the Greens/European Free Alliance

C.   Union for Europe of the Nations Group

D.   Independence/Democracy Group

15.   How many standing committees does the European Parliament have?

A.   20

B.   17

C.   15

D.   22

16.   How many MEPs represent the Parliament in the Conciliation Committee?

A.   15

B.   25

C.   30

D.   50

17.   The European Centre for Parliamentary Research and Documentation is administered ....

A.   By the Robert Schuman Centre for Advanced Studies

B.   By the Parliamentary Assembly of the Council of Europe

C.   By the European Parliament

D.   Jointly by the European Parliament and the Parliamentary Assembly of the Council of Europe

18.   What does the abbreviation "STOA" stand for?

A.   One of the trade unions representing EP employees

B.   EP unit carrying out scientific and technological policy options assessment

C.   The European Parliament's research and documentation centre

D.   One of the political groups in the European Parliament

19.   What does the abbreviation "COSAC" stand for?

A.   A consultation and coordination body

B.   A decision-making body comprising the speakers of national parliaments of the Member States

C.   An organisation dealing with aviation safety matters

D.   A European employees' organisation

20.   Who was elected President of the European Parliament in July 2004?

A.   Pat Cox

B.   Hans-Gert Pöttering

C.   José Manuel Barroso

D.   Josep Borrell Fontelles

21.   What does the term "democratic deficit" imply?

A.   Under the Treaties in force, the Member States do not transfer real sovereignty to the EU

B.   The EU is not recognised by each and every country as a fully fledged international organisation

C.   The EU is not member of the UN

D.   The EU may seem inaccessible to the ordinary citizen

22. Who said: "The time for a Constitutional Treaty settlement has come, and that time is now"?

A. Pat Cox

B. Josep Borrell Fontelles

C. Martin Schulz

D. Hans-Gert Pöttering

23. Which of the following statements is false? The 2004 European elections saw ....

A. Centre-right parties maintain their majorities across much of the EU

B. A continuing downward trend in voter participation in European elections

C. Voter turnout generally higher in the "new" Member States than in the "old" Member States

D. Participation lowest in Slovakia

24. Who was the President of the European Parliament between 2002-2004?

A. Pat Cox

B. Josep Borrell Fontelles

C. Enrique Barón Crespo

D. Nicole Fontaine

25. Who was not President of the European Parliament or one of its predecessor bodies?

A. Paul Henri Spaak

B. Robert Schuman

C. Altiero Spinelli

D. Lord Plumb

26. In 2003 the Council, the Commission and the Parliament signed an Interinstitutional Agreement on ....

A. Better lawmaking

B. Conflict of interests

C. Joint hiring policy

D. Greater transparency in external communication

27. Which of the following procedures applies to agriculture policy?

A. Codecision

B. Cooperation

C. Consultation

D. Assent

28. Which of the following Treaties introduced the cooperation procedure?

A. Treaty of Rome

B. Single European Act

C. Maastricht Treaty

D. Amsterdam Treaty

29. The assent procedure was introduced by the ....

A. Single European Act

B. Maastricht Treaty

C. Amsterdam Treaty

D. Brussels Treaty

30. **The assent procedure may not apply in connection with ....**

A. Taxation

B. Association agreements

C. Sanctions imposed on a Member State for a serious and persistent breach of fundamental rights

D. The uniform procedure for elections to the European Parliament

31. **The Treaty of Nice has extended the scope of codecision to ....**

A. 15 areas

B. 38 areas

C. 43 areas

D. 52 areas

32. **The Council must obtain the European Parliament's assent when ....**

A. Prohibiting privileged access to the services of financial institutions

B. Passing laws regulating immigration quotas

C. Setting out taxation regimes

D. Concluding association and cooperation agreements

33. **Which of the following areas does not fall under the codecision procedure?**

A. Public health

B. Development cooperation

C. Customs cooperation

D. Harmonisation of the denomination and technical specifications of euro coins

34. **Codecision procedure does not apply to ....**

A. Liberalisation of services

B. Judicial cooperation in civil matters (except family law)

C. Sea and air transport

D. Consumer protection

35. **According to the EC Treaty, the European Parliament appoints the Ombudsman ....**

A. For a two and a half year period

B. For the duration of the Parliament's term

C. For five years

D. For an unfixed period of time

36. **Which of the following areas falls under the codecision procedure?**

A. Anti-discrimination measures under Article 13(2) of the EC Treaty

B. Establishing a Social Protection Committee

C. Adopting detailed rules for the multilateral surveillance procedure

D. Appointing Members of the Court of Auditors

37. **Which of the following statements is correct? When EU citizens exercise their right of petition, they address their petitions to the ....**

A. European Parliament

B. European Court of Justice

C. European Ombudsman

D. European Human Rights Agency

38. Which Treaty grants Parliament the right to bring actions before the Court of Justice, under the same conditions as the other institutions?

A.   Treaty of Rome

B.   Maastricht Treaty

C.   Amsterdam Treaty

D.   Treaty of Nice

39. The European Parliament has no power ....

A.   Of the purse

B.   To legislate

C.   To supervise the executive

D.   To define the principles of the common foreign and security policy of the EU

40. When debating the budget, Parliament has the power to table amendments to ....

A.   Non-compulsory expenditure but only to pro-pose modifications to compulsory expenditure

B.   Compulsory expenditure but only to propose modifications to non-compulsory expenditure

C.   Both compulsory and non-compulsory expenditures

D.   Compulsory expenditures

41. Under the EU Treaty, what role does the European Parliament play in accession procedures?

A.   Initiates the commencement of accession negotiations

B.   Consultation

C.   May give assent, by an absolute majority of its component members

D.   Signs the accession treaty on behalf of the European Union's institutions

42. Under the EC Treaty, what role may the European Parliament play in "enhanced cooperation"?

A.   None

B.   Opinion

C.   Consultative

D.   Consultative or assent

43. On what basis does the President of the European Parliament participate at European Council meetings?

A.   Provisions laid down in the Rules of Procedure of the EP

B.   Provisions inserted by the Brussels Treaty into the EC Treaty

C.   Rules set out in the Interinstitutional Agreement of 9 May 1999

D.   Simple practice

44. In which area does the Parliament not have a right of consultation?

A.   Immigration

B.   Movement of capital to or from third countries

C.   Judicial co-operation in criminal matters

D.   Economic, financial and technical co-operation with third countries

45. The .... is not obliged to provide the European Parliament with a yearly activity report.

A.   Commission

B.   Supervisory Committee of the OLAF

C.   Ombudsman

D.   European Court of Justice

B.   Maastricht Treaty

C.   Amsterdam Treaty

D.   Treaty of Nice

46.   The texts of acts adopted jointly by Parliament and the Council are signed by ....

A.   The President

B.   The President and by the Vice-Presidents

C.   The President and by the Secretary-General

D.   The President and by the leaders of the European Parliament's political groups

49.   Which of the following statements is correct?

A.   The European Parliament is left out of the European Social Dialogue

B.   The Members of the EP sit in national delegations

C.   The European Parliament has not yet entered into an Interinstitutional Agreement

D.   The Secretary General of the EP is Mr Gerhard Stahl

47.   The European Parliament is not entitled to ....

A.   Invite the Commission to draw up reports on particular problems concerning the social situation

B.   Request the Commission to submit legislative proposals

C.   Investigate, under certain circumstances, alleged contraventions or maladministration in the implementation of Community law

D.   Censure the Commissioners individually

50.   Which of the following statements is false?

A.   Parliament has several powers of control

B.   Every citizen of the EU residing in a Member State of which he/she is not a national has the right to vote in elections to the European Parliament in the Member State in which he/she resides

C.   A motion of censure against the Commission requires a two-thirds majority of the votes cast, representing a majority of Parliament's members present for the vote

D.   Parliament finally adopts the budget of the EU and monitors its implementation

48.   Which Treaty empowered the European Parliament to approve or reject the nomination of the Commission President?

A.   Single European Act

EUROPEAN COMMISSION

55 QUESTIONS – ANSWERS PAGE 214

1. **Who is not a Vice-President in the Barroso Commission?**

A. Margot Wallström

B. Jacques Barrot

C. Markos Kyprianou

D. Franco Frattini

2. **When did the Barroso Commission take office?**

A. 1 November 2004

B. 22 November 2004

C. 1 January 2005

D. 15 December 2004

3. **According to the Code of Conduct of Commissioners, what should a Commissioner do with the royalties resulting from a book they publish during their term of office?**

A. They dispose of it as they wish

B. They must pay it to a charity organization of their choice

C. They must not accept any royalty

D. The Code of Conduct does not have any provisions on this issue

4. **What is the maximum value of gifts a Commissioner may accept and keep?**

A. €150

B. €500

C. There is no such limit

D. They have to hand over all gifts they receive

5. **What does a Commissioner's declaration of interests not have to include?**

A. Assets and stocks

B. Spouse's professional activity

C. Posts in foundations or similar bodies

D. Children's financial interests

6. **How many Commissioners were there on 30 June 2004?**

A. 15

B. 25

C. 30

D. 35

7. **Which Treaty was the one that "aligned" the Commission's and the Parliament's terms of office?**

A. Amsterdam Treaty

B. Maastricht Treaty

C. Treaty of Nice

D. Single European Act

8. **What is the generally used name for Commission reports with concrete proposals for law-making in a policy area?**

A. Green paper

B. White paper

C. Blue paper

D. Grey paper

9. **How many Directorates-General (DG) and services are there in the European Commission?**

A. 25 DG, 8 services

B. 26 DG, 9 services

C. 25 DG, 9 services

D. 26 DG, 8 services

10. **The Commission may not take decisions by ....**

A. Written procedure

B. Empowerment

C. Delegation

D. Referral

11. **Which one of these is not a main area of the Commission's 2002 "Better law-making" action plan?**

A. Simplifying and improving the regulatory environment

B. Promoting a culture of dialogue and participation

C. Re-organising and reducing the acquis communautaire

D. Systematising impact assessment by the Commission

12. **What is CONECCS?**

A. Database concerning Consultation, the European Commission and Civil Society

B. Commission Network for European and Caribbean Cooperation Systems

C. Consultative body of the European Community's Cultural Service

D. "Connect Europe" – the Commission's Computer System initiative

13. **Which of the following statements is false? According to the Code of Conduct for consultants, lobbyists, in their dealings with the European Commission, should ....**

A. Honour confidential information given to them

B. Refrain from contacts with law-makers outside Commission premises

C. Not obtain information from EU institutions by dishonest means

D. Only employ EU personnel subject to the rules and confidentiality requirements of the EU institution

14. **The European Anti-Fraud Office (OLAF) may conduct investigations ....**

A. Against civil servants of EU institutions but only on its own initiative

B. Into almost any financial issue on the European Union's territory

C. Only when national investigators refuse to act and a procedure has been initiated

D. Into almost any issue adversely affecting the Community's financial interests

15. Who is the Commissioner for Fisheries and Maritime Affairs?

A.   Dalia Grybauskait

B.   Mariann Fischer Boel

C.   Joe Borg

D.   Vladimír Špidla

16. What is Louis Michel's portfolio?

A.   Financial Programming and Budget

B.   Energy

C.   Development and Humanitarian Aid

D.   Taxation and Customs Union

17. Approximately what percentage do women represent in the Barroso Commission?

A.   One fifth

B.   One fourth

C.   One third

D.   One sixth

18. Who of the Barroso Commission's following members was not in the Prodi Commission?

A.   Joaquín Almunia

B.   Günter Verheugen

C.   Margot Wallström

D.   Viviane Reding

19. What do Günter Verheugen and Olli Rehn have in common?

A.   They have been / are Commissioners responsible for enlargement policy

B.   They have both been Ministers of Foreign Affairs

C.   They have been / are Commissioners for economic affairs

D.   They are both former Ministers of Finance

20. The Commissioner responsible for sport issues is the one holding the portfolio of ....

A.   Health and Consumer Protection

B.   Education, Training, Culture and Multilingualism

C.   Employment, Social Affairs and Equal Opportunities

D.   Information Society and Media

21. How many Presidents has the European Commission had before J. M. Durão Barroso?

A.   8

B.   10

C.   12

D.   11

22. According to the EC Treaty, what obligation does the Commission have regarding its activities?

A.   The Commission President has to give an account to the Parliament of its activities at least once a year

B.   Twice a year the Commission must publish a half-yearly report

C. The Commission must publish an annual report on the activities of the Community

D. The Treaty does not set out requirements in this field, yet each year the Commission publishes an annual report

26. A Commissioner's vacancy may not arise by ....

A. Resignation

B. Death

C. Compulsory retirement

D. Retirement in the interest of the service

23. What right does the Court of Justice have vis-à-vis the Commissioners?

A. It may establish a serious misconduct but only the Council may dismiss the Commissioners

B. It may compulsorily retire the Commissioners

C. The Court of Justice has no jurisdiction over the Commissioners

D. It may establish a Commissioner's responsibility without compulsory retiring

27. Which of the following is not a Commission internal service?

A. Press and communication

B. Infrastructures and Logistics

C. Group of Policy Advisers

D. Personnel and Administration

24. What is the name of the Commission's representative offices and in how many countries are they present?

A. Delegations in 135 countries

B. Representations in 87 countries

C. Delegations in 123 countries

D. Representations in 118 countries

28. Since when has the Commission been surveying public opinion in Member States by standard Eurobarometer?

A. 1958

B. 1981

C. 1965

D. 1973

25. Which one of the following is not a general service operated by the Commission?

A. Translation Centre for the Bodies of the European Union

B. Eurostat

C. Publications Office

D. European Anti-Fraud Office

29. Who is the chief negotiator with the World Trade Organisation (WTO) on behalf of the EU?

A. Commission only

B. Commission and Member States

C. Council

D. Mixed committee of Commission officials and Members of Parliament

30. Which Council decision lays down the procedures for the exercise of implementing powers conferred on the Commission?

A.   1985/45/EEC

B.   1987/373/EEC

C.   1999/468/EC

D.   2004/352/EEC

31. What was the name of the project to re-organise the European Commission and in which year was it presented?

A.   Green Paper on Reform, 2000

B.   White Paper on Reform, 2000

C.   White Paper on a Better Administration, 2001

D.   Green Paper on Pre-enlargement Restructuring, 2001

32. Which day of the week do Commissioners meet and where?

A.   Monday, Brussels or Strasbourg

B.   Tuesday, Brussels, Strasbourg or Luxembourg

C.   Wednesday, Brussels or Strasbourg

D.   Monday, Brussels or Luxembourg

33. Article 217(4) of the EC Treaty was amended by the Treaty of Nice as follows: "A Member of the Commission shall resign if the .... so requests, after obtaining the approval of the ...."

A.   Council by qualified majority, European Council

B.   Absolute majority of the European Parliament, Council

C.   Court of Justice, Council

D.   President, College

34. Which one of these areas does not fall under the European Community's exclusive competence?

A.   Conservation of marine biological resources

B.   Commercial policy

C.   Conclusion of international agreements

D.   Environmental policy

35. Which national administration was used as a model when the European Commission was set up?

A.   Italian

B.   French

C.   British

D.   German

36. What was the White Paper on Governance about?

A.   More democratic forms of governance at all levels

B.   Government reforms needed to meet the EU's economic goals

C.   Proposals for cooperation between the EU and Middle-East countries

D.   Reform of the Staff Regulation

37. What is Europe Direct?

A.   The common term for the direct agricultural subventions

B.   Council directive on political direct marketing

C.   A free information service about the European Union

D.   Strategic project for enhancing trans-European rail networks

38. **According to Article 202 of the EC Treaty, which institution has implementing powers for the rules the Council lays down?**

A. The Commission exclusively

B. The Commission and the European Parliament

C. The Commission, except for rules governing the euro

D. The Commission and in some cases the Council

39. **Who has to approve the candidate Commissioners?**

A. The European Parliament with an absolute majority

B. The European Parliament and eventually the Council

C. The Parliamentary Committees and the plenary of the European Parliament

D. The Council of Ministers meeting in the composition of Heads of State or Government

40. **According to the Treaty of Nice, which institutions may conclude an inter-institutional agreement?**

A. Any two from the Commission, Parliament, Council

B. Commission, Parliament, Council, as long as all three of them are signatories to it

C. The Commission and the Council

D. The Parliament and the Commission

41. **What is the Berlaymont?**

A. The Commission's headquarters in Brussels

B. The hall where the Constitutional Treaty was signed

C. The city where several informal European Councils have been held

D. The area in Luxembourg where most EU institutions are located

42. **When was Jacques Delors President of the European Commission?**

A. From 1994 to 1999

B. From 1985 to 1994

C. From 1999 to 2004

D. From 1980 to 1989

43. **Who was the President of the Commission when it resigned following an investigation into administrative failings?**

A. Jacques Santer

B. Jacques Delors

C. Romano Prodi

D. Roy Jenkins

44. **How many Commission members are there in the Economic Policy Committee (EPC)?**

A. None

B. One

C. Two

D. Four

45. **According to the Constitutional Treaty, what role will the future Foreign Affairs Minister have in the Commission?**

A. Vice-President

B.   President

C.   Commissioner for External Relations

D.   Secretary General

46. What did the Molitor Group deal with?

A.   Disarmament negotiations with the Newly Independent States

B.   Preparing proposals for improved food safety regulations

C.   Proposals on how to simplify European legislation

D.   Commission surveillance of implementation of internal market regulations

47. Who made up the Troika before the Amsterdam Treaty?

A.   The Commission President, the High Representative and the Council presidency

B.   The EU presidency, the previous and next presidencies

C.   The Commission President, the President of the European Parliament and the Council President

D.   The President of the European Council, the High Representative and the President of the European Parliament

48. What does not characterise the European Commission?

A.   It is the guardian of the Treaties

B.   It has power of management and negotiation

C.   It has its own power of decision-making

D.   It has sole right of initiative in all three pillars

49. According to Article 218(2) of the EC Treaty, who adopts the Commission's Rules of Procedure?

A.   The Commission, with the approval of the Council

B.   The Council, based on the Commission's proposal

C.   The Commission itself

D.   The Commission, after taking into account the European Parliament's opinion

50. Approximately how many officials ("fonctionnaires") are working for the European Commission?

A.   24,000

B.   33,000

C.   17,000

D.   42,000

51. Which of the following statements is incorrect?

A.   Each Commissioner is individually responsible for the decisions taken under his or her portfolio

B.   The President ensures that the Commission acts consistently and efficiently

C.   The Commission works under the political guidance of its President

D.   The President decides on the Commission's internal organisation

52. Regarding the Commissioners' portfolios, which statement is correct?

A.   The responsibilities incumbent upon the Commissioners are set out in the EC Treaty

B.   The Treaty requires that the portfolios be shuf-

fled according to the Commissioner's competencies and previous experience in the given
area

C. The President may reshuffle the portfolios
during the Commission's term of office

D. A Commissioner's portfolio may only be
changed by his or her prior written approval

**53. According to the provisions laid down
in the Commission's Rules of
Procedure, how many Commissioners
are required to constitute a quorum?**

A. One third of the total number

B. Simple majority and the President

C. Simple majority

D. Simple majority and the President or one of the
Vice-Presidents

**54. Apart from Commissioners, who else
attends the Commission's meetings?**

A. A representative of the Council Presidency and
of the European Parliament

B. The Secretary General of the Commission and
of the Council

C. The President or one of the Vice-Presidents of
the European Parliament

D. The Secretary General of the Commission

**55. The Legal Service of the Commission
must be consulted on ....**

A. All drafts for legal instruments and documents
which may have legal implications

B. All drafts and proposals

C. All drafts and proposals in the framework of
the codecision procedure

D. All proposals prepared by the Commission
having a binding legal nature

COURT OF JUSTICE, COURT OF FIRST INSTANCE;
COMMUNITY LEGAL ORDER

60 QUESTIONS – ANSWERS PAGE 226

1. Which statement is false?

A. In special cases the Advocate General's opinion
is binding on the Court

B. There are eight Advocates General at the Court

C. The members of the Court of First Instance may
be called upon to perform the tasks of an
Advocate General

D. Every three years there must be a partial
replacement of the Advocates General

**2. What did the Court rule in the
Kupferberg case?**

A. Free trade agreements are directly applicable in
all Member States

B.   Political groups in the European Parliament with less than twelve members cannot form a technical group

C.   Discrimination is prohibited against persons currently not in the labour market

D.   The Economic and Social Committee may not seek preliminary ruling from the Court

3.   According to the Constitutional Treaty, what will be the name of binding regulations with a general application in all Member States?

A.   European framework law

B.   European law

C.   European regulation

D.   European decision

4.   What is the name of the procedure according to which a national court, when in any doubt about the interpretation or validity of an EU law, may and sometimes must ask the Court of Justice for advice?

A.   Referral for opinion

B.   Preliminary ruling

C.   Interpretation procedure

D.   Summary proceedings

5.   Which institution has jurisdiction in disputes concerning the fulfilment by Member States of obligations under the Statute of the European Investment Bank?

A.   The Council acting by two-thirds majority

B.   Court of Justice and Court of First Instance, depending on the case

C.   Court of First Instance only

D.   Court of Justice only

6.   Article 226 of the EC Treaty provides that "[i]f the Commission considers that a Member State has failed to fulfil an obligation under this Treaty, it shall deliver a .... on the matter after giving the State concerned the opportunity to submit its ...."

A.   Decision, appeal

B.   Reasoned opinion, observations

C.   Reasoned decision, arguments

D.   Reasoned decision, pleas

7.   Which statement is false?

A.   All regulations, directives and decisions must be published in the Official Journal of the European Union

B.   A regulation is binding in its entirety and directly applicable in all Member States

C.   A directive leaves to the national authorities the choice of form and methods concerning its transposition

D.   A decision is binding in its entirety upon those to whom it is addressed

8.   Which statement is true?

A.   Regulations of the Council and of the Commission always enter into force on the date specified in them

B.   Regulations, directives and decisions adopted by codecision procedure must be signed by the President of the European Parliament and by the President of the Council before publication in the Official Journal

C.   Directives and decisions must be notified to those to whom they are addressed and take effect on the 20th day after notification

D.   Council, Commission and Parliament decisions must be published in the Official Journal of the European Union

9.   What did the Court rule in the Marleasing case?

A.   With regard to the implementation of the provisions of the Treaty, the system of internal Community measures may not be separated from that of external relations

B.   Member States are obliged to interpret national legislation according to European directives even if they have yet to be incorporated into that national legislation

C.   The rule on equal treatment with nationals is one of the fundamental legal provisions of the Community

D.   The question of a possible infringement of fundamental rights by a measure of the Community institutions can only be judged in the light of Community law itself

10.   Which case dealt with transfer rules between football clubs?

A.   Bosman case, 1995

B.   Marschall case, 1997

C.   Gebhard case, 1995

D.   Martínez Sala case, 1998

11.   Who is signatory to the European Convention on Human Rights?

A.   The EU and the Member States

B.   The EU is but the Member States are not

C.   The EU will be as soon as the Constitutional Treaty comes into force

D.   Only the Member States

12.   Which statement is true?

A.   Today only the European Communities have legal personality but the Constitutional Treaty will change it

B.   Today the European Union has legal personality which the Constitutional Treaty will change

C.   Today the European Communities only have legal personality regarding trade-related issues

D.   Today only Member States have legal personality but the European Communities do not

13.   Which institutions may issue directives?

A.   Council, Parliament, Commission, European Central Bank

B.   Council and Parliament

C.   Council, Commission

D.   Council, Parliament, Commission

14.   If a fundamental right is found to be breached, the Court of Justice declares the act concerned to be void, with .... and .... effect.

A.   Immediate, universal

B.   Retroactive, universal

C.   Retroactive, direct

D.   Immediate, retrospective

15.   What was the Casagrande case about?

A.   Free movement of workers

B.   Direct effect of Community legal acts

C.   Discrimination against persons in the educational system

D.   Interpretation of a competition law regulation

16.   What does the acquis communautaire not include?

A.   The content, principles and political objectives of the Treaties

B.   Legal acts of Member States regarding the transposition of Community measures

C.   Case law of the Court of Justice

D.   The declarations and resolutions adopted by the Union

17.   Which one of the following is not considered as primary legislation?

A.   Budgetary Treaty of 1975

B.   Single European Act

C.   Commission, Parliament and Council inter-institutional agreement of 1999

D.   Act of Accession of Greece

18.   In which field is the term "home state regulation" used?

A.   Immigration

B.   Development policy

C.   Free movement of workers

D.   Cross-border commerce

19.   When did the Court rule in the Van Gend & Loos case?

A.   1963

B.   1967

C.   1960

D.   1964

20.   Which statement is false?

A.   The Court of First Instance may give legal opinion to some Community institutions

B.   The Court of First Instance was set up in 1989

C.   Regarding the Court of First Instance, the Treaty of Nice provides for the creation of judicial panels to examine at first Instance certain types of actions in specific matters

D.   The Court of First Instance may have more judges than the number of Member States

21.   What is the Cassis de Dijon and when did the Court rule in that case?

A.   French football team, 1976

B.   French mustard, 1982

C.   French liquor, 1979

D.   Belgian refreshment drink, 1980

22.   Which body may waive the immunity of the judges of the Court?

A.   The Court and the Council

B.   The Court sitting as a full Court

C.   A special judicial panel created for this purpose

D.   The Council with two-thirds majority

23.   What is the name of the special judicial panel that has been created for legal disputes between the Communities and its servants?

A.   Specialised panel on Civil Service

B.   European Court of Institutional Affairs

C.   European Union Civil Service Tribunal

D.   Court of European Officials

24. Which body may initiate the amendment of the Statute of the Court of Justice and what quorum is required from the Council?

A. Council or Court of Justice, qualified majority

B. Commission or Council, unanimity

C. Commission, Council or Parliament, qualified majority

D. Commission or Court of Justice, unanimity

25. The Court of Justice has no jurisdiction in disputes between ....

A. Member States

B. The EU and Member States

C. The Institutions

D. EU citizens

26. The Court of First Instance has no jurisdiction regarding ....

A. Indirect actions

B. Disputes between the Communities and their servants

C. Declaration of failure to act

D. Declaration for annulment

27. What was the Court's ruling about in the Factortame case?

A. Article 133 of the EC Treaty

B. Direct effect of Community law

C. Consumer rights

D. State aids

28. Who elects the President of the Court and how long is his/her term?

A. Council, 3 years

B. Court, 3 years

C. Council and Parliament, 6 years

D. Court, 6 years

29. What was the Court's ruling about in the Internationale Handelsgesellschaft and Simmenthal cases?

A. The national court should discard a law which is contrary to Community law

B. The principles on which the European Convention for the Protection of Human Rights and Fundamental Freedoms is based must be taken into consideration in Community law

C. Measures adopted by the Parliament for the purpose of allocating appropriations are intended to finance the pre-election information campaign

D. Articles 30 and 36 of the Treaty do not preclude a Member State restricting the consumption of additives by subjecting their use to prior authorisation

30. Which body may not bring an action for annulment before the Court of Justice?

A. Member States

B. European Central Bank

C. European Parliament

D. Council

31. According to Article 231 of the EC Treaty, an action for annulment may not be brought to the Court of Justice on ground of ....

A. Lack of competence

B. Infringement of an essential procedural requirement

C. Non-transposition of a legal act by a Member State

D. Infringement of any rule of law relating to its application

32. Which case dealt with the European Parliament's right of consultation?

A. Van Eycke case

B. Isoglucose case

C. Foto-Frost case

D. Colson case

33. Who has been the President of the Court of Justice since 2003?

A. Jean-Pierre Puissochet

B. José Narciso da Cunha Rodrigues

C. Christine Stix-Hackl

D. Vassilios Skouris

34. How many cases did the Court of Justice complete in 2004?

A. 665

B. 397

C. 475

D. 984

35. Generally, which is the largest group of cases at the Court of First Instance?

A. Staff cases

B. Intellectual property

C. Actions for annulment

D. Actions for damages

36. Which of the following formations does the Court of Justice not have?

A. Chamber of seven

B. Chamber of five

C. Full court

D. Grand Chamber

37. The Statute of the Court of Justice provides that "[a] Judge may be deprived of his office [...] only if, in the unanimous opinion of the .... , he no longer fulfils the requisite conditions or meets the obligations arising from his office."

A. Council and the Judges of the Court

B. Judges of the Court

C. Council

D. Judges and Advocates General of the Court

38. Approximately how many officials work for the Court of Justice and Court of First Instance?

A. 700

B. 1800

C. 2700

D. 4500

39. In the case of direct actions and appeals, when does the Judge-Rapporteur draw up his preliminary report?

A.   After the objection to admissibility

B.   After the interim measures

C.   After the intervention

D.   After the end of the written procedure

40. When was the Court of Justice of the European Communities established?

A.   1952

B.   1967

C.   1957

D.   1989

41. When was the European Free Trade Agreement (EFTA) Court established and where is it based?

A.   1994, Luxembourg

B.   1972, Basel

C.   1983, Brussels

D.   1967, The Hague

42. How many judges does the EFTA Court have and how long is their mandate?

A.   15, 3 years

B.   3, 6 years

C.   28, 6 years

D.   12, 3 years

43. When was the European Court of Human Rights established?

A.   1950

B.   1978

C.   1959

D.   1967

44. What are the main working languages of the International Court of Human Rights?

A.   English, French

B.   English only

C.   English, French, Russian, Chinese, Arabic, Spanish

D.   English, French, Spanish, German, Italian

45. What was the Francovich case about?

A.   Inadequate or non-transposition of a directive

B.   Free flow of capital

C.   Compensation for damage caused by a civil servant of the Community

D.   Freedom to provide services for lawyers

46. What is the legal basis of the European Community's power of enforcement and that of the Member States?

A.   Article 300 of the EC Treaty

B.   Article 10 of the EC Treaty

C.   Article 251 of the EC Treaty

D.   Article 12 of the EU Treaty

47. **The Constitutional Treaty will change the name of the Court of First instance to ....**

A. General Court

B. High Court

C. General Tribunal

D. European Tribunal

48. **The Court of Justice does not have jurisdiction to review the legality of framework decisions and decisions in actions brought by a Member State or the Commission on grounds of ....**

A. Internal security

B. Lack of competence

C. Misuse of powers

D. Infringement of an essential procedural requirement

49. **According to the Constitutional Treaty, what will be the name of the European Court of Justice?**

A. Court of Justice of Europe

B. Remains unchanged

C. European Court

D. Court of Justice of the European Union

50. **What rights does the Ombudsman have regarding the Court of Justice and Court of First Instance? The Ombudsman may ....**

A. Carry out examinations of all kinds

B. Not carry out any examination regarding these two institutions

C. Not carry out examinations when these bodies act in their judicial role

D. Not carry out examinations in cases where a Community institution is involved

51. **Which Treaty included fundamental rights and employment for the first time?**

A. Amsterdam Treaty

B. Maastricht Treaty

C. Treaty of Rome

D. Single European Act

52. **Regarding enhanced cooperation, the Treaty of Nice did not require that ....**

A. Member States which intend to establish it may not make use of the institutions

B. It does not undermine the internal market

C. It remains within the limits of the powers of the Union or of the Community

D. It does not concern the areas which fall within the exclusive competence of the Community

53. **Article 5 of the EC Treaty provides that "[i]n areas which do not fall within its exclusive competence, the Community shall take action, in accordance with the principle of .... , only if and in so far as the objectives of the proposed action cannot be sufficiently achieved by the Member States and can [...] be better achieved by the Community."**

A. Proportionality

B. Parallelism

C. Subsidiarity

D. Good lawmaking

54. **Which of the following is not considered an "Amsterdam leftover"?**

A.   Weighting of votes in the Council

B.   Size and composition of the Commission

C.   Extension of qualified majority voting

D.   Number of European Parliament Members

55. **In which of the following areas did the Single European Act (SEA) not replace unanimity?**

A.   Freedom to provide services

B.   Common customs tariff

C.   Common sea and air transport policy

D.   Free movement for students

56. **The Amsterdam Treaty does not extend codecision to ....**

A.   Environment protection measures

B.   Implementation of the Regional Development Fund

C.   Vocational training measures

D.   Competition policy

57. **Citizenship of the European Union does not include ....**

A.   The right to move and reside freely within the territory of the Member States

B.   The right to petition the European Parliament

C.   The right to stand as a candidate in national elections in the Member State in which the citizen resides

D.   The right to diplomatic protection in the territory of a third country

58. **Views of all or individual Council members regarding the interpretation of the Council's decisions are set out in a(n) ....**

A.   Non-binding annex

B.   Personal opinion

C.   Addendum to the act

D.   Declaration

59. **When did the European Coal and Steel Community (ECSC) Treaty expire?**

A.   1 January 2000

B.   23 July 2002

C.   20 October 2003

D.   17 February 1999

60. **The right of all citizens of the Union to access European Parliament, Council and Commission documents was inserted by the .... in Article .....**

A.   Treaty of Nice, 289

B.   Amsterdam Treaty, 255

C.   Single European Act, 51

D.   Maastricht Treaty, 188

EUROPEAN COURT OF AUDITORS (ECA)
20 QUESTIONS – ANSWERS PAGE 240

1. Which Treaty established the European Court of Auditors (ECA)?

A. Treaty of Rome

B. Brussels Treaty

C. Single European Act

D. Maastricht Treaty

2. Which of the following statements is correct? The ECA ....

A. Is outside the institutional framework of the EU

B. Became operational in 1975

C. Was established in 1977

D. Has its headquarters in Luxembourg

3. When did the ECA get promoted to the rank of an institution?

A. 1993

B. 1995

C. 1999

D. 2003

4. What change was brought into effect by the Treaty of Nice in relation to the ECA?

A. The ECA's reporting obligation

B. The Statement of Assurance

C. The membership of the ECA

D. The Cooperation Committee

5. How many levels does the control of the European Union's budget have?

A. Two

B. Three

C. Five

D. Six

6. The ECA examines the ....

A. Functioning of the institutions

B. Budgetary activity of the Council and the European Parliament

C. Legality and regularity of Community income and expenditure

D. Financial interplay between the Member States

7. When the ECA suspects that fraud or irregularities have occurred, the information obtained is forwarded to the ....

A. OLAF

B. European Commission

C. European Parliament

D. European Court of Justice

8. What kind of powers of sanction is conferred on the Court of Auditors?

A. It may require that the infringement be brought to an end

B. It may impose fines

C.   It may order interim measures

D.   It has no powers of sanction

C.   6

D.   8

9.   **Which of the following statements is incorrect?**

A.   The Commission and the ECA implement the EU budget

B.   The ECA carries out an independent external control of the EU's accounts

C.   The ECA does not have any powers of sanction

D.   The ECA is outside the institutional framework of the European Court of Justice

13.   **The President of the ECA is appointed for a period of .... years.**

A.   2

B.   3

C.   4

D.   6

14.   **What does the independence of the ECA members mean?**

A.   OLAF is not entitled to instruct ECA members

B.   When performing their duties, ECA members may not take instructions from any government or other body

C.   ECA members may take instructions only from the President of the ECA

D.   ECA members are bound by no obligations

10.   **How many members does the ECA have?**

A.   8

B.   10

C.   25

D.   40

11.   **According to the EC Treaty, what kind of qualification does a member of the ECA need to have?**

A.   Political science

B.   Law

C.   Audit

D.   There is no Treaty provision for qualification criteria

15.   **The members of the ECA may engage .... during their term of office.**

A.   In any other occupations

B.   In any other occupations paid or unpaid

C.   Only in scientific or educational occupations

D.   In no other occupations either paid or unpaid

16.   **Which body is entitled to deprive a member of the ECA of his/her office?**

A.   Council

B.   The ECA itself

C.   Court of Justice

12.   **The members of the ECA are appointed for a period of .... years.**

A.   4

B.   5

D.   The government which has delegated the ECA member

19.   The ECA draws up an annual report ....

A.   On or prior to 1 July each year

B.   Before the Commission submits the preliminary draft budget

C.   After the next year's EU budget has been drawn up

D.   After the close of each financial year

17.   What does the abbreviation "INTO-SAI" stand for?

A.   International body of the supreme auditing institutions

B.   Abbreviation for the Italian name of the ECA

C.   ECA unit dealing with statistical and analytical matters

D.   International auditing standards

20.   What role does the Contact Committee play?

A.   Liaises between the institutions

B.   Promotes cooperation between the SAIs and the ECA

C.   Implements joint initiatives of the ECA and the Commission

D.   Promotes peer-to-peer exchange of information between the ECA and OLAF

18.   What does the abbreviation "DAS" stand for?

A.   Auditing and statistical records processed by the EUROSTAT

B.   Statement of Assurance

C.   Decentralised Auditing System

D.   Defined Auditing Standards

ADVISORY BODIES, AGENCIES

40 QUESTIONS – ANSWERS PAGE 245

1.   The Committee of the Regions (CoR) is the guardian of ....

A.   The Treaties

B.   The principle of subsidiarity

C.   Welfare in the regions

D.   Sustainable social and economic development in the regions

2.   The CoR was set up by the ....

A.   Treaty of Rome

B.   Single European Act

C.   Maastricht Treaty

D.   Amsterdam Treaty

3. **The CoR became operational in ....**

A. 1992

B. 1994

C. 1997

D. 1999

4. **The CoR must be consulted on ....
policy areas.**

A. 5

B. 10

C. 15

D. 18

5. **How many members does the CoR of
EU25 have?**

A. 212

B. 312

C. 317

D. 350

6. **The maximum number of seats in the
Committee of the Regions is fixed at ....**

A. 350

B. 400

C. 450

D. 500

7. **The members of the CoR are
appointed for .... years by the ....**

A. 4, Member States

B. 4, Council

C. 5, Member States

D. 5, Council

8. **No member of the CoR may at the
same time ....**

A. Be a Member of the European Parliament

B. Be a member of the National Assembly of a
Member State

C. Be politically accountable to an elected Assembly

D. Hold a regional or local authority electoral
mandate

9. **Which of the following is not a political group in the Committee of the
Regions?**

A. Party of European Socialists Group

B. European People's Party Group

C. Union for Europe of the Nations Group

D. European Alliance Group

10. **RELEX (one of the specialised
Commissions of the CoR) is responsible for ....**

A. Interinstitutional relations

B. Legislative matters

C. Economic and social policy

D. External relations

11. **Which of the following statements is
false?**

A. The Bureau is responsible for implementing the
political programme of the CoR

B.   The President of the CoR is elected for a term of 2 years

C.   There are 4 political groups in the CoR

D.   There are 12 specialised Commissions within the CoR

12.   Who is the President of the Committee of the Regions?

A.   Peter Straub

B.   Anne-Marie Sigmund

C.   Hubert Weber

D.   Danuta Hübner

13.   What does the abbreviation CAFA stand for?

A.   CoR body dealing with financial and administrative matters

B.   Trade union within the CoR

C.   Specialised Commission within the CoR dealing with foreign affairs

D.   Consultative committee bringing together external experts assisting the Bureau of the CoR

14.   In the Pujol report the CoR proposed that ....

A.   Its opinions be legally binding instruments

B.   It be obligatorily consulted on matters falling under the common agricultural and fisheries policy of the EU

C.   Its Plenary sessions take place in the premises of the European Parliament

D.   It should be given legal standing

15.   The European Economic and Social Committee (EESC) was set up by the ....

A.   Treaty of Rome

B.   Merger Treaty

C.   Single European Act

D.   Maastricht Treaty

16.   Which statement characterises best the role that the EESC plays?

A.   The engine of economic prosperity and social progress in the EU

B.   The guardian of economic and social welfare in the EU

C.   A bridge between Europe and organised civil society

D.   The watchdog of the acquis

17.   Which of the following statements is incorrect? The EESC ....

A.   Is a non-political organisation

B.   Was established earlier than the CoR

C.   Has not yet issued a report on its own initiative

D.   Has an advisory status

18.   Which Treaty made it possible for the EESC to be consulted by the European Parliament?

A.   Single European Act

B.   Amsterdam Treaty

C.   Maastricht Treaty

D.   Treaty of Nice

19. **The Netherlands delegates to the EESC Assembly as many members as ....**

A. Hungary

B. Spain

C. Estonia

D. Ireland

20. **The maximum number of seats in the EESC is fixed at ....**

A. 222

B. 300

C. 350

D. The maximum number of seats will be fixed in 2009

21. **The Members of the EESC are appointed by the ....**

A. Council acting unanimously

B. Council acting by a qualified majority

C. Member States

D. Commission

22. **The Members of the EESC are bound by ....**

A. Instructions from the Member States

B. Instructions from the Council only

C. Instructions from the Commission

D. No mandatory instructions

23. **EESC Group I consists of .... delegates**

A. Employers'

B. Workers'

C. Trade unions'

D. Civil society

24. **How many sections does the European Economic and Social Committee have?**

A. 6

B. 11

C. 13

D. 15

25. **EESC section INT deals with ....**

A. Internal affairs

B. External relations

C. Single Market, production and consumption

D. Employment and social affairs

26. **When the Council or Commission consult the EESC, they may set it a time limit of at least ....**

A. Two weeks

B. One month

C. Three months

D. Six months

27. **There is no obligation imposed on the Council and the Commission to consult the EESC on ....**

A. Agricultural policy

B. Approximation of laws for the internal market

C. Immigration and asylum

D. Harmonisation of indirect taxation

28. Which of the following statements is correct?

A. The President of the EESC is Peter Straub

B. As a general rule, the EESC adopts texts and decisions by a qualified majority

C. Every two years the EESC elects a Bureau made up of 37 members

D. The EESC meets in Plenary sessions ten times a year

29. Which of the following statements is incorrect?

A. Plenary sessions are open to the public

B. The meetings of the ESSC sections are closed to the public

C. Certain debates that do not concern consultative work may be declared confidential by the EESC

D. The EESC seeks transparency on all its activities

30. What does the abbreviation ECOSOC stand for?

A. An advisory body of the EU

B. A UNESCO organ

C. An OECD organ

D. A UN organ

31. How many agencies does the European Union have?

A. 13

B. 18

C. 21

D. 15 (plus EUROPOL and EUROJUST)

32. Where is the European Centre for the Development of Vocational Training (Cedefop) located?

A. Thessaloniki

B. Vienna

C. Luxembourg

D. Dublin

33. The headquarters of the .... is in Alicante (Spain).

A. European Agency for Reconstruction

B. European Medicines Agency

C. European Food Safety Authority

D. Office for Harmonisation in the Internal Market

34. The European Council in Brussels on 12 and 13 December 2003 decided to extend the remit of .... to convert it into a Fundamental Rights Agency.

A. MCDDA

B. EUMC

C. ENISA

D. EFSA

35. Which statement is incorrect? TAIEX ....

A. Is not one of the agencies of the EU

B. Has been operational since 1996

C. Provides technical assistance in the field of approximation, application and enforcement of legislation

D. Is a unit of DG Enterprise and Industry of the Commission

36. On 30 June 2005, ... European Union Agency for Fundamental Rights.

A. The European Monitoring Centre on Racism and Xenophobia was renamed

B. The Commission submitted a proposal for a Council Regulation establishing the

C. The Council of Europe and the EU created the

D. Amnesty International called for the creation of a

37. The Agency for the Management of Operational Cooperation at the External Borders of the Member States of the EU (FRONTEX) is located in ....

A. Riga

B. Budapest

C. Nicosia

D. Warsaw

38. The European Union Institute for Security Studies (EUISS) ....

A. Is dependent on Member States' governments

B. Was created by a Council Joint Action in 2001

C. Does not deal with the development of a transatlantic dialogue

D. Is located in Brussels

39. Regarding the Office for Harmonisation in the Internal Market (Trade Marks and Designs, OHIM), which of the following statements is false?

A. The Spanish name of the agency is OAMI

B. Applications for trade marks and designs can be filed on-line

C. Application for a Community Trade Mark can only be made in English, French, German, Italian, or Spanish

D. Community design is a unitary system wherein one application provides design protection throughout the European Union

40. The European Centre for Disease Prevention and Control (ECDC) ....

A. Has an extended network of partners including Iceland

B. Helps strengthen Europe's research efforts against cancer

C. Is located in Stockholm

D. Is headed by a former Latvian health expert

EUROPEAN CENTRAL BANK (ECB)
EUROPEAN INVESTMENT BANK (EIB)
EUROPEAN BANK FOR RECONSTRUCTION AND DEVELOPMENT (EBRD)
35 QUESTIONS – ANSWERS PAGE 252

1.   When was the European Investment Bank (EIB) set up?

A.   1958

B.   1952

C.   1967

D.   1989

2.   Which statement is false?

A.   The EIB is the European Union's long-term lending institution

B.   The EIB contributes to European integration and social cohesion

C.   The EIB supports capital investment furthering EU economic objectives

D.   The members of the European Investment Bank are the members of the European Economic Area

3.   The EIB is active as a financing institution in approximately .... non-EU member countries.

A.   150

B.   78

C.   163

D.   138

4.   What kind of financial resources does the EIB provide?

A.   Loans and aids

B.   Aids only

C.   Loans and refundable subventions

D.   Loans only

5.   The European Investment Fund is part of the .... and was established in .....

A.   European Central Bank Group, 2000

B.   European Investment Bank Group, 1994

C.   European System of Central Banks, 1995

D.   European Investment Network, 1996

6.   The European Investment Fund specialises in .... and guarantees for .... and takes part in financing the new technology sector.

A.   Long-term loans, non-member countries

B.   Bonds, Member States

C.   Venture capital, small and medium enterprises

D.   Investments, large enterprises

7. Who was not president of the EIB?

A. Paride Formentini

B. Torsten Gersfelt

C. Yves Le Portz

D. Philippe Maystadt

8. Who make up the EIB's Management Committee and how long is their mandate?

A. President and five Vice-Presidents, 5 years

B. President and three Vice-Presidents, 3 years

C. President and eight Vice-Presidents, 6 years

D. President and two Vice-Presidents, 4 years

9. How many members and alternates does the EIB's Board of Directors have?

A. 12, 8

B. 25, 15

C. 30, 18

D. 26, 16

10. Since 1 May 2004, the Board of Directors makes decisions by a majority consisting of at least .... of members entitled to vote and representing at least .... of the subscribed capital.

A. One third, 50%

B. Half, 65%

C. One third, 65%

D. Half, 50%

11. Where is the EIB located?

A. Frankfurt

B. Luxembourg

C. London

D. Paris

12. Which statement is false?

A. The Council may invite the European Investment Bank to reconsider its lending policy towards a Member State

B. The European Investment Bank has legal personality

C. The Court of Justice does not have jurisdiction in disputes concerning the fulfilment by Member States of obligations under the Statute of the European Investment Bank

D. The European Investment Bank enjoys in the territories of the Member States such privileges and immunities as are necessary for the performance of its tasks

13. According to the Constitutional Treaty, the European Investment Bank may request the adoption of ....

A. Laws and opinions

B. Laws and framework laws

C. Framework laws and decisions

D. Recommendations and decisions

14. According to the Constitutional Treaty, how much will the EIB's capital be?

A. €87 billion

B. €120 billion

C. €245 billion

D. €163 billion

15. According to the Constitutional Treaty, what does the EIB not finance?

A. Projects for developing less-developed regions

B. Projects involving venture capital

C. Projects for modernising or converting undertakings

D. Projects with common interests to Member States

16. What make up the European System of Central Banks (ESCB)?

A. The European Central Bank and the national central banks of EU Member States

B. The European Central Bank and the national central banks of EU Member States that adopted the euro

C. National central banks of EU Member States that adopted the euro

D. National central banks of EU Member States

17. Who make up the Eurosystem?

A. National central banks of EU Member States

B. National central banks of EU Member States that adopted the euro

C. The European Central Bank and the national central banks of EU Member States that adopted the euro

D. The European Central Bank and the national central banks of EU Member States

18. What is the name of the supreme decision-making body of the European Central Bank?

A. Governing Board

B. Board of Governors

C. Board of Executives

D. Governing Council

19. Where is the International Monetary Fund located and when was it founded?

A. Vienna, 1962

B. Frankfurt, 1958

C. Tokyo, 1952

D. Washington D.C., 1946

20. What does the abbreviation TARGET stand for?

A. Trans-continental Automatic Repurchase Generation and Economic Transfers

B. Trans-European Automated Real-time Gross settlement Express Transfer

C. Time-based Asset and Resource Generation for European Trade

D. Total Assets and Revenues in General Economic Terms

21. What is the name of the guidelines adopted by the Council to provide the framework for defining the economic policy objectives and orientations of the Member States and the European Community?

A. General Financial Planning

B. Broad Economic Policy Guidelines

C. Strategic Economic Objectives

D. Financial and Economic Goals

22. According to the EC Treaty, what is the main objective of the European Central Bank?

A. To keep a low level of inflation

B. To curb unemployment

C. To maintain price stability

D. To maintain a stable exchange rate mechanism

23. Which one of the following is not a basic task to be carried out through the ESCB?

A. Conducting intra-Community exchange operations

B. Holding and managing the official foreign reserves of the Member States

C. Defining and implementing the monetary policy of the Community

D. Promoting the smooth operation of payment systems

24. Which statement is false? The ECB....

A. Defines and implements the monetary policy for the euro area

B. Holds and manages the official foreign reserves of the euro area countries

C. Has the exclusive right to authorise the issuance of bankcoins within the euro area

D. Collects statistical information necessary for fulfilling its tasks

25. Who is currently the president of the ECB?

A. Willem F. Duisenberg

B. Jean-Claude Trichet

C. Erkki Liikanen

D. Axel A. Weber

26. The Executive Board of the ECB consists of the ....

A. President, Vice-President and four other members

B. President, three Vice-Presidents and four other members

C. President, two Vice-Presidents and three other members

D. President, five Vice-Presidents and five other members

27. Members of the ECB's Executive Board are appointed by ....

A. Common accord of the Heads of State or Government of the euro area countries

B. Common accord of the Heads of State or Government of EU Member States

C. Two thirds majority of the Heads of State or Government of the euro area countries

D. Two thirds majority of the Heads of State or Government of EU Member States

28. Responsibilities of the ECB's Executive Board do not include ....

A. Preparation of Governing Council meetings

B. Appointment of Governing Council members

C. Management of the day-to-day business of the ECB

D. The implementation of monetary policy for the euro area

29.   Which one the following is not a basic principle for the European Central Bank?

A.   Transparency

B.   Efficiency

C.   Integrity

D.   Competitiveness

30.   When was the European Central Bank inaugurated?

A.   1996

B.   2000

C.   1998

D.   2002

31.   The European Bank for Reconstruction and Development (EBRD) does not promote ....

A.   Structural and sectoral reforms

B.   Competition, privatisation and entrepreneurship

C.   Small and medium-sized enterprises in need of venture capital

D.   Infrastructure development needed to support the private sector

32.   In which of the following countries does the EBRD not operate?

A.   Serbia and Montenegro

B.   Turkey

C.   Tajikistan

D.   Ukraine

33.   Who owns the EBRD?

A.   Member and shareholder countries, the European Community

B.   Member and shareholder countries, the European Investment Bank

C.   Member and shareholder countries, the European Community and the European Investment Bank

D.   The European Community and the European Investment Bank

34.   Who is the president of the EBRD?

A.   Jean Lemierre

B.   Noreen Doyle

C.   Steven Kaempfer

D.   Fabrizio Saccomanni

35.   When was the European Bank for Reconstruction and Development (EBRD) founded and where is it located?

A.   1991, London

B.   1989, Paris

C.   1990, Frankfurt

D.   1992, Zurich

POLICIES OF THE EUROPEAN UNION

AGRICULTURE

30 QUESTIONS – ANSWERS PAGE 258

1. The Common Agricultural Policy (CAP) became effective as of ....

A. 1958

B. 1960

C. 1962

D. 1993

2. Which of the following statements is false? The CAP ....

A. Directly relates to the Single Market

B. Is financed from the EAGG

C. Aims to increase production quantity

D. Is the one with the largest budget of all the EU policy areas

3. Which of the following statements is not an objective of the CAP?

A. Stabilising markets

B. Assuring the availability of supplies

C. Ensuring that supplies reach consumers at reasonable prices

D. Strengthening the market position of the EU in the international arena

4. What does the principle of "financial solidarity" mean in the context of the common agricultural market?

A. All expenses resulting from the CAP are borne by the Community budget

B. Member States which are better off are expected to contribute a greater share to the CAP budget

C. Any Member States falling victim to a natural disaster will receive financial assistance from other Member States

D. When applying product quotas, Member States assume solidarity with the ACP countries

5. The EAGGF was set up in ....

A. 1958

B. 1962

C. 1964

D. 1993

6. Which of the following statements is incorrect? The Guidance Section of the EAGGF ....

A. Is less important than the Guarantee Section

B. Is one of the structural funds

C. Funds expenditure concerning the common organisation of the markets

D. Aims at promoting regional development and reducing disparities between areas in Europe

7. SAPARD supports sustainable agricultural and rural development in....

A. The severely disadvantaged areas

B. Areas whose average per capita GDP is below 75% of the European Union average

C. The Central and Eastern European applicant countries during the pre-accession period

D. The ACP countries

8. Which of the following statements is incorrect in the context of the 2003 CAP reform?

A. Application arrangements for subsidy payments will be simplified

B. Environmentally friendly farming practices will be better acknowledged and rewarded

C. Competitiveness, food quality and environment standards are in the spotlight

D. Subsidies will be linked to production

9. What is the bottom-line of "modulation"?

A. Old premiums paid under the CAP will be merged into a 'single farm payment'

B. Funds saved through cutting support to big producers are shifted to the rural development pillar of the CAP

C. Modulation will stop the agricultural dumping that destroys the livelihoods of small farmers in the poorest countries

D. Environmentally friendly farming practices will be better acknowledged and rewarded

10. What does the term "cross compliance" imply?

A. Farmers may receive direct payments provided that they meet the standards on public health, environment and animal welfare

B. Farmers must observe international agricultural patterns to receive production aids

C. CAP schemes may not run counter to the relevant EC competition rules

D. Farmers may receive a single payment only if they have received certain direct payments

11. The IACS ....

A. Replaced IAPS

B.   Enables the farmers' payment applications to be checked

C.   Co-finances payment schemes

D.   Is managed by the Commission and monitored by the European Parliament

12.   What does the abbreviation ECCP stand for?

A.   European Soil Protection Programme

B.   A programme containing plans for how the EU will meet its Kyoto Protocol commitment to reduce greenhouse gas emissions

C.   OECD unit dealing with agricultural and rural development matters

D.   A programme setting out 'Indicator Reporting' on the integration of Environmental concerns into Agricultural policy

13.   Since Agenda 2000, the Common Agricultural Policy has had two pillars:

A.   Agriculture (first pillar), and rural development (second pillar)

B.   Farming (first pillar), and sustainable development (second pillar)

C.   Market and income policy (first pillar), and sustainable development of rural areas (second pillar)

D.   Agriculture and forestry (first pillar), and sustainable rural development (second pillar)

14.   The multilateral trade talks held between 2 and 4 March 2005 in Mombasa (Kenya) were to ....

A.   Push forward the Doha Development Round

B.   Settle dispute between the G90 and the G20

C.   Prepare the Davos World Economic Forum

D.   Reach an agreement on the "Singapore issues"

15.   Which of the following statements is correct?

A.   The majority of EU citizens believes that granting more funds for direct support for farmers is a good thing

B.   Most EU citizens are unhappy with the recent changes in the Common Agricultural Policy

C.   Most EU15 citizens believes that the current funding schemes favour farmers from EU10

D.   The majority of EU citizens would give a green light to GMOs

16.   What is the WTO "Amber Box"?

A.   A category of programmes on which spending is not limited by international trade agreements

B.   Blue box with conditions

C.   Supports exempt from 'de minimis' provisions

D.   Production or trade distorting domestic support measures

17.   Agriculture is covered by the .... procedure.

A.   Consultation

B.   Cooperation

C.   Codecision

D.   Information

18.   Which country is the largest producer and collector of cow's milk in the EU?

A.   Denmark

B.   France

C.   Germany

D.   Poland

19. Agricultural production employs around .... % of EU25 workforce.

A.   8

B.   15

C.   20

D.   23

20. What does the abbreviation TAC stand for?

A.   The maximum amount of fish that can be taken during a certain period of time

B.   The European Parliament's agricultural committee

C.   OECD unit dealing with matters with trade, agriculture and commerce implications

D.   Agriculture Agreement (WTO)

21. The 2005 budget for the CAP is EUR .... billion.

A.   28.6

B.   35.8

C.   44.7

D.   49.7

22. Which of the following statements is correct? The European Food Safety Agency is not ....

A.   Located in Parma, Italy

B.   Making laws

C.   Dealing with requests for risk assessments from the European Commission

D.   A fully-fledged independent agency of the EU

23. The ISPA ....

A.   Covers the period between 2000-2006

B.   Has an annual budget of EUR 250 million

C.   Is accessible to Ireland, Spain, Greece and Portugal

D.   Is located in Parma

24. The CMOs ....

A.   Constitute the "second pillar" of the CAP

B.   Are designed to increase production output

C.   Ensure that consumers are provided with secure food supplies

D.   Were laid down in Agenda 2000

25. Compensatory allowances ....

A.   May be paid to farmers from Ireland, Spain, Greece and Portugal only

B.   Are paid to farmers in naturally less favoured areas

C.   Have been set out under the PHARE directive

D.   Are offered to EU exporters to cover the difference between the internal EU price and the world market price

26. FADN ....

A.   Is the main channel for the EU's financial and technical cooperation with Central and Eastern European Countries

B.   Brings together national agricultural accountancy offices

C.   Is located in Stockholm

D.   Enables the market to be stabilised with minimal effect on traditional marketing channels

27. **Which of the following is not an objective for rural development policy set in Commission Communication on the Financial Perspectives for the period 2007-2013?**

A. Promoting an agricultural system based on drastic restrictions on farm inputs such as fertilisers and pesticides (organic farming)

B. Increasing the competitiveness of the agricultural sector

C. Enhancing the environment and countryside

D. Enhancing the quality of life in rural areas and promoting diversification of economic activities

28. **Which statement is incorrect?**

A. Financial discipline ensures that the EU's farm budget fixed until 2013 is not overshot

B. New Member States may complement direct aid up to the level applicable prior to accession

C. The single farm payment is independent from production

D. Semi-subsistence farms produce for own consumption and do not bring products to market

29. **The abbreviation "PDO"**

A. Stands for a term used to describe foodstuffs

B. Refers to periods in which a production-linked aid was granted

C. Was replaced with the abbreviation 'PGI' in 2004

D. Stands for national organisations in the Member States dealing with production development matters

30. **The 2002 reform of the Common Fisheries Policy does not entail ....**

A. A long term approach

B. A new policy for the fleets

C. The streamlining of the system of procurement for fisheries goods and services

D. The stakeholders' greater involvement

EMPLOYMENT, SOCIAL AFFAIRS AND EQUAL OPPORTUNITIES

35 QUESTIONS – ANSWERS PAGE 265

1. **Which Treaty added the "promotion of employment" to the list of the European Union's objectives?**

A. Treaty of Nice

B. Maastricht Treaty

C. Amsterdam Treaty

D. Brussels Treaty

2. **According to the EC Treaty, Member States must regard promoting employment as ....**

A. A common concern

B. A fundamental principle of the Community

C. A prerequisite for greater social cohesion and prosperity

D. A necessary step to achieving full employment

in a way consistent with the broad guidelines of the economic policies of the Member States and of the Community

C.   Single European Act

D.   Maastricht Treaty

3.   What does the so-called "Luxembourg Process" call for?

A.   Action to coordinate and monitor the employment policies in the Member States on a yearly basis

B.   The establishment of the European Employment Service

C.   Measures aimed at harmonising labour laws in the Member States

D.   Revising the Lisbon objectives

7.   The first Employment Policy Guidelines were adopted ....

A.   In 1998

B.   In 1999

C.   Before the Amsterdam Treaty entered into force

D.   After the entry into force of the Amsterdam Treaty

4.   The so-called "Cardiff Process" was initiated ....

A.   In 1998

B.   In 1999

C.   Before the "Luxembourg Process"

D.   After the "Cologne Process"

8.   The first Employment Policy Guidelines were built on .... pillars.

A.   3

B.   4

C.   5

D.   6

5.   The European Employment Pact was adopted at the ....

A.   Luxembourg Summit

B.   Cardiff Summit

C.   Cologne Summit

D.   Lisbon Summit

9.   Which of the following terms is not linked to the Open Method of Coordination?

A.   Convergence

B.   Country surveillance

C.   Management by objectives

D.   Awareness raising

6.   The European Employment Strategy was formally created by the ....

A.   Amsterdam Treaty

B.   Treaty of Nice

10.   What changes did the 2004 Employment Guidelines make to the main objectives set out by the 2003 Employment Guidelines?

A.   None

B.   Repealed them

C. Exempted the new Member States from observing them

D. The Council decided not to adopt Employment Guidelines in 2004

11. Under the EC Treaty, the European Employment Committee is responsible for ....

A. Advising the European Parliament on matters relating to employment policies in the Member States

B. Establishing the Employment Guidelines

C. Supervising the drawing up of National Action Plans

D. Monitoring the employment situation and employment policies in the Member States and the Community

12. Which of the following statements is incorrect? There is no directive on ....

A. Economically dependent workers

B. Employee participation in profits

C. Equitable wage

D. European Works Councils

13. The Commission proposes to amend the Working Time Directive to the effect that ....

A. Previous principles such as health and safety of workers be revoked

B. Individual opt-out from the 48 hour week would not be allowed

C. Member States could extend the standard reference period for calculating the average working week of 48 hours from 4 months to up to 3 years

D. The "inactive" part of on-call time would not be counted as working time

14. The EC Treaty provides that the European Council must each year adopt a conclusion on the employment situation in the Community based on ....

A. A joint annual report by the Council and the Commission

B. The National Action Plans drawn up by the Member States

C. A joint memorandum by the Council and the European Parliament

D. A recommendation by the Council

15. The provisions of the Agreement on Social Policy annexed to the .... were introduced in the ....

A. Single European Act, Maastricht Treaty

B. Amsterdam Treaty, Maastricht Treaty

C. Maastricht Treaty, Amsterdam Treaty

D. Amsterdam Treaty, Treaty of Nice

16. Which Treaty provided for the establishment of the Social Protection Committee?

A. Amsterdam Treaty

B. Maastricht Treaty

C. Treaty of Nice

D. Single European Act

17. When did the Commission put forward the third scoreboard on implementing the Social Policy Agenda?

A. 2000

B. 2001

C. 2002

D. 2003

18. The European Social Fund was set up by the ....

A. Treaty of Rome

B. Single European Act

C. Amsterdam Treaty

D. Treaty of Nice

19. In 1999, the European Council that was held in Cologne decided to begin drafting a ....

A. European Social Charter

B. European Convention on Human Rights

C. Charter of Fundamental Rights

D. Constitution for Europe

20. What is the purpose of the EQUAL Community Initiative?

A. To integrate and combat discrimination against women

B. To finance job creation schemes in the new Member States

C. To co-finance the European Social Fund

D. To test and promote new means of combating all forms of discrimination and inequalities in the labour market

21. What is the purpose of the Tripartite Social Summit for Growth and Employment?

A. To ensure a continuous concertation between the Council, the Commission and the social partners on economic, social and employment matters

B. To revise the Growth and Stability Pact on a yearly basis

C. To ensure a continuous dialogue and exchange of best practice between the Council and the European employees' and employers' organisations

D. To set out the Broad Economic Policy Guidelines and the Employment Guidelines

22. Who initiated the Val Duchesse social dialogue process?

A. Jacques Delors

B. Jacques Chirac

C. Pat Cox

D. Romano Prodi

23. In 2002, the general cross-industry organisations (UNICE/UEAPME, CEEP and ETUC) concluded a framework agreement on ....

A. Parental leave

B. Fixed-term work

C. Telework

D. The organisation of working time of mobile workers in civil aviation

24. Which of the following is not an objective of the European Social Agenda?

A. Full employment

B. Fighting all forms of poverty and discrimination

C. Modernising social protection

D. Reinforcing the social dimension of enlargement

25. **Which of the following statements is incorrect? The Lisbon Strategy ....**

A. Aims at making the EU the most competitive and the most dynamic knowledge-based economy in the world

B. Targets more and better jobs in the EU

C. Has an indefinite term

D. Intends not to harm the achievements of the European welfare state

26. **Who chaired the High Level Group that put forward a report "Facing the Challenge - The Lisbon Strategy for Growth and Employment"?**

A. Vladimir Špidla

B. Anna Diamantopoulou

C. Wim Kok

D. Valéry Giscard d'Estaing

27. **The 22 and 23 March 2005 European Council agreed to .... the Lisbon process.**

A. Break off

B. Speed up

C. Re-launch

D. Withdraw from

28. **Which of the following statements is correct? Enlargement has raised the EU population by .... %, to more than .... million people, but only increased its GDP by .... %.**

A. 20, 450, 4.5

B. 18, 550, 5.5

C. 25, 480, 0.5

D. 22, 468, 8

29. **Which European Council adopted the Commission Communication "European Initiative for Growth - Investing in Networks and Knowledge for Growth and Jobs"?**

A. Brussels European Council (2003)

B. Stockholm European Council (2001)

C. Cologne European Council (1999)

D. Lisbon European Council (2000)

30. **On 1 June 2004 the Council reached political agreement to focus action on four specific objectives highlighted in the "Employment Task Force" report. Which of the following objectives is not one of the said four?**

A. Increased adaptability

B. Making the work pay

C. Improving employment governance

D. Investing in human capital

31. **The "ENEA pilot project" is designed to test the feasibility and usefulness of the establishment of European exchange programmes for....**

A. The elderly

B. People with disabilities

C. Women

D. Ethnic or national minorities

32. **Which of the following statements is correct?**

A. Females are more likely than males to be unemployed in most Member States

B. Males are more likely than females to be unemployed in most Member States

C. Females are more likely to be unemployed in most new Member States

D. Females are more likely to be unemployed than disabled people in most Member States

33. **Council Decision 2000/750/EC of 27 November 2000 on a "Community action programme to combat discrimination 2001-2006" does not deal with discrimination based on ....**

A. Religion or belief

B. Gender

C. Sexual orientation

D. Age

34. **What doest the abbreviation MISSOC stand for?**

A. Community initiative to promote the development of information society in the social field

B. One of the EU-level cross-industry organisations

C. Free alliance of consultancy firms and NGOs engaging in activities relating to employment and social affairs

D. A system that aims at promoting a continuous exchange of information on social protection

35. **DELSA is a(n)....**

A. Association for European law students

B. Unit within the OECD

C. Community initiative to promote the development of the information society in the social field

D. Civil organisation for the development of employment and labour conditions in society

INTERNAL MARKET

40 QUESTIONS – ANSWERS PAGE 271

1. **The Common Market was created in ....**

A. 1951

B. 1952

C. 1957

D. 1958

2. **Which Treaty introduced the notion of an "Internal Market"?**

A. Treaty of Rome

B. Single European Act

C. Maastricht Treaty

D. Amsterdam Treaty

3. **The Common Customs Tariff has been in place since ....**

A. 1 July 1968

B. 1 July 1966

C. 1 July 1987

D. 1 January 1993

4. **Which principle was laid down by the Court of Justice in the Cassis de Dijon judgment of 1979?**

A. Mutual recognition

B. Non-discrimination

C. Free movement of goods

D. Secondary establishment

5. **The so called "Dassonville formula" relates to ....**

A. Trademarks

B. Taxes

C. Customs duties

D. Measures having equivalent effect to quantitative restrictions

6. **.... may not constitute a "mandatory requirement" capable of justifying restrictions on imports or exports.**

A. The protection of culture

B. Fairness of commercial transactions

C. National state aid schemes

D. Improvement of working conditions

7. **In Keck and Mithouard the Court of Justice dealt with rules on ....**

A. Taxes

B. Quantitative restrictions

C. Mutual recognition

D. Selling arrangements

8. **Which Treaty has introduced the concept of "European citizenship"?**

A. Single European Act

B. Maastricht Treaty

C. Amsterdam Treaty

D. Treaty of Nice

9. **The White Paper entitled "Completing the Internal Market" did not/was not ....**

A. Follow the adoption of the Single European Act

B. Produced by the Commission headed by Jacques Delors

C. Suggest that non-tariff barriers should be eliminated by means of mutual recognition of national rules

D. Set a deadline for the creation of a single market by 31 December 1992

10. **Which statement is incorrect? The Cecchini Report ....**

A. Was named after an Italian man

B. Was based on economic models of four of the largest EU economies plus Belgium and the Netherlands

C. Provided the economic justification for completing the Internal Market

D. Was the outcome of the research programme "Cost of Europe"

11. **The so-called "new approach" is related to ....**

A.   Customs duties

B.   Taxes

C.   Standardisation and harmonisation

D.   Collective investment funds

12. **The Single Market Action Plan drawn up by the Commission in 1997 ....**

A.   Set out priority actions for improving the functioning of the Single Market by 1 January 1999

B.   Affirmed that the introduction of the European single currency must take place by 1 January 2002

C.   Confirmed that a European "Home Market" should be achieved by 1 May 2004

D.   Provided for a Directive on Services in the Internal Market, which should be adopted before 31 December 2005

13. **Which statement is incorrect? The Internal Market Strategy 2003-2006 ....**

A.   Was adopted in 2003

B.   Contains 10 priorities

C.   Does not deal with taxation issues

D.   Aims to strengthen the "basics" or "fundamentals" of the Internal Market

14. **Which of the following countries' nationals can benefit from the free movement of workers principle?**

A.   The nationals of the EFTA countries except the citizens of Switzerland

B.   Nationals of Norway, Liechtenstein, Iceland and Switzerland

C.   The nationals of the EFTA countries except the citizens of Liechtenstein

D.   Only Swiss citizens

15. **Which "new" Member States' nationals cannot take up work without a work permit during the transitional period defined in the Accession Treaties?**

A.   Hungary, Slovakia and Cyprus

B.   Poland, Malta, Latvia, Estonia and Lithuania

C.   Slovenia and the Czech Republic

D.   Poland, Cyprus and Lithuania

16. **For stays of less than three months, the only requirement from European Union citizens is that they ....**

A.   Possess a valid identity document or passport

B.   Have sufficient resources and sickness insurance

C.   Are engaged in economic activity

D.   Do not have a criminal record

17. **Who has the right to reside with a worker who is a national of one Member State and who is employed in the territory of another Member State?**

A.   The worker's spouse or registered partner and their descendants who are under the age of 21 years

B.   The worker's spouse and their descendants who are under the age of 18 years

C.   Only the worker's dependent relatives

D.   The worker's dependent relatives in the ascending line of the worker and his spouse

18. Who has the right to take up any activity as an employed person within the EU's territory?

A. The worker's spouse and those of the children who are under the age of 21 years or dependent on the worker

B. The worker's or his/her spouse's dependent relatives in the ascending lines

C. The worker's spouse

D. The family members of the worker, as defined under the national law of each Member State

19. In the context of free movement of persons, Regulation 1408/71 ....

A. Creates a single European social scheme

B. Harmonises the national social security measures

C. Harmonises the national social security measures except pension schemes

D. Co-ordinates the social security schemes of EU Member States

20. Which professional qualifications are recognised automatically as a result of harmonisation?

A. Doctors, dentists, midwives, architects

B. Nurses, pharmacists, veterinarians, notaries

C. Dentists, pharmacists, psychologists

D. Doctors, lawyers, teachers

21. A student may reside in another Member State for studying purposes on condition that he or she ....

A. Provides evidence of having sufficient means to avoid becoming a burden on the social assistance system of the host Member State

B. Is enrolled in an educational establishment, either recognised or not, for the purpose of following a vocational training course

C. Is covered by sickness insurance in respect of all risks in the host Member State

D. Does not have a criminal record

22. In the light of the judgment of the European Court of Justice in the Grzelczyk case, if a student exercising free movement applies for social assistance, the Member State may ....

A. Consider suspending his/her right of residence

B. Not refuse such an application

C. Refuse the application and, as a consequence, suspend his/her right of residence

D. Refuse the application, but this may not result in an automatic suspension of his/her right of residence

23. Which statement is incorrect? The Societas Europaea (SE) ....

A. Is a public limited liability company

B. Will be registered in the Member States in which it engages in business activities

C. Is subject to Community legislation directly applicable in all Member States

D. May be established by the merger of two or more existing public limited companies from at least two different EU Member States

24. A Community facility providing medium-term financial assistance for Members States' balances of payments is ....

A. Not available to those Member States that have not adopted the euro

B. A substitute for a short-term financing facility

C.   Part of EMR II

D.   Implemented by the Council

25. Which body is responsible for ensuring that capital moves freely between EFTA States and EU Member States?

A.   EEA Council

B.   EFTA Monitoring Committee

C.   EFTA Surveillance Authority

D.   EU-EFTA Joint Supervisory Committee (EEJSC)

26. Council Regulation (EC) No 881/2002 imposes specific restrictive measures directed against ....

A.   Certain capital movements from the applicant countries

B.   Member States limiting parallel trade in violation of EU competition law

C.   Any person who acquires knowledge or a suspicion of money laundering but fails to disclose such information

D.   Certain persons and entities associated with Usama bin Laden, the Al-Qaida network and the Taliban

27. The Financial Services Action Plan (FSAP) was adopted in .... and expired/will expire in ....

A.   1999, 2004

B.   2002, 2005

C.   2003, 2017

D.   2004, 2008

28. Which of the following legal instruments was adopted in light of the Fraud Prevention Action Plan (2004-2007)?

A.   Directive on Financial Conglomerates

B.   Directive on Collateral

C.   Directive on Insurance Intermediaries

D.   None of the above

29. Approximately how many concrete new initiatives are contained in the Green Paper on Financial Services Policy (2005-2010)?

A.   None

B.   More than ten but less than twenty

C.   More than twenty but less than fifty

D.   More than fifty

30. What do the so-called UCITS Directives cover?

A.   Retail financial services

B.   Collective investment funds

C.   Supplementary pensions

D.   Financial crime

31. A European "26th regime" for certain consumer financial products would ....

A.   Be an alternative for providers to complying with EU law

B.   Make it impossible for companies to passport business

C.   Be a voluntary code of pan-European laws

D.   Revitalise the "home country" regime

32. What is FIN-NET?

A. An out-of-court complaints network for financial services

B. A network for banks and financial institutions in the euro-zone

C. Online fraud detection database for retail financial services

D. A network providing expert guidance on insurance, investment products and services

33. The "CESAME" Group ....

A. Was set up in 2005

B. Is a forum for fraud prevention

C. Assists the Commission in the integration of securities clearing and settlement systems

D. Advises the Commission on matters relating to cross-border credit transfers in euros

34. The Lamfalussy Report dealt with ....

A. Cyber crime

B. The European Securities Market

C. Fraud and counterfeiting

D. Postal services

35. According to the Electronic Commerce Directive, Member States may restrict the freedom to provide information society services from another Member State if necessary for ....

A. The protection of consumers, excluding investors

B. The protection of public health

C. Safeguarding cultural heritage

D. Such freedom cannot be restricted in any way whatsoever

36. The abbreviation .... stands for the European Committee for Standardisation.

A. CEN

B. CENEL

C. CENELEC

D. CELEX

37. What is ETSI?

A. A fully fledged EU agency

B. A non-profit making organisation

C. The European Technology and Science Institute

D. The predecessor body of ETI

38. CENELEC ....

A. Was created in 1987

B. Was born out of the merger between CENEL-COM and CELEC

C. Was set up under EC law

D. Prepares mandatory electrotechnical standards

39. The 2004 draft Directive on Services in the Internal Market ....

A. Excluded the whole health care services sector

B. Watered down the "country of origin principle"

C. Is unlikely to undergo fundamental review by the Commission

D. Was nicknamed the "Bolkestein Directive"

40. **Which statement is false? The Third Anti-Money Laundering Directive ....**

A.   Reflects the revised Forty Recommendations of the Financial Action Task Force (FATF)

B.   Is applicable to the banking sector

C.   Is not applicable to terrorist financing

D.   Applies to all providers of goods, when payments are made in cash in excess of EUR15 000

REGIONAL POLICY

40 QUESTIONS – ANSWERS PAGE 286

1. **The Commissioner in charge of Regional Policy is of which nationality?**

A.   Polish

B.   Slovene

C.   French

D.   Spanish

2. **Article 158 of the EC Treaty provides that "[i]n order to promote its overall harmonious development, the Community shall develop and pursue its actions leading to the strengthening of its ...."**

A.   Measures against regional differences

B.   Efforts for regional development

C.   Economic and social cohesion

D.   Anti-poverty measures and financial cohesion

3. **Based on the Regulation 1164/94 of 16 May 1994, a Member State is eligible for Cohesion Fund if it ....**

A.   Has a per capita gross national product (GNP),

measured in purchasing power parities, of less than 85% of the Community average

B.   Has a programme leading to the fulfilment of the conditions of economic convergence as set out in the EC Treaty

C.   Presents projects in the field of environment and regional development

D.   Has a GDP lower than 80% of the EU25's average

4. **Which of the following countries was considered no longer eligible for the Cohesion Fund from 2004?**

A.   Greece

B.   Spain

C.   Ireland

D.   Portugal

5. **Which of the following countries was not considered eligible for the Cohesion Fund after accession?**

A.   Slovenia

B.   Czech Republic and Slovenia

C.   None of them

D.   Cyprus and Estonia

6.   **How many Member States are eligible for the Cohesion Fund in 2005?**

A.   11

B.   14

C.   13

D.   12

7.   **Which of the following statements is false regarding the Cohesion Fund?**

A.   Environment projects may be eligible

B.   Funding granted to a Member State can be suspended if the country fails to comply with its convergence programme

C.   Projects establishing or developing transport infrastructure are eligible

D.   To be eligible for funding, no country may have a public deficit higher than 4% of its GDP

8.   **Regarding EU assistance under the Cohesion Fund, which statement is false?**

A.   The total rate of the EU assistance cannot exceed 85% of public or equivalent expenditure

B.   It is always a natural or legal person who can be held responsible for implementation

C.   Exceptionally, the Commission may finance 100% of the total cost of preliminary studies and technical support measures

D.   The combined assistance of the Fund and other Community aid for a project cannot exceed 90% of the total expenditure relating to that project

9.   **Which of the following countries had the highest allocation of Cohesion Funds for the period 2004-2006?**

A.   Slovakia

B.   Hungary

C.   Czech Republic

D.   Latvia

10. **Which of the following is not included in the Commission's draft reform of the Cohesion Fund?**

A.   The Community Support Framework will be abolished and the Programme Complement will be extended

B.   The renewed Cohesion Fund will be part of multi-annual programmes instead of being decided project by project

C.   The number of Objectives will be limited from 7 to 3, the number of funds involved from 6 to 3

D.   Eligibility rules are to be defined at Member States level

11. **The term "additionality" refers to ....**

A.   The number of Member States required to take part in a Trans-European Network project

B.   An extra financial resource Member States are obliged to provide for projects under the Cohesion Fund

C.   The maximum amount of public spending a region may allocate to a project

D.   Community assistance complementing the contributions of the Member States rather than reducing them

12.   A strip of land and sea, the width of which depends on the nature of the environment and of human activity related to aquatic resources is called ....

A.   Coastal area

B.   Seashore region

C.   Bay zone

D.   Semi-peninsular territory

13.   Which of the following statements is true regarding Community Initiatives?

A.   They are aid or action programmes in regions where no Structural Fund operation is involved

B.   They are drawn up by the Commission and the Committee of the Regions

C.   An initiative may be financed by several funds

D.   They absorb 5.35% of the Structural Funds budget

14.   Which of the following is not a Community Initiative?

A.   Equal

B.   Interreg III

C.   Urban II

D.   Cordis

15.   Which of the following Committees does not take part in the implementation of the Structural Funds?

A.   Committee pursuant to Article 147 of the Treaty

B.   Committee on Environmental Structures and Economic Development

C.   Committee on the Development and Conversion of Regions

D.   Committee on Structures for Fisheries and Aquaculture

16.   What are the so-called "compensatory allowances"?

A.   Special aid granted under the European Regional Development Fund

B.   Extra aid that may be requested by the least favoured peripheral regions

C.   Aid for farmers to compensate for the handicap of difficult physical and climatic conditions

D.   Conversion assistance to maritime areas under the Financial Instrument for Fisheries Guidance

17.   Since when has the Financial Instrument for Fisheries Guidance (FIFG) been operational?

A.   1994

B.   1999

C.   1987

D.   1992

18.   Which of the following does rural development not concern?

A.   Environmental challenges

B.   Decreasing fishing vessels in maritime areas

C.   Improvement of living and working conditions

D.   Supplementary or alternative job-creating activities

19.   What is the name of the financial instrument for candidate countries in the field of agriculture?

A.   ISPA

B. PHARE

C. SAPARD

D. TEN

20. NUTS is related to ....

A. Statistical data concerning regions

B. Areas under Objective 2

C. Agricultural production and direct aids

D. Outermost regions and French overseas departments

21. Which of the following is not considered as a mountain area?

A. Areas at a lower altitude in which the slopes are so steep that the use of machinery is not possible

B. Areas in which, due to hot temperature, very difficult climatic conditions prevail and the growing season is between 4 to 6 months

C. Areas which are characterised by both altitude and slopes and in which the combination of the two handicaps gives rise to a handicap equivalent to the two preceding handicaps taken separately

D. Areas north of the 62nd parallel and certain adjacent areas

22. Which of the following created the European Social Fund?

A. Council Regulation No 1408/71

B. Single European Act

C. Maastricht Treaty

D. Treaty of Rome

23. In budgetary terms, which Structural Fund is the largest?

A. European Agricultural Guidance and Guarantee Fund

B. Financial Instrument for Fisheries Guidance

C. European Social Fund

D. European Regional Development Fund

24. More than .... of the appropriations of the Structural Funds are allocated to helping areas lagging behind in their development ("Objective ....") where the gross domestic product (GDP) is below ....% of the Community average.

A. Two thirds, 2, 85

B. Half, 1, 85

C. Half, 2, 75

D. Two thirds, 1, 75

25. Objective 2 of the Structural Funds aims to revitalise all areas facing ....

A. Long-term industrial decline

B. Structural difficulties

C. Low agricultural production rates

D. High levels of youth unemployment

26. In the 2000-2006 term, the proportion between the budget allocated to the Priority Objectives and Community Initiatives was approximately ....

A. 90:10

B. 94:6

C. 98:2

D. 88:12

27. Which of the following is not a priority under the Financial Instrument for Fisheries Guidance?

A. Processing and marketing of fisheries products

B. Coupling fisheries guidance with regional policy tools regarding unemployment of fishermen

C. Assistance for small-scale coastal fishing, protection of fish stocks in sea coast areas

D. Renewal of the fleet and modernisation of fishing vessels, adjustment of fishing activity to fish stocks

28. Trans-European Networks do not include ....

A. Cross-border cooperation

B. Telecommunications

C. Transport

D. Energy

29. Until 2007, the Council is to act .... on a proposal from the Commission and after obtaining the .... of the European Parliament and consulting the Economic and Social Committee and the Committee of the Regions, to determine some basic issues relating to both the Structural Funds and the Cohesion Fund.

A. By qualified majority, assent

B. By qualified majority, opinion

C. Unanimously, assent

D. Unanimously, opinion

30. The above mentioned basic issues do not include ....

A. General rules applicable to the Funds

B. Organisation of the Funds

C. The coordination of the Funds with one another and with other financial instruments

D. The designation of regions eligible for Structural Funds financial instruments

31. Which section of the EAGGF contributes to spending on the structural reform of agriculture and promotion of new forms of rural development?

A. Guarantee Section

B. Guidance Section

C. Both the Guidance and Guarantee Sections

D. Neither of the two

32. Which European Council decided to increase the appropriations earmarked for structural operations in 1994-99 by a further 40%?

A. Luxembourg

B. Lisbon

C. Madrid

D. Edinburgh

33. Within the framework of Interreg III, which of the following is not a chief objective?

A. Cooperation with bordering third countries

B. Transnational cooperation

C. Cross-border cooperation

D. Interregional cooperation

34. ESPON is a programme that concerns ....

A. Statistical and publication issues regarding regional policy objectives

B. Spatial planning and observation

C. Role of non-governmental organisations in rural development

D. European public opinion networks

35. The European Union Solidarity Fund has an annual budget of .... billion euros.

A. 1.5

B. 1

C. 1.8

D. 0.5

36. What is the population (in millions of inhabitants) covered by Objective 1 between 2000 and 2006?

A. 89

B. 187

C. 155

D. 211

37. Objective 3 is financed by the ....

A. ESF

B. ERDF

C. EAGGF

D. FIFG

38. Among others, ESF also finances ....

A. Equal

B. Urban II

C. Leader+

D. Objective 1 and 2

39. How many regions are there in the EU25?

A. 221

B. 273

C. 254

D. 205

40. According to the Commission proposal for the 2007-2013 period, what percent would spending on Structural Funds be in terms of the EU27's GDP?

A. 1.12

B. 0.67

C. 0.41

D. 0.89

COMPETITION POLICY

30 QUESTIONS – ANSWERS PAGE 293

1.   The process of defining the relevant product market typically begins by ....

A.   Establishing the closest substitutes to the product (or group of products)

B.   Assessing market concentration

C.   Determining the relevant geographic market

D.   Assessing cross-price elasticity

2.   The Hypothetical Monopolist Test is also called .... Test.

A.   SIEC

B.   SLC

C.   SSNIP

D.   Cellophane Fallacy

3.   Which source of competitive constraint (if any) is not taken into account when defining markets?

A.   Supply side substitutability

B.   Demand side substitutability

C.   Potential competition

D.   All sources of competitive constraints must be taken into account when defining markets

4.   Articles 81 and 82 of the EC Treaty are applied and enforced in Ireland by the ....

A.   Department of Justice (DOJ)

B.   Competition Authority

C.   Office of Fair Trading (OFT)

D.   Competition Bureau

5.   Article 81(2) of the EC Treaty provides that any agreements or decisions prohibited under Article 81(1) must be ....

A.   Brought in compliance with the Community competition rules

B.   Null and void

C.   Automatically void

D.   Declared incompatible with the common market

6.   Which of the following points is not taken into account when applying Article 81(3) of the EC Treaty?

A.   Benefits to the consumer

B.   Abuse of dominance

C.   Efficiency gains

D.   Indispensability of the restrictions

7.   When applying Community competition rules, the Commission may not ....

A.   Order interim measures

B.   Impose structural remedies on the undertakings in violation of law

C.   Issue a compulsory winding up order

D.   Accept commitments

8. **What does the requirement for uniform application of Community competition law mean?**

A.   National competition authorities may not initiate proceedings without the prior approval of the Commission

B.   The European Court of Justice has the final word on each disputed competition case

C.   National competition authorities and courts have the power to apply Articles 81 and 82 of the EC Treaty

D.   National competition authorities and courts may not take decisions running counter to the decision adopted by the Commission

9. **Which of the following statements is incorrect? The Commission is entitled to ....**

A.   Inquire into a particular type of agreement across various sectors

B.   Appoint the members of the Advisory Committee

C.   Reject a complaint on the ground that a national competition authority is dealing with the case

D.   Impose heavy fines on undertakings in violation of Articles 81 and 82 of the EC Treaty

10. **In the context of the application by the Commission of Articles 81 and 82 of the EC Treaty, third parties may submit their observations before a decision relating to .... is adopted.**

A.   Commitments

B.   Interim measures

C.   Fines

D.   Periodic penalty payments

11. **Which of the following points is not an inherent feature of the Commission's leniency programme?**

A.   First-come, first-served system

B.   "No-names" basis approach may be made

C.   Total immunity from fines is possible

D.   Maverick firms are excluded

12. **The EC Merger Regulation (ECMR) applies from ....**

A.   1 December 2003

B.   1 January 2004

C.   1 May 2004

D.   1 January 2005

13. **What does the "one-stop-shop" principle imply under the ECMR?**

A.   Each and every merger must be appraised at Community level

B.   The Commission may declare a concentration compatible with the common market by one-off action

C.   The Commission may refer the case to the relevant national Competition Authorities

D.   A proposed merger may be assessed by the Commission alone rather than being subject to different review processes in one or more Member States

14. **Which of the following statements is incorrect? The so-called "substantive test" is ....**

A.   A hybrid test

B.   Aimed to curtail the dominance test

C.   Designed to capture all anti-competitive mergers

D.   Also called SIEC test

15.   The ECMR allows the parties to file a notification prior to ....

A.   The conclusion of a binding agreement

B.   Signing a letter of intent

C.   Establishing a memorandum of understanding

D.   Publicly announcing an intention to make a public bid

16.   Under the ECMR the Commission decides to initiate proceedings ....

A.   When the relevant national Competition Authority is reluctant to initiate an investigation

B.   If it finds that the proposed concentration raises serious doubts as to its compatibility with the common market

C.   When it is evidently clear that a merger would create or strengthen dominant position

D.   If the undertakings concerned failed to notify the concentration to the Commission prior to implementation

17.   A concentration is to be suspended ....

A.   Until it has been declared compatible with the common market

B.   As long as it raises serous doubts as to its compatibility with the common market

C.   If the undertakings concerned fail to comply with the conditions and obligations attached to the clearance decision

D.   Until the Advisory Committee has given its blessing to it

18.   What is the so-called "Article 11 letter"?

A.   Administrative letter by which the Commission informs a complainant of its intention to reject the complaint

B.   Commission's communication to inform undertakings and the general public of its intention to clear a notified agreement

C.   Commission's written request for information in merger control proceedings

D.   Commission's clearance decision

19.   According to case law, very large market shares – .... – may in themselves be evidence of the existence of a dominant market position.

A.   Below 40%

B.   Between 40% and 50%

C.   50% or more

D.   More than 50%

20.   What can be measured by applying the Herfindahl-Hirschman Index?

A.   Market power

B.   Pre-merger market shares of the merging undertakings

C.   Post-merger combined market share of the merging undertakings

D.   Concentration level in a market

21.   .... arise when the merged group is able profitably to reduce value for money, choice or innovation through its own acts without the need for a co-operative response from competitors.

A.   Unilateral effects

B.   Coordinated effects

C.   Ancillary restraints

D.   Vertical restraints

22. In which case did the Court of First Instance set out the necessary conditions for a finding of collective dominance?

A.   Tetra Laval v Commission

B.   Schneider Electric v Commission

C.   Gencor v Commission

D.   Airtours v Commission

23. What does the term "merger specificity" imply when the Commission conducts assessment of efficiency claims?

A.   The consumers must not be worse off as a result of the merger

B.   Efficiencies cannot be achieved to a similar extent by less anticompetitive scenario

C.   The efficiencies could not be achieved by other means than a merger

D.   The proposed merger entails efficiencies that are likely to counteract the potential harm to consumers

24. In the context of merger control proceedings, which of the following is not a relevant criterion for the application of a "failing firm defence"?

A.   The allegedly failing firm is in financial difficulties

B.   Without a merger, the assets of the failing firm would exit the market

C.   There is no less anti-competitive alternative

D.   The merger does not result in increased market power

25. Dominance arises from a situation where undertakings can act .... their competitors, their customers and, ultimately, of consumers.

A.   In a manner that may cause competitive harm to

B.   To a considerable extent independently of

C.   To the detriment of

D.   In any way jeopardising the reasonable economic interests of

26. State aid ....

A.   Presents a threat to the running of the Internal Market

B.   Is prohibited to public bodies not involved in economic activities

C.   Is banned to entities providing services of general economic interest (as defined in the EC Treaty)

D.   Is allowed if granted by the EU

27. Which of the following is not a characteristic of State aid in the context of Article 87(1) of the EC Treaty?

A.   It is granted by the State or through State resources

B.   It favours certain undertakings or production of certain goods

C.   It causes serious and irreparable damage to effective competition

D.   It affects trade between Member States

28. Treaty exemptions to the general band on State aid include ....

A.   Social aid granted to individual consumers

B.   Capital transfers

C.   Advantages resulting from the activities of agencies for urban renewal

D.   Indemnities against operating losses

29.   The Altmark case affects the payment of state aid to ....

A.   Airline sector for restructuring purposes

B.   Chemical and pharmaceutical industry in the "new" Member States

C.   Transport operators for performance of a public service obligation

D.   Telecommunications service providers

30.   Which statement is incorrect?

A.   The overall level of State aid granted by the Member States was estimated at €53 billion in 2003

B.   EU15 spend more than EU10 in state subsidies to businesses as a percentage of their GDP

C.   The majority of aids are earmarked for manufacturing and services

D.   There is a shift away from aid to individual companies and towards horizontal objectives

ENVIRONMENT POLICY

40 QUESTIONS – ANSWERS PAGE 302

1.   Articles 174 to 176 of the EC Treaty have been the legal basis for environment policy since the ....

A.   Treaty of Rome

B.   Single European Act

C.   Amsterdam Treaty

D.   Maastricht Treaty

2.   Since when has Community action been in place in the field of the environment?

A.   1965

B.   1987

C.   1972

D.   1982

3.   The idea that Community institutions were obliged to take account of environmental considerations in all their other policies was confirmed at the .... European Council.

A.   Vienna

B.   Dublin

C.   Stockholm

D.   Helsinki

4.   The Commissioner responsible for environment is of which nationality?

A.   Swedish

B.   Dutch

C.   Slovene

D.   Greek

5. **Development that meets the needs of the present without compromising the ability of future generations to meet their own needs is called ....**

A. Prudent environmental management

B. Due energy approach

C. Sustainable development

D. Protracted control

6. **What is EPER?**

A. A waste management catalogue of hazardous pollutants and waste materials

B. An environmental agency that deals with pollution observation and database management

C. A rapid reaction agency in case of severe natural catastrophes and large scale contamination

D. A web-based register to enable the public to view data on emissions of key pollutants

7. **Which environment action programme is currently in force?**

A. 5th

B. 4th

C. 3rd

D. 6th

8. **Which of the following does the above environment action programme not consider as a priority?**

A. Health and quality of life

B. Improving nuclear safety

C. Climate change

D. Nature and biodiversity

9. **The Convention on access to information, public participation in decision making and access to justice in environmental matters was signed in ....**

A. Tartu

B. Aarhus

C. Dublin

D. Malmö

10. **On 26 January 2005, the Commission adopted its Strategic Objectives for the period ....**

A. 2005-2010

B. 2005-2009

C. 2005-2008

D. 2005-2007

11. **The CAFE programme is related to ....**

A. Air pollution

B. Water management

C. Flora and fauna protection

D. Contamination of forests

12. **TREMOVE is a ....**

A. Policy assessment model

B. Framework programme for energy forwarding facilities

C. Community initiative for lower levels of energy consumption

D. Research programme on earthquakes

13.   What is the name of the special sign a product may obtain if it meets certain environmental standards?

A.   Envirocard

B.   Green certificate

C.   Compliance license

D.   Eco-label

14.   On 29 October 2003 the Commission adopted a new EU regulatory framework for chemicals called ....

A.   REACH

B.   ARCH

C.   CHEMREG

D.   SAFE

15.   What is the name of the agreement on greenhouse gas emissions?

A.   Copenhagen Declaration

B.   Kyoto Protocol

C.   Seoul Convention

D.   Johannesburg Agreement

16.   What is the so-called Seveso II Directive about?

A.   Control of major-accident hazards

B.   Severe river contamination and protection of fish

C.   Trans-national air pollution

D.   Non-biodegradable waste

17.   In the field of civil protection, it is not among the EU's aims to ....

A.   Increase the level of self-protection of European citizens

B.   Establish a framework for effective and rapid cooperation

C.   Enhance the coherence of actions undertaken at international level

D.   Create an international emergency unit available in case of a disaster

18.   Concerning the Emission Trading Scheme, which of the following statements is false?

A.   It is an international trading system for CO_2 emissions

B.   It covers some 12,000 installations representing close to half of Europe's emissions of CO_2

C.   Emission trading must be combined with new environmental targets

D.   Participating companies can buy or sell emission allowances

19.   The Regional Environmental Reconstruction Programme concerns ....

A.   Romania and Bulgaria

B.   EuroMed countries

C.   The Balkans

D.   Newly Independent States

20.   The Financial Instrument for the Environment (LIFE) does not concern ....

A.   Nature

B.   Nuclear safety

C.   Environment

D.   Third countries

21.   The DABLAS task force concerns ....

A.   Dolomite and lasque protection

B.   Daffodil flora and the ecosystem

C.   The Danube and Black Sea

D.   Ornithology research

22.   The name of the tool to assess human exposure to environmental pollutants and potential health effects of such pollutants is called ....

A.   Environmental marking

B.   Human observation

C.   Substance assessment

D.   Biomonitoring

23.   At which European Council was it agreed to launch the so-called Green Diplomacy Network?

A.   Brussels

B.   Copenhagen

C.   Thessaloniki

D.   Seville

24.   Which region does the so-called SMAP programme concern?

A.   North Sea

B.   Mediterranean

C.   Atlantic coast

D.   Gulf of Bothnia

25.   Community policy on waste management does not involve ....

A.   Eliminating waste at source

B.   Encouraging the recycling and re-use of waste

C.   Reducing pollution caused by waste incineration

D.   Strict financial responsibility for polluters

26.   The Convention on Biological Diversity was signed in ....

A.   Rio de Janeiro, 1992

B.   Aruba, 1995

C.   Ottawa, 1990

D.   Kinshasa, 1996

27.   Which statement is true concerning the European Union Network for the Implementation and Enforcement of Environmental Law (IMPEL)?

A.   It is an informal network of the environmental authorities of Member States

B.   Only Member States take part in it

C.   Every six months the meetings are chaired by another Member State

D.   The European Commission is only an observer in it

28.   Which of the following principles should not be taken into account when the precautionary principle is invoked?

A.   Implementation should be based on the fullest possible scientific evaluation

B.   The evaluation should determine the degree of scientific uncertainty at each stage

C.   The greatest possible transparency must be
     ensured

D.   Action is always better than inaction

C.   Transport

D.   Air traffic

**29.   The Convention on the Control of
        Transboundary Movements of
        Hazardous Wastes and Their Disposal
        is called the ....**

A.   Athens Convention

B.   Barcelona Convention

C.   Basel Convention

D.   Bordeaux Convention

**33.   How many signatories does the Energy
        Charter Treaty have?**

A.   28

B.   52

C.   68

D.   104

**30.   The European air quality monitoring
        network is called ....**

A.   Airobserver

B.   Euromonitor

C.   Qualitynet

D.   Euroairnet

**34.   Concerning the Habitat Agenda, which
        statement is false?**

A.   Originally it was drafted by the European
     Communities

B.   To date, 171 countries have adopted it

C.   It was adopted at a United Nations Conference
     in Istanbul

D.   It provides a practical roadmap to an urbanis-
     ing world

31.   Eurovignette is ....

A.   A special authorisation for advanced waste
     management facilities

B.   An annual charge for heavy vehicles

C.   A certificate concerning a vehicle's conformity
     with emission rules

D.   A quality license for low noise-emission trains

**35.   To improve public access to informa-
        tion on the environment and thus con-
        tribute in the long term to the
        prevention and reduction of pollution,
        the EU set up a ....**

A.   European database on pollution, contamination
     and hazardous materials

B.   European   network   of   counter-pollution
     measures

C.   European pollutant release and transfer register

D.   Catalogue of pollution prevention methods

**32.   Environmental noise is defined as an
        unwanted or harmful outdoor sound,
        not including noise emitted by ....**

A.   Natural sources

B.   Road traffic

36. Landsat satellite programme has been operational since ....

A.   1985

B.   1981

C.   1967

D.   1972

37. The reporting system used by both EU and OECD member countries to report industrial accidents is called ....

A.   IARS

B.   MARS

C.   EARSYS

D.   REPINAC

38. The European Union's ecological network of special protected areas is known as ....

A.   Natura 2000

B.   Ecolonet

C.   Diversity Assistance

D.   Flora Cooperation

39. The system that will make available relevant and quality geographic information for the purpose of formulation and implementation of Community environmental policy-making is called ....

A.   ECOINFO

B.   GEOTRACK

C.   INSPIRE

D.   POLNET

40. Directive 2002/96/EC (the so-called WEEE directive) concerns ....

A.   Waste management for eco-toxic and electric emissions

B.   Waste, eco-intensive and environment-friendly materials' management

C.   Waste disposal and ex-ante environmental extrapolation

D.   Waste electrical and electronic equipments

RESEARCH, CULTURE
AND EDUCATION POLICY
20 QUESTIONS – ANSWERS PAGE 310

1.   The EC Treaty requires the Community and the Member States to .... their research and technological development activities so as to ensure that national policies and Community policy are ....

A.   Harmonise, mutually consistent

B.   Coordinate, mutually consistent

C.   Harmonise, sufficiently coherent

D.   Coordinate, sufficiently coherent

2.   What percentage of its GDP does the European Union devote to research and development?

A.   Approximately 1%

B.   1.56%

C.   Approximately 2%

D.   More than 2%, but less than 3%

3.   An objective for the EU to increase its investment in research and development towards 3% of GDP by 2010 was set by the .... European Council in March ....

A.   Lisbon, 2000

B.   Stockholm, 2001

C.   Barcelona, 2002

D.   Brussels, 2003

4.   Which of the following is not an objective set out in the 2003 Commission Communication on "Investing in research: an action plan for Europe"?

A.   Ensuring that actions at national level form an effective mix of policy measures

B.   Improving considerably public support to research and innovation

C.   Stimulating research through the funding of "frontier research" carried out by individual teams

D.   Improving the environment for research and innovation in Europe

5.   The 2004 Commission Communication on "Science and technology, the key to Europe's future - Guidelines for future European Union policy to support research" ....

A.   Builds specific anticipatory management techniques in view of the 7th Framework Programme

B.   Proposes new policy mix measures to be introduced

C.   Takes stock of recent experiences with the application of the Open Method of Coordination (OMC)

D.   Sets out six major objectives

6.   The European Research Area ....

A.   Kicked off in 1999

B.   Covers, among other things, education

C.   Is sponsored from EUREKA

D.   Ensures tax free exchange of scientific data between the Member States and third countries

7.   **When did the 6th Framework Programme start and when will it end?**

A.   2000, 2005

B.   2001, 2006

C.   2002, 2006

D.   2002, 2007

8.   **What is the aim of the "networks of excellence" in the context of the 6th Framework Programme?**

A.   Integrating the activities of partners networked through "virtual" centres of excellence

B.   Encouraging researchers to participate in shaping the future direction of competitive areas of R&D

C.   Constituting a critical mass in research activities focusing on clearly defined scientific and technological objectives

D.   Supporting interdisciplinary research networks ("research institutions without walls") on topics related primarily to human and community development

9.   **What is CORDIS?**

A.   Intergovernmental framework for European cooperation in the field of scientific and technical research

B.   An internet information system

C.   A software for preparing contract preparation forms

D.   Scientific and technical research body responsible for assisting the Community institutions in the field of scientific research and technological development

10.   **EURAB is ....**

A.   A pan-European network for market-oriented industrial R&D

B.   An agency

C.   An internet information system

D.   An advisory committee

11.   **The Brussels European Council held between 20 and 21 March 2003 called for .... in support of research and innovation policy.**

A.   The application of the open method of coordination

B.   Reinforced cooperation

C.   Integrated policy mix measures

D.   A new mainstreaming approach to be established

12.   **Which of the following is not an objective set out in the 7th Research Framework Programme?**

A.   Establishing horizontal and vertical mainstreaming approach in scientific and technology areas

B.   Stimulating the creativity and excellence of European research through the funding of "frontier research"

C.   Enhancing research and innovation capacity throughout Europe

D.   Gaining leadership in key scientific and technology areas by supporting cooperation between universities, industry, research centres and public authorities

13. **According to the EC Treaty, the Community contributes to the flowering of the cultures of the Member States, while .... and at the same time bringing the common cultural heritage to the fore.**

A.   Respecting their national and regional diversity

B.   Showing consideration for their cultural heritage

C.   Encouraging promotion and preservation of multiculturalism

D.   Acknowledging their exclusive competence for cultural matters

14. **Which statement is incorrect? The Culture 2000 programme ....**

A.   Ran in the period between 1 January 2000 and 31 December 2005

B.   Emphasises the role of culture as an economic factor and as a factor in social integration and citizenship

C.   Comprises 30 European countries

D.   Is implemented by the Commission

15. **The list and order of countries holding the European Capital of Culture is decided each year by the ....**

A.   European Council

B.   Council

C.   Council and the Parliament

D.   Commission

16. **What is the Erasmus Mundus programme?**

A.   A vocational training programme

B.   A higher education cooperation scheme

between EU Member States and developing countries

C.   A cooperation and mobility programme in the field of higher education

D.   Programme for improving information and communication technologies in education

17. **Which of the following actions concerns adult education?**

A.   Comenius

B.   Minerva

C.   Lingua

D.   Grundtvig

18. **What is the Bologna Process?**

A.   It aims at creating convergence at the European level through reforming national higher education systems

B.   It has the objective of identifying a small number of key indicators or benchmarks to assist national evaluation of systems in the area of adult education

C.   It is a process of closer cooperation in vocational education and training

D.   Its primary objective is to support youth exchanges

19. **The European Union's approach towards the protection of European film heritage relating to archives is based on a ....**

A.   Directive

B.   Regulation

C.   Recommendation

D.   Framework decision

20. Which of the following is not part of the Commission's set of proposals for a new generation of EU programmes for education and training, culture, youth and the audiovisual sector in 2007-2013?

A.   Integrated Action Programme in Lifelong Learning

B.   Youth in Action

C.   Children's rights

D.   Media 2007

INDUSTRY, INFORMATION TECHNOLOGY, TRANSPORT, ENERGY POLICY

20 QUESTIONS – ANSWERS PAGE 318

1.   The Multiannual Programme for Enterprise and Entrepreneurship ....

A.   Will expire in 2006

B.   Is an integral part of the European Charter for Small Enterprise

C.   Aims at improving the financial environment for business, especially SMEs

D.   Is funded by one of the structural funds of the EU

2.   The European Investment Fund ....

A.   Is a public-private partnership established in 1995

B.   Acts in a complementary role to its majority shareholder, the EBRD

C.   Manages the European Investment Facility (EIF)

D.   Is the EU's specialised vehicle providing venture capital and guarantee instruments for SMEs

3.   The "Innovation 2000 Initiative" ....

A.   Is a Community Action Programme for information networks, human capital formation and intangible corporate investment

B.   Was launched by the EIB

C.   Will be replaced by the Amsterdam Special Action Programme (ASAP)

D.   Is designed to increase the availability of and facilitate access to debt finance for small companies with job creation potential in Europe

4.   What is PAXIS?

A.   A programme promoting the setting-up and development of innovative companies across Europe

B.   Community initiative to considerably improve public support to research and innovation

C.   PAXIS is responsible for assisting contractors taking part in Community funded R&D projects with IPR issues

D.   A tool to support networks among industrial

liaison offices in public research organisations
to strengthen public-private links

**5.   The "European TrendChart on
       Innovation" ....**

A.   Is one of the EU Agencies

B.   Is managed by the EIB

C.   Collects, analyses and disseminates information
      on various innovation policy measures

D.   Is an opinion poll conducted among enterprises
      to gather their views on innovation challenges

**6.   What does the abbreviation "CIP"
       stand for?**

A.   Common Industrial Practice

B.   Common Industrial Policy

C.   Competitiveness and Innovation Framework
      Programme

D.   Intellectual Property Code

**7.   What role is the "Entrepreneurship
       and Innovation Programme" intended
       to play?**

A.   Giving absolute priority to projects located in
      regional development areas

B.   Facilitating access to finance and support
      investment in innovation activities

C.   Supporting technological solutions to ICT-
      based services at EU level

D.   Supporting new technological solutions to
      reduce greenhouse gas emissions

8.   What is IDABC?

A.   A European network on information security
      issues

B.   Single European standards for transport replac-
      ing ERTMS, ETCS, LCTC and GSM-Rail

C.   An Internet-based groupware application
      developed by the European Commission

D.   A Pan-European e-government programme

**9.   When and where was the eEurope 2005
       Action Plan launched?**

A.   2000, Lisbon

B.   2001, Göteborg

C.   2002, Seville

D.   2003, Brussels

**10.   The policies aiming at ensuring equal
       access to Information and
       Communication Technology (ICT)
       services for all, at an affordable cost
       are known as ....**

A.   eInclusion

B.   eFor@ll

C.   ACCESS

D.   EQUAL

**11.   What does the Capgemini study of 4
       March 2005 concern?**

A.   A widespread secure broadband infrastructure

B.   The use of modern information technologies
      available to healthcare professionals and
      healthcare providers, as well as policy makers

C.   The online availability and sophistication of 20
      public services

D. The use of multimedia technologies and the Internet to improve the quality of learning

12. The .... programme provides financial support for the implementation of the eEurope 2005 Action Plan.

A. DECT

B. IST

C. IDA

D. Modinis

13. The Marco Polo programme ....

A. Is designed to promote cleaner and better transport in cities

B. Supports actions in the freight transport, logistics and other relevant markets

C. Aims at developing harmonised European approaches for transport costing and project assessment

D. Facilitates the interurban and international mobility of goods and passengers

14. The 2003 Van Miert high-level group put forward recommendations on ....

A. The trans-European transport network (TEN-T)

B. The Community Road accident data base (CARE)

C. Cleaner and better transport in cities (CIVITAS II)

D. The air traffic control infrastructure modernisation (SESAME)

15. The Single European Sky legislation came into effect in ....

A. 1999

B. 2000

C. 2002

D. 2004

16. What is GALILEO?

A. A Community Programme funding the European Space Agency

B. The European Union's space programme for 2003 - 2010

C. A satellite radio navigation system

D. A ground-to-space interface for global broadband telecom systems

17. The European Energy Charter was signed in ....

A. 1991

B. 1995

C. 2000

D. 2005

18. Which of the following is not a component of the "Intelligent Energy - Europe" (EIE) programme?

A. ALTENER

B. COOPENER

C. SAVE

D. CENTEREL

19. STEER is designed to ....

A.   Further initiatives relating to the promotion of renewable energy sources and energy efficiency in the developing countries

B.   Support initiatives relating to all energy aspects of transport

C.   Promote new and renewable energy sources for production of electricity and heat

D.   Improve energy efficiency and rational use of energy, in particular in the building and industry sectors

20. Directive 2001/77/EC set a target of .... of gross inland energy consumption from renewables for the Community as a whole by 2010.

A.   2%

B.   12%

C.   22%

D.   32%

EUROPEAN MONETARY UNION
EUROPEAN SINGLE CURRENCY
20 QUESTIONS – ANSWERS PAGE 325

1. The European Exchange Rate Mechanism (ERM) ....

A.   Was launched in 1979

B.   Replaced the European Monetary System (EMS)

C.   Defined the exchange rate of European currencies in terms of central rates against the ECU

D.   Allowed participating currencies to float within a range of ±15% with respect to a central rate against the euro

2. The .... set out a plan to introduce a European Monetary Union (EMU) in three stages.

A.   Delors Report

B.   Lamfalussy Report

C.   1989 White Paper on EMU

D.   1991 ECOFIN Council

3. Which Treaty established the EMU as a formal objective?

A.   None. EMU was decided by the Madrid European Council

B.   Single European Act

C.   Maastricht Treaty

D.   Amsterdam Treaty

4.   Stage I of EMU started on ....

A.   1 January 1979

B.   1 January 1989

C.   1 July 1990

D.   7 February 1992

5.   Which statement is incorrect? Stage II of EMU ....

A.   Began on 1 January 1994

B.   Provided for the establishment of the European Monetary Institute

C.   Provided for the avoidance of excessive government deficits

D.   Set out the European System of Integrated Economic Accounts

6.   The European Monetary Institute ....

A.   Was established on 1 January 1992

B.   Was to coordinate the monetary and exchange-rate policies of the Member States

C.   Was first headed by Philippe Lamfalussy

D.   Was the forerunner of the European Central Bank

7.   The Maastricht Convergence Criteria ....

A.   Were put in place by the Maastricht European Council

B.   Serve as a basis for the assessment of whether a "new" Member State may adopt the euro

C.   Are connected to Stage III of EMU

D.   Are binding on all Member States, including Denmark, Sweden and the UK

8.   Which one is not among the Maastricht Convergence Criteria?

A.   Functioning market economy

B.   Low inflation

C.   Sound public finances

D.   Low interest rates

9.   Stage III of EMU started with .... Member States.

A.   9

B.   11

C.   12

D.   13

10.   Which statement is false?

A.   ERM II is to maintain exchange-rate stability between the euro and the participating national currencies

B.   The currencies of Cyprus, Latvia and Malta are included in ERM II

C.   Membership of ERM II is voluntary

D.   ERM II was launched during Stage II of EMU

11.   The .... European Council adopted the euro.

A.   1995 Madrid

B.   1997 Luxembourg

C.   1997 Amsterdam

D.   1998 Vienna

12.   On .... the euro replaced the ECU at the value ....

A.   15 July 1999, 1:1

B.   31 December 1999, 1:1.2

C.   1 January 1999, 1:1

D.   1 January 2000, 0.8:1

13.   Which entity/entities has/have the exclusive right to authorise the issue of euro bank notes?

A.   European Central Bank

B.   Council

C.   Council together with the European Parliament

D.   Council upon authorisation by the European Council

14.   Euro notes and coins were introduced on ....

A.   1 January 2001

B.   1 January 2001 (except in Greece)

C.   1 January 2002

D.   1 January 2002 (except in Greece)

15.   The euro banknote series comprises .... different denominations.

A.   5

B.   6

C.   8

D.   7

16.   Which of the following is not an element of the Stability and Growth Pact?

A.   Political commitment

B.   Preventive elements

C.   Deterrent mechanisms

D.   Opt-out

17.   Which measure can the Council not choose to apply in an Excessive Deficit Procedure?

A.   Require the Member State concerned to publish additional information, to be specified by the Council, before issuing bonds and securities

B.   Invite the European Central Bank to reconsider its lending policy towards the Member State concerned

C.   Require the Member State concerned to make a non-interest-bearing deposit of an appropriate size with the Community until the excessive deficit has, in the view of the Council, been corrected

D.   Impose fines of an appropriate size

18.   The European Commission has never initiated an Excessive Deficit Procedure against .....

A.   The United Kingdom

B.   Germany

C.   The Netherlands

D.   Spain

19.   What does the abbreviation "EONIA" stand for?

A.   Euro overnight index average

B.   Credit extended for a period of less than one business day

C.   A decision-making body of the ECB

D.   Euro interbank offered rate

(XEU) which was an idea laid down in the Pléven Plan

B.   The predecessor of the ERM

C.   The ISO 4217 currency code of the ECU

D.   A proposed name for the European single currency (later called euro)

20.   What was "XEU"?

A.   The code name of a European Stock Exchange

JUSTICE AND HOME AFFAIRS, AREA OF FREEDOM, SECURITY AND JUSTICE
20 QUESTIONS – ANSWERS PAGE 331

1.   To create an area for freedom, security and justice, the .... introduced a new title called "Visas, asylum, immigration and other policies related to free movement of persons" into the EC Treaty.

A.   Maastricht Treaty

B.   Amsterdam Treaty

C.   Treaty of Nice

D.   Constitutional Treaty

2.   Which of the following is not an instrument used for measures in "police and judicial cooperation in criminal matters" under the Treaty on European Union?

A.   Common position

B.   Decision

C.   Regulation

D.   Framework decision

3.   Measures implementing conventions in respect of police and judicial cooperation in criminal matters have to be adopted ....

A.   Within the Council by at least eight Member States

B.   Within the Council by all Member States

C.   Within the Council by a majority of two thirds of the Contracting Parties

D.   By the European Council

4.   How may framework decisions be adopted under Title VI of the Treaty on European Union?

A.   Unanimously by the Council

B.   By majority of the Member States

C.   By qualified majority of two thirds of the Member States

D.   Such form does not exist under Title VI

5.   When the Council adopts a decision in a matter falling within the third pillar, which procedure is used in relation to the European Parliament?

A.   Codecision

B.   Cooperation

C.   Consultation

D.   The European Parliament is not involved in any way whatsoever

6.   The "Citizenship of the Union" does not entail the right to ....

A.   Move freely and to reside on the territory of the Member States

B.   Petition the European Parliament

C.   Apply to the European institutions in his/her mother tongue and to receive a reply in that language

D.   Vote and to stand as a candidate in elections to the European Parliament and in municipal elections in the Member State in which he/she resides

7.   Which statement is incorrect? Citizenship of the Union ....

A.   Was introduced by the Maastricht Treaty

B.   Supplements national citizenship without replacing it

C.   Implies that any person who holds the nationality of an EU Member State is automatically a citizen of the EU

D.   Means that EU citizens can move and reside freely within the EU subject to no limitations and conditions

8.   A five-year agenda, agreed at the .... European Council of 1999, set out the basis for constructing an "Area of Freedom, Security and Justice" across the Union.

A.   Tampere

B.   Brussels

C.   Cologne

D.   Helsinki

9.   For how long does a third country national have to reside legally and continuously in a Member State in order for him/her to be given a long term resident status?

A.   12 months

B.   24 months

C.   2 years

D.   5 years

10.   Who may be considered a "sponsor" in the context of legal rules concerning family reunification?

A.   NGOs

B.   The European Commission

C.   A third country national residing lawfully in a Member State

D.   Any person in good financial standing with a credit institution established in the EU

11.   Which statement is incorrect? The Schengen Agreement ....

A.   Is a type of "enhanced cooperation" initiated by a group of Member States

B.   Was signed on 14 June 1985

C.   Supplemented the Schengen Convention

D. Was also signed by Iceland and Norway as associated countries

12. To which fields of the Schengen acquis does the Community method not apply?

A. Judicial cooperation in civil matters

B. Asylum, immigration

C. Judicial cooperation in criminal matters

D. External border control

13. Visas issued by the Member States ....

A. Must be printed on pastel yellow paper

B. Must be produced in a uniform format

C. May be in electronic format

D. Must display texts in English, French and German

14. Europol ....

A. Is a European FBI

B. Is the criminal intelligence agency of the Commission

C. Has no executive powers

D. Has its origins in Interpol

15. Eurojust ....

A. Was established in 2004

B. Has limited investigative powers

C. Is a permanent network of judicial authorities

D. Supervises the investigations and prosecutions between the authorities in the Member States

16. .... is an action programme for administrative cooperation at EU level in the fields of asylum, visas, immigration and external borders.

A. ANEAS

B. DAPHNE

C. AGIS

D. ARGO

17. The .... provides the legal basis for establishing the criteria and mechanism for determining the State responsible for examining an asylum application in one of the Member States of the EU by a third country national.

A. Dublin II Regulation

B. Geneva Convention

C. Hague Programme

D. Rome II Regulation

18. Which statement is false? A Member State may refuse to execute a European arrest warrant if ....

A. The person concerned was sentenced to death

B. A final judgment has already been passed by a Member State in respect of the requested person for the same offence

C. The offence is covered by an amnesty in the executing Member State

D. The person concerned may not be held criminally responsible by the executing State owing to his age

19. AGIS ....

A. Will be divided and replaced by OISIN, STOP, Grotius-Criminal, Falcone and Hippokrates

B. Runs from 2004 to 2008

C. Promotes administrative cooperation in the fields of external borders, visas, asylum and immigration

D. Supports projects of a maximum duration of two years

20. The Hague Programme ....

A. Aims to boost immigration levels

B. Seeks to strengthen freedom, security and justice in the EU

C. Launches SitCen

D. Establishes the European Refugee Fund

EXTERNAL RELATIONS
SECURITY, DEFENCE, EXTERNAL TRADE AND DEVELOPMENT
100 QUESTIONS – ANSWERS PAGE 336

1. The Commissioner responsible for the European Neighbourhood Policy is of which nationality?

A. Finnish

B. Belgian

C. French

D. Austrian

2. What does the European Neighbourhood Policy (ENP) offer to the partner countries?

A. Privileged relationship

B. Prospective membership

C. Special trade relationship

D. Human rights cooperation

3. What is the name of the document regarding the priorities for each country involved in the ENP?

A. Priority Paper

B. Country reports

C. Roadmap to Europe

D. Action Plans

4. The European Parliament report "Wider Europe - Neighbourhood: A New Framework for Relations with our Eastern and Southern Neighbours" is also known as the ....

A. Napoletano Report

B. Winterbourne Report

C. Van Orden Report

D. Zacharakis Report

5. Which of the following is not considered as a Southern Mediterranean country in the framework of the European Neighbourhood Policy?

A. Libya

B. Turkey

C. Palestinian Authority

D. Syria

6. Which of the following is not a Western Newly Independent State?

A. Ukraine

B. Moldova

C. Georgia

D. Belarus

7. The European Neighbourhood Policy does not involve ....

A. Belarus

B. Kazakhstan

C. Israel

D. Azerbaijan

8. From 2007 what will replace the TACIS and MEDA programmes in the ENP partner countries and Russia?

A. European Neighbourhood and Partnership Instrument

B. Financial Assistance and Partnership Fund

C. European Financial Instrument for Wider European Countries

D. European Aid for Neighbour and Partner Countries

9. Every year, the European Union provides over .... billion euros in external assistance to more than .... countries and territories.

A. 14, 160

B. 2, 120

C. 10, 140

D. 7, 150

10. The EuropeAid cooperation is financed by the ....

A. European Community budget and the European Development Fund

B. European Development Fund and External Aid

C. European Community budget and the United Nations

D. European Community budget and the Financial Programme for External Action

11. What is the Agadir Agreement about?

A. Humanitarian cooperation between the EU 25 and Jordan, Morocco, Algeria and Tunisia

B. Creation of a free trade area between Jordan, Morocco, Tunisia and Egypt

C. Cultural cooperation between North African countries and the EU 25

D. Political and economic cooperation between the EU and the Arab League

12. What is the name of the programme which aims at supporting the participation of the countries of the Western Balkans in the Stabilisation and Association Process?

A. CORDIS

B. HELIOS

C.   CARDS

D.   INTAS

13. Which of the following is not listed as an objective in the framework of the Tacis programme?

A.   Support for the private sector and assistance for economic development

B.   Nuclear safety

C.   Support for addressing the social consequences of transition

D.   Combating drug trafficking

14. In the Euro Mediterranean area, the Barcelona Declaration was not aiming at the ....

A.   Development of human resources

B.   Progressive establishment of a free-trade area

C.   Establishment of a common area of peace and stability

D.   Inclusion of the area into the EU's fisheries policy

15. The Mashrek countries do not include ....

A.   Egypt

B.   Tunisia

C.   Israel

D.   Palestinian Authority

16. Which statement is false concerning the MEDA II programme?

A.   It is the principal financial instrument for the

implementation of the Euro-Mediterranean Partnership

B.   Its budget is financed exclusively by the EU Member States

C.   It may apply to States, their local and regional authorities as well as stakeholders of their civil society

D.   It offers technical and financial support to accompany the reform of economic and social structures

17. What is the name of the annual discussion forum between the EU and all of Latin America and the Caribbean countries?

A.   Maracaibo Forum

B.   Lima Dialogue

C.   Rio Group

D.   Madrid Conference

18. Which country does not take part in the Mercosur?

A.   Argentina

B.   Paraguay

C.   Chile

D.   Brazil

19. The Cartagena Agreement established what is known today as the ....

A.   Andean Community

B.   Amazon Cooperation

C.   Caribbean Union

D.   Patagonia Plan

20. **Which of the following South American countries does not belong to any regional grouping?**

A. Chile

B. Uruguay

C. Venezuela

D. Bolivia

21. **The EU as a whole is the .... source of Official Development Assistance in the world.**

A. Number Two

B. Number One

C. Number Three

D. Number Four

22. **In the field of the EU's international drug policy, which of the following is not a basic principle?**

A. Shared responsibility

B. Balanced approach

C. Protection of private life

D. Emphasis on multilateralism

23. **What is the Kimberley Process about?**

A. Democratic process in Sub-Saharan Africa

B. Conflict diamonds

C. Election observation

D. Women's rights

24. **Concerning the Middle East, whom does the "Quartet" comprise?**

A. EU, USA, Israel, Palestinian Authority

B. EU, USA, UN, Council of Europe

C. UN, Council of Europe, OECD, Norway

D. EU, USA, UN, Russia

25. **What is the name of the document concerning the Middle East peace process?**

A. Cooperation Plan

B. Peace Initiative

C. Partnership for Peace

D. Road map

26. **What is the name of the treaty that aims at fighting landmines?**

A. Ottawa Convention

B. Tokyo Agreement

C. Paris Treaty

D. Delhi Solemn Declaration

27. **When was the World Trade Organisation (WTO) founded and who represents the EU Member States in it?**

A. 1995, Commission

B. 1997, Commission and Member States jointly

C. 1996, Commission and European Parliament

D. 1993, Member States themselves

28. Which round of multilateral trade negotiations is going on now in the framework of the World Trade Organisation?

A. Tokyo Round

B. Doha Round

C. Geneva Round

D. Uruguay Round

29. The so-called TRIPs Agreement, concluded within the framework of the WTO, deals with ....

A. Intellectual property

B. Agriculture

C. Textile quotas

D. Research and development

30. When did the Cotonou Agreement come into force and in which country was it signed?

A. 2001, Cameroon

B. 2000, Ivory Coast

C. 2003, Benin

D. 2002, Chad

31. The Economic Community of West African States (ECOWAS) is a regional group that does not include ....

A. Guinea Bissau

B. Burkina Faso

C. Mauritania

D. Sierra Leone

32. When was the first Lomé Convention signed and how many years did the last one cover?

A. 1980, 10

B. 1980, 5

C. 1975, 5

D. 1975, 10

33. What is the name of the Lomé Convention's predecessor?

A. Cape Verde Convention

B. Abuja Convention

C. Yaoundé Convention

D. Lagos Convention

34. What does STABEX and SYSMIN deal with regarding ACPs (African, Caribbean and Pacific countries)?

A. Regional trade cooperation and data system exchange for ACPs

B. Political stabilisation and cooperation between ACPs

C. Anti-landmine and anti-warfare projects for ACPs

D. ACP exports and mining

35. Concerning Overseas Countries and Territories (OCTs), which of the following statements is false?

A. Crozet and the Kerguelen Islands are part of the French OCTs

B. There are 21 OCTs

C. Spain does not have any OCTs

D. Bermuda is part of the British OCTs

36. Which of the following countries does not belong to the Commonwealth of Independent States (CIS)?

A.   Armenia

B.   Turkmenistan

C.   Lithuania

D.   Ukraine

37. "Visegrád group" is a denomination for countries in ....

A.   Central Europe

B.   South-East Asia

C.   The Western Balkans

D.   North America

38. The Isle of Man is ....

A.   Not an EU Member but it takes part in the customs union

B.   An EU Member but does not take part in the customs union

C.   Not an EU Member and it does not take part in the customs union either

D.   Both an EU Member and takes part in the customs union as well

39. Which of the following belongs to the EU customs territory without being an EU Member?

A.   Azores Islands

B.   Canary Islands

C.   Madeira

D.   San Marino

40. Which of the following is an EU Member without being in the EU customs territory?

A.   Channel Islands

B.   Monaco

C.   Gibraltar

D.   Andorra

41. Which of the following left the EU and is now not part of the customs area either?

A.   Mayotte

B.   San Marino

C.   Livigno commune

D.   Gibraltar

42. Which of the following has the euro as its currency?

A.   Gibraltar

B.   Isle of Man

C.   Island of Heligoland

D.   Faeroe Islands

43. Which of the following has the Swiss franc as a currency?

A.   Madeira

B.   Liechtenstein

C.   Holy See

D.   Büsingen am Hochrhein

44. **Which of the following is exempt from the EU's common value added tax (VAT) system?**

A. Monaco

B. Åland Islands

C. Azores

D. Isle of Man

45. **Which of the following statements is false concerning Mount Athos?**

A. It is part of the EU's territory

B. It is part of the EU's common VAT system

C. It is part of the EU's customs area

D. It has the euro as a currency

46. **Regarding Liechtenstein, which of the following statements is true?**

A. It is member of the European Economic Area

B. It formed a customs union with Switzerland in 1926

C. It has a border with Italy

D. It is part of the EU's common VAT system

47. **POSEICAN is a special aid programme for ....**

A. Azores

B. Campione d'Italia

C. Canary Islands

D. French Overseas Departments

48. **Regarding the sovereign bases on Cyprus, which statement is false?**

A. Article 299(6b) of the EC treaty defines their status

B. Xylotimbou and Ormidhia are part of the sovereign bases

C. The EC Treaty applies only to a limited extent to them

D. The bases can be found in the Akrotiri and Dhekelia area

49. **Regarding the Kaliningrad region, which of the following statements is false?**

A. It is under Russian jurisdiction

B. A Facilitated Transit Document (FTD) scheme applies to the transit of Russian citizens

C. It has benefited from the EU's TACIS programmes

D. It is surrounded by the Baltic Sea, Poland and Latvia

50. **Saint Pierre-et-Miquelon is ....**

A. Not part of the Euro-zone

B. A French Overseas Department

C. Part of the EU's customs territory

D. A French Overseas Territorial Community

51. **Which islands form an autonomous and demilitarised province of Finland?**

A. Åland Islands

B. Heligoland

C. Faeroe Islands

D. Channel Islands

52. **Ceuta and Melilla are Spanish enclaves in ....**

A. Morocco

B. Algeria

C. Libya

D. Egypt

53. **The Common Foreign and Security Policy (CFSP) was established in the .... and further defined and broadened in the .....**

A. Maastricht Treaty, Treaty of Nice

B. Maastricht Treaty, Amsterdam Treaty

C. Amsterdam Treaty, Treaty of Nice

D. Single European Act, Maastricht Treaty

54. **The political background to the CFSP was the so-called ....**

A. European Political Cooperation

B. Foreign Policy Coordination

C. Security and Defence Initiative

D. International Cooperation Forum

55. **Which of the following does Article V of the EU Treaty not provide as a goal in the field of CFSP?**

A. Safeguarding the common values and funda-mental interests of the Union

B. Preserving peace and strengthening the Union's defence capabilities

C. Strengthening the security of the Union

D. Developing democracy and the rule of law

56. **Article 2 of the EU Treaty provides that one of the Union's objectives is "to assert its identity on the international scene [...] including the progressive framing of a .... [...]"**

A. Common military policy

B. Common defence policy

C. Joint security initiative

D. Joint peacekeeping mission

57. **What instruments does the Maastricht Treaty provide Member States with in the field of CFSP?**

A. Framework regulations, joint decisions

B. Common declarations, joint directives

C. Common positions, joint actions

D. Common conventions, European initiatives

58. **Which of the following statements is false regarding CFSP?**

A. The Commission's role includes the right to submit legislative proposals and budget execution

B. The European Parliament may put questions and recommendations to the Council in CFSP-related issues

C. The Member States only can decide questions unanimously

D. The Court of Justice cannot rule against coun-tries unwilling to implement the CFSP

59. **Which of the following created the so-called "constructive abstention"?**

A. Amsterdam Treaty

B. Treaty of Nice

C. Council Regulation

D.   There is no legal basis for it, only a tacit agreement between the heads of state and government

B.   Commissioner for External Relations

C.   Vice-President of the Commission

D.   Vice-President of the European Parliament

60.   What is the name of the organisation set up by the Treaty of Nice that exercises political control and strategic direction of crisis management operations?

A.   Rapid Reaction Unit

B.   Crisis Analysis and Supervision Unit

C.   Political and Security Committee

D.   Joint Political Management Group

64.   What is the EUPOL PROXIMA?

A.   EU Police Cooperation with Serbia and Montenegro

B.   EU Political Cooperation with Bosnia and Herzegovina

C.   EU Political Dialogue with Albania

D.   EU Police Mission in the Former Yugoslav Republic of Macedonia

61.   What is the common name for humanitarian, rescue, peacekeeping and peace-making tasks?

A.   Freiberg tasks

B.   Munich tasks

C.   Naples tasks

D.   Petersberg tasks

65.   Concerning the European Defence Agency, which of the following statements is false?

A.   One of its functions is related to defence capabilities development

B.   It was set up by the Council

C.   It was established in 2002

D.   Its aim is to support the Member States in their effort to improve European defence capabilities

62.   The Treaty of Nice changed the minimum number of participating Member States in an enhanced cooperation from .... to .....

A.   10, two thirds

B.   Majority, 8

C.   One third, majority

D.   Two thirds, 12

66.   Regarding the European Union Military Committee (EUMC), which of the following statements is false?

A.   Regarding its institutional position, the EUMC is established within the Council

B.   The EUMC is composed of the Chiefs of Defence represented by their military representatives

C.   The EUMC meets at the level of Chiefs of Defence once every month

D.   The EUMC provides military direction to the European Union Military Staff

63.   The High Representative for CFSP is the ....

A.   Council Secretary General

67. What is the so-called EUJUST LEX?

A. EU aid provided for improving prison conditions in third countries

B. Judicial cooperation in criminal matters with the USA

C. Development programme for improving the independence of judicial authorities in South-East Asia

D. An integrated rule-of-law mission for Iraq

68. According to the so-called Helsinki "headline goal", the Union should be able to deploy within .... days, and sustain for at least .... year(s) up to .... persons.

A. 30, 2, 80,000

B. 60, 1, 60,000

C. 90, 1, 45,000

D. 45, 2, 75,000

69. Which Treaty provided the legal base for the transfer of Western European Union (WEU) competencies into the EU?

A. Amsterdam Treaty

B. Maastricht Treaty

C. Treaty of Nice

D. Constitutional Treaty

70. Who is the EU Special Representative in Bosnia and Herzegovina?

A. Lord Ashdown

B. Aldo Ajello

C. Erhard Busek

D. Michael Sahlin

71. Marc Otte is the EU Special Representative ....

A. For the Middle East peace process

B. For the South Caucasus

C. In the Former Yugoslav Republic of Macedonia

D. In Afghanistan

72. What is the generalised system of preferences?

A. Priority products the EU subsidises in third countries

B. EU priorities that must be met in order to be entitled to financial aids

C. An anti arms-proliferation policy applied by the EU

D. Tariff reduction for developing countries' products

73. A country may not have the status of .... in the Western European Union (WEU).

A. Associate Member

B. Non-voting Member

C. Observer

D. Associate Partner

74. Which of the following countries is not a Member of the WEU?

A. France

B. Italy

C. Sweden

D. United Kingdom

75.   Where is the European Union Satellite Centre located?

A.   Torrejón, Spain

B.   Aix-en-Provence, France

C.   Matosinhos, Portugal

D.   Tarquinia, Italy

76.   According to the Constitutional Treaty, who appoints the Foreign Minister?

A.   Council of Ministers by qualified majority voting and the European Parliament by simple majority

B.   European Council by qualified majority voting with the Commission President's agreement

C.   Commission as whole, approved by the European Council by qualified majority voting

D.   European Council by qualified majority voting, approved by the Commission as a whole

77.   Regarding the Constitutional Treaty, which of the following statements is false?

A.   The provisions relating to the external action of the Union are grouped together under a single title

B.   The President of the European Council will be responsible only for the non-commercial issues of foreign policy

C.   The pillar structure of the EU in the field of foreign policy will be discarded

D.   The Union will have an international legal personality

78.   In the Constitutional Treaty, ... is not included in the foreign policy section.

A.   Fostering international free trade

B.   Development cooperation policy

C.   Financial and technical cooperation with third countries

D.   Humanitarian aid

79.   The Constitutional Treaty extends the common commercial policy to .... but not to .....

A.   Intellectual property, energy

B.   Foreign direct investment, transport

C.   Health related services, textiles

D.   Fisheries, educational services

80.   What is the name of the principle according to which decisions relating to the negotiation and conclusion of agreements are subject to unanimity when these agreements contain provisions for which unanimity is required for the adoption of internal rules?

A.   Dual approval

B.   Restricted mandate

C.   Parallelism

D.   Subsidiarity

81.   CFSP funding ....

A.   Is fully provided for by the EU general budget under the supervision of the Council

B.   Is provided by the general budget of the EU except for operations having military or defence implications

C.   Will be increased by 50% until 2009

D.   Makes up 12.5% of the EU budget

82. **In the field of CFSP, the Constitutional Treaty provides that the Court of Justice ....**

A. Has full jurisdiction over CFSP issues

B. Does not have jurisdiction to rule on the legality of restrictive measures against natural persons

C. Does not have jurisdiction whether an international agreement is compatible with the Constitutional Treaty

D. Has jurisdiction to rule on the legality of restrictive measures against legal persons

83. **What does the so-called "solidarity clause" provide in the Constitutional Treaty?**

A. Should a natural disaster happen outside the EU, special funds will be allocated to provide assistance

B. Special aid programmes and help should be provided to third countries

C. Should a non-EU country be in serious and persistent breach of human rights, EU Member States will have a joint approach towards it

D. If a Member State suffers a terrorist attack, others will assist it at the request of its political authorities

84. **Which article of the EC Treaty is considered as the foundation of the Common Commercial Policy?**

A. Article 12

B. Article 251

C. Article 133

D. Article 299

85. **Which of the following countries is not a member of the Central American Common Market?**

A. Panama

B. Nicaragua

C. El Salvador

D. Honduras

86. **Which country is not a member of the Central European Free Trade Agreement (CEFTA)?**

A. Romania

B. Bulgaria

C. Croatia

D. Hungary

87. **When companies integrate social and environmental concerns in their business activities and in interaction with their stakeholders on a voluntary basis, it is called ....**

A. Corporate Social Responsibility

B. Social Awareness Scheme

C. Integrated Trade Approach

D. Business Consciousness Plan

88. **Approximately how many "developing countries" were there in 2000?**

A. 100

B. 120

C. 140

D. 170

89. The initiative according to which the EU eliminated all duties and quotas for all products originating from the least developed countries is known as ....

A.   Most Favoured Countries Scheme

B.   Everything But Arms

C.   Lowest Quota System

D.   Highest Preference Regime

90. In relation to international agricultural negotiations, which country does the so-called QUINT not include?

A.   Mexico

B.   EU

C.   Canada

D.   Japan

91. When and where was the World Summit on Sustainable Development held?

A.   Seoul, 1999

B.   Caracas, 2003

C.   Johannesburg, 2002

D.   St. Petersburg, 2001

92. When was the customs union with Turkey established?

A.   1983

B.   1985

C.   1995

D.   1975

93. Turkey does not share a border with ....

A.   Iraq

B.   Azerbaijan

C.   Armenia

D.   Jordan

94. Accession negotiations with Bulgaria were concluded at the ....

A.   Nice European Council

B.   Brussels European Council

C.   Helsinki European Council

D.   Copenhagen European Council

95. Bulgaria's currency is the ....

A.   Lei

B.   Dinar

C.   Leva

D.   Kuna

96. When did the Association Agreement enter into force with Croatia?

A.   15 October, 2004

B.   1 February, 2005

C.   1 April, 2005

D.   1 January, 2005

97. When Romania and Bulgaria join the EU, it will be the .... enlargement.

A.   4th

B.   5th

C.   7th

D.   6th

B.   Justin Mullen

C.   Cristina Gallach

D.   Joseph von Schultz

98.   Where is the European Union Institute for Security Studies (EUISS) located?

A.   London

B.   Brussels

C.   Paris

D.   Amsterdam

100. Which of the following does not participate at the so-called G8 meetings?

A.   China

B.   Japan

C.   Italy

D.   European Union

99.   The EU's counter-terrorism coordinator is ....

A.   Gijs de Vries

MISCELLANEOUS

DECISION MAKING

25 QUESTIONS – ANSWERS PAGE 355

1. **Which decision making procedure is the one most commonly used?**

A. Assent

B. Codecision

C. Budget

D. Information

2. **Which institutions may call on the Commission to initiate legislation?**

A. European Central Bank and the Council of Ministers

B. Committee of Regions and the Council of Ministers

C. Council of Ministers and the European Parliament

D. Council of Ministers and the Member States

3. **According to the EU Treaty, who may initiate a reasoned proposal to determine the existence of a serious and persistent breach of the EU's founding principles?**

A. Four fifths of the Member States, Parliament, Council

B. One third of the Member States, Commission

C. One third of the Member States, Commission, Parliament

D. Council, two thirds of the Member States, Parliament

4. **In the field of Common Foreign and Security Policy, what is the majority required from the Council to adopt joint actions?**

A. Unanimity

B. Qualified majority

C. Majority of two thirds of the Member States

D. Qualified majority with at least two thirds of Member States in favour

B. Single European Act

C. Maastricht Treaty

D. Amsterdam Treaty

5. In the consultation procedure, the Parliament ....

A. May propose any amendment to the Commission's proposal

B. May only propose amendments that the Commission approves

C. Always discusses the Commission's proposal in two readings

D. Must convene a conciliation committee with the Commission

9. The budgetary powers of the Parliament are exercised mainly on ....

A. Non-compulsory expenditure

B. Compulsory expenditure

C. Expenditure related to Community issues

D. Almost every expenditure

6. Which decision making procedure is used for legislation on the European electoral system?

A. Codecision procedure

B. Consultation procedure

C. Cooperation procedure

D. Assent procedure

10. Which procedure is used for measures implementing the Common Agricultural Policy, the Common Fisheries Policy and programmes with serious budgetary implications?

A. Budgetary procedure

B. Advisory Committee procedure

C. Management Committee procedure

D. Approval procedure

7. In which field is the legislation not passed by codecision procedure with the Council acting unanimously?

A. Social security related to the free movement of workers

B. Citizenship of the Union

C. Customs cooperation

D. Culture

11. Whom does the Legislative Committee comprise and what majority is required for its decisions?

A. Ministers from the Member States, qualified majority

B. Representatives of the Member States, qualified majority

C. Permanent Representatives, unanimity

D. Members of the European Parliament, simple majority

8. The cooperation procedure was introduced by the ....

A. Treaty of Rome

12. **Which statement is false? The simplified procedure ....**

A. Requires no Commission proposal to initiate the legislative process

B. Does not restrict the Commission to what is expressly provided for in the Treaties

C. Is used for the adoption of non-mandatory instruments

D. Applies to measures outside the Commission's own powers

13. **Regarding the adoption of the Statute for Members of the European Parliament and the Statute for the Ombudsman, the proposal is coming from the .... ; the final decision is made by the ....**

A. Parliament, Council

B. Commission, Parliament

C. Parliament, Parliament

D. Commission, Council

14. **What majority is required for the amendment of the protocol on the Statute of the Court of Justice by the Council and the Parliament?**

A. Qualified majority, codecision

B. Unanimity, assent

C. Qualified majority, information

D. Unanimity, consultation

15. **In the codecision procedure, what happens if in the second reading the Parliament proposes amendments to the common position?**

A. The Commission has to give an opinion on it

B. The Council has to decide it by a qualified majority

C. If the Council does not accept it, the Conciliation Committee is convened

D. The Parliamentary Committee has to give an opinion on it

16. **Which statement is false concerning the codecision procedure and the Conciliation Committee?**

A. If the Council does not adopt the act, the Committee is convened within 6 weeks

B. The Committee decides by a simple majority

C. The Committee is made up of 25 representatives each from the Council and Parliament

D. If the Committee accepts a joint draft, the Council and Parliament must confirm its acceptance in a third reading within six weeks

17. **The Advisory Committee has to give its opinion within ....**

A. A time-limit set by the Commission

B. Three months from the presentation of the Commission proposal

C. Ten weeks from setting up the Committee

D. A deadline set by the Committee itself, which may not exceed six weeks

18. **After the Treaty of Nice, qualified majority was not extended to ....**

A. The appointment of the Secretary General of the Council

B. The adoption of the conversion rates at which Member States' currencies are irrevocably fixed

C. Measures against discrimination

D. Economic, financial and technical cooperation with third countries

19. **In the framework of the budgetary procedure, the Council draws up a draft budget which it presents to the Parliament. What does the Parliament do after that?**

A.   It can give its opinion within 30 days and propose modifications on all expenses

B.   It can give its opinion within 45 days and can present amendments for non-compulsory expenditure

C.   It can propose modifications to the Council only for non-compulsory expenditure

D.   It must give its opinion within 60 days, failing which results in approval of the budget

20. **Regarding compulsory expenditure, which statement is true for the Council?**

A.   If the Parliament's modifications would increase expenditure, the Council has to refuse them by a qualified majority

B.   If the Parliament's modifications do not increase expenditure, the Council has to accept them by a qualified majority

C.   If the Parliament's modifications increase expenditure, the Council has to accept them by unanimity

D.   If the Parliament's proposals do not increase expenditure, the Council has to refuse them by a qualified majority

21. **In which case can the Parliament reject the budget in its entirety?**

A.   Only if it proposes a new draft budget

B.   It can only make amendments but complete rejection is not permitted

C.   Always, without restrictions

D.   It can only do so with the agreement of the majority of the Council

22. **Which Treaty placed judicial cooperation in civil matters within the scope of the codecision procedure?**

A.   Amsterdam Treaty

B.   Treaty of Nice

C.   Maastricht Treaty

D.   Amsterdam Treaty with a five-year transition

23. **What majority does a censure motion require from the European Parliament?**

A.   Majority of all Members

B.   Majority of the votes cast

C.   Two thirds of the votes cast

D.   Majority of all Members and two thirds of the votes cast

24. **When the European Union accepts Romania and Bulgaria as Member States, what will be the maximum number of votes in the Council and how many votes will be required for a qualified majority?**

A.   345, 255

B.   321, 232

C.   330, 235

D.   358, 262

25. **The Council meets in the composition of Heads of State or Government when ....**

A.   Adopting measures in the fields of the prevention of and fight against fraud affecting the financial interests of the Community

B.   Adopting the Statute of the European System of Central Banks and of the European Central Bank

C.   Nominating the person it intends to appoint as President of the Commission

D.   Determining that there is a clear risk of a

serious breach by a Member State of basic principles

STAFF REGULATIONS
10 QUESTIONS – ANSWERS PAGE 361

1.   Article 43 of the Staff Regulations provides that "[t]he ability, efficiency and conduct in the service of each official shall be the subject of a periodical report made at least once every .... as provided for by each institution in accordance with Article 110."

A.   Two years

B.   Year

C.   Three months

D.   Six months

2.   According to the Staff Regulations, termination of service is not possible by ....

A.   Dismissal for incompetence

B.   Reduction of administrative staff or reorganisation

C.   Retirement in the interests of the service

D.   Compulsory resignation

3.   Which of the following is not a precondition for an official to be appointed?

A.   Be a national of one of the Member States of the

Communities, unless an exception is authorised by the appointing authority

B.   Produce the appropriate character references as to his suitability for the performance of his duties

C.   To have fulfilled any obligations imposed by the laws concerning military service

D.   Produce evidence of fluent knowledge of two official languages

4.   Which of the following statements is true? An official ....

A.   May only seek or take instructions from a government or authority in exceptional circumstances

B.   Should neither seek nor take instructions from any government, authority, organisation or person outside his institution

C.   May seek instructions from governments, authorities, organisations or others only to the extent required by and to the benefit of the service

D.   May only seek or take instructions from governments or authorities after the prior written approval of his hierarchic supervisor

5. The .... enable[s] members of the public to file a complaint where the European Commission is in breach of it/them, so that failure to comply with the principles of sound administration set out therein can be punished.

A. Ethical Guidelines for Officials

B. Rules of Procedure

C. Basic Principles for Interaction with Citizens

D. Code of Good Administrative Behaviour

6. An official who has completed at least .... years' service is entitled to a retirement pension. He is, however, entitled to such pension irrespective of the length of service if he is over .... years, if it has not been possible to reinstate him during a period of non-active status or in the event of retirement in the interests of the service.

A. 5, 64

B. 8, 65

C. 12, 64

D. 10, 63

7. Members of the public who write to the Commission are entitled to receive a reply ....

A. Within 30 days from the date of receipt of the letter by the department

B. Preferably in English, French or German

C. Within 30 days from the date of receipt of the letter by the official

D. In the language of their initial letter, provided that it was written in one of the official languages of the European Union

8. Regarding relations with the media, ...

A. With a few exceptions, staff should generally refer the issue to the Press and Communication department

B. Staff must always refer the issue to the Press and Communication department

C. Staff may never have direct contacts or appear on their own behalf

D. Staff may give interviews or information on non-confidential issues with the prior written consent of their supervisor

9. How long is the probationary period of officials?

A. 9 months

B. 3 months

C. 6 months

D. 4 months

10. What does Regulation 1049/2001 concern?

A. Commission Rules of Procedure

B. Reform of the Staff Regulations

C. Right of access to documents

D. Governance 2002-2006

ABBREVIATIONS

30 QUESTIONS – ANSWERS PAGE 363

1. **ASEAN is an abbreviation that concerns ....**

A. Research and development

B. Environment policy

C. South-East Asia

D. The European Parliament

2. **EMEA is an EU ....**

A. Programme for developing countries

B. Fisheries regime for the Mediterranean

C. Specialised agency

D. Political group in the European Parliament

3. **CORDIS deals with ....**

A. Promotion of renewable energy sources

B. Community aid to the Western Balkans

C. Information society framework programmes

D. Research and development information

4. **Which of the following deals with asylum issues?**

A. CIREA

B. RARE

C. COGECA

D. INTAS

5. **The action programme for the vocational training of young people and their preparation for adult and working life is called ....**

A. SCENT

B. PETRA

C. SPRINT

D. VALUE

6. **The abbreviation "SAFE" stands for ....**

A. Safety actions for Europe

B. Safe atomic and fuel energy

C. Safeguarding rare fauna in Europe

D. Scientific alternatives for enterprise management

7. **Which of the following deals with the disabled and elderly?**

A. TIDE

B. DELTA

C. DECT

D. FIDE

8. **Which of the following deals with assistance to employment?**

A. Erasmus

B. Eurydice

C. EURES

D. ERICA

9.   Which of the following is not related to science?

A.   Codest

B.   FAST

C.   NAMSA

D.   MAST

10.   Which of the following programmes is not related to the environment?

A.   ACE

B.   DIANE

C.   Corine

D.   CFPE

11.   Europartnerariat concerns ....

A.   WEU-NATO partnership

B.   Less favoured regions

C.   Cooperation between the EU and Ukraine

D.   Joint scientific research programme between the EU and Israel

12.   FORCE deals with ....

A.   Cross-border regional cooperation

B.   Promoting the use of wind energy

C.   Cultural exchange programmes

D.   Vocational training

13.   JANUS deals with ....

A.   Anti-proliferation of nuclear weapons

B.   Health and safety at work

C.   Integration of women into the labour market

D.   Promoting anti-discrimination measures in Member States

14.   Lingua deals with ....

A.   Promoting the French language

B.   Inter-institutional translation tools

C.   Vocational training of interpreters

D.   Promoting language competence

15.   Which of the following education programmes deals with Latin America?

A.   Leonardo da Vinci

B.   Erasmus

C.   Tempus

D.   ALFA

16.   What does the abbreviation "NUTS" stand for?

A.   Non-uniform treaty standards

B.   National unilateral trade system

C.   Nomenclature of territorial units for statistics

D.   New uniform territorial structure

17.   Which of the following is related to public procurement?

A.   SIMAP

B.   UCLAF

C.   EURAM

D.   FLAIR

18. Which of the following does not deal with fisheries?

A. FAR

B. INFCE

C. IBSFC

D. FIFG

19. Which of the following is not a political group in the European Parliament?

A. ALDE

B. UEN

C. SDR

D. PES

20. Which of the following abbreviations does not denominate a group of countries?

A. SADCC

B. SAHEL

C. ARE

D. CONTADORA

21. The abbreviation "COPA" stands for ....

A. Common Organisation of Agricultural Production

B. Community Orientation and Production Aid

C. Official Community Production Assessment

D. Committee of Agricultural Organisations

22. The abbreviation "NOW" stands for ....

A. Numerical Occlusive Warranty

B. New Opportunities for Women

C. National Organisation of Waste

D. National Office for Water Management

23. The programme to support artistic and cultural activities having a European dimension is called ....

A. Comedi

B. Kaleidoscope

C. Konver

D. Recite

24. The programme for exchange, assistance and training for the protection of the Euro against counterfeiting is called ....

A. Hercule

B. Daphne

C. Pericles

D. Xerxes

25. What does the CARE programme concern?

A. Road accidents

B. Aviation safety

C. Train schedules

D. Maritime transport

26. What is CENELEC related to?

A. Decision making database

B. Standardisation

C. Election observation

D. Legislative process

27.   The abbreviation "ERDF" stands for ....

A.   European Resource for Destabilised Fisheries areas

B.   European Restructuring and Development Framework

C.   European Research and Development Financial assistance

D.   European Regional Development Fund

28.   The Esprit programme deals with ....

A.   Cultural heritage

B.   The integration of minorities

C.   Information technology

D.   The internal market

29.   Which of the following programmes deals with technology in education?

A.   Eureka

B.   Poseidom

C.   Horizon

D.   Neptune

30.   The abbreviation "EPSO" stands for ....

A.   European Personnel Selection Office

B.   European Privacy Safety Organisation

C.   Eastern Pacific Standardisation Office

D.   Enlargement Policy for Southern and Occidental nations

MEMBER STATES

25 QUESTIONS – ANSWERS PAGE 367

1.   Approximately what proportion is the EU's territory compared to the United States'?

A.   One fifth

B.   One third

C.   Half

D.   One fourth

2.   Which one of the following is not a bordering country of the EU?

A.   Macedonia

B.   Moldova   — now borders Romania

C.   Turkey

D.   Ukraine

NONE OF ABOVE

3.   Approximately how many times is the EU's population as a whole bigger than the population of the Czech Republic?

A.   35

B.   55

C.   45

D.   65

4.   What is the life expectancy at birth in Europe for the total population?

A.   76.7 years

B.   79.9 years

C.   78.1 years

D.   81.2 years

5.   What percentage does agriculture represent in the EU25's GDP?

A.   14.5%

B.   2.3%

C.   8.4%

D.   21.6%

6.   Which of the following is not a harbour in the EU?

A.   Vilnius

B.   Helsinki

C.   Talinn

D.   Antwerp

7.   Which is the southernmost Member State in the EU25 (taking its capital as a reference)?

A.   Cyprus

B.   Greece

C.   Malta

D.   Italy

8.   Which of the following Member States is the biggest in size?

A.   Austria

B.   Hungary

C.   Ireland

D.   Portugal

9.   Tartu is in ....

A.   Lithuania

B.   Estonia

C.   Latvia

D.   Finland

10.   Which two countries have very similar flags in terms of their colour?

A.   Estonia, Slovakia

B.   Ireland, Slovenia

C.   Luxembourg, The Netherlands

D.   Lithuania, Portugal

11.   Which is the EU's smallest Member State in terms of population?

A.   Luxembourg

B.   Estonia

C.   Cyprus

D.   Malta

12.   How many times is Turkey's population bigger than Bulgaria's?

A.   10

B.   5

C.   7

D.   9

13. **Which EU Member States' flags are split vertically into two?**

A.   Poland, Denmark

B.   Finland, Latvia

C.   Malta, Portugal

D.   Cyprus, Austria

14. **Which of the following countries is not Romania's neighbour?**

A.   Ukraine

B.   Bulgaria

C.   Bosnia and Herzegovina

D.   Serbia and Montenegro

15. **Which is the EU25's second largest country by size?**

A.   Poland

B.   Spain

C.   Italy

D.   Germany

16. **What percentage is the EU 25's population of the world's?**

A.   7.3%

B.   12.5%

C.   18.5%

D.   4.2%

17. **Which country is the EU 25's leading trading partner?**

A.   USA

B.   Russia

C.   China

D.   Japan

18. **How many EU Member States are landlocked?**

A.   4

B.   5

C.   6

D.   3

19. **Which EU Member State has the highest number of EU Member States as neighbours?**

A.   Germany

B.   Czech Republic

C.   Luxembourg

D.   Austria

20. **In which institution's symbol can we find a balance?**

A.   Court of Justice, Court of First Instance

B.   Court of Justice, Court of First Instance, Eurojust

C.   Court of Justice, Court of First Instance, Court of Auditors, Eurojust, Europol

D.   Eurojust, Europol, Court of Auditors

21. **Which EU Member States have the following colours in their flags: red, dark blue and white?**

A.   France, Slovakia, United Kingdom, Estonia, Hungary

B.   Czech Republic, France, The Netherlands, Slovakia, Slovenia, United Kingdom

C.   France, Slovenia, Slovakia, Czech Republic, Luxembourg, Sweden

D.   Estonia, The Netherlands, France, United Kingdom, Slovenia

22.   How many EU Member States are crossed by the Danube?

A.   2

B.   5

C.   4

D.   6

23.   What is the name of the border river between Germany and France?

A.   Danube

B.   Seine

C.   Elbe

D.   Rhine

24.   Where is the Europa island?

A.   North-West of Ireland

B.   South of Greenland

C.   Greece

D.   Off southern Africa

25.   Approximately how many lakes does Finland have?

A.   25,000

B.   40,000

C.   75,000

D.   60,000

CONSTITUTIONAL TREATY

100 QUESTIONS – ANSWERS PAGE 370

1. The Declaration on the future of the Union was annexed to the ....

A. Treaty of Nice

B. Presidency Conclusions of the Laeken European Council

C. Presidency Conclusions of the Brussels European Council

D. Amsterdam Treaty

2. Which of the following issues did the above Declaration not call to be addressed?

A. Reshuffling the competences between the European Union and Member States

B. Simplification of the Treaties

C. The status of the Charter of Fundamental Rights of the European Union

D. The role of national parliaments

3. Who was the European Convention chaired by?

A. José Manuel Barroso

B. Wim Kok

C. Roman Herzog

D. Valéry Giscard d'Estaing

4. How many full members did the Convention responsible for the drafting of the Charter of Fundamental Rights have and in which year did it finish its work?

A. 324, 1998

B. 85, 1999

C. 168, 2001

D. 62, 2000

5. The final draft Treaty establishing a Constitution for Europe was submitted to the .... presidency.

A. Italian

B. Danish

C. Greek

D. Spanish

9. Not counting the Preamble, how many main parts does the Constitutional Treaty have?

A. 5

B. 8

C. 7

D. 4

6. How many representatives did candidate countries have all together in the European Convention (not including alternates)?

A. 33

B. 18

C. 39

D. 26

10. Part II includes ....

A. Fundamental rights and citizenship of the Union

B. The European Charter of Fundamental Rights

C. Association of the overseas countries and territories

D. Declaration on the creation of a European external action service

7. Which of the following statements is true?

A. The candidate countries took part in the discussions with full voting and veto rights

B. One representative of the Spanish, Danish and Greek governments was member of the Praesidium

C. The Convention met in Laeken once or twice a month

D. There were four representatives of the European Commission in the Praesidium

11. Which of the following does Part III not include?

A. Non-discrimination and citizenship

B. Clauses of general application

C. The exercise of Union competences

D. Internal policies and action

12. When was the draft Constitutional Treaty signed?

A. 29 October 2004

B. 12 December 2003

C. 18 June 2004

D. 23 November 2004

8. Which of the following was not a working group set up by the Convention?

A. Complementary powers

B. The area of freedom, security and justice

C. Increasing the European Union's competitiveness

D. The role of the principle of subsidiarity

13. **Which Member State was the first to approve the Constitutional Treaty?**

A. Hungary

B. Lithuania

C. Slovenia

D. Latvia

14. **The Preamble of the Constitutional Treaty is a quote from ....**

A. Thucydides

B. Pausanias

C. Herodotus

D. Plutarch

15. **According to the Constitutional Treaty, which of the following is not listed among the values of the Union?**

A. Respect for equality

B. Respect for human dignity

C. Respect for rights of persons belonging to ethnic or religious minorities

D. Respect for the rule of law

16. **The Union values play an important role in ....**

A. Legal proceedings between European citizens

B. Failure by a Community institution to respect these values

C. External relations with third countries

D. The accession of a new Member State

17. **"The Union and the Member States shall, in full mutual respect, assist each** other in carrying out tasks which flow from the Constitution." This principle is called ....

A. Mutual assistance

B. Joint efforts

C. Sincere cooperation

D. Due diligence

18. **Giving the Union legal personality means the merging of the .... and the .....**

A. European Community, Second Pillar

B. European Community, European Coal and Steel Community, Euratom

C. European Community, European Union

D. European Union, Euratom

19. **Before the Constitutional Treaty, the principle of the Union law's primacy over national laws was declared by ....**

A. The Treaty of Nice

B. A Council Regulation

C. Court case law

D. The German Constitutional Court

20. **According to the Constitutional Treaty, which of the following is not an aim the Union seeks to promote?**

A. Peace

B. Democracy

C. Its values

D. Well-being of its peoples

21. The Constitutional Treaty provides that "[t]he Union shall accede to the ....".

A. European Convention for the Protection of Human Rights and Fundamental Freedoms

B. Universal Declaration of Human Rights

C. Declaration of the Principles of International Cultural Co-operation

D. International Covenant on Civil and Political Rights

22. "The content and form of Union action shall not exceed what is necessary to achieve the objectives of the Constitution" is the principle of ....

A. Subsidiarity

B. Conferral

C. Shared competences

D. Proportionality

23. How many exclusive Union competences did the Constitutional Treaty add?

A. Two

B. Three

C. One

D. None

24. Which of the following is not a shared competence according to the Constitutional Treaty?

A. Trans-European networks

B. Consumer protection

C. Conservation of marine biological resources

D. Common safety concerns in public health matters

25. Enhanced cooperation may take place in areas of ....

A. Shared competence and supporting, coordinating or complementary action

B. Shared competence only

C. Exclusive Union competences

D. Supporting, coordinating or complementary action

26. "If action by the Union should prove necessary [...] to attain one of the objectives set out in the Constitution, and the Constitution has not provided the necessary powers, the Council of Ministers [...] shall adopt the appropriate measures." This is called ....

A. Flexibility clause

B. Supplementary competence

C. Complementary proceedings

D. Reinforced assistance

27. In the case of the above action, the European Parliament has to ....

A. Give its consent

B. Be informed

C. Monitor the adopted measures

D. Be consulted

28. Which of the following statements is true?

A. The Constitutional Treaty includes the Copenhagen criteria regarding membership of the Union

B. A Member State can be deprived of membership if it persistently infringes the Union's fundamental values

C. Requests for accession are submitted for approval to the European Parliament, which decides by simple majority of the votes cast

D. The Constitutional Treaty provides a definition for the term "European country"

29. In the case of voluntary withdrawal from the Union, the Council of Ministers concludes this agreement on the part of the Union, acting by ...., and after .... the European Parliament.

A. Qualified majority, informing

B. Unanimity, informing

C. Unanimity, obtaining the consent of

D. Qualified majority, obtaining the consent of

30. The Constitutional Treaty reduces the number of legal acts from more than .... to .....

A. 18, 7

B. 15, 6

C. 23, 5

D. 21, 8

31. Regarding delegated European regulations, which institution(s) may have the right to revoke the delegation?

A. Council, Commission, European Parliament

B. Council

C. Commission, European Parliament

D. European Parliament, Council

32. In the field of common foreign and security policy, what kind of legal acts

can be adopted pursuant to the Constitutional Treaty?

A. European decisions

B. European laws

C. European regulations

D. Framework laws

33. In the area of freedom, security and justice, what kind of legal acts can be adopted pursuant to the Constitutional Treaty?

A. European regulations and laws

B. European decisions and laws

C. European decisions and framework laws

D. European laws and framework laws

34. When the Union mobilises all instruments at its disposal in case of a disaster, which of the following does the "Solidarity clause" not list as a goal?

A. Protect democratic institutions and the civilian population from any terrorist attack

B. Assist a Member State in its territory, at the request of its political authorities in the event of a terrorist attack

C. Prevent bio-terrorism or the spread of contagious diseases

D. Prevent the terrorist threat in the territory of the Member States

35. "In all its activities, the Union shall observe the principle of the equality of its citizens, who shall receive equal attention from its institutions, bodies, offices and agencies" is called the principle of ....

A. Legitimate interests

B.   Democratic equality

C.   Citizens' participation

D.   Equal representation

36.   The principle of "Representative democracy" does not include that ....

A.   Every citizen has the right to reside freely in any Member State of the Union

B.   Political parties at European level contribute to forming European political awareness

C.   Citizens are directly represented at Union level in the European Parliament

D.   Every citizen has the right to participate in the democratic life of the Union

37.   The principle of "Participatory democracy" does not include that ....

A.   The institutions give representative associations the opportunity to publicly exchange their views in all areas of Union action

B.   The institutions maintain an open, transparent and regular dialogue with civil society

C.   Representative associations shall always be consulted on issues that concern the transparency and coherence of Union legal acts

D.   The Commission carries out broad consultations with parties concerned

38.   According to the Constitutional Treaty, not less than .... million citizens who are nationals of .... Member States may take the initiative of inviting the Commission to submit any appropriate proposal on some specific matters.

A.   One, a significant number of

B.   Five, eight

C.   Ten, at least five

D.   Twenty, at least one tenth of the total number of

39.   According to the Constitutional Treaty, the .... contributes to social dialogue.

A.   Multilateral Social Dialogue

B.   Tripartite Social Summit for Growth and Employment

C.   Trade Unions and Employers' Representative Associations

D.   Bilateral Social Forum for Equal Opportunities

40.   According to the Constitutional Treaty, the "European Parliament shall meet in public, as shall the Council when considering and voting on .... ."

A.   A draft legislative act

B.   Legislative acts whose disclosure is not excluded by a European law

C.   Any legislative act

D.   Non-legislative acts and European framework laws

41.   The Constitutional Treaty provides that apart from churches and religious associations, the Union equally respects the status of ....

A.   Philosophical and non-confessional organisations

B.   Civil religious organisations and communities

C.   Civil non-confessional organisations and religious communities

D.   Recognised confessional organisations

42. As opposed to the ...., the Constitutional Treaty recognises the .... as one of the "main" institutions of the European Union.

A. Economic and Social Committee, Committee of the Regions

B. European Council, European Central Bank

C. Committee of the Regions, Court of Auditors

D. Court of Auditors, European Council

43. According to the Constitutional Treaty, Members of the Economic and Social Committee and the Committee of the Regions are .... for a term of .... years.

A. Elected, 4

B. Elected, 5

C. Appointed, 5

D. Appointed, 4

44. According to the Constitutional Treaty, a panel should give an opinion on candidates' suitability to perform the duties of Judge and Advocate-General of the Court of Justice and the General Court. How many members should this panel have and how many of them should be proposed by the European Parliament?

A. 5, 1

B. 12, 3

C. 3, none

D. 7, 1

45. According to the Constitutional Treaty, which of the following statements is true? The European Parliament, the Council or the Commission may, to submit its opinion, set the Economic and Social Committee ....

A. A time-limit. Should the Committee fail to give an opinion upon expiry, it shall prevent further action

B. A mutually agreed time-limit by which it is shall compulsorily give its opinion

C. A time-limit of not less than one month

D. An indicative time-limit of less than three months

46. According to the Constitutional Treaty, the codecision procedure will be called ....

A. Regular procedure

B. Special reading procedure

C. Joint decision process

D. Ordinary legislative procedure

47. According to the Constitutional Treaty, which of the following will be decided by qualified majority voting?

A. Citizenship

B. Taxation

C. Non-discrimination issues

D. Freedom of movement for workers

48. Which of the following will not be decided by qualified majority voting?

A. Common policy on asylum and temporary protection

B. Measures concerning operational cooperation between police authorities

C. The Union's policy with regard to border checks

D. Judicial cooperation in criminal matters

49. Concerning the budgetary procedure in the Constitutional Treaty, which of the following statements is false?

A. The Parliament makes the final decision, acting by a majority of the members and two thirds of the votes cast

B. The Commission must submit annually to the European Parliament and to the Council of Ministers an evaluation report

C. The budgetary procedure will become part of the (what is currently known as) codecision procedure

D. The distinction between mandatory and non-mandatory expenditure will be eliminated

50. Regarding the European Parliament, the Constitutional Treaty provides that the minimum number of MEPs per country shall be .... , the maximum in aggregate shall be ...., and no Member State may have more than ....

A. 4, 736, 94

B. 5, 732, 98

C. 4, 732, 96

D. 6, 750, 96

51. Regarding the Constitutional Treaty's provisions on the European Parliament and the Committee of Inquiry it may set up, which of the following statements is false?

A. The Parliament's hearings and its investigation has to be secret when the alleged facts are being examined before a court

B. A European law of the European Parliament shall lay down the detailed provisions governing the exercise of the right of inquiry

C. One fourth of the Parliament's component Members may request that such a Committee be set up

D. The Committee ceases to exist on submission of its report

52. The European Council is convened by its President ....

A. When the President deems it necessary

B. Twice a year

C. Four times a year or when the situation so requires

D. When the situation so requires

53. The European Council President is elected by .... for a term of ....

A. Qualified majority, 5 years

B. Qualified majority, 2.5 years

C. Unanimity, 5 years

D. Unanimity, 2.5 years

54. Which of the following tasks is the European Council President not responsible for?

A. Present a report to the European Parliament after each of the meetings of the European Council

B. Ensure the preparation and continuity of the work of the European Council in cooperation with the President of the Commission

C. Endeavour to facilitate cohesion and consensus within the European Council

D. Provide exclusive representation of the Union in external affairs and diplomatic relations

55. Which of the following statements is false regarding the Constitutional Treaty's provisions on the European Council?

A. In case of a vote that requires unanimity, an abstention may prevent the adoption of an act

B. The European Council establishes its procedural rules by simple majority

C. As a rule, decisions of the European Council are taken by consensus

D. Any member of the European Council may also act on behalf of not more than one other member

56. A qualified majority in the Council means at least .... % of the members comprising at least .... of them and representing Member States comprising at least ....% of the population of the Union.

A. 65, 10, 58

B. 63, 12, 54

C. 55, 15, 65

D. 62, one third, 55

57. When the Council does not act on a proposal from the Commission or from the Union Minister for Foreign Affairs, the above qualified majority is defined as at least .... % of the members of the Council representing Member States comprising at least .... % of the population of the Union.

A. 55, 65

B. 72, 65

C. 67, 55

D. 75, 62

58. According to the Constitutional Treaty, the Presidency of Council configurations, other than that of Foreign Affairs, must be held by Member State representatives in the Council on the basis of ....

A. The list established by a unanimous European decision of the European Council

B. Equal rotation, in accordance with the alphabetical order of Member States

C. Equal rotation between a group of three Member States for fifteen months

D. Equal rotation, in accordance with the conditions established by a European decision

59. The Union Minister for Foreign Affairs is also going to be the ....

A. European Council President

B. Commissioner Responsible for External Affairs and Development

C. Vice-chairman of the Foreign Affairs Council

D. Vice-president of the Commission

60. Supposing the Constitutional Treaty comes into effect in 2007 and the number of Member States is 27, how many Members will the European Commission have in 2015, not including its President and the Union Minister for Foreign Affairs?

A. 18

B. 25

C. 23

D. 16

61. Concerning the Commission President, which of the following statements is false?

A. When proposing the candidate for President of the Commission, the European Council takes into account the elections to the European Parliament

B. The President appoints each Vice-President from among the members of the Commission

C. On the basis of the European Parliament's consent, the Commission is appointed by the European Council

D. The Council to adopt the list of persons whom it proposes for appointment as members of the Commission, by common accord with the President-elect

62. Regarding the Union Minister for Foreign Affairs, he or she conducts the Union's common foreign and security policy and contributes by his or her proposals to the development of that policy, which he or she carries out as mandated by the .....

A. College of Commissioners

B. Council

C. Commission President

D. European Council

63. The ...., acting by ...., with the agreement of the President of the Commission, appoints the Union Minister for Foreign Affairs.

A. Council and the European Parliament, The majority of its component members

B. European Council, Qualified majority

C. Council, Unanimity

D. European Council, Unanimity

64. In fulfilling his or her mandate, the Union Minister for Foreign Affairs is assisted by a ....

A. European Diplomatic Corps

B. Union Foreign Network

C. European External Action Service

D. Foreign Relations Office

65. According to the Protocol on the Role of National Parliaments, annexed to the Constitutional Treaty, which of the following is not forwarded to national Parliaments upon publication?

A. Implementing measures

B. Annual legislative programme

C. Green papers

D. Communications

66. According to the Protocol mentioned in the previous question, which of the following is not considered as a "draft European legislative act"?

A. Requests from the Court of Justice

B. Initiatives from a group of Member States

C. Recommendations from the European Central Bank

D. Requests from the Court of Auditors

67. In the framework of the "Simplified revision procedure", how much time do national Parliaments have from the date of notification to make known their eventual opposition?

A. 6 months

B. 6 weeks

C. 15 weeks

D.   3 months

C.   14

D.   7

68. Which of the following is not possible under the "Simplified revision procedure"?

A.   The European Council may authorise the Council to act by a qualified majority in an area under unanimity

B.   The European Council may authorise that the Council adopts laws by ordinary procedure previously under special legislative procedure

C.   The Government of any Member State may submit proposals for revising the provisions on the internal policies of the Union

D.   The European Council may adopt a decision amending all or part of the provisions on Union policies, which, provided it has been adopted by unanimity, comes into force on the day indicated thereof

69. "Any national Parliament or any chamber of a national Parliament may […] send […] a reasoned opinion stating why it considers that the draft in question does not comply with the principle of subsidiarity." This is called ....

A.   Early Warning System

B.   Legality Control Procedure

C.   Democratic Supervision

D.   Principle of Double Legitimacy

70. Supposing the EU has 28 Member States, how many National Parliaments are needed for a legislative proposal to be reviewed concerning the area of freedom, security and justice?

A.   13

B.   9

71. Which of the following statements is true?

A.   Provisions of the Constitutional Treaty applicable to each individual policy refer to the possibility of adopting "acts" or "measures"

B.   The Constitutional Treaty includes new legal bases which explicitly empower the Union to act in certain areas

C.   As a general rule, Council decisions are to be taken by unanimity

D.   The Commission will no longer retain the sole right of initiative for laws under (what is currently known as) the codecision procedure

72. Which of the following statements is false in the context of the free movement of persons and combating discrimination?

A.   The Union may define the basic principles on which incentive measures may be adopted

B.   The Council shall adopt the necessary provisions to secure diplomatic and consular protection of citizens of the Union in third countries

C.   The Union may adopt measures concerning passports and identity cards

D.   With regard to measures needed to combat discrimination, the Council must obtain the prior consent of the European Parliament

73. According to the Constitutional Treaty, ... in the field of social security.

A.   Provisions concerning pensioners and students are adopted by qualified majority voting

B.   Provisions concerning employees may be adopted by the Article I-18 procedure

C.   The legal basis is extended to cover self-employed migrant workers

D.   Unanimous voting prevails

C.   Supports Member States' efforts to promote joint initiatives

D.   Contributes to this objective by European regulations and decisions

74.   Regarding European intellectual property rights, the Constitutional Treaty ....

A.   Calls for uniform protection throughout the Union by means of European laws and framework laws

B.   Provides that a non-centralised authorisation procedure is required

C.   Provides that English, French and German be used as official languages for the procedures

D.   Stipulates that coordination and supervision arrangements are to be carried out by the Office for Harmonisation in the Internal Market (OHIM)

77.   "The Commission may, in close contact with the Member States, take any useful initiative to promote such coordination, in particular initiatives aiming at the establishment of guidelines and indicators, the organisation of exchange of best practice, and the preparation of the necessary elements for periodic monitoring and evaluation. The European Parliament shall be kept fully informed." This is called ....

A.   European Social Dialogue

B.   Reinforced Cooperation

C.   Enhanced Cooperation

D.   Open Method of Coordination

75.   In the field of research and technological cooperation, the Constitutional Treaty ....

A.   Provides that the Commission's coordination may not extend to biotechnology issues

B.   Provides that Member States should encourage cooperation among each other

C.   Requires the European Parliament's approval by two thirds of its component Members when multi-annual programmes are involved

D.   Adds a provision on the promotion of cross-border cooperation between researchers

78.   In which of the following areas is the above tool not used?

A.   Promotion of coordination in research and technological development activities

B.   Prevention of occupational accidents and diseases

C.   Union action to improve public health

D.   Creation of a favourable environment for the development of undertakings in tourism

76.   Regarding European space policy, the Constitutional Treaty provides that the Union ....

A.   Should establish any appropriate relations with the European Space Agency

B.   Only supports efforts needed for the exploration but not the exploitation of space

79.   Regarding internal policy, in which of the following areas has no new legal base been created?

A.   Special quantitative restrictions for agricultural products

B.   Measures to support Member States' action in civil protection

QUESTIONS – CONSTITUTIONAL TREATY

C. Administrative cooperation to implement Union law

D. Adoption of laws related to services of general economic interest

80. Regarding economic policy in the Constitutional Treaty, which of the following statements is false?

A. When the Council of Ministers addresses a recommendation to a Member State, the latter does not take part in the vote

B. Qualified majority in questions relating to the economic policy requires two thirds of the Member States to vote in favour

C. Decisions concerning excessive deficits are based on a proposal from the Commission

D. The Commission may address warnings to any Member State whose economic policy contravenes the broad guidelines

81. Based on the Constitutional Treaty's provisions, which of the following issues is not decided by unanimity?

A. Adoption of measures to replace the existing protocol on excessive deficits

B. Common positions on monetary union matters within the competent international financial institutions

C. Appointment of members of the European Central Bank's Executive Board

D. Establishing the substitution rate between the euro and the national currency of the Member State adopting the euro

82. The denomination "Member States with a derogation" refers to Member States ....

A. In respect of which the Council has not decided

that they fulfil the necessary conditions for the adoption of the euro

B. In respect of which the Council has decided that they do not fulfil the necessary conditions for the adoption of the euro

C. Which have decided not to accept the euro as their currency

D. Which, based on objective data, do not fulfil the conditions required for the adoption of the euro

83. Which of the following does not belong to the list of particularly serious crimes with a cross-border dimension, listed in the Constitutional Treaty?

A. Drug trafficking

B. Counterfeiting of means of payment

C. Crimes against humanity

D. Computer crime

84. In order to combat crimes affecting the financial interests of the Union, a European law of the Council may establish a(n) ....

A. Eurojust Financial Operations Unit

B. European Public Prosecutor's Office

C. OLAF International Fraud Force

D. Anti-Counterfeit and Fraud Bureau

85. Regarding the common commercial policy in the Constitutional Treaty, which of the following statements is false?

A. It is extended to foreign direct investment excluding transport

B. The European Parliament is involved in the decision-making process

C.   Qualified majority is required for agreements in the field of trade in cultural services

D.   Decisions relating to the conclusion of agreements in some areas are subject to unanimity

86.   The Constitutional Treaty provides that the Union may conclude an agreement with third countries or international organisations to achieve one of the objectives referred to in the Constitution. This is called ....

A.   Tacit constitutional requirement

B.   Indirect obligations

C.   Implicit international prerogative

D.   Implied external powers

87.   According to the Constitutional Treaty, who provides the resources for the common foreign and security policy?

A.   Member States only

B.   Union only

C.   Members States and the Union

D.   Union and some Member States on a voluntary basis

88.   According to the Constitutional Treaty, who may submit proposals in the field of common foreign and security policy?

A.   The Commission, supported by the Union Minister for Foreign Affairs

B.   The Commission only

C.   The Commission, the Union Minister for Foreign Affairs or one third of Member States

D.   The Union Minister for Foreign Affairs, supported by the Commission

89.   The Union does not conduct the common foreign and security policy by ....

A.   Adopting European framework laws concerning arrangements for implementation

B.   Strengthening systematic cooperation between Member States

C.   Adopting European decisions defining positions to be taken by the Union

D.   Defining the general guidelines

90.   The Council may adopt a European decision determining that there is a clear risk of a serious breach by a Member State of the values on the basis of a ....

A.   Reasoned initiative signed by four fifths of the Members of the European Parliament

B.   Reasoned initiative of one third of the Member States

C.   Joint proposal from the Commission and Union Minister for Foreign Affairs

D.   Joint proposal of the European Council President and the Commission President

91.   For the adoption of a European decision concerning the existence of a serious and persistent breach by a Member State of the values mentioned in Article I-2, qualified majority is defined as at least .... % of the members of the Council, representing the participating Member States, comprising at least .... % of the population of these States.

A.   72, 65

B.   65, 55

C.   75, 62

D.   67, 62

92. Regarding withdrawal from the Union, which of the following statements is false?

A. Withdrawal of membership is only possible on a voluntary basis

B. The agreement concerning withdrawal is concluded by the Council, acting by a qualified majority, after obtaining the consent of the European Parliament

C. If a State which has withdrawn from the Union asks to rejoin, its request will be subject to the same procedure as the one set out for the withdrawal

D. As a rule, the Constitution ceases to apply to the State in question from the date of entry into force of the withdrawal agreement or, failing that, two years after the notification

93. Blocking minority in enhanced cooperation requires at least the minimum number of Council members representing more than .... , failing which the qualified majority shall be deemed attained.

A. One third of the population of the Member States

B. 30% of the population of the Member States plus one member

C. 35% of the population of the participating Member States plus one member

D. One fourth of the population of the participating Member States, but at least 30% of all Member States

94. Which of the following will still remain in force when the Constitutional Treaty enters into force?

A. Treaty of 22 April 1970 amending certain budgetary provisions

B. Act of 25 March 1993 amending the Protocol on the Statute of the European Investment Bank

C. Treaty establishing the European Atomic Energy Community

D. Protocol of 8 April 1965 on the privileges and immunities of the European Communities

95. According to the Constitutional Treaty, insofar as the Charter of Fundamental Rights recognises fundamental rights as they result from the ...., those rights must be interpreted in harmony with those ....

A. Community jurisprudence, Principles

B. Constitutional traditions common to the Member States, Traditions

C. Union's inherent principles, Values

D. Values recognised by the international community, Merits

96. "Nothing in this Charter shall be interpreted as implying any right to engage in any activity or to perform any act aimed at the destruction of any of the rights and freedoms recognised in this Charter or at their limitation to a greater extent than is provided for herein." According to the Constitutional Treaty, this principle is called ....

A. Rule of "Nemo plus iuris"

B. Limited exhaustion of rights

C. Principle of proportionality

D. Prohibition of abuse of rights

97. Which of the following does the Constitutional Treaty not list under the

title "Prohibition of slavery and forced labour"?

A. No one may be required to perform labour without due payment, unless ordered so by law

B. Trafficking in human beings is prohibited

C. No one may be held in slavery or servitude

D. No one may be required to perform forced or compulsory labour

98. Which of the following "diversities" does the Constitutional Treaty not enumerate in the section on the Charter of Fundamental Rights?

A. Religious

B. Cultural

C. Linguistic

D. Intellectual

99. In the course of ordinary revision procedure, the proposals for the amend-

ment of the Constitutional Treaty is submitted to the .... by the .....

A. Council and European Parliament, Commission

B. Council, Commission

C. European Council, Member State or institution who proposed the amendment

D. European Council, Council

100. According to the Constitutional Treaty, if, ... after the signature of the Treaty establishing a Constitution for Europe, ... of the Member States have ratified it and one or more Member States have encountered difficulties in proceeding with ratification, the matter will be referred to the European Council.

A. Four years, four fifths

B. Two years, four fifths

C. Two years, three quarters

D. Four years, three quarters

VERBAL REASONING

50 QUESTIONS – ANSWERS PAGE 388

50 QUESTIONS – ANSWERS PAGE 388

In each question below, which statement is true or can be best derived from the question text?
Please note that each question should be considered independently and no further information or knowledge should be considered when answering.

1. The European Council welcomed the fact that, following the opening session of the Intergovernmental Conference in Rome, work in the Conference was now underway. It recalled its support for the approach and timetable put forward by the Presidency in line with the conclusions of the European Council meeting in Thessaloniki. The European Council invited ministers to continue actively the political discussions.
(Presidency Conclusions, Brussels European Council, 2003)

A. The Intergovernmental Conference was launched in Rome

B. The Thessaloniki European Council is due to follow the Intergovernmental Conference

C. The European Council consists of ministers of Member States

D. The timetable put forward by the Presidency is supported by the Intergovernmental Conference

2. Bruges can seem a dream-like vision of the Middle Ages, with its houses of mellow time-worn brick, its majestic public buildings and its canals where swans glide gracefully over the dark waters. The medieval illusion is complete when melodious chimes ring out from the belfries of the city's ancient churches. In summer and even during out-of-season weekends a metamorphosis takes place, when visitors fill the streets and squares and the whole town buzzes with activity.
(Michelin Guide)

A. Bruges is in the Flemish speaking area of Belgium

B.   Bruges had been built in the middle ages but was destroyed in the following centuries

C.   The churches in Bruges were built several hundred years ago and some of them still have managed to preserve their belfry

D.   Bruges has an excellent atmosphere that attracts a large number of tourists all year

3.   **The foreign occupation of Lebanon began in 1976, when Syria's dictator, Hafez Assad, sent his army to intervene in Lebanon's brutal three-cornered civil war between Maronite Christians, Muslims and Palestinians. The mass protests that forced Lebanon's pro-Syrian government to resign this week would probably not have happened but for a powerful shock: last month's murder of Rafik Hariri, the country's former prime minister and most popular politician. This was the catalyst for a chain reaction.**
(The Economist, 3 March 2005)

A.   Lebanon's government had always been against supporting Syria

B.   Lebanon had suffered a civil war in which Syria intervened

C.   Rafik Hariri was Lebanon's president in 1976 but he was overthrown by Maronite Christians

D.   Lebanon has had widespread relations with Arab nations in the Middle East

4.   **Belgian chocolates and pralines (chocolate with creamy or nutty fillings) need no introduction, but Brussels and Liege waffles are appreciated just as much. The country's bakeries offer a great variety of different kinds of bread and a number of regional specialities. They include couque (sugary, spicy bread from Brussels and hard spiced bread with honey from Dinant), craquelin (sugar-filled brioche), noeud (butter biscuit**

with brown sugar), cramique (milk bread with raisins), pistolet (small round loaf), and mastel (rusk bread with aniseed).
(Michelin Guide)

A.   Liege is mostly famous for its waffles, whereas Brussels is more known for chocolate and pralines

B.   Craquelin and pistolet are both Belgian specialities that are like a small cake or loaf

C.   The noeud is mainly sold in the Liege area and occasionally in other regions as well

D.   Craquelin is a rusk bread with aniseed and sugar topping

5.   **Iraqis now have their first democratically elected government in 50 years – appointed, as it happens, on Saddam Hussein's 68th birthday. Even so, five cabinet jobs, including that of defence minister, are still being disputed, and will be filled temporarily until final agreement is reached. One of the main hold-ups had been the demands by the Shia-led party of Iyad Allawi, the outgoing, interim prime minister, for a large share of the cabinet seats. Mr Allawi and his allies will not now take part in the government, and are likely to form the main opposition block in the Parliament.**
(The Economist, 29 April 2005)

A.   Iyad Allawi is an extrovert person who was presiding the Shia-led party

B.   Until recently, Iraq's prime minister had been Iyad Allawi

C.   The interim, democratically elected Iraqi government was appointed on the same day when Saddam Hussein took power

D.   Iyad Allawi's allies will take part in the government only at a later stage and until then they will form the main opposition block

6. **Teaching hospitals are an important component of the health care system. They are the vital sites of education and research and bring to bear considerable and varied expertise to clinical care. However, it has not been clear to everyone that they do in fact deliver care of higher quality than that delivered by non-teaching hospitals. This applies not only for the care of the more complex and sophisticated illnesses, where better quality may be expected, but also for the care of more "routine" conditions.**

A. Teaching hospitals only provide higher levels of health care for everyday conditions

B. Teaching hospitals, compared to non-teaching ones, provide higher level of health care in all sorts of illnesses

C. Teaching hospitals have too many students, which restricts the provision of efficient health care

D. There should be more teaching hospitals in order to have a higher level of health care

7. **In 1986 the Community received fresh impetus from the third round of enlargement to include Spain and Portugal and later the conclusion of the Single Act, a Community Treaty setting new targets for the enlarged Community (single market, economic and social cohesion etc.) with the result that a radical reform of the Community's financial system on sound policy footing was envisaged. In February 1987, the reform was presented by the Commission as an overall proposal in the "Delors package".**
(ScadPlus)

A. The Single European Act was initiated by Portugal and aimed at setting new targets for the Community

B. Jacques Delors served two terms as the president of the European Commission

C. The Delors package, aiming at higher spending on regional policy, was fostered by the accession of Spain and Portugal to the Community

D. There had been two enlargements before the accession of Spain and Portugal to the European Community

8. **Developing the competitiveness of the European economy in line with the Lisbon agenda requires a renewed commitment of the public and private sectors to the objective of investing 3% of GDP in research, with a particular emphasis on technological innovation including environmental technology, on developing human capital through higher investment in education and research, along the lines recommended by the Council on 22 September 2003. (Presidency Conclusions, Brussels European Council, 2003)**

A. The current level of investment in research and technological innovation is currently less than three percent of GDP

B. The Council of Ministers with the portfolio of environmental issues held a meeting on 22 September 2003

C. Development of human capital means a greater investment into financial markets and the education industry

D. The Lisbon agenda was aiming at boosting the European economy in order to make it the most competitive market in the world

9. **According to projections by the United Nations, on present trends the median age of Americans, now 35, will rise by only five years by 2050, and the population will grow by over 40%. Japan's median age, on the other hand, will rise by 12 years to 53, and its population will fall by 14%. Germany's is due to drop by 4% and Italy's by 22%. Falling and ageing populations will make it harder to boost demand. As people age and their children grow up,**

they tend to save more and spend less, though usually after retirement a prolonged period of dissaving sets in.
(The Economist, 18 September 2003)

A. The current median age in Japan is higher than that of the USA

B. Germany's population is expected to fall by 22%, whereas Italy's is likely to fall by 14%

C. According to the United Nations, the median age of Americans is expected to rise by more than 40% by 2050

D. People tend to spend more than before once their children have grown up

10. **The first independent Slovene state dates back much further: when the Romans had been driven out by Mongolian Avars, who had in turn been driven out by Slavs, it was in AD 623 that king Samo established a kingdom (tribal confederation) stretching from Lake Balaton (now in Hungary) to the Mediterranean, which had its centre in the present Czech Republic. The territory fell under the Frankish Empire late in the 8th century, and in the 10th century it became the independent duchy of Carantania under Holy Roman Emperor Otto I. From this period onwards, until 1414, a special ceremony of the enthronement of princes, conducted in Slovene, took place.**
(DG Enlargement)

A. Otto I ruled in the 15th century as the Emperor of Rome

B. King Samo's country stretched to areas that today belong to Hungary and the Czech Republic

C. The Mongolian Avars destroyed the Frankish Empire late in the 8th century

D. The special ceremony conducted for princes in the Slovene language first took place in 1414

11. **The protection of intellectual property is, of course, governed by many international conventions. The World Intellectual Property Organisation (WIPO) and, more recently, the World Trade Organisation (WTO) are responsible for implementing numerous international conventions and treaties. The first convention, the Paris Convention for the Protection of Industrial Property, dates back to 1883, and since then several conventions and treaties have been signed which cover various aspects of the protection of intellectual property, such as the protection of literary and artistic works (Berne Convention) and the protection of performers, producers of phonograms and broadcasting organisations (the Rome Convention).**
(ScadPlus)

A. Artistic works and broadcasting organisations are protected by the Berne Convention

B. The first convention to protect industrial property was signed in Paris

C. The World Intellectual Property Organisation and the World Trade Organisation have their headquarters in Paris and Rome

D. Performers are generally protected by the Paris Convention and in some special cases, the Rome Convention

12. **The removal of technical barriers to trade is a precondition for the completion of the internal market. Since the adoption of the new approach to technical harmonisation and standardisation in 1985, the harmonisation of European industrial standards in the sixteen areas covered by European technical legislation has become an essential instrument for the achievement of this objective. This approach was subsequently complemented by a coherent policy on certification and tests, setting out clear, consistent and transparent principles which apply to**

the product certification procedures to be used at Community level.
(ScadPlus)

A. There are more than twenty areas where technical legislation has to be implemented in order to remove technical barriers to trade

B. The completion of the internal market entails the harmonisation of industrial standards and a policy on certification and tests

C. Product certification procedures require the adoption of a new approach to technical harmonisation

D. The completion of the internal market was achieved in 1985 when technical standards were harmonised

13. **The annual allocation to Romania under ISPA is between EUR 208-270 million for the period 2000-2006. The sectors benefiting from ISPA are transport and the environment, with both sectors receiving around half of the annual allocation. The ISPA programme is designed principally to support municipalities in the field of the environment and the central authorities in the field of transport. In order to bring Romania up to EU standards, ISPA will concentrate on the "heavy investment" directives (mainly drinking water, treatment of waste-water, solid-waste management and air pollution).**
(DG Enlargement)

A. The ISPA programme mainly concerns the transport and energy sector for the period 2000-2006

B. Romania is due to become a member of the European Union in 2007

C. Romania receives around 104-135 million euros for the period 2000-2006 from ISPA to improve its environment sector

D. Wastewater treatment is not included in the so-called "heavy investment" issues tackled by the ISPA programme

14. **In the past decade, the effects budget for a typical blockbuster has ballooned from $5 million to $50 million. As digital effects (DFX) have become more complex and accessible, the barriers between fanciful computer-animated films and ostensibly realistic ones have crumbled. DFX now allow film-makers to not only manipulate reality, but to build it from scratch.**
(Popular Science)

A. Digital effects have become more complex but fewer filmmakers can afford their application

B. There is a limit to the extent digital effects can change "reality" in a movie

C. Movie effects have seen a tenfold increase in terms of their budget over the last ten years

D. There is still a huge difference between computer-animated movies and real ones

15. **Both man and machine are approaching the future at an ever-accelerating clip. Almost every year, our vehicles break speed records. This past fall, the X-43A scramjet-powered aircraft reached a speed of nearly Mach 10, beating a record of Mach 6.8 set only six months before. Today's fastest supercomputer, IBM's Blue Gene, is about 450,000 times as speedy as the ruling machine of 30 years ago and twice as fleet as the fastest machine of just one year ago. We build passenger trains that travel 267 miles an hour and rocket cars that break the speed of sound.**
(Society of Broadcast Engineers)

A. The fastest aircraft reached a speed more than three times higher than six months before

B. Today, the fastest computer is manufactured by IBM and it has doubled in speed in just one year

C. Aircrafts, computers and trains have undergone an incredible development that is soon coming to an end

D. Passenger trains have managed to break the speed of sound

16. **In Latvia, by the end of the nineties, the macroeconomic situation had stabilised and offered a favourable basis: GDP growth (over 5%), low inflation (less than 3%), low budget deficit (around 3%), acceptable level of foreign debt (total stock of 46% of GDP in 2001), and stable currency (pegged to the IMF Special Drawing Rights). Interest rates lowered to less than 10% in 2002.**
(DG Enlargement)

A. The inflation rate and budget deficit in Latvia were around 3%, which is considered an acceptable level

B. The International Monetary Fund (IMF) was founded in 1946 in Bretton Woods

C. Latvia's GDP growth was due to the low level of inflation and the acceptable level of foreign debt

D. Latvia's currency was interlinked with the so-called special drawing rights, which prevented fluctuations

17. **Qori Kalis, a glacier that lies at above 18,000 feet in the Peruvian Andes, is melting at a rate of nearly 700 feet a year. In 2002, Ohio State University paleoclimatologist Lonnie Thompson discovered a perfectly preserved Distichia muscoides, a moss-type plant that carbon dating measured as 5,200 years old, on the Qori Kalis. "The find was remarkable," he says. "This tells us the glacier hasn't been this small for more than 5,000 years."**
(Impact Lab)

A. Qori Kalis is a paleo-climatologist at Ohio State University who made a discovery about a moss-type plant

B. Carbon dating is generally used to determine the size of glaciers

C. Half of the Peruvian Andes is covered by snow all year long

D. Concerning the size of the glacier, the Ohio

State University professor based his conclusion on a moss-type plant

18. **Freedom of movement for persons was not brought about only in the context of the European Communities. In 1985, Germany, France and the Benelux countries signed the Schengen Agreement on an intergovernmental basis. That Agreement, which was supplemented by an implementing convention in 1990, was to introduce genuine freedom of movement for all citizens of the European Communities within the Schengen area and to deal with visa, immigration and asylum issues.**
(Commission)

A. The village of Schengen, where the Agreement was signed in 1985, is on the Luxembourgish-German border

B. The Schengen Agreement aimed to introduce freedom of movement for all citizens of the European Communities

C. In 1990, the Schengen Agreement was replaced by a so-called implementing convention

D. The Schengen Agreement was originally signed by five countries

19. **The transport industry occupies an important position in the Community, accounting for 7% of its GNP, 7% of its total employment, 40% of Member States' investment and 30% of Community energy consumption. Demand, particularly in intra-Community traffic, has grown more or less constantly for the last 20 years, by 2.3% a year for goods and 3.1% for passengers.**
(DG Transport)

A. The transport industry accounts for a higher percentage of the Community's GNP than it does of the Community's total employment

B. The transport industry accounts for one-third of

the Community's energy consumption and more than half of Member States' investment

C.   Demand for transport services has grown more dynamically for passengers than goods in the last twenty years

D.   Each Member State spends about 7% of its gross national product on transport services

20.   **In 2002, English track star Paula Radcliffe won the Chicago Marathon with a world-record-breaking time of two hours, 17 minutes and 18 seconds. Then, less than a year later, she ran the 2003 Flora London Marathon and finished in 2:15:25 – beating her own record by nearly two minutes and slicing an unprecedented three minutes off her closest competitor. In a sport where speed improvements are marked in seconds, not minutes, Radcliffe redefines the rate of human performance gains. Prior to her record-smashing run, it had taken 16 years for women to knock a minute and 20 seconds off the world record.**
(Popular Science)

A.   Paula Radcliffe had managed to keep her record for 16 years

B.   Paula Radcliffe won the London Marathon in 2002 and 2003 as well

C.   The Chicago Marathon was held after the London Marathon

D.   Paula Radcliffe broke the world record twice

21.   **Over the next few months two reports on Kosovo are due to be presented to the UN Security Council. If they paint a generally positive picture, Kofi Annan, the UN secretary-general, will appoint a "status envoy" to shuttle between Belgrade and Pristina, talking over what is now being dubbed Kosovo's "future", not its "final status". The envoy will probably be a former politician well acquainted with**

the Balkans. One possibility is Giuliano Amato, a former Italian prime minister who chaired an international commission on the Balkans that released its report this week. The report advocates Kosovo's independence, to be achieved in four stages.
(The Economist, 14 April 2005)

A.   Kosovo's independence is one of the principal issues in the United Nations Security Council and on Kofi Annan's agenda

B.   Once Kosovo's final status has been resolved, talks will turn to its "future"

C.   The former Italian prime minister may become a special representative commissioned by the United Nations

D.   There have been severe tensions between Kosovo and Pristina in recent years

22.   **Germany is no longer a safe bet for more European integration. Politicians and the media seem surprised at how much sovereignty has shifted to Brussels. Few had noticed that Germany's Basic Law now includes a clause allowing nationals to be extradited to other EU countries. Such discoveries increase Euroscepticism.**
(The Economist, 14 April 2005)

A.   It is no longer obvious that Germany and its citizens will support European integration without any reservation

B.   Germany's constitution allows for foreign nationals to be extradited to other European Union Member States

C.   Euroscepticism is term used for the less supportive attitude towards European integration and the European Union as such

D.   Germans generally support the idea that a large part of their sovereignty has been transferred to the European Union

23. **For 50 years, America and the nations of Western Europe have been lumped together as rich countries, sharing the same basic demographic features: stable populations, low and declining fertility, increasing numbers of old people. For much of that period, this was true. But in the 1980s, the two sides began to diverge. The effect was muted at first, because demographic change is slow. But it is also remorseless, and is now beginning to show up.** *(The Economist, 22 August 2002)*

A. Demographic changes are relatively easy to predict

B. Declining fertility in Western Europe was due to the economic well-being of the society

C. For half a century, America and Western Europe had similar populations

D. Declining fertility and increasing numbers of old people have led to demographic changes that are more and more apparent

24. **Doc Ock, the tentacled villain at the heart of the movie Spider-Man 2, nearly succeeded where thousands of scientists and 50 years of work have so far failed: in building a nuclear fusion reactor. But non-villainous scientists may be about to save their reputation. This year a multinational team is scheduled to begin constructing ITER, the International Thermonuclear Experimental Reactor, a project designed to demonstrate that fusion can generate almost limitless amounts of electricity without the risks and long-lived radioactive waste linked with nuclear fission reactors.** *(Popular Science)*

A. Doc Ock is the chief scientist leading the project on the International Thermonuclear Experimental Reactor

B. Scientists were inspired by the movie Spider Man 2 to create a new alternative energy source

C. Researchers may succeed in achieving what the

scientist in Spider Man 2 was about to create: a fusion reactor

D. The ITER project may be very beneficial for generating electricity but it also leaves radioactive waste behind

25. **One vital exercise of preventive "soft power" over the past decade has been the spending of more than $7 billion by the United States to secure nuclear and other weapons materials and know-how in the countries of the former Soviet Union. Although the problem is on their doorstep, the Europeans collectively have mustered less than $1 billion. America has committed itself to another $10 billion over the next decade; Europeans, alongside the rest of the G8, including Canada and Japan, have promised to find a matching amount, but the pledges do not yet add up.** *(The Economist, 21 November 2002)*

A. Europeans have given or pledged less than 15% of what the USA has spent on securing nuclear weapons

B. Canada and Japan do not take part in the so-called G8 but they wish to participate in the prevention efforts

C. America plans to spend a further 7 billion dollars on the non-proliferation of nuclear weapons

D. Almost all countries of the former Soviet Union have bought nuclear and other weapons, let alone the know-how

26. **To the average EU insider the big concerns at the moment are as follows: referendums on the European constitution, the success or failure of the new European Commission and the future of EU budget negotiations. Back in Britain, however, it seemed that everyone from taxi-drivers to middle-class housewives had only one**

thought about Brussels. And this is that the whole place is a massive sink-hole of corruption, a funnel into which British taxpayers' money is poured, to be sprayed liberally about by corrupt bureaucrats on a variety of undeserving causes. In Brussels, the reaction to all this is often to dismiss it as typical British Euroscepticism, stoked up by its malign American-owned press. But the image of the European Union as corrupt is not confined to Britain, as any Danish, Dutch or German politician will know. So is it true?
(*The Economist, 7 April 2005*)

A. Only the British think the European Union is badly affected by corruption

B. Experts dealing with European issues tend to have a different view on what is an important issue than the "laymen"

C. Brussels based officials tend to attribute British Euroscepticism to the fact that television channels are owned by Americans

D. All European taxpayers are concerned by the negotiations on the European Union's budget

27. In the dimly lit cyber-café at Sciences-Po, hot-house of the French elite, no Gauloise smoke fills the air, no dog-eared copies of Sartre lie on the tables. French students are doing what all students do: surfing the web via Google. Now President Jacques Chirac wants to stop this American cultural invasion by setting up a rival French search-engine. The idea was prompted by Google's plan to put online millions of texts from American and British university libraries.
(*The Economist, 31 March 2005*)

A. French students are doing the same thing as most other students in the world, i.e. surfing the internet

B. Mr. Chirac would like to put online texts in French the same way as Google

C. Sartre used to be the most popular French

philosopher among students but very few read his works now

D. American and British university libraries are strongly opposing Google's plan to put their texts on the web

28. Most people require about 8 hours sleep a night, but some lucky oddballs function well on 4 hours or even less. A new study in fruit flies provides evidence that genetics plays a strong role in determining who can get by with little rest. A single mutation in a gene that's also found in people can reduce the insects' sleep needs by about two-thirds. Although researchers have been studying sleep for decades, they've made little progress in teasing out the genetic components that control this phenomenon. A sleeping fly simply sits motionless, usually for many hours a day.
(*Science News*)

A. Everybody needs at least four hours' sleep every day

B. A sleeping fly, as a recent study has found, does not move for more than 8 hours

C. Those who require four hours' sleep a night are likely to have a mutation in the same gene that reduces sleep needs of insects as well

D. Scientists have made little progress in discovering the genetic components of insects' sleep needs

29. Although vitamin pills can provide much or all of the U.S. recommended daily intake (RDI) of vitamin D for children and adults – 200 to 600 International Unit (IU), depending on age – bone and mineral researchers have lately been recommending that people get much, much more. In fact, some scientists have advised the federal government to boost the vitamin

D RDI up to at least 1,000 IU and to bump up the certified-safe limit beyond the current 2,000 IU.

A.   The maximum certified vitamin D intake is currently 600 international units

B.   Scientists have proposed to increase the recommended level of vitamin D intake per day to at least thousand international units

C.   According to mineral researchers, only sun can provide sufficient levels of vitamin D

D.   Children usually get less vitamin D than adults because of unhealthy nutritition

30.   Unprecedented advances in the life sciences and the potential for the misuse of the scientific enterprise for bioterrorism or bio-warfare have created a pressing need for an international consensus on the steps that must be taken to reduce this grave threat to humanity. Counter-bioterrorism measures must include providing ethical guidance – especially for scientists, physicians, scientific institutions, and others engaged in research and development in the life sciences throughout the world.
(Science Magazine)

A.   An ethical guidance is likely to stop scientists from getting involved in bio-warfare issues

B.   There is an international consensus that bio-warfare is linked to terrorism

C.   The latest progress in life sciences has fostered the need for measures against the misuse of the achievements

D.   Scientists and physicians are more likely to be involved in bioterrorism than those not dealing with life sciences

31.   Migration is well established as a mechanism by which animals cope with seasonal variations in food supply. It is has also been suggested as a possible way of reducing the burden of para-

sitism in a range of hosts, either by weeding out infected individuals or by allowing them to escape from environments in which parasites have accumulated. Evidence has been provided that one of the more spectacular examples of migration – that of the monarch butterfly in North America – may have evolved at least in part as such a mechanism.
(Science Magazine)

A.   Parasitism may only be reduced by weeding out infected hosts

B.   The monarch butterfly migrates every winter to North America

C.   Evidence has shown that the real reason why the monarch butterfly migrates is to cope with seasonal variations in the food supply

D.   Animals migrate in order to overcome difficulties caused by changing seasons

32.   In the first 60 years of the 20th century, commercial whaling wiped out 97 percent of the Southern Hemisphere's blue whales, notes Rodrigo Hucke-Gaete of the Southern University of Chile in Valdivia and his survey team. As of 2000, the International Whaling Commission (IWC) estimated that 700 to 1,400 blue whales remain in the Southern Hemisphere.
(Science News)

A.   The International Whaling Commission was created to preserve and protect whales

B.   Mr. Hucke-Gaete and his survey team work at the Southern University of Chile

C.   Commercial whaling started in the first half of the 20th century

D.   Commercial whaling has destroyed 97% of blue whales in the Pacific Ocean

33.   After a period of uncertainty, some positive signs are emerging in Europe. An improvement in the international economic environment, low levels of

inflation, stabilised oil prices and better conditions in the financial markets are key factors behind a pick-up in economic activity, which is expected to strengthen in the course of 2004. Since the situation remains fragile, a message of confidence in the European Union's economic potential is needed. Maintaining sound macroeconomic policies, accelerating structural reforms and promoting investment in infrastructure and human capital are key policies.
(Presidency Conclusions, Brussels European Council, 2003)

A.   Reinforcing measures are needed to be taken in order to stabilise the positive tendencies

B.   Oil prices have been severely fluctuating in the recent years

C.   The uncertainty that has been going on for several years still does not seem to be coming to an end

D.   The most important goals are to improve the financial markets, the free flow of capital and keep a low level of inflation

34.   A new study suggests that most people inhale substantially more organic contaminants, including cancer-causing benzene, than is indicated by standard environmental risk assessments based on outdoor measurements. "Ambient measurements at central sites aren't good predictors of [personal] exposure," says John Adgate of the University of Minnesota in Minneapolis. "Actual exposures are higher." To monitor urban air quality, environmental agencies typically measure pollutant concentrations in samples collected at centralized outdoor locations and extrapolate individuals' average exposures from those measurements. That's a reasonable approach for studying ozone and other pollutants that form out-of-doors or

that come almost exclusively from identifiable industrial sources.
(Science News)

A.   The extrapolation method of assessment is only reliable in the case of ozone

B.   Urban air quality is usually measured at outdoor locations and conclusions are not as reliable as it had been presumed before

C.   A recent study has shown that people inhale a lot more benzene than ten years ago

D.   Environmental agencies have the exclusive right to measure pollutant concentrations in centralized areas

35.   As SANCO Commissioner Markos Kyprianou underlined at the launch of the EU Platform, "Today's overweight teenagers are tomorrow's middle aged heart attack victims". Tackling this serious public health issue will also have an impact on the EU's economy and health care services. Obesity, poor nutrition and lack of exercise and associated health problems such as cardio-vascular disease, type 2 diabetes, respiratory problems and an increased risk of cancer are already linked to 2-8% of EU health care costs.
(Commission en Direct, no. 358, p. 4)

A.   Obesity and malnutrition not only cause serious health risks but also increased spending on health care

B.   The Commissioner for Health and Consumer protection is of Greek nationality

C.   Overweight teenagers usually suffer from cardio-vascular diseases which entail a higher risk of cancer

D.   The EU spends 2-8% of its budget on health care costs

36.   In the context of integrating migration issues in our Union's relations with third countries, the European Council

reaffirms that the EU dialogue and actions with third countries in the field of migration should be part of an overall integrated, comprehensive and balanced approach, which should be differentiated, taking account of the existing situation in the different regions and in each individual partner country. In this respect, the European Council recognises the importance of developing an evaluation mechanism to monitor relations with third countries which do not cooperate with the EU in combating illegal immigration. *(Presidency Conclusions, Thessaloniki European Council, 2003)*

A.   Migration issues have been part of the EU's policy towards third countries

B.   The EU has extensive relations with a number of third countries in various continents

C.   The EU affirms its intention to reconsider relations with third countries that do not show efforts against illegal immigration

D.   The European Council considers it necessary to combat illegal immigration and establish a comprehensive approach in its foreign policy

37. **The European Council calls in particular on the Council, along with the European Parliament where appropriate, to adopt as rapidly as possible during 2000 pending legislation on the legal framework for electronic commerce, on copyright and related rights, on e-money, on the distance selling of financial services, on jurisdiction and the enforcement of judgments, and the dual-use export-control regime.** *(Presidency Conclusions, Lisbon European Council, 2000)*

A.   The European Council expressed its wish to have legislation passed on several issues on, among other things, distance selling of financial services

B.   E-money is a concept used for electronic commerce and on-line banking issues

C.   The European Council voiced its concern over the lack of legislation in areas like international cooperation in criminal matters

D.   The Council must always consult the European Parliament when passing legislation on copyright and related rights

38. **As inhabitants of rugged shores, mussels have an amazing capacity to stick to rocks, despite the constant pounding of waves. These organisms are also notorious for sticking to ships, glass, and, well, just about anything – even Teflon. Researchers at Purdue University in West Lafayette say they have uncovered the secret to what makes mussel glue so strong. It's iron. Once they understand the glue's chemistry, researchers might develop more effective antifouling paints to prevent mussels, barnacles, and other hangers-on from sticking to ships. Another payoff could be stronger biomaterials, particularly sutures and other wound-closing products.** *(Science News)*

A.   Teflon is the only material a mussel is unable to stick itself to

B.   Barnacles are posing a real danger to the safety of maritime shipping

C.   The fact that scientists have managed to reveal the chemistry of mussels' glue may help in developing special paints to prevent them from sticking to ships

D.   Mussels can glue themselves to anything with a special kind of iron web

39. **The decline of newspapers predates the internet. But the second – broadband – generation of the internet is not only accelerating it but is also changing the business in a way that the previous rivals to newspapers – radio and TV – never did. Older people, whom Mr Murdoch calls "digital immigrants", may not have noticed, but**

young "digital natives" increasingly get their news from web portals such as Yahoo! or Google, and from newer web media such as blogs. Short for "web logs", these are online journal entries of thoughts and web links that anybody can post. Whereas 56% of Americans haven't heard of blogs, and only 3% read them daily, among the young they are standard fare, with 44% of online Americans aged 18-29 reading them often, according to a poll by CNN/USA Today/Gallup.
(The Economist, 21 April 2005)

A. Newspapers started to decline when the internet became more and more widespread

B. The internet changes journalism the same way as radio and TV once did

C. More than half of Americans have never heard of web logs, or "blogs"

D. Older people increasingly tend to get their news from web portals

40. Money is so often at the root of family squabbles. The European Union is no exception. Ever since Margaret Thatcher wielded her handbag in the 1980s to demand her money back, the budget has caused friction. The then Mrs Thatcher won a rebate for Britain at the Fontainebleau summit in 1984. But summits at Edinburgh in 1992 and Berlin in 1999 saw more budget rows. Now it may happen again, as EU leaders wrestle with the "financial perspective for 2007-13".
(The Economist, 3 March 2005)

A. The 1999 Berlin summit dealt with budgetary issues related to the Agenda 2000 and enlargement

B. The discussion about the European budget perspective was launched at the Edinburgh summit

C. EU leaders have had disagreements on financial issues since the very beginning of their cooperation

D. Britain has been getting a rebate from the European budget since 1984

41. Beethoven first joined Prince Lichnowsky's household and studied under Haydn, Albrechtsberger, and possibly Salieri. His music is usually divided into three periods. In the first (1792–1802), which includes the first two symphonies, the first six quartets, and the 'Pathétique' and 'Moonlight' sonatas, his style gradually develops its own individuality. His second period (1803–12) begins with the 'Eroica' symphony (1803), and includes his next five symphonies, the difficult 'Kreutzer' sonata (1803), the Violin Concerto, the 'Archduke' trio (1811), and the 'Razumovsky' quartets. His third great period begins in 1813, and includes the Mass, the 'Choral' symphony (1823), and the last five quartets.
(Biography.com)

A. Beethoven was born in 1770

B. The second period of Beethoven's music began with the Kreutzer sonata

C. Salieri had most probably died before Beethoven was born

D. Beethoven composed the Moonlight sonata in the early period of his life

42. Certain cells lining the lungs and other membrane-covered areas make and store mucus. These cells, called goblet cells, routinely release small amounts of the slippery substance. But the cells also secrete bursts of mucus in response to irritants. The mechanism behind the switch from healthy burst to aberrant secretion, as seen in people with asthma, remains unknown.
(Science News)

A. All cells in the lungs store mucus

B. Aberrant secretion of mucus has been recently discovered by scientists

C.   Goblet cells are the only ones that do not release any slippery substance

D.   The cause and mechanism of asthma is not yet known

43.   **The removal of technical barriers to trade is a precondition for the completion of the internal market. Since the adoption of the new approach to technical harmonisation and standardisation in 1985, the harmonisation of European industrial standards in the sixteen areas covered by European technical legislation has become an essential instrument for the achievement of this objective. This approach was subsequently complemented by a coherent policy on certification and tests, setting out clear, consistent and transparent principles which apply to the product certification procedures to be used at Community level.**
(ScadPlus)

A.   There are more than twenty areas where technical legislation has to be implemented in order to remove technical barriers to trade

B.   The completion of the internal market entails the harmonisation of industrial standards and a policy on certification and tests

C.   Product certification procedures require the adoption of a new approach to technical harmonisation

D.   The completion of the internal market was achieved in 1985 when technical standards were harmonised

44.   **Early in the history of the planet, when only single-celled life forms such as bacteria were around, there was little oxygen in the air. About halfway through Earth's 4.6 billion years, oxygen began to rapidly accumulate in the atmosphere. The first eukaryotes with**

several different types of cells emerged at the same time.
(Science News)

A.   In the very beginning of Earth's history, little else but bacteria were present

B.   The age of the Earth is 4.6 million years

C.   Oxygen started to accumulate "only" a billion years ago

D.   Eukaryotes, like bacteria, have only one cell

45.   **The EU has from the outset taken a pro-active role in the negotiations and unreservedly supported the implementation of the Doha Declaration. The recently adopted reform of the CAP and proposals for reform in other sectors are the best proof that for the EU the path towards less trade-distorting support need not be an external constraint, but a desired policy orientation. Internally, the path chosen meets the domestic challenges of promoting competitiveness for EU agriculture while at the same time meeting the highest environmental, quality and animal welfare standards that our citizens expect.**
(Reviving the DDA Negotiations – the EU Perspective, 2003)

A.   According to the Doha Declaration, EU agriculture is not competitive enough

B.   The Common Agricultural Policy (CAP) had undergone several reforms in the past

C.   Regarding agriculture, the EU did not have any substantial objection to the implementation of the Doha Declaration

D.   The EU considers that less trade-distorting support is indeed nothing else but an external constraint

46.   **The European Commission is working with Member States to ensure that the European Union achieves its goals for**

reduction in carbon emissions agreed at the Kyoto environmental conference. Climate change is one of the principal themes of the European Union's Sixth Environmental Action Programme, to be completed by 2012, alongside protecting nature and biodiversity, contributing to the quality of life and social well-being for citizens, better resource efficiency and resource and waste management.
(DG Environment)

A.   The Sixth Environmental Action Programme was launched in 2002 for a ten-year period

B.   The Kyoto conference dealt with reduction of carbon emissions and climate change

C.   Resource and waste management is one of the main priorities of the Sixth Environmental Action Programme

D.   The European Commission imposes very strict environmental standards on EU Member States

47.   **The European Ombudsman was established by the Maastricht Treaty to deal with complaints about maladministration by the institutions and bodies of the European Community. The first ombudsman was elected in 1995 and has since then dealt with over 12,000 grievances from citizens, companies, organisations and public authorities. A complaint must be made within two years of the date when the facts on which the complaint is based became known and the institution or body concerned had already been contacted.**
(Commission)

A.   The Maastricht Treaty created the European Ombudsman who entered into office when the Treaty entered into force

B.   A complaint can be made directly to the Ombudsman without any further conditions to meet

C.   Only EU citizens and public authorities may seek legal assistance from the Ombudsman

D.   The Ombudsman only deals with issues that are related to maladministration by the Community institutions and bodies

48.   **In 1985, the Dooge Committee Report, drawn up in preparation for the Intergovernmental Conference which was to lead to the Single European Act (SEA), contained a number of proposals concerning foreign policy. The provisions introduced by the SEA established an institutional basis for the European Political Cooperation, the group of European correspondents and a secretariat working under the direct authority of the Council presidency.**
(ScadPlus)

A.   The Single European Act was signed in 1986 and entered into force in 1987

B.   The Dooge Committee proposed to place the European Political Cooperation's secretariat under the Council presidency

C.   The Intergovernmental Conference call for the creation of the Dooge Committee to give proposals for the reform of foreign policy

D.   It was the Single European Act that actually created a specialised group of European correspondents in the field of foreign policy

49.   **Picasso studied at Barcelona and Madrid, and in 1901 set up a studio in Montmartre, Paris. His 'blue period' (1902-4), a series of striking studies of the poor in haunting attitudes of despair and gloom, gave way to the gay, life-affirming 'pink period' (1904-6), full of harlequins, acrobats, and the incidents of circus life. He then turned to brown, and began to work in sculpture. His break with tradition came with 'Les Demoiselles d'Avignon' (1906-7, New York), the first exemplar of analytical Cubism, a movement**

which he developed with Braque
(1909-14).
(Biography.com)

A.   Picasso painted 'Les Demoiselles d'Avignon' in
      1904 in Paris

B.   Picasso had a blue, pink and brown period of
      painting

C.   Cubism was a brand new style of painting and
      architecture Picasso had invented

D.   Picasso had lived in Paris before pursuing his
      studies in Spain

50.   **Many of the European Union's most
      ardent supporters still see the EU as a
      crucial bulwark against the return of
      war to Europe. In pressing the case for
      monetary union, Mr Kohl argued that
      adopting the euro was ultimately a
      question of war and peace in Europe.**

**When efforts to write a European con-
stitution looked like stalling, Elmar
Brok, a prominent German member of
the EU's constitutional convention
(and confidant of Mr Kohl), gave
warning that if Europe failed to agree
on a constitution, it risked sliding back
into the kind of national rivalries that
had led to the outbreak of the first
world war.**
(The Economist, 23 September 2004)

A.   Mr. Kohl was the federal chancellor of Germany
      for several years

B.   European politicians many times see the
      European Union as a tool against the return of
      war to the continent

C.   The constitutional convention was co-chaired
      by Mr. Elmar Brok

D.   The euro was the first tangible sign of the
      European monetary union

NUMERICAL REASONING

50 QUESTIONS – ANSWERS PAGE XXX

1. Judy is five times as old as Henry. In
    two years, she'll be three times as old,
    and in six years she'll only be twice as
    old. How old will Judy be in seven
    years?

    A.   17

    B.   12

    C.   9

    D.   25

2. An amoeba, placed in a jar, multiplies
    at a highly accelerated rate. After 15
    seconds the amoeba splits; 15 seconds
    later the two amoebae split; 15 seconds
    after that the four amoebae split and
    so on. After two hours the jar is
    halfway full. How long will it take to
    fill the jar completely?

    A.   1 hour

    B.   1 minute

    C.   90 seconds

    D.   15 seconds

3. If there are four empty seats in a
    movie theatre, how many ways can
    four people sit in these seats?

    A.   24

    B.   12

    C.   8

    D.   9

4. There are ten gloves of each of the fol-
    lowing colours in a drawer: blue,
    green, red, yellow and white, for a
    total of 50 gloves. If the gloves are ran-
    domly distributed in the drawer and
    are not in pairs or any other grouping,
    what is the minimum number of
    gloves you must draw in order to be
    certain you have at least two gloves of
    the same colour?

    A.   40

    B.   10

    C.   11

    D.   6

5. If no one in Restoland owns an odd number of dishes, no one owns more than 274 dishes and no two people own the same number of dishes, what is the maximum number of people in Restoland?

A. 548

B. 138

C. 549

D. 274

6. What is the average wealth of a team of six people who have 1250 euros, 1915 euros, 450 euros, 25 euros, 875 euros and 3885 euros?

A. 1200 euros

B. 1400 euros

C. 1680 euros

D. 2000 euros

7. Eight books have 88 pages each. How many pages are there if you don't count the two cover pages?

A. 704

B. 696

C. 688

D. 720

8. When the time in Paris is 14:00, the time in London is 13:00 and 16:00 in Moscow. If a man takes an airplane in Moscow at 20:00, what will be the local time in London when he arrives after three hours of flight?

A. 19:00

B. 21:00

C. 20:00

D. 22:00

9. Taking the above example, if the same man leaves London by car at 23:00, what will be local time when he arrives in Paris after a five-hour drive?

A. 06:00

B. 05:00

C. 03:00

D. 04:00

10. When the local time in Paris is 23:00, the time in Bangkok is 05:00 the next day. How much time does the trip take if a man takes an airplane in Bangkok at 20:00 and arrives in London at 22:00 local time?

A. 10 hours

B. 9 hours

C. 12 hours

D. 6 hours

11. How many hours does a man sleep in five weeks if he sleeps seven hours on weekdays and nine hours on week-ends?

A. 265

B. 274

C. 255

D. 280

12. If a 4 sq m office can be rented for 125 euros per square metre per month and a 7 sq m office can be rented for 117 euros per square metre per month, how much would it be to rent three smaller offices and two bigger offices for four months?

A. 6,584 euros

B. 12,552 euros

C. 2,436 euros

D. 10,458 euros

13. If the size of a bathroom floor is 8.5 metres by 4.5 metres, and one tile is 40 sq cm, how many tiles do you need? (A "broken" tile is considered as one.)

A. 95

B. 96

C. 957

D. 9601

14. If a beer bottle has a volume of 0.25 litre, a wine bottle has a volume of 0.75 litre and a mineral water bottle has a volume of 1 litre, how many bottles are there if we have 18 litres of beer, 9 litres of wine and 23 litres of water?

A. 83

B. 90

C. 97

D. 107

15. If a car consumes 9 litres of fuel per hour at a speed of 120 km/h and 5 litres of fuel per hour at 100 km/h, how long was the trip if it consumed 45 litres in 9 hours without stopping?

A. 900 km

B. 780 km

C. 600 km

D. Cannot say

16. If the interest rate for a savings account is 7% per year, how much interest will there be after three years with an initial saving of 1000 euros?

A. 145 euros

B. 225 euros

C. 210 euros

D. 248 euros

17. A man jogs for an hour at 9 km/h five days a week and walks an hour at 6 km/h every 2nd week. What will be his average speed in a 4 week period?

A. 7.8 km/h

B. 7.3 km/h

C. 8.7 km/h

D. 8.2 km/h

18. If a man swims 3000 metres, how many turns does he have to do in a 35 metre-long pool?

A. 92

B. 77

C. 80

D. 84

19. If a maximum of two pears fit in a blue jar, twelve plums in a green jar and three melons in a red jar, how many jars do I need for 48 plums and 6 melons if a pear is twice as big as a plum, a melon is four times the size of a plum and I want to use only red jars?

A.   8

B.   10

C.   12

D.   6

20. What is the average age of a group of EU knowledge test takers whose individual ages are 22yrs, 25yrs, 30yrs, 45yrs and 48yrs?

A.   25

B.   32

C.   34

D.   37

21. You made up your mind to prepare for taking an EU knowledge test in five weeks. You recorded the hours spent on preparing each week in a table (below). What was the average time (in hours) you prepared per week?

Week	1	2	3	4	5
Hours	14	16	20	15	25

A.   14

B.   18

C.   20

D.   25

22. With reference to the table for question 21, supposing you spent 30% of your study time on taking EU tests, which week did you spend the most time with this activity?

A.   5th week

B.   3rd week

C.   2nd week

D.   3rd and 5th week

***

TABLE FOR QUESTIONS 23-27

	Total area (sq. km)	Population (1000 inhabitants)	GDP/ inhabitants	Inflation %
A	30 500	5 300	27 530	2.8
B	93 000	10 200	11 840	9.1
C	90 000	10 200	16 920	4.9
D	450 000	8 999	23 130	2.0
E	200 001	59 000	23 160	1.9

23. Approximately how many people in countries A and D are unemployed if the unemployment rate is 2% in country A and 4% in country D?

A.   215,000

B.   380,000

C.   466,000

D.   652,000

24. In which country is the density of population the lowest?

A.   Country A

B.   Country C

C.   Country D

D.   Country E

25. **What is the average inflation rate in all five countries?**

A.   2.5%

B.   4.1%

C.   5.1%

D.   6.3%

26. **What percentage of the total population of all five countries live in country E?**

A.   45%

B.   50%

C.   Less than 60%

D.   More than 60%

27. **What is the ratio between the total area of country D and country C?**

A.   1 : 4

B.   4 : 1

C.   5 : 1

D.   1 : 5

28. **Which flavour sold in the largest quantity and which flavour sold in the smallest quantity in July 2005?**

A.   Flavour C and flavour B

B   Flavour B and flavour C

C.   Flavour B and flavour A

D.   Flavour A and flavour C

29. **How many litres of flavour B did Company Y sell in July 2005?**

A.   0

B.   10

C.   100

D.   1000

30. **What percentage of revenue is due to flavour A and flavour C?**

A.   50%

B.   60%

C.   75%

D.   Cannot say

TABLE FOR QUESTIONS 28-32

CARBONATED SOFT DRINKS IN 100 L SOLD IN JULY 2005 IN A TOTAL QUANTITY OF 18,000 L

	Flavour A	Flavour B	Flavour C
Company X	50	30	8
Company Y	10	?	0
Company Z	42	20	10

31. **If the total quantity sold of flavour A and flavour C increased by 20% in August 2005, and assuming that the quantity sold of flavour B remained the same, then how many litres would the total quantity sold of flavour B and flavour C be?**

A.   5,896

B.   Approximately 6,200

C.   Cannot say

D.   8,160

32. If the quantity sold by Company Z of flavour C increased by 50% and the quantity sold by Company X of flavour A decreased by 10%, then what change would occur in the total quantity sold of all flavours?

A.   No change

B.   The total quantity would increase

C.   The total quantity would decrease

D.   Cannot say

TABLE FOR QUESTIONS 33-37

PRODUCTION AND TRADE DATA IN NOVEMBER 2005
(WIRE & WIRE LTD.)

All lengths in metres (100s)	Bare copper wire	Tinned copper wire	PTFE silver plated copper cable	Gold plated copper wire
Production (100s)	100	150	30	20
Production costs per m in €	1	2	4	10
income per m in €	2	3	10	20
export (100s)	80	90	10	20

33. How much income did Wire & Wire Ltd. generate from the export of bare copper wire and PTFE silver plated copper cable in November 2005?

A.   EUR 2,600

B.   EUR 26,000

C.   EUR 32,000

D.   EUR 320,000

34. What is the ratio between the total production of all types of wire and the quantity sold for export?

A.   3 : 2

B.   2 : 3

C.   4 : 3

D.   3 : 4

35. How much profit was made by Wire and Wire Ltd. from PTFE silver plated copper cable and gold plated copper wire in November 2005? (Profit is the difference between income and production costs.)

A.   19,000

B.   38,000

C.   30,000

D.   26,000

36. Which export product shows the poorest profit margin? (The profit margin is the profit as a percentage of income.)

A.   Bare copper wire

B.   Tinned copper wire

C.   PTFE silver plated copper cable

D.   Gold plated copper wire

37. Which type of product was sold in the largest volume by Cable & Cable Ltd. in November 2005?

A.   Bare copper wire

B.   Tinned copper wire

C.   PTFE silver plated copper cable

D.   Cannot say

TABLE FOR QUESTIONS 38-42

INCOME FROM CERTAIN INDUSTRIAL PRODUCTS (in billion euros)

Products	2001	2002	2003	2004	2005
Cars	50	52	53	55	58
Buses	33	35	32	32	32
Trucks	40	44	45	46	49
Boats	8	12	11	15	14
Airplanes	40	40	30	40	50
Helicopters	20	22	20	22	20

38. Assuming that the trend in the helicopter industry will not change, the income for 2037 would most likely be about ....

A. EUR 22 billion

B. EUR 20 billion

C. EUR 44 billion

D. Cannot say

39. How much profit is made from the aircraft industry in 2003, if the production costs amount to 60% of the income received? (Profit is the difference between income and production costs.)

A. EUR 10 billion

B. EUR 15 billion

C. EUR 20 billion

D. EUR 25 billion

40. Among the following, the greatest increase in income occurred for ....

A. Cars between 2001 and 2002

B. Buses between 2002 and 2003

C. Airplanes between 2003 and 2004

D. Helicopters between 2002 and 2003

41. How many industries made a gain of 20% or more between 2002 and 2004?

A. 0

B. 1

C. 2

D. 3

42. Between which years does the production of any type of industry increase or decrease the most in absolute terms?

A. 2002 and 2003

B. 2003 and 2004

C. 2004 and 2005

D. Cannot say

TABLE FOR QUESTIONS 43-45

POPULATION DATA IN 2005

	Pop. in millions	Live births (per 1000 pop.)	Deaths (per 1000 pop.)	Under 18yrs (%)	65yrs or over (%)
Country A	40	12	10	20	19
Country B	22	4	5	22	18
Country C	35	6	5	25	20
Country D	80	20	18	18	22
Country E	100	30	28	20	20

43. In which country is the fertility rate the highest?

A.   Country A

B.   Country C

C.   Cannot say

D.   Country E

44. Which country experiences the highest population decline?

A.   Country B

B.   Country C

C.   Country D

D.   Country E

45. Which country/countries has/have the largest elderly population?

A.   Country A

B.   Country D

C.   Country E

D.   Country D and Country E

TABLE FOR QUESTIONS 46-50

Juices sold in 2004 (m. boxes)	Grapefruits	Orange	Pear
Company A	12	20	14
Company B	4	37	19
Company C	27	23	8

Income from all juices sold (millions in €)	2003	2004	2005
Company A	180	200	220
Company B	225	240	210
Company C	280	225	300

46. How much money in million euros did Company B get in 2004 from pear juice if all juices are sold at the same price?

A.   80

B.   76

C.   120

D.   48

47. Which company had the highest income between 2003 and 2005?

A.   Company C

B.   Company A and B the same

C.   Company B

D.   Company A

48. Which company sold its juices at the lowest average price in 2004?

A.   Company A

B.   Company C

C.   Company A and C the same

D.   Company B

49. If grapefruits are the same price as oranges and a third of the price of pears how many million euros income did Company C have in 2004 from oranges?

A.   45

B.   Cannot tell

C.   109

D.   70

50. **Supposing Company A sold 10% less in 2003 and 20% more juice in 2005 than in 2004, in which year was the average price of a single juice the highest?**

    A.   2003

    B.   2004

    C.   2005

    D.   2003 and 2004 equally

MIXED QUESTIONS

MIXED I

50 QUESTIONS – ANSWERS PAGE 395

1. The European Free Trade Agreement (EFTA) Court is situated in ....

A. The Hague

B. Strasbourg

C. Oslo

D. Luxembourg

2. Which Member State's constitution requires a referendum before the country participates in the economic and monetary union?

A. Sweden

B. Denmark

C. Slovenia

D. Poland

3. Who is the President of the European Court of Justice?

A. Cunha Rodrigues

B. Vassilios Skouris

C. Francis Jacobs

D. Roger Briesch

4. Which of the following is not considered as a "candidate country"?

A. Croatia

B. Bulgaria

C. Serbia

D. Turkey

5. The Community Plant Variety Office is located in ....

A. Angers

B. Lisbon

C. Alicante

D. Parma

6. **The aim of starting a dialogue between pupils, teachers and European Union personalities on their vision for Europe and its future is carried out through the programme called ....**

A. Spring Day

B. My Europe

C. FutureMe

D. Dream Europe

7. **The European Centre for Parliamentary Research and Documentation is administered by/jointly by ....**

A. The Robert Schuman Centre for Advanced Studies

B. The Parliamentary Assembly of the Council of Europe

C. The European Parliament

D. The European Parliament and the Parliamentary Assembly of the Council of Europe

8. **Which entity/entities has/have the exclusive right to authorise the issue of euro bank notes?**

A. European Central Bank

B. Council

C. Council together with the European Parliament

D. Council upon authorisation by the European Council

9. **Which of the following countries does not use the euro as its currency?**

A. Monaco

B. Montenegro

C. San Marino

D. Faeroe Islands

10. **Which of the following is the POSEI-DOM programme aimed at?**

A. Madeira

B. Azores

C. Canary Islands

D. French Overseas Departments

11. **The so-called Isoglucose case dealt with ....**

A. Free movement of goods

B. Direct aids to farmers

C. Direct applicability of directives

D. The European Parliament's right of consultation

12. **Employment was inserted into the EC Treaty by the ....**

A. Amsterdam Treaty

B. Treaty of Nice

C. Single European Act

D. Constitutional Treaty

13. Which of the following is not a political group in the Committee of the Regions?

A. Party of European Socialist Group

B. European People's Party Group

C. Euroipean Alliance Group

D. Union for Europe of the Nations Group

14. The WTO agreement dealing with intellectual property and trade issues is called ....

A. GATT

B. Uruguay Agreement

C. TRIPS

D. Doha Agreement

15. To which fields of the Schengen acquis does the Community method not apply?

A. Judicial cooperation in civil matters

B. Asylum, immigration

C. Judicial cooperation in criminal matters

D. External border control

16. Since Agenda 2000, the second pillar of the agricultural policy is ....

A. Farming

B. Sustainable development of rural areas

C. Market and income policy

D. Agriculture and forestry

17. The Kyoto Protocol concerns ....

A. Nuclear waste management

B. Greenhouse gas emissions

C. Noise emission thresholds

D. River pollution standards

18. The enterprise for acquisition of imagery of Earth from space is called ....

A. Landsat

B. Galileo

C. Digital Image

D. SpaceNav

19. How many times more members did the European Convention have compared to the Convention that drafted the Charter of Fundamental Rights?

A. 4

B. 3

C. 2

D. 5

20. The European Council in Brussels on 12 and 13 December 2003 decided to extend the remit of .... to convert it into a Fundamental Rights Agency.

A. MCDDA

B. EUMC

C. ENISA

D. EFSA

21. The European Parliament prize for outstanding achievement in advancing the peace process is called ....

A. European Achievement Prize

B. Sakharov Prize

C. Europa Nostra Prize

D. Macquari Prize

22. How many advocates general does the Court of Justice have?

A. 8

B. 20

C. 15

D. 12

23. Which of the following Member States has or will have the highest number of members in the Committee of the Regions?

A. Bulgaria

B. Czech Republic

C. Romania

D. Belgium

24. According to the EC Treaty, how much time needs to elapse between a country's application for membership and the signature of the accession treaty?

A. At least 4 years

B. 8 years

C. There is no such rule

D. Minimum 5, maximum 10 years

25. Gijs de Vries is the ....

A. EU's special envoy to Kosovo

B. EU's counter-terrorism coordinator

C. Secretary General of the Commission

D. Vice-Secretary General of the Commission

26. Which Treaty expired on 23 July 2002?

A. European Coal and Steel Community (ECSC) Treaty

B. Treaty establishing a European Atomic Energy Community (Euratom)

C. Single European Act

D. None

27. The Short and Medium-term Priority Environmental Action Programme (SMAP) is a framework programme ....

A. For the protection of the Mediterranean environment

B. For the period 2005-2010

C. Mainly promoting aquatic biodiversity

D. Run jointly by the EU and the UN

28. Lebanon belongs to the so-called .... countries.

A. Maghreb

B. ACP

C. Mashrek

D. Lomé Convention

29. Which Member State held two referendums on the Treaty of Nice?

A.   United Kingdom

B.   Spain

C.   Ireland

D.   France

30. Which of the following does not belong to the EU's custom territory?

A.   Channel Islands

B.   Gibraltar

C.   Mount Athos

D.   Andorra

31. Which of the following Member States is the smallest?

A.   Hungary

B.   Portugal

C.   Austria

D.   Ireland

32. The European Parliament can consult the Economic and Social Committee since the ....

A.   Amsterdam Treaty

B.   Maastricht Treaty

C.   Single European Act

D.   Treaty of Nice

33. Which statement is incorrect?

A.   Financial discipline ensures that the EU's farm budget fixed until 2013 is not overshot

B.   "New" Member States may complement direct aid up to the level applicable prior to accession

C.   The single farm payment is independent from production

D.   Semi-subsistence farms produce for own consumption and do not bring products to market

34. The Charter of Fundamental Rights was first presented to the .... European Council.

A.   Thessaloniki

B.   Laeken

C.   Nice

D.   Rome

35. In order to finance the additional rural development measures, direct payments for bigger farms will be reduced. This is called ....

A.   Decoupling

B.   Agricultural levying

C.   Modulation

D.   Sustainable farming

36. The Treaty of Brussels of 22 July 1975 gave the European Parliament the right to ....

A.   Give its assent for the accession of new Member States

B.   Reject the budget

C.   Reject the Commission as a body

D.   Propose substantial amendments to the non-compulsory expenditure

37. **In which year did the Association Agreement with Malta enter into force?**

A. 1967

B. 1985

C. 1988

D. 1971

38. **When did/will the EU open formal accession negotiations with Turkey?**

A. There is no exact date yet

B. Once Turkey has fulfilled all Copenhagen criteria

C. On 3 October 2005

D. On 1 January 2007

39. **The Commissioner responsible for .... is of Estonian nationality.**

A. Employment, Social Affairs and Equal Opportunities

B. Science and Research

C. Administrative Affairs, Audit and Anti-Fraud

D. Taxation and Customs Union

40. **Which countries have only blue and white colours in their flag?**

A. Luxembourg, Netherlands

B. Finland, Netherlands

C. Greece, Finland

D. Luxembourg, Greece

41. **The Constitutional Treaty creates the position of a ....**

A. European Foreign Affairs Minister

B. European Minister for Foreign Affairs

C. Foreign Minister of the European Union

D. Union Minister for Foreign Affairs

42. **How many Commissioners will there be in 2008 if Romania and Bulgaria join the EU in 2007?**

A. 25

B. 18

C. 27

D. 21

43. **"Jobs, Jobs, Jobs" was said by ....**

A. V. I. Lenin

B. Wim Kok

C. Tony Blair

D. Romano Prodi

44. **The enlargement towards Romania and Bulgaria will be the ....**

A. 6th

B. 5th

C. 7th

D. 8th

45. **Which of the following countries did not sign the Schengen Agreement?**

A. United Kingdom

B.   Switzerland

C.   Iceland

D.   Norway

**46.   Which year was or will be the European
         Year of People with Disabilities?**

A.   2003

B.   2005

C.   2007

D.   2001

**47.   The plan for a unified European army
         and establishing a European Defence
         Community is known as the ....**

A.   Fouchet Plan

B.   Schuman Plan

C.   Pléven Plan

D.   De Gaulle Plan

**48.   The Brussels European Council held
         between 20 and 21 March 2003 called
         for .... in support of research and inno-
         vation policy.**

A.   The application of the open method of coordi-
      nation

B.   Reinforced cooperation

C.   Integrated policy mix measures

D.   A new mainstreaming approach to be estab-
      lished

**49.   In the context of free movement of per-
         sons, Regulation 1408/71 ....**

A.   Creates a single European social scheme

B.   Harmonises national social security measures

C.   Harmonises national social security measures
      except pension schemes

D.   Co-ordinates the social security schemes of EU
      Member States

**50.   The Commission DG Competition's
         Merger Task Force, dissolved in 2004,
         chose .... as its informal emblem.**

A.   A stylised map of Europe

B.   Justitia's sword and scales

C.   A piranha

D.   Two hands holding the ends of a knotted rope

MIXED II

50 QUESTIONS – ANSWERS PAGE 396

1.   When was the Treaty of Rome signed?

A.   1 January 1958

B.   9 May 1950

C.   15 February 1951

D.   25 March 1957

2.   Which year was the agreement on the Western European Union (WEU) signed and where?

A.   1946, Berlin

B.   1957, Paris

C.   1951, Berlin

D.   1948, Brussels

3.   How many Articles do the Treaty on European Union and the Treaty establishing the European Community have, as amended by the Treaty of Nice?

A.   53, 314

B.   42, 451

C.   78, 299

D.   67, 343

4.   The Council meets in .... different configurations.

A.   9

B.   15

C.   25

D.   27

5.   In which field is legislation not passed by codecision procedure with the Council acting unanimously?

A.   Social security related to the free movement of workers

B.   Citizenship of the Union

C.   Customs cooperation

D.   Culture

6.   The Secretary-General of the Council ....

A.   Is Mr. Charlie McCreevy

B.   Participates in General Affairs and External Relations Council meetings

C.   Chairs European Council meetings

D.   Is appointed by the European Parliament

7.   The Conciliation Committee ....

A.   Is to reconcile the differences between the Council, the Parliament and the Commission

B.   Comprises 30 members

C.   Has a role in the third stage of the codecision procedure

D.   Is convened by the President of the Council and the President of the European Parliament

8.   The ANTICI Group assists ....

A.   The Secretary General of the Council

B.   COREPER II

C.   The Mertens Group

D.   The ECOFIN Council

9.   Which Treaty empowered the European Parliament to approve or reject the nomination of the Commission President?

A.   Single European Act

B.   Maastricht Treaty

C.   Amsterdam Treaty

D.   Treaty of Nice

10.   In which case can the Parliament reject the budget in its entirety?

A.   Only if it proposes a new draft budget

B.   It can only make amendments but full rejection is not permitted

C.   Always, without restrictions

D.   It can only do so with the agreement of the majority of the Council

11.   How many Commissioners were there on 30 June 2004?

A.   15

B.   25

C.   30

D.   35

12.   Which one of the following is not a general service operated by the Commission?

A.   Translation Centre for the Bodies of the European Union

B.   Eurostat

C.   Publications Office

D.   European Anti-Fraud Office

13.   What characterises the European Commission?

A.   Guardian of the Treaties

B.   Power of management and negotiation

C.   Own power of decision-making

D.   Sole right of initiative in all three pillars

14.   When was the Court of Justice of the European Communities established?

A.   1952

B.   1967

C.   1957

D.   1989

15.   When the European Court of Auditors suspects that frauds or irregularities have occurred, the information obtained is forwarded to the ....

A.   OLAF

B.   European Commission

C.   European Parliament

D.   European Court of Justice

16. Which organ is referred to as the guardian of the principle of subsidiarity?

A.   Commission

B.   European Parliament

C.   The Council

D.   Committee of the Regions

17. There is no obligation imposed on the Council and the Commission to consult the European Economic and Social Committee on ....

A.   Agricultural policy

B.   Approximation of laws for the internal market

C.   Immigration and asylum

D.   Harmonisation of indirect taxation

18. In the 2004 film Ocean's Twelve, Catherine Zeta-Jones played Isabel Lahiri, a(n) .... agent on the trail of Danny Ocean and company.

A.   Europol

B.   Eurojust

C.   OLAF

D.   None of the three organs has yet been featured in works of fiction

19. .... may not constitute a "mandatory requirement" capable of justifying restrictions on imports or exports.

A.   The protection of culture

B.   Fairness of commercial transactions

C.   National state aid schemes

D.   Improvement of working conditions

20. Who has the right to reside with a worker who is a national of one Member State and who is employed in the territory of another Member State?

A.   The worker's spouse or registered partner and their descendants who are under the age of 21 years

B.   The worker's spouse and their descendants who are under the age of 18 years

C.   Only the worker's dependent relatives

D.   The worker's dependent relatives in the ascending line of the worker and his spouse

21. The 22 and 23 March 2005 European Council agreed to .... the Lisbon process.

A.   Break off

B.   Speed up

C.   Re-launch

D.   Withdraw from

22. The European Employment Strategy was formally created by the ....

A.   Amsterdam Treaty

B.   Treaty of Nice

C.   Single European Act

D.   Maastricht Treaty

23. A Community facility providing medium-term financial assistance for Member States' balances of payments ....

A.   Is not available to those Member States that have not adopted the euro

B.   Is a substitute for a short-term financing facility

C.   Is part of EMR II

D.   Is implemented by the Council

24.   EUREKA ....

A.   Finances new means of combating all forms of discrimination and inequalities in the labour market

B.   Supports the competitiveness of European companies through international collaboration, in networks of innovation

C.   Promotes administrative cooperation at EU level in the fields of asylum, visas, immigration and external borders

D.   Assists the candidate countries in the preparation for accession

25.   .... arise when the merged group is able profitably to reduce value for money, choice or innovation through its own acts without the need for a co-operative response from competitors.

A.   Unilateral effects

B.   Coordinated effects

C.   Ancillary restraints

D.   Vertical restraints

26.   Which statement is incorrect? Stage II of EMU ....

A.   Began on 1 January 1994

B.   Provided for the establishment of the European Monetary Institute

C.   Provided for the avoidance of excessive government deficits

D.   Set out the European System of Integrated Economic Accounts

27.   Which one is not among the Maastricht Convergence Criteria?

A.   Functioning market economy

B.   Low inflation

C.   Sound public finances

D.   Low interest rates

28.   .... aims at creating convergence at the European level through reforming national higher education systems.

A.   The Bologna Process

B.   Rome II

C.   Spring Day

D.   Sapientia

29.   What does the term "democratic deficit" imply?

A.   Under the Treaties in force, the Member States do not transfer real sovereignty to the EU

B.   The EU is not recognised by each and every country as a fully fledged international organisation

C.   The EU is not member of the UN

D.   The EU may seem inaccessible to the ordinary citizen

30.   Which of the following procedures applies to agricultural policy?

A.   Consultation

B.   Assent

C.   Cooperation

D.   None of the three

31. **Which of the following areas falls under the codecision procedure?**

A. Anti-discrimination measures under Article 13(2) of the EC Treaty

B. Establishing a Social Protection Committee

C. Adopting detailed rules for the multilateral surveillance procedure

D. Appointing Members of the Court of Auditors

32. **The policies aimed at ensuring equal access to ICT services for all at an affordable cost are known as ....**

A. eInclusion

B. eFor@ll

C. ACCESS

D. EQUAL

33. **STEER is designed to ....**

A. Further initiatives relating to the promotion of renewable energy sources and energy efficiency in the developing countries

B. Support initiatives relating to all energy aspects of transport

C. Promote new and renewable energy sources for production of electricity and heat

D. Improve energy efficiency and rational use of energy, in particular in the building and industry sectors

34. **The European Investment Fund ....**

A. Is a public-private partnership established in 1995

B. Acts in a complementary role to its majority shareholder, the EBRD

C. Manages the European Investment Facility (EIF)

D. Is the EU's specialised vehicle providing venture capital and guarantee instruments for SMEs

35. **How may framework decisions be adopted under Title VI of the Treaty on European Union?**

A. Unanimously by the Council

B. By majority of the Member States

C. By qualified majority of two thirds of the Member States

D. Such form does not exist under Title VI

36. **The Hague Programme ....**

A. Aims to boost immigration levels

B. Seeks to strengthen freedom, security and justice in the EU

C. Launches SitCen

D. Establishes the European Refugee Fund

37. **What was the Court's ruling about in the Factortame case?**

A. Article 133 of the EC Treaty

B. Direct effect of Community law

C. Consumer rights

D. State aids

38. **Which of the following countries had the highest allocation of Cohesion Funds for the period 2004-2006?**

A. Slovenia

B. Hungary

C. Estonia

D. Latvia

39. **What is the population (in millions of inhabitants) covered by Objective 1 between 2000 and 2006?**

A. 81

B. 180

C. 155

D. 111

40. **Which of the following is not a Community Initiative?**

A. Equal

B. Interreg III

C. Urban II

D. Cordis

41. **What is CONECCS?**

A. Database concerning Consultation, the European Commission and Civil Society

B. Commission Network for European and Caribbean Cooperation Systems

C. Consultative body of the European Community's Cultural Service

D. "Connect Europe" – the Commission's Computer System initiative

42. **When did the 6th Research Framework Programme start and when will it end?**

A. 2000, 2005

B. 2001, 2006

C. 2002, 2006

D. 2002, 2007

43. **As a rule, when entering the EU from a non-EU country, a passenger may bring perfume having no commercial character up to .... grams in his/her personal luggage.**

A. 50

B. 100

C. 200

D. There is no such limit for perfumes

44. **The European Union – Russia Energy Dialogue has been in place since ....**

A. 1995

B. 2000

C. 2001

D. 2004

45. **Which of the following countries had not held a referendum on the Constitutional Treaty by October 2005?**

A. Luxembourg

B. France

C. United Kingdom

D. The Netherlands

46. **Which of the following countries are members of NATO but not members of the European Union?**

A. Norway, Iceland, Turkey

B. Norway, Turkey, Hungary

C. Iceland, Greece, France

D. USA, Latvia, Cyprus

47. Which of the following countries is not a neighbour of Croatia?

A. Bosnia and Herzegovina

B. Serbia and Montenegro

C. Slovenia

D. Albania

49. The Nice summit determined that once the EU has reached .... members, all summits will take place in Brussels.

A. 27

B. 20

C. 25

D. 18

48. On 1 January 2007 the EU Presidency moves to ....

A. Finland

B. Portugal

C. Germany

D. France

50. One Euro is worth approximately .... Japanese Yen.

A. 45

B. 10

C. 254

D. 133

MIXED III

50 QUESTIONS – ANSWERS PAGE 397

1. Which body has the task of exercising democratic control over EU institutions, possibly by setting up committees of inquiry?

A. European Council

B. European Commission

C. European Parliament

D. European Ombudsman

2. "...." is established Community shorthand for the work of committees, made up of representatives of Member States and chaired by the Commission, whose function it is to implement EU laws and policies.

A. Conciliation

B. Comitology

C. Concertation

D. COREPER I

3. **Which statement is incorrect in respect of the European Central Bank?**

A. It independently manages the European monetary policy

B. Its main objective is to ensure price stability

C. It lends money for investment projects of European interest

D. It is based in Frankfurt in Germany

4. **Who may request from the European Court of Justice the annulment or cancellation of an EU legislative act?**

A. The Commission and the European Council

B. The Court of First Instance at the request of a Member State

C. Only the Council

D. A Member State, the Commission, the Council or the European Parliament

5. **The European Public Prosecutor ....**

A. Was created on 1 March 2005

B. Will have authority to send for trial in the national courts the perpetrators of the offences being prosecuted

C. Will work jointly with the Advocate General of the European Court of Justice

D. Was planned to be created but eventually the plan was dismissed by the Brussels European Council

6. **Where is the Agency for the Management of Operational Cooperation at the External Borders of the Member States of the EU (FRONTEX) located?**

A. Riga

B. Budapest

C. Nicosia

D. Warsaw

7. **The European Union Institute for Security Studies (EUISS) ....**

A. Is dependent on Member States' governments

B. Was created by a Council Joint Action in 2001

C. Does not deal with the development of a transatlantic dialogue

D. Is located in Brussels

8. **How many judges does the European Union Civil Service Tribunal have?**

A. 7

B. 9

C. 5

D. 11

9. **To which institution is the term "orientation générale" connected?**

A. European Council

B. Council

C. European Parliament

D. Commission

10. **Which body is headed by Max-Peter Ratzel?**

A. OHIM

B. EIB

C. EUROPOL

D. ECB

11. Which court has its headquarters in The Hague?

A. European Court of Justice

B. European Court of Human Rights

C. International Court of Justice

D. International Court of Human Rights

12. The .... sets the minimum threshold for establishing enhanced cooperation at eight Member States.

A. Constitutional Treaty

B. Maastricht Treaty

C. Amsterdam Treaty

D. Treaty of Nice

13. Whom does a formal trialogue bring together in Conciliation?

A. The two co-Chairmen of the Conciliation Committee and a Commissioner

B. The Chairman of the Conciliation Committee, one Member of the Parliament and one representative of the Council

C. The Presidents of the Council, the Parliament and the Commission

D. The Three Wise Men

14. Which procedure applies when adopting implementing decisions regarding the European Social Fund?

A. Cooperation

B. Consultation

C. Codecision

D. Assent

15. What is OLAF?

A. The predecessor body of UCLAF

B. A creation of the Commission

C. A European FBI

D. One of the EU institutions

16. When a trader supplies a service to a private consumer, the trader is responsible for applying VAT at the rate of the Member State where ....

A. He has his place of establishment

B. He actually engages in business activity

C. The consumer resides

D. More favourable tax rules apply

17. Interreg III ....

A. Is exclusively funded by the European Regional Development Fund (ERDF)

B. Aims to promote economic and social regeneration of regions in crisis

C. Is a Community Initiative Programme (CIP)

D. Is a supplementary tool for INTERACT

18. The European Commission has named 2006 the European Year for ....

A. Equal opportunities for all

B. Mobility of workers

C. People with disabilities

D. Children

19. The .... was launched in June 2004 to simplify access to necessary medical care when travelling in the EU.

A. FSO

B. Pink Chip

C. European Travel Insurance Card

D. European Health Insurance Card

20. Who said: "A modern Budget for Europe is not one that 10 years from now is still spending 40 per cent of its money on the CAP"?

A. Franz Fischler (former Commissioner for Agriculture)

B. Jacques Chirac (French President)

C. Tony Blair (UK Prime Minister, President of the European Council)

D. Szabolcs Fazakas MEP (Chairman of Committee on Budgetary Control)

21. In 2004 the average growth of the euro area was .... %, while the US economy grew by 4.3%, Japan by 4.4%, India by 6.4% and China by 9%.

A. 2.2

B. 3.2

C. 4.2

D. 5.2

22. In June 2005 the EU25 employment rate was 62.9% and the employment rate in the USA was .... %.

A. 61.1

B. 64.3

C. 71.2

D. 80.3

23. In which Member State was unemployment the highest (as of May 2005)?

A. Slovakia

B. Czech Republic

C. Poland

D. Hungary

24. Microeconomic guidelines as part of the Integrated Guidelines for Growth and Jobs (2005-2008) do not aim to ....

A. Extend and deepen the internal market

B. Ensure open and competitive markets inside and outside Europe

C. Facilitate all forms of innovation

D. Promote greater coherence between macroeconomic and structural policies

25. Which statement is false? INTI ....

A. Is a funding programme

B. Encourages the creation of transnational partnerships and networks

C. Programmes may be co-financed by ARGO

D. Covers some of the Member States only

26. In addition to the place of fattening, slaughtering and cutting, the beef label also has to include precise information about ....

A. Where the animal was born and reared

B. When the animal was born

C. Whether the animal has been fed on GMOs

D.   Whether the animal received medication

27.   According to the Commission's proposal to reform the registration, evaluation and authorisation of chemicals (REACH), ...

A.   No authorisation will be required for bio-accumulative substances

B.   There will be three types of evaluation

C.   All substances imported in quantities of five tonnes or more per year will have to be registered

D.   A European Chemicals Agency will be established

28.   Regarding the patentability of software and other computer-related inventions, the European Parliament ....; the European Commission will .... proposal.

A.   Rejected the proposal, Present a revised

B.   Proposed major amendments, Present a revised

C.   Proposed minor amendments, Insist on its original

D.   Rejected the proposal, Not present a new

29.   Which of the following statements is true concerning the European Driving Licence?

A.   Under Council Directive 115/2005, Member States must issue such licences before 1 January 2007

B.   The European Parliament supported the idea but no concrete measures have yet been taken

C.   According to the proposal, it must contain biometric data of its bearer

D.   It can also be used as a personal identification document in the Schengen area

30.   In ...., the euro became the sole currency of .... EU Member States.

A.   February 2001, 11

B.   February 2001, 12

C.   February 2002, 11

D.   February 2002, 12

31.   Which of the following countries is not a net contributor to the EU budget?

A.   Luxembourg

B.   Italy

C.   Denmark

D.   Austria

32.   Which Member State is not a member in the Exchange Rate Mechanism (as of August 2005)?

A.   Lithuania

B.   Slovakia

C.   Slovenia

D.   Malta

33.   Regarding the EU's budget, the maximum call-in rate for the VAT resource is ....%.

A.   0.25

B.   0.5

C.   0.75

D.   1

34. Member States themselves manage approximately ....% of the expenditure of the Community budget.

A. 80

B. 70

C. 60

D. 65

35. The Community action programme to promote activities in the field of the protection of the Community's financial interests is called the .... programme.

A. Pericles

B. Antigone

C. Hercule

D. Electra

36. Which of the following is not an own resource of the Community budget?

A. Customs duties

B. Direct community VAT

C. Agricultural levies

D. GNP-based additional resource

37. The ceiling of resources on Community level is ....% of GNI, but in 2006 the actual spending will be ....% of the GNI.

A. 0.84, 0.81

B. 1, 0.83

C. 1.32, 1.26

D. 1.24, 1.09

38. In 2006, 4.5% of the Community budget goes to .....

A. Internal policies

B. External action

C. Pre-accession strategy

D. Administrative expenses

39. ALTER-EU concerns ....

A. Energy resources

B. Democratic deficit

C. Transparency and ethics

D. Environment-friendly vehicles

40. The "Orange Revolution" is related to ....

A. Ukraine

B. Cuba

C. Georgia

D. Brazil

41. The Accession Treaty of Romania and Bulgaria was signed in ....

A. July 2005

B. December 2004

C. October 2004

D. April 2005

42. How many chapters is the acquis communautaire broken down into in the framework of accession negotiations with Turkey and Croatia ....

A. 28

B.   31

C.   35

D.   39

43.   In September 2005, the United Nations Summit on the Millennium Development Goals (MDGs) was held in ....

A.   New York

B.   Cape Town

C.   Mombassa

D.   Rio de Janeiro

44.   Which statement is correct in relation to the ".eu"?

A.   It is a Top Level Domain

B.   It is not available to natural persons

C.   It is unlikely to become operational before the end of 2006

D.   It will be operated by the ".eu Registry" run by the Commission

45.   Which of the following criteria is not required for a European official to be deemed financially liable?

A.   Breach a legal obligation

B.   Be found guilty by the European Civil Service Tribunal

C.   Cause financial damage to the Communities

D.   Be guilty of serious personal misconduct

46.   What is the name of the network that helps citizens and businesses get mis-applications of EU internal market laws corrected?

A.   EURASSISTANCE

B.   INTERSOLUTION

C.   FIXNET

D.   SOLVIT

47.   The service that aims to help students, job seekers, workers, parents, guidance counsellors and teachers to find out information about studying in Europe is called .....

A.   STUDIA

B.   INFOSOC

C.   PLOTEUS

D.   UNISERV

48.   The colour of the Official Journal's English language edition is .....

A.   Magenta

B.   Purple

C.   Dark green

D.   Red

49.   A European official cannot be employed as ....

A.   Auxiliary staff

B.   Part-time worker

C.   Freelance expert

D.   Assistant

50. **The European Space Agency's budget**
for 2005 is about EUR .... million.

A.   3000

B.   10,000

C.   30,000

D.   300,000

EUROPEAN INTEGRATION: HISTORY, ENLARGEMENTS

ANSWERS

Question No	A	B	C	D
1.			X	
2.	X			
3.		X		
4.				X
5.			X	
6.	X			
7.			X	
8.	X			
9.				X
10.		X		
11.			X	
12.				X
13.		X		
14.	X			
15.				X
16.	X			
17.			X	
18.		X		
19.			X	
20.			X	
21.				X
22.	X			
23.			X	
24.		X		
25.				X

Question No	A	B	C	D
26.		X		
27.	X			
28.				X
29.			X	
30.		X		
31.	X			
32.		X		
33.			X	
34.				X
35.				X
36.			X	
37.		X		
38.	X			
39.				X
40.	X			
41.				X
42.			X	
43.			X	
44.		X		
45.				X
46.	X			
47.		X		
48.	X			
49.			X	
50.				X

Question No	A	B	C	D
51.		X		
52.		X		
53.	X			
54.				X
55.			X	
56.				X
57.	X			
58.		X		
59.		X		
60.	X			
61.			X	
62.			X	
63.				X
64.	X			
65.		X		
66.			X	
67.				X
68.			X	
69.	X			
70.	X			
71.		X		
72.			X	
73.				X
74.	X			
75.			X	

1.   C

The North Atlantic Treaty Organisation (NATO) was founded on 4 April 1949 by ten countries: Belgium, Canada, Denmark, France, Iceland, Italy, Luxembourg, Netherlands, Norway, Portugal, United Kingdom and the United States of America. Today NATO has 26 members.

2.   A

NATO members are (those not in the EU are marked in italics): Belgium, *Canada*, Denmark, France, *Iceland*, Italy, Luxembourg, Netherlands, Norway, Portugal, United Kingdom, *United States of America*, Greece, *Turkey*, Germany, Spain, Czech Republic, Poland, Hungary, *Bulgaria*, Estonia, Latvia, Lithuania, *Romania*, Slovakia, Slovenia.

3.   B

Paul-Henri Spaak (1899-1972) was a Belgian statesman and Socialist leader, who later became the first president of the Council of Europe's Parliamentary Assembly. He had also been Belgian foreign minister and he was the first President of the General Assembly of the United Nations.

4.   D

René Pléven was a French politician, twice premier of the Fourth Republic (1950–51, 1951–52). He is best known for his sponsorship of the Pléven Plan for a unified European army and establishing a European Defence Community.

5.   C

The Treaty of Paris, establishing the European Coal and Steel Community (ECSC), was signed on 18 April 1951 and entered into force on 23 July 1952. As the Treaty was signed for a limited period of 50 years, it expired on 23 July 2002.

6.   A

At the European Summit in The Hague in 1969, the Heads of State and Government of the EC agreed to prepare a plan for the creation of the economic and monetary union. In October 1970 the Werner Report, drawn up by a working group chaired by Luxembourg's President and Minister for the Treasury, was presented. However, the monetary union failed at this stage, due to several reasons but mainly the 1973 oil crisis.

7.   C

The Single European Act (SEA) of 1986, incorporating the first significant update of the founding Treaties, aimed at creating the Single European Market by 31 December 1992.

8.   A

Greece signed its Association Agreement with the EEC in 1961 and became the Community's tenth Member State by the EC's second enlargement in 1981. It is worth noting that the Commission had given a negative opinion on economic grounds against accepting Greece as a new Member State, but the Council was persuaded by Prime Minister Constantine Karamanlis to overrule the Commission in order to safeguard democracy against another military coup.

9.   D

The Elysée Treaty, also known as the Treaty of Friendship, was concluded by Charles de Gaulle and Konrad Adenauer in 1963. It set the seal on reconciliation between the two countries. With it, Germany and France established a new foundation for relations that ended centuries of rivalry between them. On 22 January 2003, the 40th anniversary of the signing of the Treaty was celebrated.

10.   B

Born in Rome, Altiero Spinelli was a lifelong advocate of European federalism. In 1970 he became a member of the European Commission, with responsibility for industrial policy. He resigned in 1976 and in 1979 he was elected to the European Parliament as an Independent of the Left.

11.   C

The United Kingdom, Ireland and Denmark joined the EC in 1973. According to the referenda held in Ireland and Denmark, 83.1% and 63.3% of the population was in favour of accession. However, voters in Norway turned down the government's intention to join by having only 46.5% in favour. This was the first enlargement in the Community's history, followed by four others:

1981:   Greece;
1986:   Spain and Portugal;
1995:   Austria, Finland and Sweden;
2004:   Estonia, Latvia, Lithuania, Poland, the Czech Republic, Hungary, Slovakia, Slovenia, Malta and Cyprus

12.   D

The Treaty of Rome, establishing the European Communities comprising the European Economic Community (EEC), the European Atomic Energy Community (Euratom) and the European Coal and Steel Community (ECSC), was signed on 25 March 1957 by the founding six members and entered into force on 1 January 1958. The Treaty of Rome has been amended by several Treaties and it will be replaced by the Constitutional Treaty should it enter into force.

13.   B

The Association Agreement ("Ankara Agreement", not to be confused with the Accession Agreement which Turkey will only sign upon acceding to the EU) signed between the Community and Turkey in 1963 and the protocol added in 1970 lay down basic objectives in their relations, such as the continuous and balanced strengthening of trade and economic relations and the establishment of a customs union in three phases, along with the free movement of workers. For socio-economic reasons however, it has not been possible to achieve this according to the timetable set. Turkey was accepted as a candidate country at the 1999 European Council and the decision to commence accession negotiations in October 2005 was made at the 2004 European Council.

14.   A

Walter Hallstein was the first President of the European Commission of the European Economic Community from 1 January 1958. Louis Armand was the first president of the Euratom. Christian Fouchet, former French Interior Minister, was the one assigned by President De Gaulle to elaborate a plan on closer political cooperation on European level, which he carried out in 1961-62, referred to as the Fouchet plan since. Jean Rey, after the Merger Treaty of the three Communities signed in 1965 (entered into force in 1967), was the first President of the "merged" new Commission.

15.   D

The Yaoundé Convention, an Association Agreement valid for five years, was signed between the Community and 17 African States and Madagascar in Yaoundé, Cameroon in 1963. The European Development Fund (EDF) is the main instrument for Community aid for development cooperation in the African, Caribbean and Pacific (ACP) countries and the Overseas Countries and Territories (OCT). Articles 131 and 136 of the 1957 Treaty of Rome provided for its creation with a view to granting technical and financial assistance to African countries that were still colonised at that time and with which certain countries had historical links. Each EDF is concluded for a period of around five years. Since the conclusion of the first partnership convention in 1964, the EDF cycles have generally followed that of the partnership agreements /conventions.

First EDF: 1959-1964

Second EDF: 1964-1970 (Yaoundé I Convention)
Third EDF: 1970-1975 (Yaoundé II Convention)
Fourth EDF: 1975-1980 (Lomé I Convention)
Fifth EDF: 1980-1985 (Lomé II Convention)
Sixth EDF: 1985-1990 (Lomé III Convention)
Seventh EDF: 1990-1995 (Lomé IV Convention)
Eighth EDF: 1995-2000 (Lomé IV Convention and the revised Lomé IV)
Ninth EDR: 2000-2005 (Cotonou Convention) *(ScadPlus)*

16.   A

The founding Treaties have been amended on several occasions, in particular when new Member States joined the Community. There have also been more far-reaching reforms bringing major institutional changes and introducing new areas of responsibility for the European institutions, the first of which – the Merger Treaty, signed in Brussels on 8 April 1965 and in force from 1 July 1967 – provided for a Single Commission and a Single Council of the then three European Communities. *(http://europa.eu.int/abc)*

17.   C

For a comprehensive list of the Presidents of the European Commission, please refer to the section on the European Commission.

18.   B

A loose arrangement which was never recognised by the Commission or the European Court of Justice, the 1966 Luxembourg Compromise effectively extended the life of the national veto beyond the transitional period allowed in the Treaty of Rome. Its genesis was the impasse known as the "empty chair crisis", when France boycotted Council meetings for the last six months of 1965 in protest against bureaucratic supranationalism and the advent of qualified majority voting, thereby immobilising the Community. President Charles de

Gaulle took the line that the Treaty of Rome was ambiguous or flawed, and that it was unthinkable that France should be outvoted by foreigners. Under the Luxembourg Compromise any decision which affected "a very important national interest" would be deferred until a unanimously acceptable solution could be found, regardless of whether the Treaty prescribed majority voting. *(EuroKnow)*

19.   C

After the collapse of previous attempts at currency union in Europe, Roy Jenkins launched the EMS in his first year as president of the Commission in 1977. It came into force in 1979. The two components of the EMS were the ECU (the embryonic single currency) and the Exchange Rate Mechanism (ERM), a revised system of fixed but adjustable exchange rates. All the EU Member States participated in the EMS and the ECU, but membership of the ERM was neither mandatory nor universal. The launch of the euro in 1999 rendered the EMS obsolete, replacing both the ECU and the ERM with a regime of irrevocably fixed exchange rates, leading by 2002 to the issue of euro notes and coin and the abolition of national currencies. *(EuroKnow)*

20.   C

Before direct election Members of the European Parliament (MEPs) were appointed by each of the Member States' national parliaments. All Members thus had a dual mandate. The Summit Conference in Paris on 9-10 December 1974 decided that direct elections "should take place in or after 1978" and asked Parliament to submit new proposals to replace its draft Convention of 1960. In January 1975 Parliament adopted a new draft, on the basis of which the Heads of State or Government, after settling a number of differences, reached agreement at their meeting of 12-13 July 1976. The Decision and Act on European elections by direct universal suffrage were signed in Brussels on 20 September 1976. After ratification by all the Member States, the text came into force on 1 July 1978. The first elections took place between 7 and 10 June 1979. *(http://europarl.eu.int/facts)*

21.   D

To assess the size of the gains from achieving the Single Market, a study was commissioned entitled "The Costs of non-Europe" and since known as the Cecchini Report (1988). This examined and tried to measure the economic costs of the barriers to be removed by the Single European Act. The Report also considered that second-round macro-economic effects following an improvement in government budgets could also add significantly to the benefits. It projected that the "single market" would add 4.5 percent to the GDP of the 12-nation EU, adding 1.8 million jobs. This later proved to be too optimistic, yet significant advantages of the single market were apparent.

22.   A

Jacques Delors served two terms from 1985-1990 and from 1990-1995. Before that, under President François Mitterrand, Delors served as economy and finance minister (1981-83) and economy, finance, and budget minister (1983-84), helping to revive the French economy.

23.   C

Greece joined the EC in 1981 as the 10th Member State. Spain and Portugal joined as the 11th and 12th Member States, whereas Denmark, along with the United Kingdom and Ireland, had been members since 1973.

24.   B

The Single European Act (SEA) entered into force on 1 January 1987. The French president of the time was François Mitterand, who served 14 years in office from 1981 to 1995; therefore he was also in office at the time when the Maastricht Treaty entered into force (1 November 1993).

25.   D

In 1985, the EC had 10 Member States, among which the most northern was the United Kingdom, the most eastern was Greece. Sweden and Cyprus were not members at the time.

26.   B

The European Free Trade Association (EFTA) was founded by Austria, Denmark, Norway, Portugal, Sweden, Switzerland and the UK in 1960. Finland became an associate member in 1961 (it later became a full member in 1986), and Iceland joined in 1970. The United Kingdom, Denmark and Ireland joined the European Community in 1973, and therefore ceased to be EFTA members. Portugal also left EFTA for the European Community in 1986. Liechtenstein joined in 1991 (previously its interests in EFTA had been represented by Switzerland). Finally, Austria, Sweden and Finland joined the European Union in 1995 and hence ceased to be EFTA members.

27.   A

The **Council of Europe**, an international organisation of 46 Member States in the European region, was founded on 5 May 1949 by the Treaty of London. Membership is open to all European states which accept the principle of the rule of law and guarantee fundamental human rights and freedoms to their citizens. One of the main successes of the Council was the European Convention on Human Rights in 1950, which serves as the basis for the European Court of Human Rights. The seat of the Council of Europe is in Strasbourg on the Franco-German border. Originally meeting in Strasbourg's University Palace, it is now domiciled in the Palace of Europe. The Council of Europe is not to be confused with the Council of the European Union, or with the European Council.

The **European Council**, sometimes informally called the European Summit, is a meeting of the heads of state or government of the EU Member States and the President of the European Commission. In 1974, a Summit meeting was held in Paris where it was decided to hold meetings three times a year as the "European Council". The first of such summits was held in Dublin the following year. On average four European Councils are held every year. Traditionally the summits of the European Councils have been held in the country currently holding the Presidency of the Council of the European Union. However, in late 2000 it was agreed at the Nice European Council that in the future, half the European Councils would be held in Brussels and eventually all would be held there.

The ten founding members of the Council of Europe were: Belgium, Denmark, France, Ireland, Italy, Luxembourg, Netherlands, Norway, Sweden, United Kingdom.

Members that joined before the first European Council of 1975 are: Greece (9 August 1949), Turkey (9 August 1949), Iceland (9 March 1950), Federal Republic of Germany (13 July 1950), Austria (16 April 1956), Cyprus (24 May 1961), Switzerland (6 May 1963), Malta (29 April 1965). Therefore the correct answer is 18. (*Wikipedia*)

28.   D

The European Court of Human Rights was created in Strasbourg to systematise the hearing of human rights complaints from Council of Europe member states. The Court's mission is to enforce the Convention for the Protection of Human Rights and Fundamental Freedoms, ratified in 1953. The ECHR should not be mistaken for the European Court of Justice, an institution of the European Union for the resolution of disputes under EU law. The Court consists of a number of judges equal to the number of Council of Europe member states, which currently stand at forty-six. Despite this correspondence, however, there are no requirements that each state be represented at the Court, nor are there limits to the number of judges belonging to any nationality.

29.   C

The Maastricht Treaty (formally, the Treaty on European Union) was signed on 7 February 1992 at Maastricht in the Netherlands, where the final negotiations had taken place during December 1991. It led to the creation of the European Union

and was the result of separate negotiations on monetary union and on political union.

The Treaty led to the creation of the euro, and introduced the three-pillar structure (the Community pillar, the Common Foreign and Security Policy or CFSP pillar, and the Justice and Home Affairs or JHA pillar). The CFSP pillar was built on the foundation of European Political Cooperation (EPC), but brought it under a treaty and extended it. The JHA pillar introduced cooperation in law enforcement, criminal justice, civil judicial matters, and asylum and immigration.

Ratification of the Treaty encountered difficulties in various states. A referendum in France only narrowly supported it, with 51.05% in favour, and Denmark rejected the original treaty. In the United Kingdom, ratification was done by Parliament, where the Maastricht rebels nearly defeated John Major's government's policy on the matter. (*Wikipedia*)

30.   B

The Schengen Treaty is an agreement signed on 14 June 1985, by five European Community countries (Belgium, the Netherlands, Luxembourg, France and Germany). The agreement was signed on board the ship *Princess Marie-Astrid* on the Moselle River, near Schengen, a small town in Luxembourg on the border with France and Germany.

Its goal was to end border checkpoints and controls within the Schengen area and harmonise external border controls. It was created outside the European Union (European Communities at the time) framework, because of the failure to achieve unanimity in this subject among all of the countries of the European Community.

31.   A

In cooperation with the Council of Europe, each year is dedicated to a special subject on a European level, which entails programmes, initiatives and more consciousness on the given issue. 1990 was the European year of tourism etc. More recent European years are:
•   2003: People with disabilities
•   2004: Education through sport
•   2005: Citizenship through Education

- 2006: Workers' Mobility
- 2007: Equal Opportunities for All

32.   B

The European City of Culture was the result of an initiative by the Greek Minister of Culture, Melina Mercouri. It was launched at intergovernmental level in 1985 by the Council of Ministers, which has designated at least one European City of Culture each year since then. During the German Presidency the event was integrated into the Community framework and a new selection procedure was introduced. At the same time, the European City of Culture was renamed the Cultural Capital of Europe. Council decision 1419/99/EC of 25 May 1999 entered into force as of 2005.

The selection procedure is based on a rotation principle, with individual EU Member States able to suggest one or more Cultural Capitals for a particular year, possibly stating preferences. An independent international, seven-member Selection Panel examines the candidacies collated each year by the European Commission. The panel consists of two members of the European Parliament, two members of the Council, two members of the Commission and one member of the Committee of the Regions. The panel makes a recommendation to the European Parliament, the Council and the Commission. Within a period of three months after receipt of this report, the European Parliament may forward an opinion on the nominations. The Commission then submits its recommendation to the Council. (For further questions and information on this topic, please consult the section on Research, Culture and Education Policy.)

33.   C

Applications for EU membership:
- Turkey (April 1987)
- Cyprus (July 1990)
- Malta (July 1990, reactivated 1998)
- Switzerland applied in May 1992 but, following the negative outcome of the 1992 referendum on the country's accession to the European Economic Area, the Swiss Government did not pursue its application to accede to the EU, but neither did it withdraw it
- Hungary (March 1994)
- Poland (April 1994)
- Romania and Slovakia (June 1995)
- Latvia (October 1995)
- Estonia (November 1995)
- Bulgaria and Lithuania (December 1995)
- Czech Republic (January 1996)
- Slovenia (June 1996)
- Croatia (February 2003)

34.   D

The Copenhagen European Council of June 1993 laid down the basic criteria for accession which future members would have to meet in addition to the conditions in the Treaty. These are:
- stability of institutions and respect for and protection of minorities;
- existence of a functioning market economy and the ability to cope with competitive pressure and market forces within the Union;
- ability to take on the obligations of membership, including adherence to the aims of political, economic and monetary union and adoption of the common rules, standards and policies that make up the body of EU law – the acquis communautaire.

35.   D

36.   C

The Berlin European Council of March 1999 decided to increase pre-accession aid substantially and to create two specific instruments, ISPA (for transport and environment) and SAPARD (for agriculture and rural development) to supplement the PHARE programme (originally created in 1989 to assist Poland and Hungary), which would now concentrate on strengthening administrative and judicial systems and aiding investment related to the adoption of the acquis communautaire. Assistance was stepped up with the adoption, in 2002, of the Action Plans for building administrative, judicial and institutional capacity and the special transition facility for institution-building endorsed by the European Council in October 2002. From 2001, the CARDS programme (Community Assistance for Reconstruction, Development and Stability in the Balkans) has provided financial assistance to countries in the Balkans.

37.   B

The accession process was formally opened on 30 March 1998 and detailed negotiations began the following day with six candidate countries (named after the Luxembourg European Council in December 1997, the so-called Luxembourg six: Cyprus, Estonia, Hungary, Poland, the Czech Republic and Slovenia), in the form of bilateral intergovernmental conferences composed of representatives of the Union and the applicant country concerned and the Commission negotiating team. Negotiations with Bulgaria, Latvia, Lithuania, Malta, Romania and Slovakia (the so-called Helsinki six, Helsinki European Council, December 1999) were formally launched in February 2000. The negotiations were preceded by a screening exercise aimed at explaining existing EU legislation to the candidate countries and checking whether they were willing to accept it and able to apply it. The negotiations cover the 31 chapters into which the acquis is broken down.

38.   A

The European Council of Nice (in December 2000) reaffirmed the "Roadmap" for the negotiations proposed by the Commission and endorsed the target date for membership of the most advanced candidate countries in 2004, confirming Parliament's view that the best prepared candidate countries should be able to participate in the 2004 European Parliament elections. It also defined the framework for the institutional reform necessary for enlargement. Negotiations with ten countries (Cyprus, Czech Republic, Estonia, Hungary, Latvia, Lithuania, Malta, Poland, Slovakia and Slovenia) were closed at the Copenhagen meeting of the European Council in December 2002. The Treaty of Accession for these countries was signed on 16 April 2003 and they became Member States on 1

May 2004 following completion of the ratification procedures.

39.   D

The European conference brought together countries aspiring to join the EU: the ten candidate countries from Central Europe and Eastern Europe, Cyprus, Malta and Turkey (invited but declined to participate). The Conference was a multilateral forum for discussing issues of common interest, such as foreign and security policy, justice and home affairs, regional cooperation or economic matters. The conference met for the first time in London on 12 March 1998. The second meeting took place in Luxembourg on 6 October 1998 and the third one in Brussels on 19 July 1999, at the level of foreign affairs ministers.

40.   A

In July 1997, the Commission presented Agenda 2000, a single framework in which the Commission outlined

- the broad perspective for the development of the European Union and its policies after the year 2000;
- the challenges of enlargement;
- the main conclusions and recommendations from the individual opinions on the applicant countries and the Commission's views on the launching of the accession process;
- reinforcement of the pre-accession strategy;
- the impact of enlargement on the EU as a whole;
- the future financial framework beyond 2000, taking into account the prospect of an enlarged Union.

For further information, see:
http://europa.eu.int/ScadPlus/leg/en/s60000.htm

41.   D

Accession of Romania and Bulgaria is scheduled for 2007; Croatia has been recently accepted as a candidate country and accession talks were started on the same day as with Turkey, officially on 3 October 2005.

42.   C

Twinning is used in several fields; however in the framework of enlargement, twinning helped and helps the applicant countries to acquire the structures, human resources and management skills needed to implement the acquis through secondment of experts from the Member States.

43.   C

Finland: 5,214,512 (July 2004 est.)
Bulgaria: 7,517,973 (July 2004 est.)
Sweden: 8,986,400 (July 2004 est.)
Belgium: 10,348,276 (July 2004 est.)

44.   B

Romania, with a population of 22,355,551 (July 2004 est.), has a territory of 237,500 sq km.

45.   D

Apart from those listed, Hungary is also a neighbour of Croatia.

46.   A

In 1997 the Council reached agreement on the procedure for the negotiations. Sessions are held at the level of ministers or deputies, i.e. permanent representatives, for the Member States, and Ambassadors or chief negotiators for the applicants.

The negotiations with each applicant proceed on their own merits. The pace of each negotiation depends on the level of preparation by each applicant country and the complexity of the issues being negotiated. For this reason, it is not possible to estimate the likely length of each negotiation in advance. The Commission proposes common negotiating positions for the EU for each chapter relating to matters of Community competence.

Each applicant country draws up its position on each of the 31 chapters of the EU acquis. Each applicant appoints a Chief Negotiator with a supporting team of experts.

On the EU's side, the European Commission proposes the draft negotiating positions. The Commission itself is in close contact with the applicant countries in order to seek solutions to problems arising during the negotiations. Within the Commission, the work is coordinated by the Directorate General for Enlargement. The draft negotiating positions are then approved unanimously by the Council.

After an agreement is reached (that may contain extra financial aid from the Community to help adjustment to the acquis, or derogations for some months or years), the chapter is temporarily closed. This means that until the end of negotiations, any chapter may be re-opened or re-adjusted, due to new needs on either side or the constantly evolving and changing nature of the acquis communautaire.

When negotiations are finished and all chapters are closed, the results are eventually incorporated in an Accession Treaty. This is submitted to the Council for approval and to the European Parliament for assent. After signature, the Accession Treaty passes to the Member States and to the applicant country or countries for ratification involving, in some cases, referenda. It takes effect, and the applicant becomes a Member State, on the date of accession.

The negotiation chapters are the following:
1: Free Movement of Goods
2: Freedom of Movement for Persons
3: Freedom to Provide Services
4: Free Movement of Capital
5: Company Law
6: Competition Policy
7: Agriculture
8: Fisheries
9: Transport Policy
10: Taxation
11: Economic and Monetary Union
12: Statistics
13: Employment and social policy
14: Energy
15: Industrial Policy
16: Small and Medium-sized Enterprises
17: Science and Research
18: Education and Training

19: Telecom and IT
20: Culture and Audiovisual Policy
21: Regional policy and co-ordination of structural instruments
22: Environment
23: Consumer protection
24: Justice and Home Affairs
25: Customs Union
26: External Relations
27: Common Foreign and Security Policy
28: Financial Control
29: Finance and Budgetary Provisions
30: Institutions
31: Other

For further information, see:
http://europa.eu.int/comm/enlargement/negotiations/ind ex.htm

47.   B

The French referendum on the Maastricht Treaty (signed on 7 February 1992) was held on 20 September 1992 with a positive result of 51.5% of the French voters in favour and 48.95% against it.

48.   A

CFCU is the Central Financing and Contracting Unit set up in all candidate countries for the administration of tenders, contracts and payments for all Institution Building and some investment projects.

49.   C

Reports by the Commission on progress towards accession by each of the candidate countries were first published on 4 November 1998.

The European Council in Luxembourg (December 1997) decided that "From the end of 1998, the Commission will make regular reports to the Council, together with any necessary recommendations for opening bilateral intergovernmental conferences, reviewing the progress of each Central and East European candidate State towards accession in the light of the Copenhagen criteria, in particular the rate at which it is adopting the Union

acquis. […] In that context, the Commission will continue to follow the method adopted by Agenda 2000 in evaluating candidate States' ability to meet the economic criteria and fulfil the obligations deriving from accession. "

50.   D

Referenda on EU-accession took place as follows (the number of those in favour in parenthesis):
Malta: 8 March 2003 (53%)
Slovenia: 23 March 2003 (89%)
Hungary: 12 April 2003 (84%)
Lithuania: 11 May 2003 (90%)
Slovakia: 16-17 May 2003 (92.5%)
Poland: 7-8 June 2003 (77.5%)
Czech Republic: 15-16 June 2003 (77%)
Estonia: 14 September 2003 (66.9%)
Latvia: 20 September 2003 (67%)
Cyprus: no referendum, only parliamentary ratification

51.   B

The EU initially paid 25% of the direct income aid for farmers in the applicant countries in 2004, 30% in 2005, and it will pay 35% in 2006. After this, the figure will increase by 10% every year until 2013. Based on the agreement the new Member States managed to reach in October and later in December 2003, they are allowed to pay out more from their own budgets and money allocated for rural development to a maximum of 55% in 2004, 60% in 2005, and 65% in 2007 (except for Slovenia and Cyprus, allowed to do so from the date of accession).

52.   B

At the Fontainebleau European Council in France on 25 and 26 June 1984, the then ten Member States (Germany, Belgium, Denmark, France, Greece, Ireland, Italy, Luxembourg, the Netherlands and the UK) agreed on the rebate to be granted to the UK to reduce its contribution to the Community budget. This agreement was marked by the speech by the British Prime Minister, Margaret Thatcher, in which her aim was clearly stated: "I want my money back". The UK's reduced contribution seems less relevant today, and the Commission has presented a new regulatory framework for the system of own resources and the correction of budgetary imbalances. (*ScadPlus*)

53.   A

Opt-out is a permanent exemption from a Treaty provision, as opposed to a temporary "derogation". Notable examples have been the opt-outs of the UK and Denmark from the single currency stage of EMU, Denmark's opt-out on EU measures affecting defence, and the UK's opt-out (subsequently revoked) from the Social Chapter. These exemptions were contained in protocols to the 1992 Maastricht Treaty. The 1997 Amsterdam Treaty contained opt-outs exempting the UK and Ireland from its provisions abolishing internal borders. More radically, that Treaty also introduced the principle of "flexibility", enabling a majority of Member States to develop closer links in new policy areas without involving the other Member States.

54.   D

The OSCE is the name given since 1994 to the collective official peace, security and human rights movement of 55 states (originally 35), as reflected in the 1975 Helsinki Final Act and several subsequent conferences. Originally known as the CSCE (Conference on Security and Co-operation in Europe), its purpose during the Cold War was to reduce tensions in Europe between NATO and the Warsaw Pact countries and to establish human rights principles behind the Iron Curtain – an endeavour viewed idealistically in the West, if cynically by the Soviet bloc.

The Charter of Paris for a New Europe, signed in 1990, was intended to mark a watershed. It reaffirmed the Helsinki Agreement, committed the participants to democracy and free markets and signalled the impending transformation of the CSCE into a structured institution, with a council, a committee, a secretariat, a parliamentary assembly and a Conflict Prevention Centre, all with headquarters in European cities. The EU is not strictly speaking a member of the OSCE, although the Commission president Jacques Delors signed the Charter of Paris; of the participants all but two (the USA and Canada) are European states or former Soviet republics. (*EuroKnow*)

55.   C

An association agreement is an agreement between the Community and a non-EU state or group of states. Such an agreement may be designed to pave the way to possible membership of the EU, in which case it is called a Europe Agreement; for example this was the case for Hungary, Poland and the Czech Republic. It may denote an aid and technical co-operation agreement, as with certain North African and Middle Eastern countries; or a more comprehensive agreement with trade, aid, cultural and social dimensions, as with the African, Caribbean and Pacific signatories to the Lomé Convention. The EEA Treaty also counts as an Association Agreement.

Europe Agreements provide for gradual integration into the Community, mutual free trade within ten years and progress towards compatibility with Community law, within the framework of free elections, open markets and the rule of law. The process is carried forward by financial assistance and regular political meetings at head of state, ministerial, diplomatic and parliamentary levels.

56.   D

Safeguard clauses have been used during all preceding enlargements. This instrument is designed as a kind of a rapid reaction facility and is a means of ensuring that the EU can tackle unforeseen developments to protect the functioning of the enlarged EU.

In addition to a general economic safeguard clause which can be invoked by any Member State, two other specific clauses are available for three years after the 2004 enlargement in cases where a new Member State fails to implement commitments made in the negotiations in the areas of the internal market or justice and home affairs.

To prevent invoking safeguard clauses the EU will continue with its administrative assistance to candidate countries to further strengthen their institutions, mainly those dealing with justice, border controls, the customs union, veterinary services, nuclear safety and food safety. The Commission will report six months before accession on the progress made in every candidate country. Interim reports are prepared every two months.

57.   A

Every year in Aachen a well-known European receives a prize for his or her work for European integration, known as the Charlemagne Prize. In 2003, the prize went to Giscard d'Estaing and in 2004 the outgoing President of the European Parliament, Pat Cox, was the winner. In 2005, the prize was awarded to the President of Italy, Carlo Azeglio Ciampi.

For further information, see:
www.aachen.de/EN/city_citizens/prizes_honours/charle magne_prize/

58.   B

Fouchet, a French diplomat, was the "spokesperson" of Charles de Gaulle's designs for Europe in 1961 and 1962. De Gaulle had two aims: to sever Europe's dependence for military security on the Atlantic Alliance and the USA; and to restructure the Community by turning it into a voluntary union of independent states, based in Paris, with extensive national veto powers over all common policies. The Fouchet proposals envisaged the emasculation of the Commission and the Council of Ministers and the subjection of Community law to national law.

The five other Member States of the Common Market rejected Fouchet's plan, prompting a violent attack by de Gaulle on Commission President Walter Hallstein; this in turn led to widespread ministerial resignations in France. There followed the vetoing of the UK's application to join the Community in 1963, the French boycott of Community institutions in 1965 (the "empty chair"crisis), the "Luxembourg Compromise" in 1966 and finally a decade and a half of institutional paralysis in Europe, lasting for a dozen years after de Gaulle's death. To this day the spectre of Fouchet's plan is evoked in Brussels whenever a proposal surfaces that smacks too much of national autonomy. (*EuroKnow*)

59.   B

A theory of European integration according to which functions of government are gradually and continuously transferred from the national to the supra-national level as on national level they cannot adequately be undertaken. This is due to the smallness of their size, lower economies of scale, inefficiency etc. This theory tends to exaggerate the importance of size and underestimate the importance of democratic accountability in giving legitimacy and authority to states.

60.   A

Preceded by the Genscher-Colombo Plan, the Stuttgart Declaration of 1983 was made by the European Council and presaged the transformation of the Community into the European Union. It began the process of curtailing the national right of veto, increasing the powers of the European Parliament and advancing the single market, as well as urging greater co-operation in the political, economic, industrial and security fields. The Declaration led to the Dooge Committee on institutional reform and the Adonnino Committee on a People's Europe, both of which made proposals which were to find expression in the Single European Act of 1986 and the Maastricht Treaty of 1992.

61.   C

In accordance with the Laeken Declaration (European Council, December 2001) a Convention was organised in order to prepare for the next IGC (Intergovernmental Conference) which, like the Convention that established the Charter of fundamental rights, involved representatives from national governments and parliaments in the Member States and candidate countries and representatives from the European Parliament and the Commission. Its inaugural session was held on 28 February 2002 and work came to an end after 17 months of discussions. The Convention drew up a draft Treaty establishing a European Constitution which was presented by its President, Mr Giscard d'Estaing, to the Thessaloniki European Council.

For further information, see:
http://europa.eu.int/comm/laeken_council/index_en.htm

taking enhanced cooperation within the area of defence according to special rules.
(*ScadPlus*)

62.   C

On 9 May 1950, Robert Schuman presented his proposal on the creation of a European Coal and Steel Community. This proposal, known as the "Schuman declaration", is considered to be the beginning of the creation of what is now the European Union. Today, 9 May has become a European symbol (Europe Day) which along with the single currency (the euro), the flag and the anthem, identifies the political entity of the European Union.

64.   A

In 1954 plans to create a European Defence Community (to replace the national armies of Germany, France, Italy and the Benelux countries with a common defence force) collapsed when France refused to ratify the Treaty. The "Six" thereupon turned their attention to the idea of a customs union, meeting at Messina (Italy) in 1955 to entrust Paul-Henri Spaak of Belgium with the production of the report which led to the 1957 Treaty of Rome and the formation of the EEC.

63.   D

Set up in 1948 by the Treaty of Brussels, the WEU is a European organisation for the purposes of cooperation on defence and security. It consists of 28 countries with four different statuses: Member States, Associate Members, Observers and Associate Partners. All EU countries are full Member States except Denmark, Ireland Austria, Finland and Sweden, which have observer status. The six Associate Members are the Czech Republic, Hungary, Iceland, Norway, Poland and Turkey, and there are seven Associate Partners: Bulgaria, Estonia, Latvia, Lithuania, Romania, Slovakia and Slovenia.

The Amsterdam Treaty made the WEU an "integral part of the development of the Union" by giving it an operational capability in the field of defence. The WEU played a major role in the first Petersberg tasks, such as the police detachment in Mostar or cooperation with the police in Albania. However, it now seems to have abandoned that role in favour of developing the Union's own structures and capabilities in the sphere of the common foreign and security policy (CFSP). The WEU's subsidiary bodies, the Security Studies Institute and the Satellite Centre, were transferred to the Union on 1 January 2002. The Treaty of Nice also deleted from the Treaty on European Union a number of provisions concerning relations between the WEU and the Union. The WEU's main remaining area of responsibility is Article V – collective defence.

The mutual defence clause was integrated into the EU Constitution for those members under-

65.   B

The Treaty of Nice, agreed by the Heads of State and Government at the Nice European Council on 11 December 2000 and signed on 26 February 2001, was the culmination of eleven months of negotiations that took place during an Intergovernmental Conference (IGC) opened in February 2000. It entered into force on 1 February 2003 after being ratified by the fifteen Member States of the European Union (EU) according to their respective constitutional rules.

66.   C

The Charter of Fundamental Rights of the European Union, proclaimed in Nice on 7 December 2000, summarises the common values of the Member States of the European Union. Roman Herzog, a former president of the Federal Republic of Germany, was elected chairman by the members of the Convention and was responsible for the work programme and preparatory proceedings.

- The Cologne European Council (3 and 4 June 1999) concluded that the fundamental rights applicable at European Union level should be consolidated in a charter, to give them greater visibility.
- The Tampere European Council (15 and 16 October 1999) was entirely devoted to the

creation of an area of freedom, security and justice in the European Union. Agreement was reached at the summit on determining the composition, method of work and practical arrangements for the body entrusted with drawing up a draft Charter of Fundamental Rights.

- The new body, referred to as the Convention, held its first meeting on 17 December 1999.
- The Biarritz European Council (13 and 14 October 2000) unanimously approved the draft and sent it to the European Parliament and the Commission.
- The presidents of the European Parliament, the Council and the Commission signed and solemnly proclaimed the Charter in Nice (7 December 2000) on behalf of the three institutions. However, the Heads of State or Government, meeting in Nice, decided not to include any reference to the Charter in the Treaty. This means that although its political value had been recognised (for the first time the traditional civil and political rights and economic and social rights have been brought together in a single document), the text still had no binding legal force.

The Convention consisted of 62 members:

- 15 representatives of the Heads of State or Government of the Member States;
- 1 representative of the President of the European Commission;
- 16 members of the European Parliament;
- 30 members of national parliaments (two for each national parliament).

The Court of Justice of the European Communities, the Council of Europe and the European Court of Human Rights had observer status (two representatives per institution).

Hearings were also organised for:

- the European Economic and Social Committee;
- the Committee of the Regions;
- the European Ombudsman;
- the applicant countries;
- other invited bodies, social groups and experts.

For the first time a single document brings together all of the rights previously to be found in a variety of legislative instruments, such as national laws and international conventions from the Council of Europe, the United Nations and the International Labour Organisation. By making fundamental rights and freedoms clearer and more vis-

ible, the Charter helps to develop the concept of citizenship of the European Union and to create an area of freedom, security and justice (as stated in the preamble). The Charter enhances legal security as regards the protection of fundamental rights, where in the past such protection was guaranteed only by the case law of the Court of Justice and Article 6 of the Treaty on European Union. The Charter now comprises Part II of the Constitutional Treaty.

(*ScadPlus*)

For further information, see:
http://www.europarl.eu.int/charter/default_en.htm

67.   D

The referendum held on 19 October 2002 reversed the previous June 2001 "No" vote and enabled Ireland to ratify the Treaty of Nice; turnout increased by about 14% from the 2001 referendum and compared to the June 2001, the size of the "Yes" vote doubled whereas the "No" vote remained roughly the same. Consequently, the Treaty of Nice could enter into force, which took place on 1 February 2003.

68.   C

The Ioannina compromise takes its name from an informal meeting of foreign ministers in the Greek city of Ioannina on 29 March 1994. Among the decisions taken at the meeting was a Council decision concerning the specific question of qualified majority voting in an enlarged 16-member Community. The decision was later adjusted in the light of Norway's decision not to join. The resulting compromise lays down that if members of the Council representing between 23 votes (the old blocking minority threshold) and 26 votes (the new threshold) express their intention of opposing the taking of a decision by the Council by qualified majority, the Council will do all within its power, within a reasonable space of time, to reach a satisfactory solution that can be adopted by at least 65 votes out of 87. Following the re-weighting of votes in the Council of Ministers, the Treaty of Nice puts an end to the Ioannina compromise.

(*ScadPlus*)

69.   A

A member of the European Free Trade Association since 1970 and the European Economic Area since 1992, Iceland is strongly opposed to membership of the European Union, since that would mean accepting the Common Fisheries Policy, which would effectively destroy Iceland's all-important fishing industry.

70.   A

71.   B

The Dublin Convention was an intergovernmental agreement between the EU Member States on asylum. The Convention obliges the country through which asylum seekers first enter the EU to handle applications for asylum on behalf of all other Member States, unless there are good reasons why the case should be handled by another state. This procedure is designed to prevent refugees from making multiple asylum applications or targeting more friendly/lenient countries. The agreement was reached in 1990, but only became binding in 1997.

72.   C

See answer key no. 19 above.

73.   D

A report from 1975, written by the former Belgian Prime Minister Leo Tindemans, contained proposals for direct elections to the European Parliament and other integration proposals which have since been accepted, for example, the Monetary Union and the Common Foreign and Security Policy. Tindemans was elected to the European Parliament for the Belgian CVP party.

74.   A

The Council for Mutual Economic Assistance (COMECON / Comecon / CMEA / CEMA), 1949 – 1991, was an economic organisation of communist states and a kind of Eastern European equivalent to the European Economic Community. The military counterpart to the Comecon was the Warsaw Pact.

75.   C

Malta signed its Association Agreement with the European Communities in 1970 (entered into force in 1971) and became a Member State in 2004.

INSTITUTIONS OF THE EUROPEAN UNION

COUNCIL OF THE EUROPEAN UNION, EUROPEAN COUNCIL

ANSWERS

Question No	A	B	C	D
1.		X		
2.				X
3.			X	
4.				X
5.		X		
6.	X			
7.			X	
8.				X
9.			X	
10.				X
11.	X			
12.	X			
13.			X	
14.	X			
15.		X		
16.				X
17.			X	
18.	X			
19.			X	
20.		X		

Question No	A	B	C	D
21.				X
22.				X
23.	X			
24.				X
25.				X
26.	X			
27.		X		
28.	X			
29.			X	
30.	X			
31.			X	
32.		X		
33.			X	
34.		X		
35.		X		
36.				X
37.				X
38.			X	
39.	X			
40.		X		

1.   B

The Council is the European Union's main, but not exclusive decision-making and legislative institution. For a wide range of Community issues, the Council exercises its legislative power in codecision with the European Parliament.

2.   D

According to Article 202 of the EC Treaty, to ensure that the objectives set out in the EC Treaty are attained the Council must "ensure coordination of the general economic policies of the Member States".

3.   C

The Council's headquarters in Brussels is named after Justus Lipsius (Joost Lips, 1547-1606), the Dutch humanist and classical scholar.

4.   D

The Council of Europe was established on 5 May 1949, whereas NATO was established a month earlier, on 4 April 1949.

5.   B

The Nordic Council was established in 1953 and functions as an advisory body to the Nordic parliaments and governments, dealing with questions concerning co-operation between the Nordic countries in the economic, legislative, social and cultural fields and issues regarding environmental protection and communications. Denmark, Finland, Iceland, Norway and Sweden, as well as three territories with self-rule – the Faeroe Islands and Greenland under Denmark and the Åland Islands under Finland – are members of the Nordic Council. The official working languages of the Nordic Council are Swedish, Danish, and Norwegian.

6.   A

7.   C

8.   D

Italy held the EU Presidency in the second half of 2003 and Prime Minister Berlusconi was the President of the European Council.

9.   C

The president of the Council is the Foreign Minister of the Member State holding the Council Presidency.

10.   D

At its June 2002 meeting in Seville, the European Council decided to reduce the number of Council formations from 16 to 9 (see next answer).

11.   A

There are currently *nine* formations:
- General Affairs and External Relations (or GAERC)
- Economic and Financial Affairs (or ECOFIN)
- Agriculture and Fisheries
- Justice and Home Affairs Council (or JHA)
- Employment, Social Policy, Health and Consumer Affairs Council (or EPSCO)
- Competitiveness
- Transport, Telecommunications and Energy
- Environment
- Education, Youth and Culture (or EYC)

12.   A

For a fuller account of the Council formations see answer no.11 above.

13.   C

ECOFIN: Economic and Financial Affairs, Council formation bringing together Economics and Finance Ministers of the Member States.

14.   A

The creation of the Competitiveness Council in June 2002, through the merging of three previous configurations (Internal Market, Industry and Research) was a response to the perceived need for a more coherent and better coordinated handling of these matters related to the European Union's competitiveness. Depending on the items on the agenda, this Council is composed of European Affairs Ministers, Industry Ministers, Research Ministers, etc. It meets about five or six times a year.

Since then, this Council has assumed a horizontal role in ensuring an integrated approach to the enhancement of competitiveness and growth in Europe. In that spirit, it reviews on a regular basis both horizontal and sectoral competitiveness issues on the basis of analyses provided by the Commission and give its views on how competitiveness issues can be properly taken into account in all policy initiatives which have an impact on enterprises. It also deals with legislative proposals in its different fields of activity, where it decides by qualified majority, mostly in codecision with the European Parliament. (*Council Press*)

15.   B

The Secretary General of the Council (who holds the position of High Representative for CFSP) participates in General Affairs and External Relations Council meetings. Article 207(2) of the EC Treaty provides that "[t]he Council shall be assisted by a General Secretariat, under the responsibility of a Secretary-General, High Representative for the common foreign and security policy, who shall be assisted by a Deputy Secretary-General responsible for the running of the General Secretariat. The Secretary-General and the Deputy Secretary-General shall be appointed by the Council acting by a qualified majority". The current Secretary-General of the Council is Mr. Javier Solana.

16.   D

At its sessions on General Affairs, the Council deals with dossiers that affect more than one of the Union's policies, such as negotiations on EU enlargement, preparation of the Union's multi–annual budgetary perspective or institutional and administrative issues. It also exercises a role in coordinating work on different policy areas carried out by the Council's other configurations, and handles any dossier entrusted to it by the European Council. At its sessions on External Relations, the Council deals with the whole of the Union's external action, including common foreign and security policy, European security and defence policy, foreign trade and development cooperation. (*Council*)

17.   C

COREPER is an auxiliary body of the Council, for which it carries out preparation and implementation work. Its function of carrying out the tasks assigned to it by the Council does not give it the power to take decisions which belongs, under the Treaty, to the Council. This means that COREPER is neither an EU institution nor a decision-making body with its own competences. Therefore the guidelines worked out by COREPER may always be called into question by the Council.

18.   A

COREPER meetings take place on a weekly basis. As a rule, COREPER I meets Wednesdays and sometimes Fridays, while COREPER II meets Thursdays. In the weeks preceding the meetings of the Council for General Affairs and the ECOFIN Council, COREPER II meets Wednesdays.

19.   C

The personal assistants of the COREPER members who meet on the day before the COREPER meetings under the name of the MERTENS Group (for COREPER I) and the ANTICI Group (for COREPER II) prepare the COREPER discussions.

20.   B

The "Article 133" Committee was set up in the area of the Common Commercial Policy. Upon authorisation by the Council, the Commission, in consultation with this Committee, conducts negotiations on the conclusion of an agreement between the Community and one or several states or international organisations within the scope of the Common Trade Policy.

21.   D

Set up by Article 36 of the EU Treaty, the coordinating committee for police and judicial cooperation in criminal matters (Article 36 Committee), in addition to its coordinating activities, submits opinions to the Council and contributes to the preparation of Council work.

22.   D

As of 1 November 2004, to pass a vote by qualified majority (QMV), 232 votes should be gathered out of the total of 321 votes (72.27%) and the decision should be backed by a majority of Member States. Further, any Member State may request verification that the Member States constituting a qualified majority represent at least 62% of the EU population. The following number of votes are allocated to the Member States: France, Germany, Italy and the United Kingdom – each 29 votes; Poland and Spain – each 27 votes; Netherlands – each 13 votes; Belgium, Czech Republic, Greece, Hungary and

Portugal – each 12 votes; Austria and Sweden – each 10 votes; Denmark, Finland, Ireland, Lithuania and Slovakia – each 7 votes; Cyprus, Estonia, Latvia, Luxembourg and Slovenia – each 4 votes; Malta – 3 votes.

23.   A

For a fuller account of the voting system in the Council, see answer no. 22 above.

24.   D

Article 47(1) of the EC Treaty provides that "[i]n order to make it easier for persons to take up and pursue activities as self-employed persons, the Council shall, acting in accordance with the procedure referred to in Article 251, issue directives for the mutual recognition of diplomas, certificates and other evidence of formal qualifications."

25.   D

Under Article 202 of the EC Treaty, the Council may confer on the Commission powers for the implementation of the rules laid down by the Council. Also, the Council may impose certain requirements in respect of the exercise of these powers and may reserve the right, in specific cases, to exercise directly implementing powers itself. These procedures "must be consonant with principles and rules to be laid down in advance by the Council, acting unanimously on a proposal from the Commission and after obtaining the opinion of the European Parliament."

26.   A

The Treaty of Nice introduced qualified majority voting with regard to particular "Community incentive measures" to combat discriminatory treatment on the grounds of gender, race or ethnic origin, religion or faith, disability, age or sexual orientation. (See Article 13(2) of the EC Treaty.)

27.   B

According to Article 11(2) of the EC Treaty, autho-risation to establish enhanced cooperation is granted by the Council, acting by a qualified majority on a proposal from the Commission and after consulting the European Parliament. When enhanced cooperation relates to an area covered by the procedure referred to in Article 251 of this Treaty (i.e. codecision procedure), the assent of the European Parliament is required.

28.   A

Although the Council is not obliged to take the European Parliament's opinion into consideration, it cannot pass a decision without first seeking the Parliament's opinion.

29.   C

The assent procedure was introduced by the Single European Act as a way of giving the right of veto to the European Parliament over certain important decisions taken by the Council such as EU mem-bership, uniform electoral procedures, enhanced cooperation in areas falling under codecision pro-cedure, etc. The procedure requires the European Parliament to give its assent by an absolute majority of its total membership in favour of the legislative act in question before the Council could adopt it.

Article 7(1) of the EU Treaty provides that on a reasoned proposal by one third of the Member States, by the European Parliament or by the Commission, the Council, acting by a majority of four fifths of its members after obtaining the assent of the European Parliament, may determine that there is a clear risk of a serious breach by a Member State of principles of liberty, democracy, respect for human rights and fundamental freedoms, and the rule of law, and address appropriate recommen-dations to that State.

30.   A

Article 99(2) of the EC Treaty provides that the Council must inform the European Parliament of its recommendation setting out the broad economic policy guidelines.

31.   C

For a fuller account of the budgetary procedure, see Article 272 of the EC Treaty.

32.   B

In cases where the European Parliament does not have the agreement of the Council on every amendment included in its opinion submitted to the Council (first reading), the Council adopts a common position and communicates it to the Parliament. (For a fuller account of the codecision procedure, see Article 251 of the EC Treaty.)

33.   C

Conciliation is the third and final stage of the code-cision procedure. Under Article 251(3) of the EC Treaty, codecision procedure applies if the Council does not approve all the amendments of the European Parliament adopted at its second read-ing. The Conciliation Committee is made up of twenty-five Members of the Council and an equal number of representatives from the European Parliament (i.e. it has 50 members). As a general rule, the Conciliation Committee has to be con-vened by the President of the Council, in agreement with the President of the European Parliament, within 6 weeks after the Council's second reading.

34.   B

Article 251(4) of the EC Treaty provides that "[t]he Conciliation Committee [...] shall have the task of reaching agreement on a joint text, by a qualified majority of the Members of the Council or their representatives and by a majority of the representatives of the European Parliament."

35. B

The European Council was first recognised in the Single European Act (1986).

36. D

A decision was taken at the 2000 Nice Summit to move all summit meetings to Brussels once the EU has reached 18 Member States.

37. D

See answer no. 36 above.

38. C

According to the Treaties in force, the European Council is not an EU institution. The Constitutional Treaty establishes the European Council as an institution, distinct from the Council.

Under Article 4 of the EU Treaty, the European Council provides the EU with the necessary impetus for its development and defines its general political guidelines and it meets at least twice a year, under the chairmanship of the Head of State or Government of the Member State which holds the Presidency of the Council. In practice, the European Council meets at least four times a year (in line with the decision of the 2002 Seville summit), and special meetings may also be held if exceptional circumstances so require. Since 2000, the March European Council deals with economic, social and environmental issues in line with the Lisbon Strategy.

39. A

Article 207 of the EC Treaty provides that "[a] committee consisting of the Permanent Representatives of the Member States shall be responsible for preparing the work of the Council and for carrying out the tasks assigned to it by the Council. The Committee may adopt procedural decisions in cases provided for in the Council's Rules of Procedure." Prior to submitting any text to the Council for adoption, COREPER attempts to achieve agreement at its level. As a rule, the Council will confirm this agreement.

40. B

Before the entry into force of the Amsterdam Treaty the "Troika" consisted of the Member State holding the Presidency of the Council, the previous and the subsequent Presidents. In its present form the Presidency is assisted by the Secretary-General of the Council, in his capacity as High Representative for the common foreign and security policy, and by the President of the Commission.

EUROPEAN PARLIAMENT
ANSWERS

Question No	A	B	C	D
1.		X		
2.				X
3.		X		
4.			X	
5.		X		
6.		X		
7.			X	
8.			X	
9.	X			
10.			X	
11.	X			
12.				X
13.	X			
14.		X		
15.	X			
16.		X		
17.				X
18.		X		
19.	X			
20.				X
21.				X
22.	X			
23.			X	
24.	X			
25.			X	

Question No	A	B	C	D
26.	X			
27.			X	
28.		X		
29.	X			
30.	X			
31.			X	
32.				X
33.				X
34.	X			
35.		X		
36.	X			
37.	X			
38.				X
39.				X
40.	X			
41.			X	
42.				X
43.				X
44.		X		
45.				X
46.		X		
47.				X
48.		X		
49.	X			
50.			X	

1.   B

The current 2004 - 2009 legislature is the 6th term of the directly elected European Parliament.

2.   D

The European Parliament was elected by direct universal suffrage for the first time in 1979.

3. B

In 1979, 410 Members were elected in the nine Member States (Germany, France, Italy, Belgium, the Netherlands, Luxembourg, Denmark, Ireland and the United Kingdom).

4. C

According to Article 190(4) of the EC Treaty (provision inserted by the Maastricht Treaty), the European Parliament is responsible for drawing up a proposal for elections by direct universal suffrage in accordance with a uniform procedure in all Member States or in accordance with principles common to all Member States. The Council lays down (acting unanimously after obtaining the absolute majority based assent of the European Parliament) the appropriate provisions and the Member States adopt such provisions in accordance with their respective constitutional requirements.

5. B

According to the decision of national governments reached at the EU summit in Edinburgh in 1992, the seat of the Parliament is in Strasbourg. A protocol annexed to the Amsterdam Treaty confirmed the Edinburgh decision which is: "The European Parliament shall have its seat in Strasbourg where the twelve periods of monthly plenary sessions, including the budget session, shall be held. The periods of additional plenary sessions shall be held in Brussels. The committees of the European Parliament shall meet in Brussels. The General Secretariat of the European Parliament and its departments shall remain in Luxembourg."

6. B

The Amsterdam Treaty set the maximum number of MEPs at 700.

7. C

The Treaty of Nice set the maximum number of MEPs at 732.

8. C

The term of office of the President, the Vice-Presidents and the Quaestors is two and a half years.

9. A

The Bureau consists of the President and the fourteen Vice-Presidents of Parliament. The Quaestors are members of the Bureau only in an advisory capacity.

10. C

The EP elects five Quaestors. The term of office of Quaestors, as well as of the other officials, is two and a half years.

11. A

A quorum exists when at least one third of the component Members of Parliament are present in the Chamber.

12. D

According to Rule 29 of the Rules of Procedure of the European Parliament, a political group in the European Parliament needs to comprise Members elected in at least one-fifth of Member States.

For further information, see:
http://www.europarl.eu.int/home/default_en.htm

13. A

Under the above Rules of Procedure the minimum number of Members required to form a political group is 19.

14. B

Greens/EFA is the fourth largest political group in the EP.

Political groups in the EP are as follows:

- Group of the European People's Party (Christian Democrats) and European Democrats (EPP-ED) (268 members)
- Group of the Party of European Socialists (PES) (202 members)
- Group of the Alliance of Liberals and Democrats for Europe (ELDR) (88 members)
- Group of the Greens/European Free Alliance (Greens/EFA) (42 members)
- Confederal Group of the European United Left/Nordic Green Left (EUL/NGL) (41 members)
- Independence/Democracy Group (ID) (36 members)
- Union for Europe of the Nations Group (UENG) (27 members)
- The non-attached/independent members (NI) (28 members)

15. A

Parliamentary Committees: Internal Policies (17)
- BUDG – Budgets
- CONT – Budgetary Control
- ECON – Economic and Monetary Affairs
- EMPL – Employment and Social Affairs
- ENVI – the Environment, Public Health and Food Safety
- ITRE – Industry, Research and Energy
- IMCO – Internal Market and Consumer Protection
- TRAN – Transport and Tourism
- REGI – Regional Development
- AGRI – Agriculture
- PECH – Fisheries
- CULT – Culture and Education
- JURI – Legal Affairs
- LIBE – Civil Liberties, Justice and Home Affairs
- AFCO – Constitutional Affairs
- FEMM – Women's Rights and Gender Equality
- PETI – Petitions

Parliamentary Committees: External Policies (3)
- AFET – Foreign Affairs
  - DROI – Subcommittee on Human Rights
  - SEDE – Subcommittee on Security and Defence
- DEVE – Development
- INTA – International Trade

Since the adoption of the Maastricht Treaty, temporary *Committees of Inquiry* may also be set up by a vote of Parliament (e.g. on transport, on BSE, Echelon, Human Genetics, Safety at Sea).

16. B

The Conciliation Committee has 50 members: 25 Members of the European Parliament and 25 representatives from the Council, corresponding to the number of Member States.

17. D

The European Centre for Parliamentary Research and Documentation (ECPRD) is a cooperative body operating under the aegis of the European Parliament and the Parliamentary Assembly of the Council of Europe. It is primarily an international network of research and documentation departments, but it also brings together officials responsible for information gathering and dissemination and the preparation of legislation. Its aim is to facilitate contacts and exchanges between the officials of member parliaments. The ECPRD was founded in 1977 in Vienna by the Conference of Speakers of European Parliamentary Assemblies, which delegated the task of setting up and administering the Centre to the Presidents of the European Parliament and the Parliamentary Assembly of the Council of Europe.

18.   B

STOA: the Parliament's own Scientific and Technological Options Assessment unit. STOA's work is carried out in partnership with external experts. These can be research institutes, universities, laboratories, consultancies or individual researchers contracted to help prepare specific projects. These increasingly comprise round-table expert discussions, conferences and workshops with associated or consequent studies at which members of Parliament and invited experts from EU institutions, international institutions, universities, specialist institutes, academies and other sources of expertise worldwide can jointly participate in the analysis of current issues. (*European Parliament*)

19.   A

Proposed by the President of the French National Assembly, the conference has met every six months since 1989, bringing together the National Parliaments' bodies specialising in European Community Affairs and six MEPs, headed by the two Vice-Presidents responsible for relations with national parliaments. Convened by the parliament of the country holding the presidency of the Community and prepared jointly by the EP and the parliaments of the presidency "troika", each conference discusses the major topics of European integration. COSAC is not a decision-making but a consultation and coordination body that adopts its decisions by consensus.
(*http://www.europarl.eu.int/factsheets/1_3_5_en.htm*)

20.   D

On 20 July 2004 Josep Borrell Fontelles was elected President of the European Parliament with 388 MEPs voting for him (with 700 votes cast). Borrell's victory was expected following an agreement between the Parliament's two biggest groups – the European People's Party (EPP-ED) and European Socialists (PES) – to share the Parliament's presidency. Under the deal, centre-right MEPs agreed to support Borrell to lead the Parliament for the first half of its term and Socialist MEPs are to return the favour and support a centre-right candidate (probably German MEP Hans-Gert Pöttering) for the second half. (*EurActiv*)

21.   D

The democratic deficit is a concept invoked principally in the argument that the European Union suffers from a lack of democracy and seems inaccessible and not transparent enough to the ordinary citizen because its method of operating is so complex. The view is that the Community institutional set-up is dominated by an institution combining legislative and government powers (the Council) and an institution that lacks democratic legitimacy (the Commission – even though its Members are appointed by the Member States and are collectively accountable to Parliament). As European integration has progressed, the question of democratic legitimacy has become increasingly sensitive. The Maastricht, Amsterdam and Nice Treaties have triggered the inclusion of the principle of democratic legitimacy within the institutional system by reinforcing the powers of Parliament with regard to the appointment and control of the Commission and successively extending the scope of the codecision procedure.

The Constitutional Treaty aims at putting an end to the democratic deficit problem by making the codecision procedure the ordinary legislative procedure in EU lawmaking.
(*ScadPlus*)

22.   A

On 25 March 2004, Pat Cox, the President of the EP, made this statement urging EU leaders to find the political will with the aim of completing the negotiations on the Constitutional Treaty before the European elections.

23.   C

The participation figure was about 45.5 per cent for the EU as a whole, with a participation of 47.1 per cent in the EU-15 and of 26.4 per cent of eligible voters in the "new" Member States.

24.   A

Pat Cox MEP (liberal) was the President of the EP for a term between 2002 and 2004.

25.   C

From 1976 to 1986 Altiero Spinelli, founder of the Movimento Federalista Europeo (European Federalist Movement), was a Member of the European Parliament, but he was never elected President.

Presidents of the Common Assembly (1952-1958)

Dates in office	Name	Group	Country
1952-1954	Paul Henri Spaak	Socialist	Belgium
1954 (died in office August 19)	Alcide De Gasperi	Christian Democrat	Italy
1954-1956	Giuseppe Pella	Christian Democrat	Italy
1956-1958	Hans Furler	Christian Democrat	Germany

Presidents of the Parliamentary Assembly (1958-1962)

Dates in office	Name	Group	Country
1958-1960	Robert Schuman	Christian Democrat	France
1960-1962	Hans Furler	Christian Democrat	Germany

Presidents of the appointed Parliament (1962-1979)

Dates in office	Name	Group	Country
1962-1964	Gaetano Martino	Liberal	Italy
1964-1965	Jean Pierre Duvieusart	Christian Democrat	Belgium
1965-1966	Victor Leemans	Christian Democrat	Netherlands
1966-1969	Alain Poher	Christian Democrat	France
1969-1971	Mario Scelba	Christian Democrat	Italy
1971-1973	Walter Behrendt	Socialist	Germany
1973-1975	Cornelis Berkhouwer	Liberal	Netherlands
1975-1977	Georges Spénale	Socialist	France
1977-1979	Emilio Colombo	Christian Democrat	Italy

Presidents of the directly elected Parliament (1979–)

Dates in office	Name	Group	Country
1979-1982	Simone Veil	LDR	France
1982-1984	Piet Dankert	Socialist	Netherlands
1984-1987	Pierre Pflimlin	UDF/RPR	France
1987-1989	Lord Plumb	ED	UK
1989-1992	Enrique Barón Crespo	Socialist	Spain
1992-1994	Egon Klepsch	EPP	Germany
1994-1997	Klaus Hänsch	Socialist	Germany
1997-1999	José Maria Gil-Robles	EPP	Spain
1999-2002	Nicole Fontaine	EPP	France
2002-2004	Pat Cox	ELDR	Ireland
2004-2006	Josep Borrell Fontelles	PES	Spain

26.   A

The Interinstitutional Agreement sets out best practice and lays down new objectives and commitments, including:

*   The improvement of interinstitutional coordination and transparency
*   The establishment of a sound framework for "alternative instruments"
*   The increased use of impact analyses in the Community decision-making process
*   The desire to establish a mandatory time limit for transposing directives into national law

27.   C

The consultation procedure continues to apply to agriculture, taxation, competition, harmonisation of legislation not related to the internal market, industrial policy, aspects of social and environmental policy (subject to unanimity), most aspects of creating an area of freedom, security and justice, and adoption of general rules and principles for "comitology". This procedure also applies to the "framework-decision" instrument created by the Amsterdam Treaty under the third pillar for the purpose of approximation of laws and regulations. (*Eur-lex – Process and players*)

28.   B

29.   A

30.   A

The assent procedure mainly applies to the accession of new Member States (Article 49 of the EU Treaty), association agreements and other fundamental agreements with third countries (Article 300 of the EC Treaty), and the appointment of the President of the Commission. It is also required with regard to citizenship issues, the specific tasks of the European Central Bank (ECB), amendments to the Statutes of the European System of Central Banks and the ECB, the Structural and Cohesion Funds, and the uniform procedure for elections to the European Parliament. Since entry into force of the Amsterdam Treaty, the Parliament's assent has also been required for sanctions imposed on a Member State for a serious and persistent breach of fundamental rights under the new Article 7 of the EU Treaty. The Treaty of Nice has made the Parliament's assent mandatory where reinforced cooperation between certain Member States is envisaged in an area which is subject to the codecision procedure.

31.   C

The Amsterdam Treaty strengthened the legislative role of the Parliament vis-à-vis the Council. The number of areas subject to the codecision procedure under Article 251 of the EC Treaty was more than doubled from 15 to 38 and later increased to 43 by the Treaty of Nice. Codecision procedure is set to become the legislative procedure par excellence following the entry into force of the Constitution.

32.   D

Article 310 of the EC Treaty provides that the Community may conclude with one or more States or international organisations agreements that establish an association involving reciprocal rights and obligations, common action and special procedure. According to Article 300(3) of the EC Treaty, such agreements may be concluded only after the assent of the European Parliament has been obtained.

33.   D

Under Article 106(2) of the EC Treaty, the adoption of legal rules on harmonisation of the denomination and technical specifications of euro coins are subject to the cooperation procedure.

34.   A

According to Article 52(1) of the EC Treaty, "[i]n order to achieve the liberalisation of a specific service, the Council shall, on a proposal from the Commission and after consulting the Economic and Social Committee and the European Parliament, issue directives acting by a qualified majority."

35.   B

Article 195(2) of the EC Treaty provides that "[t]he Ombudsman shall be appointed after each election of the European Parliament for the duration of its term of office."

36.   A

Article 13(2) of the EC Treaty provides that Community incentive measures (except any harmonisation of national laws) targeted to support action taken by the Member States in order to contribute to the achievement of the objectives set out in the first paragraph of Article 13 (i.e. action to combat discrimination), are subject to codecision procedure.

37.   A

Article 194 of the EC Treaty provides that any citizen of the Union, and any natural or legal person residing or having its registered office in a Member State, shall have the right to address, individually or in association with other citizens or persons, a petition to the European Parliament on a matter which comes within the Community's fields of activity and which affects him, her or it directly.

38.   D

According to the amendments brought about by the The Treaty of Nice, Article 230 of the EC Treaty provides that any natural or legal person may, under the same conditions, institute proceedings against a decision addressed to that person or against a decision which, although in the form of a regulation or a decision addressed to another person, is of direct and individual concern to the former.

39.   D

According to Article 13 of the EU Treaty, the European Council defines the principles of and general guidelines for the common foreign and security policy, including for matters with defence implications.

40.   A

Article 272(4) of the EC Treaty provides that Parliament has the right to amend the draft budget, acting by a majority of its Members, and to propose to the Council, acting by an absolute majority of the votes cast, modifications to the draft budget relating to expenditure necessarily resulting from the EC or from acts adopted in accordance with it (i.e. compulsory expenditures).

41.   C

Article 49 of the EU Treaty provides that any European state that respects the principles set out in Article 6(1) of the EU Treaty (i.e. liberty, democracy, respect for human rights and fundamental freedoms, as well as the rule of law) may apply to become a member of the EU by addressing its application to the Council which will act unanimously after consulting the Commission and after receiving the assent of the European Parliament acting by an absolute majority of its component members.

42.   D

If no Member State objects or calls for a unanimous decision in the European Council ("emergency brake"), enhanced cooperation (aimed at implementing a joint action or a common position on issues that do not have any military or defence implications) is adopted by the Council through qualified majority voting on a proposal from the Commission and after consulting the European Parliament. Further, when enhanced cooperation relates to an area covered by codecision procedure, the assent of the European Parliament must be obtained.

43.   D

As a matter of fact, there is no legal basis for the President's presence at European Council meetings, he/she only participates on the basis of tradition.

44.   B

As regards the movement of capital to or from third countries (see Article 57(2) of the EC Treaty), Parliament does not have a say at all.

45.   D

The European Court of Justice (ECJ) has no such reporting obligation towards any of the EU institutions.

46.   C

Rule 66 of the Rules of Procedure of the European Parliament provides that the text of acts adopted jointly by Parliament and the Council must be signed by the President and by the Secretary-General, once it has been verified that all the procedures have been duly completed.

47.   D

Under Article 201 of the EC Treaty, if the motion of censure is carried by a two-thirds majority of the votes cast, representing a majority of the Members of the European Parliament, the Members of the Commission must resign as a body. It is understood that Commissioners cannot be censured individually.

48.   C

The Amsterdam Treaty gave the Parliament power to approve or reject the nomination of the Commission President.

49.   A

Article 139 of the EC Treaty confers no role on the European Parliament in respect of the European Social Dialogue.

50.   C

A motion of censure requires the support of an absolute majority of the European Parliament's component members and two-thirds of the votes cast. To date, no motion of censure has been adopted by the Parliament. However, in March 1999, following a report on the Commission's management by a committee of independent experts mandated by Parliament, the Commission opted to resign rather than face formal censure by Parliament.

EUROPEAN COMMISSION
ANSWERS

Question No	A	B	C	D
1.			X	
2.		X		
3.		X		
4.	X			
5.				X
6.			X	
7.	X			
8.		X		
9.		X		
10.				X
11.			X	
12.	X			
13.		X		
14.				X
15.			X	
16.			X	
17.		X		
18.	X			
19.	X			
20.		X		
21.		X		
22.			X	
23.		X		
24.			X	
25.	X			
26.				X
27.	X			
28.				X

Question No	A	B	C	D
29.	X			
30.			X	
31.		X		
32.			X	
33.				X
34.				X
35.		X		
36.	X			
37.			X	
38.				X
39.		X		
40.		X		
41.	X			
42.		X		
43.	X			
44.			X	
45.	X			
46.			X	
47.		X		
48.				X
49.		X		
50.	X			
51.	X			
52.			X	
53.			X	
54.				X
55.	X			

1.   C

Markos Kyprianou, Commissioner responsible for Health and Consumer Protection, does not have the role of Vice-President. The Vice-Presidents of the Barroso Commission are:
- Jacques Barrot (French), Transport
- Siim Kallas (Estonian), Administrative Affairs, Audit and Anti-Fraud
- Günter Verheugen (German), Enterprise and Industry
- Margot Wallström (Swedish), Institutional Relations and Communication Strategy
- Franco Frattini (Italian), Justice, Freedom and Security

2.   B

After heated debates, political discussions and re-nomination of some Commissioners, the Barroso

Commission took office on 22 November 2004 after the approval of the European Parliament as required by the Treaty.

3.   B

According to Article 1.1.1 of the Code of Conduct of Commissioners:

"Commissioners shall notify the President if they are intending to publish a book during their term as Commissioner. Royalties from copyright in a work published in connection with their duties shall be paid over to a charity of their choice."

For further information, see:

http://europa.eu.int/comm/commission_barroso/code_of _conduct/code_conduct_en.pdf

4.   A

Article 1.2.5 of the Code of Conduct of Commissioners (see above) sets out:

"Acceptance of gifts, decorations or honours. Commissioners shall not accept any gift with a value of more than EUR 150. When, in accordance with diplomatic usage, they receive gifts worth more than this amount, they shall hand them over to the Commission's Protocol department. In case of doubt as to the value of a gift, an evaluation shall be undertaken under the authority of the Director of the Office for Infrastructure and Logistics in Brussels, whose decision on the matter shall be final. The Commission's Protocol department shall keep a public register of gifts with a value of more than EUR 150. Commissioners shall notify the President of the Commission of any decoration, prize or honour awarded to them."

5.   D

Annex I of the Code of Conduct of Commissioners (see above) requires the Commissioners to declare their interests in the following fields:

Outside activities (posts in foundations or similar bodies, posts held over the last 10 years, posts currently held, posts held in educational institutions, posts held over the last 10 years)

Financial interests (shares, name of company,

number of shares, total current value, other stock, company, number of securities, total current value)

Assets (real estate, other property)

Spouse's professional activity

6.   C

The Prodi Commission, according to the previous system where each Member State could delegate one Commissioner and the "big five" could delegate two, had twenty Commissioners. However, due to the fact that their mandate was from 1 November 1999 until 31 October 2004 and the enlargement took place on 1 May 2004, ten new Commissioners from the ten "new" Member States temporarily joined the college, creating a thirty-member Commission. As soon as the Barroso Commission took office on 22 November 2004, the "one Commissioner per Member State" principle was applied; therefore the number of Commissioners was reduced to and is today 25.

7.   A

It was the Maastricht Treaty that brought the terms of office of the European Parliament and the Commission into close alignment: the College of Commissioners serves a five-year term and takes up office six months after European Parliament elections. This latter is held on a fixed basis in June every five years. The Members of the European Parliament (MEPs) are elected for a term of 5 years.

8.   B

Commission Green Papers are documents intended to stimulate debate and launch a process of consultation at European level on a particular topic (such as social policy, the single currency, telecommunications). These consultations may then lead to the publication of a White Paper, translating the conclusions of the debate into practical proposals for Community action.

Blue papers do not exist in the legislative domain. However, the names of all pre-selected candidates for traineeship at an EU institution appear in a database, which is available to all

Commission departments for the final selection process. This database is known as the virtual "Blue Book" and contains approximately 2500-3000 names.

9.   B

The European Commission is divided into 26 Directorates-General (generally referred to as DGs) and nine Services, which are divided into Directorates and Directorates are further divided into Units.

10.   D

Decisions are taken collectively on proposals coming from one or more Commissioners. The Commission decides by simple majority; if there is equality of votes, the voice of the President is decisive.

There are four ways to take decisions:
- Firstly, at meetings (normally convened once a week) – a vote can be requested by any member of the Commission;
- Secondly, by written procedure – the proposal is circulated in writing to all the members of the Commission, who then communicate their reservations and/or amendments within a certain time limit. A member of the Commission can request a discussion, if s/he thinks it would be useful. If no reservations or amendments are communicated, the proposal is adopted by the Commission;
- Thirdly, by empowerment – the Commission can empower one or more of its members to make a decision, as long as the principle of collective responsibility is respected. These powers of decision can, under certain conditions, be sub-delegated to directors-general and heads of service in the same way;
- Fourthly, by delegation – the Commission can delegate the taking of certain decisions to directors-general and heads of service, who would then act on its behalf.

(http://europa.eu.int/comm/atwork/basicfacts)

11.   C

In order to make European lawmaking more efficient, transparent and clear, the Commission has introduced several new features to its processes. The three main areas of its "Better lawmaking" action plan, adopted in June 2002 are:
- simplifying and improving the regulatory environment – in order to improve access to EU law;
- promoting a culture of dialogue and participation, in order for everyone concerned, even the smallest voices, to be heard during the lawmaking process;
- systematising impact assessment by the Commission, in order to ensure that both the benefits and costs of implementing a piece of legislation are clear in advance.

(http://europa.eu.int/comm/atwork/basicfacts)

12.   A

The database "Consultation, the European Commission and Civil Society" (CONECCS) provides information about civil society actors, operating at European Union level, who represent views on a wide range of European policy. CONECCS offers this information at two levels:
- A list of non-profit Pan European civil society organizations – a "Who is who?" and "Who does what?" in the representation of European civil society interests.
- A list of the Commission's formal and other structured civil society consultation bodies; in other words, its regular dialogue partners in the process of policy development.

For further information, see:
http://europa.eu.int/comm/civil_society/coneccs/

13.   B

In their dealings with the EU, according to the Code of Conduct for consultants, the practitioners must:
- identify themselves by name and by company;
- declare the interest represented;
- neither intentionally misrepresent their status nor the nature of their inquiries to offi-

cials of the EU institutions nor create any false impression in relation thereto;
- neither directly nor indirectly misrepresent links with EU institutions;
- honour confidential information given to them;
- not disseminate false or misleading information knowingly or recklessly and shall exercise proper care to avoid doing so inadvertently;
- not sell for profit to third parties copies of documents obtained from EU institutions;
- not obtain information from EU institutions by dishonest means;
- avoid any professional conflicts of interest;
- neither directly nor indirectly offer nor give any financial inducement to:
  - any EU official, nor
  - Member of the European Parliament, nor
  - their staff;
- neither propose nor undertake any action which would constitute an improper influence on them;
- only employ EU personnel subject to the rules and confidentiality requirements of the EU institution.

14.   D

In order to strengthen the means of fraud prevention, the Commission established within itself the European Anti-Fraud Office (OLAF) by EC, ECSC Decision 1999/352 of 28 April 1999. OLAF was given responsibility for conducting administrative anti-fraud investigations by having conferred on it a special independent status.

For further information, see:
http://europa.eu.int/comm/dgs/olaf/mission/mission/index_en.html

15.   C

Joe Borg (born in 1952), former Maltese Minister of Foreign Affairs, is the Barroso Commission's Commissioner for Fisheries and Maritime Affairs.

16.   C

Louis Michel (born in 1947), former Belgian Minister of Foreign Affairs, is the European Commissioner for Development and Humanitarian Aid.

17.   B

Based on Mr. Barroso's special request to the Member States to designate women Commissioners, there are six women in his College:

Margot Wallström, Swedish, Institutional Relations and Communication Strategy

Viviane Reding, Luxembourgish, Information Society and Media

Danuta Hübner, Polish, Regional Policy

Dalia Grybauskait, Lithuanian, Financial Programming and Budget

Neelie Kroes, Dutch, Competition

Mariann Fischer Boel, Danish, Agriculture and Rural Development

Benita Ferrero-Waldner, Austrian, External Relations and European Neighborhood Policy

18.   A

Joaquín Almunia (Spanish, born in 1948), is now the Commissioner responsible for Economic and Monetary Affairs. In the Prodi Commission, Günter Verheugen was responsible for enlargement, Viviane Reding was responsible for culture, and Margaret Wallström was responsible for environment.

19.   A

Günter Verheugen (German, born in 1944), currently Vice-President of the European Commission in charge of Enterprise and Industry was responsible for enlargement issues in the Prodi Commission. His colleague, Olli Rehn (Finnish, born in 1962) is currently the Commissioner responsible for the European Union's enlargement policy.

20.   B

Ján Figel (Slovak, born in 1960) is the Commissioner responsible for Education, Training, Culture and Multilingualism. His area of responsibility also covers sport, youth and relations with civil society. As he puts it, "there is one recurring theme throughout my whole portfolio – the citizens and their quality of life. The building of a citizen-friendly environment will be at the centre of all my activities."

21.   B

No.	Name	Commission	Assumed office	Left office	Member State
1	Walter Hallstein	Hallstein Commission	1958	1967	West Germany
2	Jean Ray	Ray Commission	1967	1970	Belgium
3	Franco Maria Malfatti	Malfatti Commission	1970	1972	Italy
4	Sicco L. Mansholt	Mansholt Commission	1972	1972	Netherlands
5	Francois-Xavier Ortoli	Ortoli Commission	1973	1977	France
6	Roy Jenkins	Jenkins Commission	1977	1981	United Kingdom
7	Gaston Edmont Thorn	Thorn Commission	12 January 1981	1985	Luxembourg
8	Jacques Delors	Delors Commission	1985	1995	France
9	Jacques Santer	Santer Commission	1995	15 March 1999	Luxembourg
10	Romano Prodi	Prodi Commission	September 1999	22 November 2004	Italy
11	José Manuel Durão Barroso	Barroso Commission	22 November 2004	(Present office-holder)	Portugal

Wikipedia

22.   C

Article 212 of the EC Treaty provides:
"The Commission shall publish annually, not later than one month before the opening of the session of the European Parliament, a general report on the activities of the Community."

23.   B

Article 216 of the EC Treaty provides:
"If any Member of the Commission no longer fulfils the conditions required for the performance of his duties or if he has been guilty of serious misconduct, the Court of Justice may, on application by the Council or the Commission, compulsorily retire him."

24.   C

The External Service has come a long way since the opening of the first diplomatic mission in London in late 1955 by the High Authority of the European Coal and Steel Community. Following the entry into force in 1967 of the Treaty merging the executive institutions of the three European Communities (Merger Treaty), the new single Commission took over the already existing delegations and in the course of the following decades set up delegations in all the major capitals and seats of International Organizations in the world. During the same period a network of delegates was created to implement co-operation and partnership agreements concluded with countries or groups of countries. Until recently, however, not all of them had the full status of diplomatic mission.

Reflecting the growing importance of external representation and the increasing number of tasks conferred upon delegations, the Commission in 1994 decided to establish a Unified External Service, a single management system for all its Delegations operating in third countries and with International Organizations.

The External Service, originally set up essentially to represent the European Commission in trade negotiations and in some industrialized countries, and to undertake development co-operation activities under the Yaoundé and Lomé Conventions, has evolved over time to reflect the growing ambition and capacity of the European Union in external relations. The establishment of the Single Market and the development of new policy areas, in particular the Common Foreign and Security Policy (CFSP) have created new challenges and expectations for the external representation of the Union. This trend was reinforced by the creation in the Amsterdam Treaty of the European Security and Defense Policy and the High representative for CFSP.

For further information, see:
http://europa.eu.int/comm/external_relations/

25.   A

Established in 1994, the Translation Centre's mission is to meet the translation needs of the other decentralised Community agencies; however, it does not work under the auspices of the Commission. In addition it participates in the Inter-institutional Committee for Translation and Interpretation, which works to promote collaboration between the services based on the principle of subsidiarity and to achieve economies of scale in the translation field.

For further information, see:
http://www.cdt.eu.int/

26.   D

Second sub-paragraph of Article 215 EC, as amended by the Treaty of Nice, provides:
"A vacancy caused by resignation, compulsory retirement or death shall be filled for the remainder of the Member's term of office by a new Member appointed by the Council, acting by a qualified majority. The Council may, acting unanimously, decide that such a vacancy need not be filled."

27.   A

The Commission applies the following grouping on its website:

POLICIES

Agriculture and Rural Development
Competition
Economic and Financial Affairs
Education and Culture

Employment, Social Affairs and Equal Opportunities
Enterprise and Industry
Environment
Fisheries and Maritime Affairs
Health and Consumer Protection
Information Society and Media
Internal Market and Services
Joint Research Centre
Justice, Freedom and Security
Regional Policy
Research
Taxation and Customs Union
Transport and Energy

EXTERNAL RELATIONS

Development
Enlargement
EuropeAid - Co-operation Office
External Relations
Humanitarian Aid Office - ECHO
Trade

GENERAL SERVICES

European Anti-Fraud Office
Eurostat
Press and Communication
Publications Office
Secretariat General

INTERNAL SERVICES

Budget
Group of Policy Advisers
Informatics
Infrastructures and Logistics
Internal Audit Service
Interpretation
Legal Service
Personnel and Administration
Translation
(http://www.europarl.eu.int/comm/dgs_en.htm)

28.   D

According to the Eurobarometer, the following surveys exist:

Standard Eurobarometer (EB)

The standard Eurobarometer was established in 1973. Each survey consists of approximately 1000 face-to-face interviews per Member State (except Germany: 2000, Luxembourg: 600, United Kingdom 1300 including 300 in Northern Ireland). Conducted between 2 and 5 times per year, with reports published twice yearly.

Special Eurobarometer (EB)

Special Eurobarometer reports are based on in-depth thematic studies carried out for various services of the European Commission or other EU institutions and integrated in Standard Eurobarometer's polling waves.

Candidate Countries Eurobarometer (CCEB)

First wave carried out in October 2001 in all the 13 countries applying for membership. Its methodology is almost identical to that of the Standard Eurobarometer. One report is published each year, excluding the special reports. It replaces the Central and Eastern Eurobarometer (CEEB).

Flash Eurobarometer (EB)

Ad hoc thematic telephone interviews conducted at the request of any service of the European Commission or other EU Institutions. The Flash Eurobarometer surveys enable the Commission to obtain results relatively quickly and to focus on specific target groups, as and when required (e.g. doctors, SMEs, etc.)

Qualitative Study

The qualitative studies investigate in-depth the motivations, the feelings, the reactions of selected social groups towards a given subject or concept, by listening and analysing their way of expressing themselves in discussion groups or with non-directive interviews.

For further information, see:

http://europa.eu.int/comm/public_opinion/description_en.htm

29.   A

The external trade administration of the European Commission, Directorate General Trade, is the negotiator, responsible for conducting trade negotiations. It is also the enforcer, responsible for ensuring compliance by third countries with international trade accords. The final decision maker, however, is the Council. Before negotiations start, it issues "directives for negotiation" to guide the Commission in its work and decides ultimately, whether to adopt an accord. The European Parliament is associated with the overall conduct of

European Union trade policy and it is kept regularly informed by the Commission.

30.   C

1999/468/EC Council Decision of 28 June 1999 laying down the procedures for the exercise of implementing powers conferred on the Commission, which is also known as the Comitology Decision. You may find a detailed description of Comitology in the section dealing with the decision-making procedures.

31.   B

After comprehensive internal consultation, the Commission presented its White Paper on Reform at the beginning of 2000. "A culture based on service" ,the administrative reform proposals introduce a new approach to management based on the principles of responsibility, accountability, efficiency and transparency. The White Paper included an Action Plan of nearly 100 specific actions and a challenging schedule for implementation. The White Paper eventually led to the New Staff Regulations.

The strategy indicated in the White Paper had three main objectives:

*   Improving the effectiveness of the organisation through better priority setting and matching of tasks with resources. A new activity-based management (ABM) approach is proposed with the aim of clearly defining the Commission's priorities and ensuring that the human and financial resources for achieving them are available;
*   Maximising staff performance through considerable changes in human resource management and staff policy;
*   An overhaul of financial management to improve efficiency and accountability. A new audit service is to be created, overseen by the Vice-President for Reform, designed to ensure the Commission is getting value for money and this money is not being misused.

32.   C

The Commissioners meet on Wednesday each week in Brussels. During the European Parliament's plenary sessions the meeting is usually held in Strasbourg. Preparing the agenda and the documents on the agenda for the meeting is one of the fundamental tasks of the Secretariat-General's registry. This agenda is adopted each week by the President of the Commission on the basis of the Commission's annual work programme. The final agenda is circulated to the Members of the Commission by no later than 17.00 on the day before the meeting.

33.   D

Article 217(4) of the EC Treaty provides the following:

"A Member of the Commission shall resign if the President so requests, after obtaining the approval of the College."

This change was introduced by the Treaty of Nice as the Commission president had no such right before.

34.   D

When the European Community has an exclusive competence, Member States are not permitted to make their own laws concerning that area. In case of a shared competence both the EC and the Member States may make laws, but the former suppress any adopted national law, and suppress the right to make national laws in the area covered by a "European law". In case of subsidiarity, it may apply only in cases where the area concerned does not fall within the Community's exclusive competence.

The Community's exclusive competences are the following:

*   competition rules within the internal market;
*   customs union;
*   conclusion of international agreements;
*   monetary policy for Euro countries;
*   conservation of marine biological resources under the common fisheries policy;
*   common commercial policy – however, Article 133(6) EC provides the following exception (emphasis added):

"An agreement may not be concluded by the Council if it includes provisions which would go beyond the Community's internal powers, in particular by leading to harmonisation of the laws or regulations of the Member States in an area for which this Treaty rules out such harmonisation.

In this regard, by way of derogation from the first subparagraph of paragraph 5, agreements relating to trade in cultural and audiovisual services, educational services, and social and human health services, shall fall within the shared competence of the Community and its Member States. Consequently, in addition to a Community decision taken in accordance with the relevant provisions of Article 300, the negotiation of such agreements shall require the common accord of the Member States. Agreements thus negotiated shall be concluded jointly by the Community and the Member States.

The negotiation and conclusion of international agreements in the field of transport shall continue to be governed by the provisions of Title V and Article 300."

35.   B

The Commission is constructed like the French central administration, in a very hierarchical structure where civil servants are supposed to be linked only to their next-in-command. The lower levels are not allowed to make decisions, but must rely on orders from above. Within the framework of a constant and ongoing process, the Commission makes significant efforts to improve the efficiency and openness of the administration.

36.   A

The Commission adopted its White Paper on European Governance in July 2001 with the aim of establishing more democratic forms of governance at all levels: global, European, national, regional and local. The White Paper forwards a set of proposals focusing on the role of the EU institutions, better involvement, better regulation, and the contribution the European Union can make to world governance. Most of the Commission's governance reforms are to be implemented immediately under the existing treaties. These efforts are to complement the phase of institutional reform launched by the Laeken

Declaration of December 2001, continuing with the Convention on the Future of the European Union, and culminating in the Intergovernmental Conference of 2004 and eventually the Constitutional Treaty.

For further information, see:
http://europa.eu.int/eur-lex/en/com/cnc/2001/com2001_0428en01.pdf

37.   C

Europe Direct is a Commission campaign since 1998 to make citizens aware of their rights under EU law regarding free movement, citizenship etc. and to answer citizens' questions. The Commission has established a free service for information on the European Union. The free phone number is: 00-800-6-7-8-9-10-11 from any Member State or (+32) 2-299-96-96 from outside the EU.

For further information, see:
http://europa.eu.int/europedirect/index_en.htm

38.   D

Article 202 of the EC Treaty provides the following (emphasis added):

"To ensure that the objectives set out in this Treaty are attained the Council shall, in accordance with the provisions of this Treaty:
–   ensure coordination of the general economic policies of the Member States,
–   have power to take decisions,
–   confer on the Commission, in the acts which the Council adopts, *powers for the implementation of the rules which the Council lays down*. The Council may impose certain requirements in respect of the exercise of these powers. *The Council may also reserve the right, in specific cases, to exercise directly implementing powers itself.* The procedures referred to above must be consonant with principles and rules to be laid down in advance by the Council, acting unanimously on a proposal from the Commission and after obtaining the opinion of the European Parliament."

39.   B

The President appoints the Commissioners in agreement with the governments of the Member States. He entrusts each of them with particular policy areas. After a series of individual hearings before Parliamentary committees, the candidate-Commissioners are subject as a body to a vote of approval by the European Parliament. The President and the other Members of the Commission are then appointed by the Council.

The Constitutional Treaty has adopted a similar solution to that of the Treaty of Nice, by maintaining one Commissioner per Member State up to a certain size, and subsequent capping of the size of the College, with equal rotation between Member States.

The Constitutional Treaty provides that the first Commission appointed under the provisions of the Constitution (probably the Commission in 2009) shall consist of one national from each Member State, including its President and the Foreign Affairs Minister.

As from 2014 the Commission will be reduced in size and consist of a number of members corresponding to two-thirds of the number of Member States. The European Council unanimously may nevertheless decide to change this number.

In the reduced-size Commission, the Commissioners will be selected according to a system of equal rotation between Member States. This system will be established by a European decision adopted unanimously by the European Council. Member States shall be treated on a strictly equal footing regarding the sequence of, and the time spent by, their nationals as members of the Commission. Each successive Commission must reflect adequately the demographic and geographical range of all the Member States.
(*ScadPlus*)

40.   B

Instead of amending the existing Treaties, the Commission, Parliament and the Council may adopt semi-constitutional law by reaching a common agreement. These so-called "inter-institutional agreements" are binding on the contracting institutions.

41.   A

The Berlaymont building, designed by Jean Gilson and Jean and André Polak, is the star-shaped, recently re-opened headquarters of the Commission in Brussels. The 13 storey building is again housing the Commissioners on the upper floor, but it had to be evacuated in 1992 and renovated following the discovery of asbestos. Situated on the Rue de la Loi in Brussels, it has a surface of more than 240,000 square metres.

The area in Luxembourg where most EU institutions are located is called Kirchberg.

42.   B

Jacques Delors (born 1925) was Commission President from 1985 to 1994, serving two entire terms in this position. He was French Finance Minister from 1981 to 1985. He chaired a working group on monetary union and is seen as one of the fathers of the single currency because of his responsibility for the so-called Delors report in 1989. He was also head of the Economic and Monetary Committee in the European Parliament from 1979 – 81. Delors now heads a think-tank in Paris called "Notre Europe".

43.   A

As Prime Minister of Luxembourg (1984-1995), Jacques Santer (Luxembourgish, born in 1937) led the negotiations on the Single European Act, which set aside the twenty-year old Luxembourg Compromise. Santer subsequently became President of the Commission when the United Kingdom vetoed the nomination of the Belgian Prime Minister Jean-Luc Dehaene, preferring the equally federalist but supposedly weaker Santer. He and the rest of his Commission resigned on 15 March 1999 following an investigation by an independent group of experts into administrative failings due to incompetence and malpractice. From 1999 to 2004, Santer was a Christian Democratic member of the European Parliament.

44.   C

The Committee (EPC) was set up by a Council decision dated 18 February 1974 (74/122/EEC). Revised statutes have been adopted by the Council on 18 June 2003 (2003/475/EC). The Economic Policy Committee (EPC) has been set up to prepare the work of the ECOFIN Council in coordinating the economic policies of the Member States and the Community, along with providing advice to the Commission and the Council.

The Committee is asked to focus on structural policies for improving growth potential and employment in the Community. The Committee provides support for the Council in the formulation of the Broad Economic Policy Guidelines, and contributes to the multilateral surveillance procedure, the Macro-economic Dialogue and the Luxembourg process including the preparation of the Employment Guidelines, the Recommendations for Member States' employment policies and the Joint Employment Report.

The Committee is composed of two members of each Member State, generally senior officials from national ministries of finance or economics and from national central banks. The Commission's Directorate General for Economic and Financial Affairs (ECFIN) and the European Central Bank also second two members. The present Chairman is Jan-Willem Oosterwijk, Secretary General at the Dutch Ministry of Economic Affairs.

For further information, see:
http://europa.eu.int/comm/economy_finance/epc/epc_en.htm

45.   A

The Foreign Affairs Minister would, as the Convention and Intergovernmental Conference put it, be "double-hatted", being both the Council's representative for the Common Foreign and Security Policy (CFSP) and one of the Commission's Vice-Presidents. As such, the Foreign Affairs Minister would be responsible for the Union's common foreign and security policy and would have a right of initiative in foreign policy matters. He or she would also implement that policy under mandate from the Council of Ministers. The Minister would have a similar role in the area of the European Security and Defence Policy (ESDP).

For further questions and details on the subject, please refer to the section on the Constitutional Treaty.

46.   C

The Molitor Group was a Commission working group established in 1994 to simplify the laws of the Community and to respect the principles that laws and policy should be made at the most local level possible (subsidiarity) and European law-making should not go beyond what is strictly necessary to achieve the aims of the Treaties (proportionality). The group itself was named after its German chairman, Bernhard Molitor.

47.   B

The Council is often represented by the so-called "Troika". Before the Amsterdam Treaty, it was made up of the EU presidency, supported by the previous and next presidencies. Since the Amsterdam Treaty, the High Representative supported by the Council's presidency and the Commission President have been referred to this way.

48.   D

Article 211 of the EC Treaty provides the following:

"In order to ensure the proper functioning and development of the common market, the Commission shall:

–   ensure that the provisions of this Treaty and the measures taken by the institutions pursuant thereto are applied,
–   formulate recommendations or deliver opinions on matters dealt with in this Treaty, if it expressly so provides or if the Commission considers it necessary,
–   have its own power of decision and participate in the shaping of measures taken by the Council and by the European Parliament in the manner provided for in this Treaty,
–   exercise the powers conferred on it by the Council for the implementation of the rules laid down by the latter."

Regarding the right of initiative, the Commission

has exclusive rights only in areas under the Community pillar whereas it shares this right with the Member States in the other two.

49.   C

Article 218(2) of the EC Treaty provides the following:

"The Commission shall adopt its Rules of Procedure so as to ensure that both it and its departments operate in accordance with the provisions of this Treaty. It shall ensure that these Rules are published."

50.   A

The day-to-day work of the Commission is done by its administrative officials, civil servants, experts, translators, interpreters and secretarial staff. Their number is approximately 24,000, which may sound a lot, but in fact it is less than the number of staff employed by most medium-sized city councils in Europe.

51.   A

Article 217(1) of the EC Treaty provides:

"The Commission shall work under the political guidance of its President, who shall decide on its internal organisation in order to ensure that it acts consistently, efficiently and on the basis of collegiality."

Also, Article 1 of the Commission's Rules of Procedure provides:

"The Commission shall act collectively in accordance with these Rules and in compliance with the political guidelines laid down by the President."

52.   C

Article 217(2) of the EC Treaty provides:

"The responsibilities incumbent upon the Commission shall be structured and allocated among its Members by its President. The President may reshuffle the allocation of those responsibilities during the Commission's term of office."

53.   C

Article 7 of the Commission's Rules of Procedure provides:

"The number of Members present required to constitute a quorum shall be equal to a majority of the number of Members specified in the Treaty."

54.   D

Article 10 of the Commission's Rules of Procedure provides:

"Save as otherwise decided by the Commission, the Secretary-General shall attend meetings. Attendance of other persons shall be determined in accordance with the rules to give effect to these Rules of Procedure.

In the absence of a Member of the Commission, his Chef de cabinet may attend the meeting and, at the invitation of the President, state the views of the absent Member.

The Commission may decide to hear any other person."

55.   A

Article 21 of the Commission's Rules of Procedure provides (emphasis added):

"In order to ensure the effectiveness of Commission action, departments shall work in close cooperation and in coordinated fashion in the preparation or implementation of Commission decisions.

Before submitting a document to the Commission, the department responsible shall, in sufficient time, consult other departments which are associated or concerned by virtue of their powers or responsibilities or the nature of the subject, and shall inform the Secretariat-General where it is not consulted. The Legal Service shall be consulted on all drafts or proposals for legal instruments and on all documents which may have legal implications. The Directorates-General responsible for the budget, personnel and administration shall be consulted on all documents which may have implications concerning the budget and finances or personnel and administration respectively. The Directorate-General responsible for

financial control shall likewise be consulted, as need be.

The department responsible shall endeavour to

COURT OF JUSTICE AND COURT OF FIRST INSTANCE; COMMUNITY LEGAL ORDER
ANSWERS

Question No	A	B	C	D
1.	X			
2.	X			
3.		X		
4.		X		
5.				X
6.		X		
7.	X			
8.		X		
9.		X		
10.	X			
11.				X
12.	X			
13.				X
14.		X		
15.			X	
16.		X		
17.			X	
18.				X
19.	X			
20.	X			
21.			X	
22.		X		
23.			X	
24.				X
25.				X
26.	X			
27.		X		
28.		X		
29.	X			
30.		X		

Question No	A	B	C	D
31.	X			
32.		X		
33.				X
34.	X			
35.			X	
36.	X			
37.				X
38.		X		
39.				X
40.			X	
41.	X			
42.		X		
43.			X	
44.	X			
45.	X			
46.		X		
47.	X			
48.	X			
49.				X
50.			X	
51.	X			
52.	X			
53.			X	
54.				X
55.				X
56				X
57.			X	
58.				X
59.		X		
60.		X		

1.   A

Article 222 of the EC Treaty provides:

"The Court of Justice shall be assisted by eight Advocates-General. Should the Court of Justice so request, the Council, acting unanimously, may increase the number of Advocates-General. It shall be the duty of the Advocate-General, acting with complete impartiality and independence, to make, in open court, reasoned submissions on cases which, in accordance with the Statute of the Court of Justice, require his involvement."

The Advocates General therefore prepare court cases with written opinions, which are not binding upon the Court, but usually influence its decisions.

2.   A

In the Kupferberg case (Case 104/81, 26 October 1982) the Court ruled that free trade agreements are directly applicable in all Member States; they therefore automatically have primacy over national law in the same way that an EU rule has precedence over national rules.

The Court stated that "since, according to Article 228(2) of the Treaty, the Member States are bound, in the same manner as the institutions of the Community, by the international agreements which the latter are empowered to conclude. This ensures respect for commitments arising from an agreement concluded by the community institutions. It fulfils an obligation not only in relation to the non-member country concerned but also and above all in relation to the community which has assumed responsibility for the due performance of the agreement. That is why the provisions of such an agreement form an integral part of the Community legal system."

3.   B

Article I-33(1) of the Constitutional Treaty provides (emphasis added):

"The legal acts of the Union
1. To exercise the Union's competences the institutions shall use as legal instruments, in accordance with Part III, European laws, European framework laws, European regulations, European decisions, recommendations and opinions.

A **European law** shall be a legislative act of general application. It shall be binding in its entirety and directly applicable in all Member States.

A **European framework law** shall be a legislative act binding, as to the result to be achieved, upon each Member State to which it is addressed, but shall leave to the national authorities the choice of form and methods.

A **European regulation** shall be a non-legislative act of general application for the implementation of legislative acts and of certain provisions of the Constitution. It may either be binding in its entirety and directly applicable in all Member States, or be binding, as to the result to be achieved, upon each Member State to which it is addressed, but shall leave to the national authorities the choice of form and methods.

A **European decision** shall be a non-legislative act, binding in its entirety. A decision which specifies those to whom it is addressed shall be binding only on them.

Recommendations and **opinions** shall have no binding force."

4.   B

Article 234 of the EC Treaty provides:

"The Court of Justice shall have jurisdiction to give preliminary rulings concerning:
(a) the interpretation of this Treaty;
(b) the validity and interpretation of acts of the institutions of the Community and of the ECB;
(c) the interpretation of the statutes of bodies established by an act of the Council, where those statutes so provide.

Where such a question is raised before any court or tribunal of a Member State, that court or tribunal may, if it considers that a decision on the question is necessary to enable it to give judgment, request the Court of Justice to give a ruling thereon.

Where any such question is raised in a case pending before a court or tribunal of a Member State against whose decisions there is no judicial remedy under national law, that court or tribunal shall bring the matter before the Court of Justice."

5.   D

Article 237 of the EC Treaty provides:

"The Court of Justice shall, within the limits here-inafter laid down, have jurisdiction in disputes concerning:
(a)   the fulfilment by Member States of obligations under the Statute of the European Investment Bank. In this connection, the Board of Directors of the Bank shall enjoy the powers conferred upon the Commission by Article 226;
(b)   measures adopted by the Board of Governors of the European Investment Bank. In this connection, any Member State, the Commission or the Board of Directors of the Bank may institute proceedings under the conditions laid down in Article 230;
(c)   measures adopted by the Board of Directors of the European Investment Bank. Proceedings against such measures may be instituted only by Member States or by the Commission, under the conditions laid down in Article 230, and solely on the grounds of non-compliance with the procedure provided for in Article 21(2), (5), (6) and (7) of the Statute of the Bank;
(d)   the fulfilment by national central banks of obligations under this Treaty and the Statute of the ESCB. In this connection the powers of the Council of the ECB in respect of national central banks shall be the same as those conferred upon the Commission in respect of Member States by Article 226. If the Court of Justice finds that a national central bank has failed to fulfil an obligation under this Treaty, that bank shall be required to take the necessary measures to comply with the judgment of the Court of Justice."

6.   B

Article 226 of the EC Treaty provides:
"If the Commission considers that a Member State has failed to fulfil an obligation under this Treaty, it shall deliver a reasoned opinion on the matter after giving the State concerned the opportunity to submit its observations.
If the State concerned does not comply with the

opinion within the period laid down by the Commission, the latter may bring the matter before the Court of Justice."

7.   A

Directives are to be transposed into national law through the Member States' parliaments and governments within a general deadline of 18 months. If a country refuses to adopt a directive, it may become law in that particular country anyway. If the rules are sufficiently precise, they may be looked upon as directly applicable. The Court's jurisprudence has proclaimed many directives to be directly applicable and even declared that the Member States are liable to pay compensation if they have not implemented a directive in time. The Constitutional Treaty proposes renaming directives as framework laws (see answer no. 3).
Article 249 of the EC Treaty provides:
"In order to carry out their task and in accordance with the provisions of this Treaty, the European Parliament acting jointly with the Council, the Council and the Commission shall make regulations and issue directives, take decisions, make recommendations or deliver opinions.
A regulation shall have general application. It shall be binding in its entirety and directly applicable in all Member States.
A directive shall be binding, as to the result to be achieved, upon each Member State to which it is addressed, but shall leave to the national authorities the choice of form and methods.
A decision shall be binding in its entirety upon those to whom it is addressed.
Recommendations and opinions shall have no binding force."
Regarding the publication of the above legislative acts, please refer to the next answer.

8.   B

Article 254 of the EC Treaty provides (emphasis added):
"1.   Regulations, directives and decisions adopted *in accordance with the procedure referred to in Article 251* shall be signed by the President of the European Parliament and by the President of the

Council and published in the Official Journal of the European Union. They shall enter into force on the date specified in them or, in the absence thereof, on the 20th day following that of their publication.

2. Regulations of the *Council and of the Commission*, as well as directives of those institutions which are addressed to all Member States, shall be published in the Official Journal of the European Union. They shall enter into force on the date specified in them or, in the absence thereof, on the 20th day following that of their publication.

3. Other directives, and decisions, shall be notified to those to whom they are addressed and shall take effect upon such notification."

9.   B

The Court of Justice ruled that Member States are obliged to interpret national legislation according to European directives even if they have yet to be incorporated into that national legislation. (Case C-106/89, 13 November 1990, modified in C-91/92, 14 July 1994)

The Court ruled:

"The Member States' obligation arising from a directive to achieve the result envisaged by the directive and their duty under Article 5 of the Treaty to take all appropriate measures, whether general or particular, to ensure the fulfilment of that obligation, is binding on all the authorities of Member States including, for matters within their jurisdiction, the courts. It follows that, in applying national law, whether the provisions in question were adopted before or after the directive, the national court called upon to interpret it is required to do so, as far as possible, in the light of the wording and the purpose of the directive in order to achieve the result pursued by it and thereby comply with the third paragraph of Article 189 of the Treaty."

Answer A (Case 22-70, 31 March 1971) concerns the Commission of the European Communities v Council of the European Communities case.

Answer C (2/74, 21 June 1974) concerns the Jean Reyners v Belgian State case.

Answer D (Case 44/79, 13 December 1979) concerns the Liselotte Hauer v Land Rheinland-Pfalz case.

10.   A

The Court ruled (Case C-415/93, 15 December 1995) against transfer rules between football clubs. Professional football is an economic activity covered by the Treaties. Jean-Marc Bosman was a professional football player for the football club Liege RC. The club demanded a transfer fee of 11,743,000 BFR (€291,101) for him to move club. According to the Court, rules providing a transfer fee after the expiry of the contract are not compatible with the principle of free movement of workers. In order to promote the development of young players of the home nation some football associations limited the number of foreign players each club team was allowed to field. The Court also ruled that limiting the number of professional players who are nationals of other Member States is precluded by the Treaty.

11.   D

The Council of Europe adopted the European Convention on Human Rights and Fundamental Freedoms. A Court of Human Rights was established in Strasbourg to adjudicate on human rights violations. The Convention was signed in Rome in 1950 and took effect from 1953. Citizens of states which have signed up to the Convention may bring cases against their own governments, alleging breaches of human rights under the Convention once all legal remedies have been exhausted in their respective home country.

All the Member States and applicant countries are signatories to the European Human Rights Convention, but due to the lack of legal personality, the EU institutions are not bound by it. However, a special convention has drafted the European Charter of Human Rights which has been included in the Constitutional Treaty in part II as a binding element.

The Constitutional Treaty, by providing legal personality to the EU as a whole, would provide a legal base for the EU to subscribe to the Council of Europe's European Convention on Human Rights. This, due to the fact that the EU has in the meantime created its own human rights catalogue, is not very likely.

The Constitutional Treaty's wording does not give primacy to the Human Rights Convention. If a conflict arises between the Council of Europe's European Court of Human Rights in Strasbourg and the European Court of Justice in Luxembourg, the judgement of the latter will hold the right to overrule according to the Constitutional Treaty. (*EUABC*)

12.   A

As opposed to the three-pillar EU, today only the European Communities have "legal personality" and thereby power to represent all Member States in binding international commitments. The Constitutional Treaty would give legal personality to the whole Union and will scrap the division between first, second and third pillar issues established by the Maastricht Treaty. This will make the EU an independent international body, in the same way as member countries have traditionally been.

13.   D

See answer no. 7.

14.   B

Article 230(1) of the EC Treaty provides:
"The Court of Justice shall review the legality of acts adopted jointly by the European Parliament and the Council, of acts of the Council, of the Commission and of the ECB, other than recommendations and opinions, and of acts of the European Parliament intended to produce legal effects vis-à-vis third parties."

Article 231 of the EC Treaty provides:
"If the action is well founded, the Court of Justice shall declare the act concerned to be void.

In the case of a regulation, however, the Court of Justice shall, if it considers this necessary, state which of the effects of the regulation which it has declared void shall be considered as definitive."

15.   C

The Treaty prohibits discrimination based on nation-

ality. However, even though prohibition had only applied to employees who were mentioned in the Treaties, the Court of Justice expanded the scope of the ban on discrimination, so that persons not currently in the labour market have been also covered. The ruling in the Casagrande case (Case 9/74, 3 July 1974) thus made discrimination against persons in the educational system illegal. At the time of that case, education was not covered by the Treaties.

With the above ruling, the Court decided that fundamental rights form part of the general principles of Community law that it is required to uphold, and that in safeguarding such rights it should be guided by the constitutional traditions of the Member States. Accordingly, no measure may have the force of law unless it is compatible with the fundamental rights recognised and protected by the Member States' constitutions. The main specific rights recognised so far by the Court are:

human dignity (*Casagrande*, 1974)
equal treatment (*Klöckner-Werke AG*, 1962)
non-discrimination (*Defrenne v Sabena*, 1976)
freedom of association (*Gewerkschaftsbund, Massa et al.* 1974)
freedom of religion and confession (*Prais*, 1976)
privacy (*National Panasonic*, 1980)
medical secrecy (*Commission v Federal Republic of Germany*, 1992)
property (*Hauer*, 1979)
freedom of profession (*Hauer*, 1979)
freedom of trade (*Internationale Handelsgesellschaft*, 1970);
freedom of industry (*Usinor*, 1984)
freedom of competition (*France*, 1985)
respect for family life (*Commission v Germany*, 1989)
entitlement to effective legal defence and a fair trial (*Johnston v Chief Constable of the Royal Ulster Constabulary*, 1986, *Pecastaing v Belgium*, 1980)
inviolability of residence (*Hoechst AG v Commission*, 1989)
freedom of expression and publication (*VBVB*, 1984)
(*http://www.europarl.eu.int/factsheets/2_1_0_en.htm*)

16.   B

The Community acquis is the body of common rights and obligations which bind all the Member

States together within the European Union. It is constantly evolving and comprises:

- the content, principles and political objectives of the Treaties;
- the legislation adopted in application of the Treaties and the case law of the Court of Justice;
- the declarations and resolutions adopted by the Union;
- measures relating to the common foreign and security policy;
- measures relating to justice and home affairs
- international agreements concluded by the Community and those concluded by the Member States between themselves in the field of the Union's activities.

The Community acquis therefore does not only comprise Community law in the strict sense, but also all acts adopted under the second and third pillars of the European Union and the common objectives laid down in the Treaties. The Union has committed itself to maintaining the Community acquis in its entirety and developing it further. (*ScadPlus*)

17.   C

The primary legislation, or Treaties, is effectively the constitutional law of the European Union. They lay down the basic policies of the Union, establish its institutional structure, legislative procedures, and the powers of the Union.

The Treaties that make up the primary legislation are (date of signature):

- ECSC Treaty, 1951 (Treaty of Paris);
- EEC Treaty, 1957 (Treaty of Rome);
- EURATOM Treaty, 1957 (Treaty of Rome);
- Merger Treaty, 1965;
- Acts of Accession of the United Kingdom, Ireland and Denmark, 1972;
- Budgetary Treaty, 1970;
- Budgetary Treaty, 1975;
- Act of Accession of Greece, 1979;
- Acts of Accession of Spain and Portugal, 1985;
- Single European Act, 1986;
- Maastricht Treaty, 1992;
- Acts of Accession of Austria, Sweden and Finland, 1994;
- Amsterdam Treaty, 1997;
- Treaty of Nice, 2001;
- Accession Treaty, 2003

18.   D

Home state regulation is a term used in European Community law relating to the cross border selling or marketing of goods and services. In a directive, or regulation, where home state regulation applies, if a firm based in country A is selling to customers living in country B, they are regulated according to the laws of country A. Home state regulation is often held to help the single market, as firms only need to be aware of their own country's laws, rather than 25 sets of national law.

19.   A

Direct effect is a principle of EU law stating that European regulations have a direct effect on EU citizens and on the laws of the Member States. The concept was defined by the European Court of Justice in its ruling in Case 26/62 Van Gend en Loos v. Nederlanse Administratie der Belastingen (5 February 1963), which stated that European Community regulations could (and should) be tried before national courts, since the regulations have a direct effect on individuals' rights and responsibilities similar to that of national laws.

The Court ruled that "[t]he European Economic Community constitutes a new legal order of international law for the benefit of which the states have limited their sovereign rights, albeit within limited fields, and the subject of which comprise not only the Member States but also their nationals. Independently of the legislation of Member States, Community law not only imposes obligations on individuals but is also intended to confer upon them rights which become part of their legal heritage. These rights arise not only where they are expressly granted by the Treaty but also by reason of obligations which the Treaty imposes in a clearly defined way upon individuals as well as upon the Member States and upon the institutions of the Community."

20.   A

The Court of First Instance (CFI) was set up in 1989 to strengthen the protection of individuals' interests by introducing a second tier of judicial authority, allowing the Court of Justice to concentrate on its basic task of ensuring the uniform interpretation and application of Community law.

The CFI is currently made up of twenty five judges appointed by common accord of the Governments of the Member States to hold office for a renewable term of six years.

The Treaty of Nice introduced greater flexibility for adapting the CFI's statute, which can be amended by the Council acting unanimously at the request of the Court or of the Commission. The approval of the rules of procedure of the Court of Justice and of the Court of First Instance is by qualified majority.

To ease the workload of the Court of Justice, the Treaty of Nice also aimed to improve the distribution of responsibilities between the Court and the CFI, making the CFI the ordinary court for all direct actions (appeals against a decision, failure to act, damages etc.), with the exception of those assigned to a judicial panel and those reserved for the Court of Justice. The Treaty also provides for the creation, based on a right of initiative shared between the Court of Justice and the Commission, of judicial panels to examine at first instance certain types of actions in specific matters to relieve the burden on the CFI. Finally, the Treaty of Nice provides for the possibility of conferring on the Court of First Instance the right to deliver preliminary rulings in certain specific areas. (*ScadPlus*)

Article 300(6), as amended by the Treaty of Nice, provides:

"The European Parliament, the Council, the Commission or a Member State may obtain the opinion of the Court of Justice as to whether an agreement envisaged is compatible with the provisions of this Treaty. Where the opinion of the Court of Justice is adverse, the agreement may enter into force only in accordance with Article 48 of the Treaty on European Union."

21.   C

In the Cassis de Dijon judgement (Case 120/78, 20 February 1979), the Court ruled that a measure could be deemed to have equivalent effect even without discrimination between imported and domestic products. In particular, imposing the technical rules of the importing State on products from other Member States is tantamount to introducing an equivalent measure since the imported products are penalised by being forced to undergo costly adjustments. The fact that there is no Community harmonisation of the rules cannot be used to justify this attitude, which effectively hinders freedom of movement, and the Court therefore laid down the principle that any product legally manufactured and marketed in a Member State in accordance with the fair and traditional rules and manufacturing processes of that country must be allowed onto the market of any other Member State. This is the principle of *mutual recognition* by the Member States of their respective rules in the absence of harmonisation. The Cassis de Dijon is otherwise a French liquor.
(*http://www.europarl.eu.int/factsheets/3_2_1_en.htm*)

22.   B

Article 3 of the Statute of the Court of Justice (Annexed to the EC Treaty) provides:

"[…] The Court, sitting as a full Court, may waive the immunity. […]"

23.   C

Article 225a of the EC Treaty and Article 140b of the Euratom Treaty empower the Council to create "judicial panels to hear and determine at first instance certain classes of action or proceeding brought in specific areas". Pursuant to those provisions of the Treaties, the Council has decided, by Decision 2004/752/EC, Euratom of 2 November 2004, to establish the European Union Civil Service Tribunal. The Civil Service Tribunal is attached to the Court of First Instance of the European Communities and has its headquarters at the Court of First Instance, has jurisdiction at first instance in disputes between the Communities and their servants referred to in Article 236 of the EC Treaty and Article 152 of the EAEC Treaty, including disputes between all bodies or agencies and their servants in respect of which jurisdiction is conferred on the Court of Justice. The Civil Service Tribunal consists of seven Judges, from among whom the president is chosen. On 6 October 2005, Paul J Mahoney was elected President of the Civil Service Ttribunal. The Judges are appointed for a period of six years which may be renewed.
(*Curia*)

24.   D

Article 245 of the EC Treaty, as amended by the Treaty of Nice, provides:

"The Statute of the Court of Justice shall be laid down in a separate Protocol.

The Council, acting unanimously at the request of the Court of Justice and after consulting the European Parliament and the Commission, or at the request of the Commission and after consulting the European Parliament and the Court of Justice, may amend the provisions of the Statute, with the exception of Title I."

25.   D

The Court of Justice rules on issues regarding:
* disputes between Member States;
* disputes between the EU and Member States;
* disputes between the Institutions;
* disputes between individuals and the EU;
* opinions on international agreements, Article 300 (228) EC Treaty;
* preliminary rulings;
* in certain special cases the Court of Justice may express an opinion on a matter outside its jurisdiction, as defined in Article 220(164) of the EC Treaty, for example on external agreements concluded by the EU.

26.   A

The Court of First Instance exercises at first instance the jurisdiction conferred on the Court of Justice:
* in disputes between the Communities and their servants referred to in Article 236 of the EC Treaty and in Article 152 of the Euratom Treaty (actions brought by staff);
* in actions brought against the Commission pursuant to the second paragraph of Article 33 and Article 35 of the ECSC Treaty by undertakings or associations of undertakings which concern individual acts relating to the application of Article 50 and Articles 57 to 76 of that Treaty (ECSC disputes);
* in actions brought against an Institution of the Communities by natural or legal persons pursuant to the second paragraph of Article

230 and the third paragraph of Article 232 of the EC Treaty. The Council Decision of 24 October 1988 establishing a Court of First Instance restricted the CFI's powers relating to the implementation of the competition rules applicable to undertakings. Following a proposal by the Court of Justice, Council Decision 93/350 Euratom, ECSC, EEC of 8 June 1993 extended the powers of the CFI to all cases brought by private individuals (actions for declaration of failure to act, for annulment and compensation). This principally concerns actions brought by individuals for declaration of failure to act in cases of State aids and trade protection measures (anti-dumping and anti-subsidy measures).
* Certain areas of competence for some actions for annulment brought by the Member States. (*http://www.europarl.eu.int/factsheets/1_3_9_en.htm*)

27.   B

The Court of Justice gave rights to citizens and companies under EU law even when Member States failed to adopt EU rules (Case C-213/89, 19 June 1990). The Court ruled as follows:

"Any provision of a national legal system and any legislative, administrative or judicial practice which might impair the effectiveness of Community law by withholding from the national court having jurisdiction to apply such law the power to do everything necessary at the moment of its application to set aside national legislative provisions which might prevent, even temporarily, Community rules from having full force and effect are incompatible with the requirements inherent in the very nature of Community law.

The full effectiveness of Community law would be just as much impaired if a rule of national law could prevent a court seized of a dispute governed by Community law from granting interim relief in order to ensure the full effectiveness of the judgment to be given on the existence of the rights claimed under Community law. It follows that a court which in those circumstances would grant interim relief, if it were not for a rule of national law, is obliged to set aside that rule."

28.   B

The fifth sub-paragraph of Article 233 of the EC Treaty provides:
"The Judges shall elect the President of the Court of Justice from among their number for a term of three years. He may be re-elected."

29.   A

The Court (Case 11/70, 17 December 1970 and 106/77, 9 March 1978) laid down that EU law should over-rule national constitutions. Since then, the principle that national laws must be amended to be in accordance with EU law, and not vice versa (the primacy of EU law) also covers national constitutions. The Constitutional Treaty contains an explicit demand that the supremacy of EU law be respected.
  Answer B: Case 222/84, 15 May 1986, Johnston case
  Answer C: Case 294/83, 23 April 1986, "Les Verts" v European Parliament case
  Answer D: Case 178/84, 12 March 1987, Commission of the European Communities v Federal Republic of Germany case

30.   B

Second sub-paragraph of Article 230 of the EC Treaty provides:
"[The Court of Justice] shall for this purpose have jurisdiction in actions brought by a Member State, the European Parliament, the Council or the Commission on grounds of lack of competence, infringement of an essential procedural requirement, infringement of this Treaty or of any rule of law relating to its application, or misuse of powers."

31.   C

See previous answer.

32.   B

In the 1979 Isoglucose case (138/79, 29 October 1980) the European Parliament won a court case annulling a legislative act because the Council had failed to wait for the Parliament's opinion under the consultation procedure. According to the consultation procedure, the European Parliament must be consulted, even though there is no obligation to follow its opinions.

33.   D

Vassilios Skouris (Greek, born in 1948) has been the President of the Court of Justice since 7 October 2003.

34.   A

Cases completed:		New cases:		Cases pending:	
2000	526	2000	503	2000	873
2001	434	2001	504	2001	943
2002	513	2002	477	2002	907
2003	494	2003	561	2003	974
2004	665	2004	531	2004	840

(*Curia*)

35.   C

Actions for annulment:		Actions for failure to act:		Actions for damages:	
2000	220	2000	6	2000	17
2001	134	2001	17	2001	21
2002	171	2002	12	2002	13
2003	174	2003	13	2003	24
2004	199	2004	15	2004	19

Arbitration clauses:		Intellectual property:		Staff cases:	
		2000	34	2000	110
2001	8	2001	37	2001	110
2002	2	2002	83	2002	112
2003	3	2003	100	2003	124
2004	7	2004	110	2004	146

Special forms of procedure:

2000	11
2001	18
2002	18
2003	28
2004	40

Total number of cases:

2000	398
2001	345
2002	411
2003	466
2004	536

(*Curia*)

36.   A

The Court of Justice may sit as a full Court, in a Grand Chamber (13 Judges) or in chambers of three or five Judges. It sits in a Grand Chamber when a Member State or a Community institution that is a party to the proceedings so requests, or in particularly complex or important cases. Other cases are heard by a chamber of three or five Judges. The Presidents of the chambers of five Judges are elected for three years, the Presidents of the chambers of three Judges for one year. The Court sits as a full Court in the very exceptional cases exhaustively provided for by the Treaty (for instance, where it must compulsorily retire the European Ombudsman or a Commissioner who has failed to fulfil his obligations) and where the Court considers that a case is of exceptional importance.
(*Curia*)

37.   D

Article 6 of the Statute of the Court of Justice provides:
"A Judge may be deprived of his office or of his right to a pension or other benefits in its stead only if, in the unanimous opinion of the Judges and Advocates General of the Court, he no longer fulfils the requisite conditions or meets the obligations arising from his office. The Judge concerned shall not take part in any such deliberations."

38.   B

39.   D

In the case of direct actions and appeals, the following procedure applies:
1.   Application
2.   Notification of the application to the defendant by the Registry
3.   Notice of action published in the Official Journal of the European Union, C Series
4.   (Interim measures)
5.   (Intervention)
6.   Defence;
7.   (Objection to admissibility)
8.   (Reply and Rejoinder)
9.   (Other pleadings)
End of written procedure
1.   The Judge-Rapporteur draws up his preliminary report
2.   General meeting (Judges and Advocates General)
3.   (Referral of case, where appropriate, to a Chamber)
4.   (Measures of inquiry)
5.   (Oral procedure waived)
6.   (Opinion waived)
7.   (Hearing; Report for the Hearing)
8.   (Opinion of the Advocate General)
9.   Deliberation by the Judges
Judgment
   (*Curia*)

40.   C

The ECSC Court was established in 1952, becoming the Court of Justice of the European Communities in 1957.

41.   A

The EFTA Court of Luxembourg (established in 1994) has jurisdiction with regard to EFTA States which are parties to the European Economic Area (EEA) Agreement – at present Iceland, Liechtenstein and Norway. The Court is mainly competent to deal with infringement actions brought by the EFTA Surveillance Authority against an EFTA State with regard to the implementation, application or interpretation of an EEA rule, for the settlement of disputes between two or more EFTA States, for appeals concerning decisions taken by the EFTA Surveillance Authority and for giving advisory opinions to courts in EFTA States on the interpretation of EEA rules. Thus the jurisdiction of the EFTA Court mainly corresponds to the jurisdiction of the Court of Justice of the European Communities over EU Member States.
(EFTA)

42.   B

The EFTA Court consists of three Judges, one nominated by each of the EFTA States party to the EEA Agreement. The Judges are appointed by common accord of the Governments for a period of six years
   The Judges elect their President for a term of three years.
   The Judges are:
   Carl Baudenbacher (Liechtenstein) – President
   Per Tresselt (Norway)
   Thorgeir Örlygsson (Iceland)
   In addition to the regular Judges, a system of ad hoc judges is established according to Article 30, fourth paragraph, of the ESA/Court Agreement for situations where a regular Judge cannot act in a particular case.
(EFTA)

43.   C

On 1 November 1998, Protocol No 11 to the European Convention for the Protection of Human Rights (1950) entered into force, establishing a single court sitting full-time and replacing the European Commission of Human Rights (1954) and the European Court of Human Rights (1959). The European Court of Human Rights is not a Community institution, it belongs to the Council of Europe.
   For further information, see:
http://www.echr.coe.int

44.   A

45.   A

According to the Francovich case (C-6/90 and C-9/90 joined cases, 19 November 1991), an individual citizen is entitled to claim compensation from a Member State which has not transposed a directive or has done so inadequately where:
*   the directive is intended to confer rights on individuals;
*   the substance of the rights can be ascertained on the basis of the directive;
*   and where there is a causal connection between the breach of the duty to transpose the directive and the loss sustained by the individual.
   Fault on the part of the Member State is then not required in order to establish liability. If the Member State has powers of discretion in transposing the law, the violation must also, in addition to the three above criteria, qualify as defective or non-existent transposition: it must be substantial and evident.
(http://www.europarl.eu.int/factsheets/1_2_1_en.htm)

46.   B

Article 10 of the EC Treaty provides:
   "Member States shall take all appropriate measures, whether general or particular, to ensure fulfilment of the obligations arising out of this

Treaty or resulting from action taken by the institutions of the Community. They shall facilitate the achievement of the Community's tasks.

They shall abstain from any measure which could jeopardise the attainment of the objectives of this Treaty."

47. A

Article I-47 of the Constitutional Treaty provides:

"The Court of Justice of the European Union shall include the Court of Justice, the General Court and specialised courts. It shall ensure that in the interpretation and application of the Constitution the law is observed."

48. A

Article 35(6) of the EU Treaty provides:

"The Court of Justice shall have jurisdiction to review the legality of framework decisions and decisions in actions brought by a Member State or the Commission on grounds of lack of competence, infringement of an essential procedural requirement, infringement of this Treaty or of any rule of law relating to its application, or misuse of powers. The proceedings provided for in this paragraph shall be instituted within two months of the publication of the measure."

49. D

Article I-19 of the Constitutional Treaty provides: "[…]

This institutional framework comprises:
— The European Parliament,
— The European Council,
— The Council of Ministers (hereinafter referred to as the 'Council'),
— The European Commission (hereinafter referred to as the 'Commission'),
— The Court of Justice of the European Union."

50. C

Article 195 of the EC Treaty provides:

"The European Parliament shall appoint an Ombudsman empowered to receive complaints from any citizen of the Union or any natural or legal person residing or having its registered office in a Member State concerning instances of maladministration in the activities of the Community institutions or bodies, with the exception of the Court of Justice and the Court of First Instance acting in their judicial role."

51. A

The Amsterdam Treaty opened the way for dialogue between the EU and its citizens by safeguarding fundamental rights (for the first time Member States failing to respect such rights may face penalties), tackling discrimination of all kinds, providing for equal opportunities for men and women, focusing on social issues and assets such as voluntary work, sport, public-service television broadcasting, disability, churches and non-confessional organisations, public credit institutions operating in certain countries and a rejection of the death penalty. The Treaty also dealt with the major issues facing our society such as employment, the environment, public health and open government.

52. A

Article 43 of the EU Treaty provides:

"Member States which intend to establish enhanced cooperation between themselves may make use of the institutions, procedures and mechanisms laid down by this Treaty and by the Treaty establishing the European Community provided that the proposed cooperation:

(a) is aimed at furthering the objectives of the Union and of the Community, at protecting and serving their interests and at reinforcing their process of integration;

(b) respects the said Treaties and the single institutional framework of the Union;

(c) respects the acquis communautaire and the

measures adopted under the other provisions of the said Treaties;

(d) remains within the limits of the powers of the Union or of the Community and does not concern the areas which fall within the exclusive competence of the Community;

(e) does not undermine the internal market as defined in Article 14(2) of the Treaty establishing the European Community, or the economic and social cohesion established in accordance with Title XVII of that Treaty;

(f) does not constitute a barrier to or discrimination in trade between the Member States and does not distort competition between them;

(g) involves a minimum of eight Member States;

(h) respects the competences, rights and obligations of those Member States which do not participate therein;

(i) does not affect the provisions of the Protocol integrating the Schengen acquis into the framework of the European Union;

(j) is open to all the Member States, in accordance with Article 43b.

Article 43a

Enhanced cooperation may be undertaken only as a last resort, when it has been established within the Council that the objectives of such cooperation cannot be attained within a reasonable period by applying the relevant provisions of the Treaties.

Article 43b

When enhanced cooperation is being established, it shall be open to all Member States. It shall also be open to them at any time, in accordance with Articles 27e and 40b of this Treaty and with Article 11a of the Treaty establishing the European Community, subject to compliance with the basic decision and with the decisions taken within that framework. The Commission and the Member States participating in enhanced cooperation shall ensure that as many Member States as possible are encouraged to take part."

53.   C

Article 5 of the EC Treaty, as amended by the Maastricht Treaty, provides:

"The Community shall act within the limits of the powers conferred upon it by this Treaty and of the objectives assigned to it therein.

In areas which do not fall within its exclusive competence, the Community shall take action, in

accordance with the principle of subsidiarity, only if and in so far as the objectives of the proposed action cannot be sufficiently achieved by the Member States and can therefore, by reason of the scale or effects of the proposed action, be better achieved by the Community.

Any action by the Community shall not go beyond what is necessary to achieve the objectives of this Treaty."

Formally, the principle of subsidiarity applies to those areas where the Community does not have exclusive competence, the principle delineating those areas where the Community should and should not act. In practice, the concept is frequently used in a more informal manner in discussions as to which competences should be given to the Community, and which retained for the Member States alone. The concept of subsidiarity therefore has both a legal and a political dimension. Consequently, there are varying views as to its legal and political consequences, and various criteria are put forward explaining the content of the principle. (*Wikipedia*)

54.   D

Certain items were left unresolved from the negotiation of the Amsterdam Treaty, namely the size and composition of the Commission, the re-weighting of votes in Council, the possible extension of qualified majority voting and changes to the institutions necessitated by enlargement. These were nicknamed the "Amsterdam leftovers". In fact, some of the changes agreed at Nice – including the size and composition of the Commission, and the weighting of votes in the Council – later proved unsatisfactory and were discussed again as " Nice leftovers" by the Convention on the Future of Europe, whose proposals formed the basis of the new Constitutional Treaty.

55.   D

The Single European Act (SEA) replaced unanimity in the following areas:

Amendment of the common customs tariff
Freedom to provide services
The free movement of capital
The common sea and air transport policy

56. D

The Amsterdam Treaty extends codecision to 15 legal bases which were already in the EC Treaty:
1. Article 12(6) prohibition of discrimination,
2. Article 18 (8a) free movement of EU citizens,
3. Article 42 (51) free movement of workers,
4. Article 47(1) (57(1)) recognition of qualifications,
5. Article 67 (73o, 100c) visa procedures,
6. Article 71 (75) transport policy, including air transport,
7. Article 141(3) (119(3)) implementation of equal pay for equal work,
8. Article 148 (125) implementation of the Social Fund,
9. Article 150(4) (127(4)) vocational training measures,
10. Article 153(4) (129a(4)) consumer protection,
11. Article 156 (129d) trans-European networks ("other measures"),
12. Article 162 (130e) implementation of the Regional Development Fund,
13. Article 172 (130o) implementation of framework research programmes,
14. Article 175(3) (130s (3)) environment protection measures,
15. Article 179 (130w) development cooperation.

It also extends codecision to eight new legal bases:
1. Article 129 (109r) measures to promote employment,
2. Article 135 (116) customs cooperation,
3. Article 137(1) (118(1)) social policy,
4. Article 152(4) 129(4) health protection, veterinary and plant health measures,
5. Article 255 (191a) principles governing access to documents,
6. Article 280 (209a) combating fraud,
7. Article 285 (213a) Community statistics,
8. Article 286 (213b) establishment of a body to monitor protection of individuals with regard to data processing.
(*http://www.europarl.eu.int/factsheets/1_1_3_en.htm*)

57. C

According to Article 17(8) of the EC Treaty, every person holding the nationality of a Member State is a citizen of the Union. Nationality is defined according to the national laws of that State. Citizenship of the Union is complementary to national citizenship and comprises a number of rights and duties in addition to those stemming from citizenship of a Member State.

For all citizens of the Union, citizenship implies:
1. The right to move and reside freely within the territory of the Member States.
2. The right to vote and to stand as a candidate in elections to the European Parliament and in municipal (but not national) elections in the Member State in which they reside, under the same conditions as nationals of that State.
3. The right to diplomatic protection in the territory of a third country (non-EU State) by the diplomatic or consular authorities of another Member State, if their own country does not have diplomatic representation there, to the same extent as that provided for nationals of that Member State.
4. The right to petition the European Parliament and the right to apply to the Ombudsman appointed by the European Parliament concerning instances of maladministration in the activities of the Community Institutions or bodies, with the exception of the Court of Justice and the Court of First Instance.
(*http://www.europarl.eu.int/factsheets/2_2_0_en.htm*)

58. D

There are two different kinds of declaration: if a declaration is concerned with the further development of the Community, such as the Declaration on Democracy and the Declaration on Fundamental Rights and Freedom, it is more or less equivalent to a resolution. Declarations of this type are mainly used to reach a wide audience or a specific group. The other type of declaration is issued in the context of the Council's decision-making process and sets out the views of all or individual Council members regarding the interpretation of the Council's decisions.
(*EurLex*)

59. B

The Treaty establishing the European Coal and Steel Community (ECSC) was signed in Paris on 18 April 1951 by Belgium, Germany, France, Italy,

Luxembourg and the Netherlands. It was concluded for a period of fifty years and, having entered into force on 23 July 1952, expired on 23 July 2002. Historically, the ECSC was the practical follow-up to the Schuman declaration of 9 May 1950, which proposed placing Franco-German production of coal and steel under a common High Authority within the framework of an organisation open to the participation of the other countries of Europe.
(*ScadPlus*)

60.   B

The term "transparency" is frequently used in Community language to mean openness in the working of the Community institutions. It is linked to a variety of demands for broader public access to information and EU documents, greater involvement in the decision-making process and more easily readable texts (simplification of the Treaties, consolidation and better drafting of legislation).

With specific reference to access to documents, the Council and the Commission adopted a code of conduct establishing common principles for the two institutions following a Council decision on 20 December 1993. On the basis of this code of conduct, the two institutions incorporated specific provisions on access to their documents into their rules of procedure.

The Amsterdam Treaty inserted a new Article 255 on transparency in the EC Treaty. This gives all citizens of the Union, plus all natural or legal persons residing or having their registered offices in a Member State, the right of access to European Parliament, Council and Commission documents.

This article was implemented by the Regulation of 30 May 2001, which is not significantly different from previous texts, in that it provides for two exceptions: cases in which access is automatically refused (for reasons of public security, defence, international relations) and cases in which access is refused except where there is an overriding public interest in disclosure (protection of commercial interests of a naturalised or legal person, for example).
(*ScadPlus*)

EUROPEAN COURT OF AUDITORS (ECA)

ANSWERS

Question No	A	B	C	D
1.		X		
2.				X
3.	X			
4.			X	
5.		X		
6.			X	
7.	X			
8.				X
9.	X			
10.			X	

Question No	A	B	C	D
11.			X	
12.			X	
13.		X		
14.		X		
15.				X
16.			X	
17.	X			
18.		X		
19.				X
20.		X		

1. B

At the initiative of Heinrich Aigner, the President of the European Parliament's Budgetary Control Committee, who since 1973 had strongly argued the case for a Community-level external audit body, the European Court of Auditors was established by the Treaty of Brussels of 22 July 1975. The Court started operating as an external Community audit body in October 1977. (*ECA*)

2. D

The ECA is located in Luxembourg.

3. A

The ECA became an institution in its own right on 1 November 1993 with the entry into force of the Maastricht Treaty.

4. C

The Treaty of Nice amended Article 247 of the EC Treaty and set the number of members of the ECA at one per Member State. The previous method of setting a precise number of members (which in fact always corresponded to the number of Member States) has therefore been replaced by a system which avoids having to amend this article with each enlargement. Article 247 of the EC Treaty has also been amended to introduce qualified majority voting for appointment by the Council of the Members of the Court of Auditors.
(*ScadPlus*)

5. B

The control of the European Union's budget has three levels: 1) internal control within each institution, 2) external control by the European Court of Auditors, and 3) a discharge procedure by the European Parliament.
   Article 248(1) of the EC Treaty provides that

"[t]he Court of Auditors shall examine the accounts of all revenue and expenditure of the Community. It shall also examine the accounts of all revenue and expenditure of all bodies set up by the Community insofar as the relevant constituent instrument does not preclude such examination."

6. C

The main role of the ECA is to monitor the correct implementation of the EU budget, i.e. the legality and regularity of Community income and expenditure. It also ensures sound financial management and contributes to the effectiveness and transparency of the Community system.
   According to Article 248(2) of the EC Treaty, the Court of Auditors must examine whether all revenue has been received and all expenditure incurred in a lawful and regular manner and whether the financial management has been sound. In doing so, it must report in particular on any cases of irregularity. The audit of revenue is carried out on the basis both of the amounts established as due and the amounts actually paid to the Community. The audit of expenditure is carried out on the basis both of commitments undertaken and payments made. These audits may be carried out before the closure of accounts for the financial year in question.
   As a general rule, all institutions of the Community, any bodies managing revenue or expenditure on behalf of the Community, any natural or legal person in receipt of payments from the budget, and the national audit bodies or, if these do not have the necessary powers, the competent national departments, must forward to the Court of Auditors, at its request, any document or information necessary to carry out its task.

7. A

When the Court of Auditors' auditors suspect, in the context of external audit, that fraud(s) or irregularities have occurred, the information obtained is forwarded as soon as possible to OLAF (European Anti-Fraud Office) so that the appropriate measures can be taken. The objective of an external audit is, on the one hand, to ensure that the public accounts are transparent and reliable and that the

operations are legal and, on the other hand, to assess whether the management operations have made it possible to achieve the objectives economically and efficiently.
(*ECA*)

8.   D

The external audit has no direct legal consequences, because the ECA does not have any powers of sanction. If ECA detects irregularities, it informs OLAF which may open an investigation into the suspected irregularities or frauds.

9.   A

The ECA is not involved in the implementation of the EU budget. Article 274 of the EC Treaty provides that "[t]he Commission shall implement the budget on its own responsibility".

10.   C

Article 247(1) of the EC Treaty provides that the ECA must consist of one national from each Member State. As a result, the ECA has 25 members, one member from each Member State of EU25, who are appointed by the Council ruling unanimously after consultation with the European Parliament.

11.   C

Article 247(2) of the EC Treaty provides that "[t]he Members of the Court of Auditors shall be chosen from among persons who belong or have belonged in their respective countries to external audit bodies or who are especially qualified for this office. Their independence must be beyond doubt."

12.   C

According to Article 247(3) of the EC Treaty, "[t]he

Members of the Court of Auditors shall be appointed for a term of six years. The Council, acting by a qualified majority after consulting the European Parliament, shall adopt the list of Members drawn up in accordance with the proposals made by each Member State. The term of office of the Members of the Court of Auditors shall be renewable."

13.   B

According to Article 247(3) of the EC Treaty, the President of the ECA is elected from among its members for a term of three years. The President may be re-elected.

14.   B

Article 247(4) of the EC Treaty: "[t]he Members of the Court of Auditors shall, in the general interest of the Community, be completely independent in the performance of their duties. In the performance of these duties, they shall neither seek nor take instructions from any government or from any other body. They shall refrain from any action incompatible with their duties."

15.   D

According to Article 247(5) of the EC Treaty, during their term of office, the members of the ECA are not entitled to engage in any other occupations, whether gainful or not.

16.   C

Article 247(7) of the EC Treaty provides that "[a] Member of the Court of Auditors may be deprived of his office or of his right to a pension or other benefits in its stead only if the Court of Justice, at the request of the Court of Auditors, finds that he no longer fulfils the requisite conditions or meets the obligations arising from his office."

17. A

The audit policies and standards of the ECA are based on the best international practice, such as the Auditing Standards published by the International Organisation of Supreme Audit Institutions (INTO-SAI) and in the International Standards on Auditing prepared by the International Auditing Practices Committee of the International Federation of Accountants (IFAC). They have been adapted, however, to reflect the Court's particular duties and responsibilities as laid down in the Treaty and the Financial Regulation and to take account of the European Community context. The policies and standards are also fully compatible with the auditing guidelines for the external audit of EC activities being developed by an ad hoc working group established by the Contact Committee of Presidents of the EU Supreme Audit Institutions.
(*Court Audit Policies and Standards – European Court of Auditors, May 2000*)

18. B

Every year, in November, the ECA publishes a report on the results of its audit of the Community accounts of the year before. Since the Maastricht Treaty these Annual Reports also need to contain a Statement of Assurance (DAS), certifying the reliability of the accounts and the legality and regularity of the underlying transactions. This DAS was expected to render the discharge procedure more meaningful and the Commission more responsible in implementing the budget. With the Maastricht Treaty coming into effect on 1 November 1993, it was the 1994 financial year that saw the DAS fully implemented for the first time.

In order to be able to give the DAS as required by the Treaty, two types of audit are carried out by the Court of Auditors: an audit as to the reliability of the accounts and an audit of the legality and regularity of the underlying transactions.

* **Audit of the reliability of the accounts:**

the objective of the audit of the accounts is to gain sufficient evidence that all transactions, assets and liabilities have been completely, correctly and accurately recorded in the accounting records and presented in the financial statements. The audit opinion will indicate whether the consolidated accounts accurately reflect the revenue and expen-

diture and give a true and fair view of the European Communities' financial situation as at 31 December. The reliability of the accounts is not dependent on the transactions being legal and regular, but whether they are completely and accurately recorded and disclosed. The audit of the accounts has always led to a result that was – though including some reservations/qualifications – overall positive, i.e. a positive Statement of Assurance.

* **Audit of the legality and regularity of the transactions:**

the objective of the audit of the legality and regularity of the underlying transactions is to gain sufficient evidence that funds have been received and spent in conformity with contractual and legislative conditions and are correctly and accurately calculated. Questions to be answered by this audit are for example: Does the underlying transaction exist? Is the recipient/beneficiary eligible? Do the costs/quantities claimed exist? Are they accurate and eligible? The opinion resulting from this audit consists of an overall conclusion on revenue and expenditure transactions. This audit not only includes expenditure at the European Union level itself but also payments on a national (Member States, third countries), regional, local or even individual level for which authorities at these levels are responsible.
(*The EU Budget - Public Perception & Fact by Terry Wynn MEP*)

19. D

Within the meaning of Article 248(4) of the EC Treaty, one of the most important and publicly conspicuous duties of the ECA is to draw up an annual report after the close of each financial year, which is forwarded to the other institutions of the Community and published, together with the replies of these institutions to the observations of the Court of Auditors, in the Official Journal of the European Communities. This document tells the public more about the activities of the Community and it is influential in drawing attention to financial and other anomalies in the Community's structure and in securing reforms. The Court of Auditors may also, at any time, submit observations, particularly in the form of special reports, on specific questions and deliver opinions at the request of one of the other institutions of the Community. It

adopts its annual reports, special reports or opinions by a majority of its Members. It also helps the European Parliament and the Council in exercising their powers of control over the implementation of the budget. Much of the content of the annual reports is concerned with the question of fraud at the expense of the Community institutions; and the sheer size of the problem of fraud is such that a major constitutional development at present under way is the creation not only of a special prosecution procedure but also of special criminal rules.
(*IP Mall*)

20.   B

Cooperation between the SAIs (the Supreme Audit Institutions of the Member States) and the ECA principally takes place within the framework of the EU Contact Committee structure. This structure consists of the *Contact Committee* composed of the Heads of the SAIs (which includes the President of the ECA), the Committee of Liaison Officers and working groups on specific audit topics. The cooperation takes due account of the independence and constitutional mandate of each institution. It promotes cooperation and implements practical joint initiatives designed to develop methodologies and strengthen the operational effectiveness of the organisations involved. The framework of the Contact Committee is also used to agree on principles how to implement the "liaison" obligations of Art 248(3) of the EC Treaty. In addition to facilitating the exchange of information between the SAIs and the ECA, the structure has made it possible to achieve considerable progress with effective cooperation between the various institutions which audit the management of Community funds. The Heads of the national SAIs and the ECA meet once a year. Their meetings are prepared by the Liaison Officers, who themselves usually meet twice a year. The Liaison Officers' tasks also include coordination of the planning of the ECA audits in the Member States, the organisation of working groups on specific audit topics and regular exchange of information. In 1996, the ECA, together with the Contact Committee, set up a parallel liaison structure with the Supreme Audit institutions of the candidate countries, to help facilitate their integration into the EU after accession.
(*ECA*)

ADVISORY BODIES, AGENCIES
ANSWERS

Question No	A	B	C	D
1.		X		
2.			X	
3.		X		
4.		X		
5.			X	
6.	X			
7.		X		
8.	X			
9.			X	
10.				X
11.				X
12.	X			
13.	X			
14.				X
15.	X			
16.			X	
17.			X	
18.		X		
19.	X			
20.			X	

Question No	A	B	C	D
21.		X		
22.				X
23.	X			
24.	X			
25.			X	
26.		X		
27.		X		
28.				X
29.		X		
30.				X
31.		X		
32.	X			
33.				X
34.		X		
35.				X
36.		X		
37.				X
38.		X		
39.			X	
40.	X			

1. B

The Committee of the Regions (CoR) is the guardian of the principle of subsidiarity (according to which the European Union does not take decisions on a subject if the local or regional authorities are capable of doing so themselves). The members of the Committee of the Regions ensure therefore that this principle is respected.
(*Committee of the Regions*)

2. C

The Committee of the Regions was established by the Maastricht Treaty signed on 7 February 1992.

3. B

The first CoR meeting took place in March 1994.

4. B

Following the entry into force of the Amsterdam Treaty, ten policy areas fall under obligatory consultation (economic and social cohesion, trans-European networks in the field of transport, energy and telecommunications, public health, education and youth, culture, employment, social policy, environment, vocational training, transport).

246   ANSWERS – ADVISORY BODIES, AGENCIES

5.   C

The CoR brings together 317 members and 317 alternate members from the 25 Member States of the EU.

6.   A

Article 263 of the EC Treaty provides that the number of members of the Committee of the Regions may not exceed 350.

7.   B

According to Article 263 of the EC Treaty, "[t]he members of the Committee and an equal number of alternate members shall be appointed for four years, on proposals from the respective Member States. Their term of office shall be renewable. The Council, acting by a qualified majority, shall adopt the list of members and alternate members drawn up in accordance with the proposals made by each Member State."

8.   A

The Treaty of Nice laid down the general membership criteria of the Committee of the Regions: CoR should consist of representatives of regional and local bodies who either hold a regional or local authority electoral mandate or are politically accountable to an elected assembly. Further, in accordance with Article 263 of the EC Treaty, no member of the CoR may at the same time be a Member of the European Parliament.

9.   C

The Union for Europe of the Nations Group is a political group in the European Parliament.
    There are four political groups in the Committee of the Regions:
- Party of European Socialists Group
- European People's Party Group

- European Liberal Democrats and Reform Party Group
- European Alliance Group

10.   D

There are six Commissions within the Committee of the Regions specialised in the following policy domains:
- COTER – Commission for Territorial Cohesion Policy
- ECOS – Commission for Economic and Social Policy
- DEVE – Commission for Sustainable Development
- EDUC – Commission for Education
- CONST – Commission for Constitutional Affairs and European Governance
- RELEX – Commission for External Relations

11.   D

For a fuller account of CoR Commissions see answer no. 10 above.

12.   A

On 11 February 2004 Peter Straub was elected President of the Committee of the Regions for a term of two years.

13.   A

Rule 64 of the Rules of Procedure of the CoR sets out the responsibilities of the Commission for Financial and Administrative Affairs (CAFA):
- Advising on and adopting, in accordance with Rule 65, the preliminary draft estimates of the Committee's expenditure and revenue submitted by the Secretary-General
- Drawing up draft Bureau implementing provisions and decisions in the financial, organisational and administrative areas, including those relating to members and alternates

14. D

In March 1994 the CoR set up a special Commission for Institutional Affairs and subsequently appointed Jordi Pujol to draft an opinion on the reform of the EU institutions. In the Pujol report the CoR proposed that it be given legal standing as an institution, which could enable the CoR to bring actions before the Court of Justice for annulment proceedings (Article 230 of the EC Treaty) and failure to act proceedings (Article 232 of the EC Treaty).

15. A

The European Economic and Social Committee was set up in 1957 by the Treaty of Rome which entered into force on 1 January 1958.

16. C

The European Economic and Social Committee is the European level institutional forum for consultation, representation, information and expression for the organised civil society. It enables representatives of Member States' economic, social and civic organisations to play an integral part in the process of shaping policy and decisions at Community level. The main tasks of this consultative body, set up by the Treaty of Rome, are to advise the Council, the Commission and the European Parliament. It is mandatory for the Committee to be consulted on those issues stipulated in the Treaties and in all cases where the institutions deem it appropriate. The Committee is also increasingly being asked to draw up exploratory opinions before proposals are adopted or policy decisions are taken. It can also issue opinions and draw up information reports on its own initiative.
(*The EESC: a bridge between Europe and organised civil society*)

17. C

According to Article 262 of the EC Treaty, the EESC may issue an opinion on its own initiative "in cases in which it considers it appropriate". In fact, on average the EESC puts forward 170 opinions and other advisory papers a year, of which about 15% are issued on its own initiative.

18. B

Following the path of progress introduced by previous Treaties, the Amsterdam Treaty further extended the scope for referral to the EESC and made it possible for the EESC to be consulted by the European Parliament: Article 262 of the EC Treaty provides that the EESC must be consulted by the Council or by the Commission where the EC Treaty so provides and may be consulted by the European Parliament.

19. A

Both the Netherlands and Hungary delegate 12 members each. The EESC brings together 317 members from the 25 Member States of the EU. Germany, France, Italy and the United Kingdom have 24 members each, Spain and Poland have 21, Belgium, Greece, the Netherlands, Portugal, Austria, Sweden, Czech Republic and Hungary 12, Denmark, Ireland, Finland, Lithuania and Slovakia 9, Estonia, Latvia and Slovenia 7, Luxembourg and Cyprus 6, Malta 5.

20. C

Article 258 of the EC Treaty provides that the number of members of the EESC may not exceed 350.

21. B

According to Article 259(1) of the EC Treaty, the members of the EESC are appointed for four years, on proposals from the Member States. The Council, acting by a qualified majority (since the Treaty of Nice), adopts the list of members drawn up in accordance with the proposals made by each Member State.

22.   D

Article 258 of the EC Treaty provides in no uncertain terms that the Members of the EESC may not be bound by any mandatory instructions and they are completely independent in the performance of their duties, in the general interest of the Community.

23.   A

The EESC consists of representatives of the various economic and social components of civil society (in particular representatives of producers, farmers, carriers, workers, dealers, craftsmen, professional occupations, consumers and the general interest), who are brought together at the following group levels:
- employers (Group I);
- wage-earners (Group II);
- delegates representing all the other socio-occupational interests (Group III).

In practice one third of the seats go to employers, one third to employees and one third to other categories (farmers, retailers, the liberal professions, consumers, etc).

24.   A

The EESC has six sections as follows:
- Agriculture, Rural Development and the Environment (NAT);
- Economic and Monetary Union and Economic and Social Cohesion (ECO);
- Employment, Social Affairs and Citizenship (SOC);
- External Relations (REX);
- Single Market, Production and Consumption (INT);
- Transport, Energy, Infrastructure and the Information Society (TEN).

Further, two more bodies have been set up recently, the Single Market Observatory (SMO) and the Consultative Commission on Industrial Change (CCIC).

25.   C

EESC INT deals with matters related to the Single Market, Production and Consumption (see specialised sections of the EESC in answer 24 above)

26.   B

Article 262 of the EC Treaty provides that "[t]he Council or the Commission shall, if it considers it necessary, set the Committee, for the submission of its opinion, a time limit which may not be less than one month from the date on which the chairman receives notification to this effect. Upon expiry of the time limit, the absence of an opinion shall not prevent further action."

27.   C

Immigration and asylum matters do not trigger consultation obligation towards the EESC. In certain areas the EC Treaty stipulates that a decision may be taken only after the Council or Commission has consulted the ESC:
- Agricultural policy (Article 37);
- Free movement of persons and services (Part Three, Title III);
- Transport policy (Part Three, Title V);
- Harmonisation of indirect taxation (Article 93);
- Approximation of laws for the internal market (Articles 94 and 95);
- Employment policy (Part Three, Title VIII);
- Social policy, education, vocational training and youth (Part Three, Title XI);
- Public health (Article 152);
- Consumer protection (Article 153);
- Trans-European networks (Article 156);
- Industrial policy (Article 157);
- Economic and social cohesion (Part Three, Title XVII);
- Research and technological development (Part Three, Title XVIII);
- The environment (Title XIX).

(*http://www.europarl.eu.int/factsheets/1_3_11_en.htm*)

28.   D

As a rule, the full Committee meets in Plenary session ten times a year. At the Plenary sessions, opinions are adopted on the basis of section opinions by a simple majority. They are forwarded to the institutions and published in the Official Journal of the European Communities.
(*EESC*)

29.   B

Rule 65(1) of the Rules of Procedure of the ESSC provides that Plenary sessions of the EESC and meetings of the specialised sections shall be public.

30.   D

The Economic and Social Council (ECOSOC) is the principal organ of the UN to coordinate the economic, social, and related work of the 14 UN specialised agencies, 10 functional commissions and five regional commissions. ECOSOC serves as the central forum for discussing international economic and social issues, and for formulating policy recommendations addressed to Member States and the United Nations system. It is responsible for promoting higher standards of living, full employment, and economic and social progress; identifying solutions to international economic, social and health problems; facilitating international cultural and educational cooperation; and encouraging universal respect for human rights and fundamental freedoms. It has the power to make or initiate studies and reports on these issues. It also has the power to assist in the preparations and organisation of major international conferences in the economic and social and related fields and to facilitate a coordinated follow-up to these conferences. With its broad mandate the ECOSOC's purview extends to over 70 per cent of the human and financial resources of the entire UN system.
(*UN*)

31.   B

At present, the 18 EU Agencies are:

CEDEFOP	European Centre for the Development of Vocational Training
EUROFOUND	European Foundation for the Improvement of Living and Working Conditions
EEA	European Environment Agency
ETF	European Training Foundation
EMCDDA	European Monitoring Centre for Drugs and Drug Addiction
EMEA	European Medicines Agency
OHIM	Office for Harmonisation in the Internal Market (Trade Marks and Designs)
EU-OSHA	European Agency for Safety and Health at Work
CPVO	Community Plant Variety Office
CdT	Translation Centre for the Bodies of the European Union
EUMC	European Monitoring Centre on Racism and Xenophobia
EAR	European Agency for Reconstruction
EFSA	European Food Safety Authority
EMSA	European Maritime Safety Agency
EASA	European Aviation Safety Agency
ENISA	European Network and Information Security Agency
ECDC	European Centre for Disease Prevention and Control
FRONTEX	Agency for the Management of Operational Cooperation at the External Borders of the Member States of the EU

For further information, see:
http://europa.eu.int/agencies/index_en.htm

32.   A

The European Centre for the Development of Vocational Training (Cedefop) is the European Union's reference centre for vocational education and training. It provides information on and analyses of vocational education and training systems, policies, research and practice. Cedefop was established in 1975 by Council Regulation (EEC) No 337/75.

Cedefop's information, research and dissemination activities support vocational education and training specialists to develop and improve vocational education and training in Europe. In 2002, Cedefop's activities grouped into four areas: research, reporting, exchanges, and information and communication.

For further information, see:
http://www.cedefop.eu.int

33.   D

The Office for Harmonisation in the Internal Market (OHIM) is located in Alicante, Spain. See also answer no. 39 below.

34.   B

In June 1999 the Cologne European Council had suggested examining the need for an Agency for human rights and democracy, an idea supported by the European Parliament. After a long debate, the representatives of the Member States meeting within the European Council in Brussels on 12 and 13 December 2003 decided to extend the remit of the European Monitoring Centre on Racism and Xenophobia (EUMC) in order to convert it into a Fundamental Rights Agency. Commission communication "The Fundamental Rights Agency - Public consultation document" (COM(2004) 693) explored the subject in greater detail.

On 26 May 2005 the European Parliament adopted a resolution based on the own-initiative report by Kinga GAL MEP on fundamental rights. Parliament felt that there should be an institutionalised link between the Council of Europe and the future Agency on Fundamental Rights, both to avoid duplication and to give the Agency all necessary input and to ensure its effectiveness. The Agency must have a strong mandate and the power to follow the development of the implementation of the Charter of Fundamental Rights within the European Union and accession countries. Parliament stressed that the Agency should also be able to cover third countries when they are involved in human rights issues affecting the Union, for example in cases where there are suspected violations of the democracy clause. It also felt that the Agency will enjoy enhanced legitimacy if its management bodies are appointed by, and answerable to, the European Parliament and report to the competent parliamentary committees.

As part of its task to promote fundamental rights, the future Agency should provide proactive support to human rights policy-making in two ways: by identifying where legislative improvements would be most welcome and by monitoring the implementation and enforcement of existing legislation.

35.   D

TAIEX is the Technical Assistance and Information Exchange unit of Directorate-General Enlargement of the European Commission. In operation since 1996, TAIEX provides centrally managed short-term technical assistance in the field of approximation, application and enforcement of legislation. Its services are complementary to the several alternative assistance programmes the European Commission offers to new Member States, candidates for accession to the European Union, and the countries of the Western Balkans.

The role of TAIEX is that of a catalyst, channelling requests for assistance as well as that of a facilitator acting as a broker between the concerned institutions and European Union Member States for the delivery of appropriate tailor-made expertise to address problems at short notice.

TAIEX is demand driven in that most of the assistance provided is in response to requests from the beneficiary Countries, the Commission Services and Member States. TAIEX is also strategy driven in that requests are addressed in accordance with the priorities identified by the Commission. The strategic approach is also evident in the large number of TAIEX's own initiatives.

The TAIEX mandate to provide assistance covers three groups of beneficiary countries:

- Cyprus, Czech Republic, Estonia, Hungary, Latvia, Lithuania, Malta, Poland, Slovak Republic, Slovenia;
- Bulgaria, Romania, Turkey and Croatia;
- Serbia and Montenegro, Former Yugoslav Republic of Macedonia, Bosnia and Herzegovina, Republic of Albania and Kosovo (as defined in UN Security Council Resolution 1244 of 10 June 1999).

The ten "new" Member States will remain beneficiary countries for TAIEX assistance, and will continue to receive TAIEX support to institution building in the first years after accession.

TAIEX's main tasks are:

- To provide technical assistance and advice on

the transposition of the acquis communautaire into the national legislation of beneficiary countries and on the subsequent administration, implementation and enforcement of such legislation.

- To provide technical training and peer assistance to the officials of the administrations of the 10 Member States, who remain beneficiaries of TAIEX assistance.
- To provide programmed technical assistance to the countries of the western Balkans.
- To be an information broker by gathering and making available information on the Community acquis.
- To provide database tools for facilitating and monitoring the approximation progress as well as to identify further technical assistance needs.

For further information, see:
http://taiex.cec.eu.int/

36.   B

37.   D

FRONTEX, the European agency for the management of operational co-operation at the external borders of the Member States, co-ordinates all activities of national border guards at the external borders of the enlarged EU.

The agency was set up by a regulation in October 2004 and after much argument, Warsaw was chosen as its seat in April 2005. FRONTEX implements the updated border code on movement of persons across borders and so facilitate the free movement of persons within the Schengen area. Agreement on the code was reached between the Council and Parliament on first reading on 23 June 2005. The agency:

- co-ordinates the activities of national border guards;
- assists in training;
- provides technical and research support;
- assists in joint return operations.

38.   B

The European Union Institute for Security Studies (EUISS) was created by a Council Joint Action on 20 July 2001. It has the status of an autonomous agency that comes under the EU's second 'pillar' – the Common Foreign and Security Policy (CFSP). Having an autonomous status and intellectual freedom, the EUISS does not represent or defend any particular national interest. Its aim is to help create a common European security culture, to enrich the strategic debate, and systematically to promote the interests of the Union.

The EUISS contributes to the development of the CFSP by performing three functions:

Research and debate on the major security and defence issues that are of relevance to the EU;

Forward-looking analysis for the Union's Council and High Representative;

Development of a transatlantic dialogue on all security issues with the countries of Europe, Canada and the United States.

For further information, see:
www.iss-eu-org

39.   C

The OHIM (OAMI) performs the tasks of registering Community Trade Marks and Community Designs.

The systems have been conceived to ensure that formalities and management are kept simple:
1.   A single application
2.   A single administrative centre
3.   A single file
4.   Application in any official EU language
5.   Defence against opposition, cancellation, and invalidity actions in the language of application or a second choice amongst English, French, German, Italian, or Spanish
6.   Links with national registrations and the Madrid Protocol system for the international registration of trade marks

Uniform laws apply, thereby providing unique protection throughout the European Union. Infringement proceedings before the courts are based on a single legislative procedure, covering all EU territories as one, single market.
(*OHIM*)

For further information, see:
http://oami.eu.int

40.   A

The Centre was established by European Parliament and Council Regulation 851/2004 of 21 April 2004, and it is located in Solna, Sweden. Mrs Zsuzsanna JAKAB (Hungarian) was nominated as the ECDC's Director by the Centre's Management Board in December 2004 and took up her post on 1 March 2005. The ECDC became operational on 20 May 2005. The agency's mission is to help strengthen Europe's defences against infectious diseases, such as influenza, SARS and HIV/AIDS. It has a small core staff but an extended network of partners across the EU and EEA/EFTA Member States. The ECDC works in partnership with national health protection bodies to strengthen and develop continent-wide disease surveillance and early warning systems. By working with experts based in these national bodies the agency pools Europe's health knowledge, so as to develop authoritative scientific opinions about the risks posed by new and emerging infectious diseases.

For further information, see:
http://www.ecdc.eu.int

EUROPEAN CENTRAL BANK (ECB)
EUROPEAN INVESTMENT BANK (EIB)
EUROPEAN BANK FOR RECONSTRUCTION AND DEVELOPMENT (EBRD)
ANSWERS

Question No	A	B	C	D
1.	X			
2.				X
3.	X			
4.				X
5.		X		
6.			X	
7.		X		
8.			X	
9.				X
10.	X			
11.		X		
12.			X	
13.		X		
14.				X
15.		X		
16.	X			
17.			X	
18.				X

Question No	A	B	C	D
19.				X
20.		X		
21.		X		
22.			X	
23.	X			
24.			X	
25.		X		
26.	X			
27.	X			
28.		X		
29.				X
30.			X	
31.			X	
32.		X		
33.			X	
34.	X			
35.	X			

1.   A

The European Investment Bank (EIB) was set up by the Treaty of Rome, therefore it has existed since 1958.

For further information, see:
http://www.eib.org

2.   D

The European Economic Area is made up of EU Member States and those of the European Free Trade Agreement (EFTA). However, only European Union Member States are members of the EIB; those of EFTA (Lichtenstein, Norway, Iceland) are not.

3.   A

As the EU's policy driven bank, EIB has grown into a major international financing institution, active in all main economic sectors, within the European Union, and in some 150 non-member countries. (*EIB*)

4.   D

The EIB is a source only of loans, it does not grant aid.

5.   B

The EIB Group, established in 2000, consists of the European Investment Bank and the European Investment Fund (EIF), established in 1994. The EIF contributes to the development of small and medium-size enterprises (SMEs) in the EU Member States and the Candidate Countries.

The EIF's activity is related to two areas, venture capital and guarantees:
- EIF's venture capital instruments consist of equity investments in venture capital funds and business incubators that support SMEs,

particularly those that are early stage and technology-oriented;
- EIF's guarantee instruments consist of providing guarantees to financial institutions that cover credits to SMEs.

6.   C

See answer above.

7.   B

Presidents of the EIB:
- Pietro Campilli (Italian), February 1958 – May 1959
- Paride Formentini (Italian), June 1959 – September 1970
- Yves Le Portz (French), September 1970 – July 1984
- Ernst-Günther Bröder (German), August 1984 – March 1993
- Sir Brian Unwin (British), April 1993 – December 1999
- Philippe Maystadt (Belgian), January 2000 –

Torsten Gersfelt is currently one of the vice-presidents of the EIB's Management Committee.

8.   C

The Management Committee is the Bank's permanent collegiate executive body with nine members (President and 8 Vice-Presidents). Under the authority of the President and the supervision of the Board of Directors, it oversees day-to-day running of the EIB, prepares decisions for Directors and ensures that these are implemented. The members of the Management Committee are responsible solely to the Bank; on a proposal from the Board of Directors, they are appointed by the Board of Governors for a renewable period of six years.

9.   D

The Board of Directors has exclusive power to take decisions regarding loans, guarantees and borrowings. Apart from supervising the proper running of the Bank, it ensures that the Bank respects the provisions of the Treaty and the Statute, along with the general directives laid down by the Governors. Its members are appointed by the Board of Governors for a renewable period of five years following nomination by the Member States and are responsible solely to the Bank.

The Board of Directors is made up of 26 Directors, with one Director nominated by each Member State and one by the European Commission. There are 16 Alternates, meaning that some of these positions will be shared by groupings of States.

In order to broaden the Board of Directors' professional expertise in certain fields, the Board may co-opt a maximum of 6 experts who participate in the Board meetings in an advisory capacity, without voting rights.

Since 1 May 2004, decisions are taken by a majority consisting of at least one third of members entitled to vote and representing at least 50% of the subscribed capital.
(*EIB*)

10.   A

See answer above.

11.   B

12.   C

Article 104(11) of the EC Treaty provides:
"[a]s long as a Member State fails to comply with a decision taken in accordance with paragraph 9, the Council may decide to apply or, as the case may be, intensify one or more of the following measures:
[…]
– to invite the European Investment Bank to reconsider its lending policy towards the Member State concerned […]"

Article 237 of the EC Treaty provides:
"The Court of Justice shall, within the limits hereinafter laid down, have jurisdiction in disputes concerning:

(a) the fulfilment by Member States of obligations under the Statute of the European Investment Bank. […]"

Article 266 of the EC Treaty provides:
"The European Investment Bank shall have legal personality."

Article 219 of the EC Treaty provides:
"The Community shall enjoy in the territories of the Member States such privileges and immunities as are necessary for the performance of its tasks, under the conditions laid down in the Protocol of 8 April 1965 on the privileges and immunities of the European Communities. The same shall apply to the European Central Bank, the European Monetary Institute, and the European Investment Bank."

13.   B

Article I-34 of the Constitutional Treaty provides:
"In the specific cases provided for in the Constitution, European laws and framework laws may be adopted at the initiative of a group of Member States or of the European Parliament, on a recommendation from the European Central Bank or at the request of the Court of Justice or the European Investment Bank."

14.   D

Article 4 of the Protocol on the Statute of the European Investment Bank, annexed to the Constitutional Treaty, provides:
"The capital of the Bank shall be 163 653 737 000 euro, subscribed by the Member States as follows: […]"

15.   B

Article III-394 of the Constitutional Treaty provides:
"The task of the European Investment Bank shall be to contribute, by having recourse to the capital markets and utilising its own resources, to the balanced and steady development of the internal

market in the Union's interest. For this purpose the European Investment Bank shall, operating on a non-profit-making basis, in particular grant loans and give guarantees which facilitate the financing of the following projects in all sectors of the economy:

(a) projects for developing less-developed regions;

(b) projects for modernising or converting undertakings or for developing fresh activities called for by the establishment or functioning of the internal market, where these projects are of such a size or nature that they cannot be entirely financed by the various means available in the individual Member States;

(c) projects of common interest to several Member States which are of such a size or nature that they cannot be entirely financed by the various means available in the individual Member States.

In carrying out its task, the European Investment Bank shall facilitate the financing of investment programmes in conjunction with assistance from the Structural Funds and other Union financial instruments."

16.   A

European System of Central Banks (ESCB) refers to the ECB and the national central banks of the EU Member States. It should be noted that national central banks of Member States which have not yet adopted the euro in accordance with the Treaty retain their powers in the field of monetary policy according to national law and are thus not involved in the conduct of the monetary policy of the Eurosystem.
(*ECB*)

For further information, see:
http://www.ecb.int

17.   C

Eurosystem is the central banking system of the euro area. It comprises the ECB and the national central banks of the Member States that have adopted the euro in Stage Three of Economic and Monetary Union (EMU).

18.   D

The Governing Council is the supreme decision-making body of the ECB. It comprises all members of the Executive Board of the ECB and the governors of the national central banks of the EU Member States that have adopted the euro.

19.   D

The International Monetary Fund (IMF) is an international organisation based in Washington, D.C. with a membership of 184 countries. It was established in 1946 to promote international monetary cooperation and exchange rate stability, to foster economic growth and high levels of employment and to help member countries to correct balance of payments imbalances. It is not affiliated with the European Union, nevertheless the two organisations have strong institutional links.

20.   B

Trans-European Automated Real-time Gross settlement Express Transfer (TARGET) system is a payment system composed of one real-time gross settlement (RTGS) system in each of the EU Member States plus the ECB payment mechanism (EPM). The national RTGS systems and the EPM are interconnected by common procedures (interlinking) to allow cross-border transfers throughout the European Union to move from one system to another.
(*ECB*)

21.   B

22.   C

Article 105(1) of the EC Treaty provides:

"The primary objective of the ESCB shall be to maintain price stability. […]"

23.   A

Articles 105(1)-(2) of the EC Treaty provide:
"[…] Without prejudice to the objective of price stability, the ESCB shall support the general economic policies in the Community with a view to contributing to the achievement of the objectives of the Community as laid down in Article 2. The ESCB shall act in accordance with the principle of an open market economy with free competition, favouring an efficient allocation of resources, and in compliance with the principles set out in Article 4.
    2. The basic tasks to be carried out through the ESCB shall be:
–   to define and implement the monetary policy of the Community,
–   to conduct foreign-exchange operations consistent with the provisions of Article 111,
–   to hold and manage the official foreign reserves of the Member States,
–   to promote the smooth operation of payment systems."

24.   C

In the euro area, the ECB has exclusive rights concerning banknotes but not coins.

25.   B

Jean-Claude Trichet has been the president of the ECB since 1 November 2003. Willem F. Duisenberg (1935–2005) was the previous president of the ECB.

26.   A

The Executive Board of the ECB comprises the President, Vice-President and four other members.

27.   A

All members of the Executive Board are appointed by common accord of the Heads of State or Government of the euro area countries.

28.   B

Responsibilities of the Executive Board are:
•   Preparing Governing Council meetings.
•   Implementing monetary policy for the euro area in accordance with the guidelines specified and decisions taken by the Governing Council. In so doing, it gives the necessary instructions to the euro area national central banks.
•   Managing the day-to-day business of the ECB.
•   Exercising certain powers delegated to it by the Governing Council, including some tasks of a regulatory nature.

29.   D

According to the ECB "[w]e at the European Central Bank are committed to performing all central bank tasks entrusted to us effectively. In so doing, we strive for the highest level of integrity, competence, efficiency and transparency."
(*ECB*)

30.   C

The European Central Bank was inaugurated on 30 June 1998. On 1 January 1999 it took over responsibility for implementing European monetary policy as defined by the European System of Central Banks
(*ESCB*).

31.   C

Through its investments, the EBRD promotes:
•   structural and sectoral reforms;
•   competition, privatisation and entrepreneurship;
•   stronger financial institutions and legal systems;
•   infrastructure development needed to support the private sector;
•   adoption of strong corporate governance, including environmental sensitivity (EBRD).

For further information, see:
http://www.ebrd.org

tal is provided by its members. Voting power is in proportion to the number of shares.

32.   B

EBRD carries out financial operations in the following countries:

Albania, Armenia, Azerbaijan, Belarus, Bosnia and Herzegovina, Bulgaria, Croatia, Czech Republic, Georgia, Estonia, Hungary, Kazakhstan, Kyrgyz Republic, Latvia, Lithuania, FYR Macedonia, Moldova, Poland, Romania, Russia, Serbia and Montenegro, Slovak Republic, Slovenia, Tajikistan, Turkmenistan, Ukraine, Uzbekistan.

33.   C

The EBRD is owned by its member/shareholder countries, the European Community and the European Investment Bank. The Bank's share capi-

34.   A

Persons named as answers B, C and D are vice-presidents of the EBRD.

35.   A

The European Bank for Reconstruction and Development (EBRD) was established in 1991 when communism was crumbling in central and Eastern Europe and ex-soviet countries needed support to nurture a new private sector in a democratic environment. Today the EBRD uses the tools of investment to help build market economies and democracies in 27 countries from central Europe to central Asia.
(*EBRD*)

POLICIES OF THE EUROPEAN UNION

AGRICULTURE

ANSWERS

Question No	A	B	C	D
1.			X	
2.			X	
3.				X
4.	X			
5.		X		
6.			X	
7.			X	
8.				X
9.		X		
10.	X			
11.		X		
12.		X		
13.			X	
14.	X			
15.	X			

Question No	A	B	C	D
16.				X
17.	X			
18.			X	
19.	X			
20.	X			
21.				X
22.		X		
23.	X			
24.			X	
25.		X		
26.		X		
27.	X			
28.				X
29.	X			
30.			X	

1.   C

The Treaty of Rome defined the general objectives of a common agricultural policy. The principles of the Common Agricultural Policy (CAP) were set out at the Stresa Conference in July 1958. In 1960, the CAP mechanisms were adopted by the six founding Member States and two years later, in 1962, the CAP came into force.
(*ScadPlus*)

2.   C

Article 33(1) of the EC Treaty outlines the objectives of the Common Agricultural Policy (CAP) as follows:
*   to increase agricultural productivity by promoting technical progress and by ensuring the rational development of agricultural production and the optimum utilisation of the factors of production, in particular labour;
*   to ensure a fair standard of living for the agricultural community, in particular by increasing the individual earnings of persons engaged in agriculture;
*   to stabilise markets;
*   to assure the availability of supplies;
*   to ensure that supplies reach consumers at reasonable prices.

Further, in order to attain these objectives, Article 34 of the EC Treaty provides for the creation of the common organisation of the agricultural markets (COM) which, depending on the product, can take one of the following forms:
*   common rules on competition;
*   compulsory co-ordination of the various national market organisations;
*   a European market organisation.

The COMs were introduced gradually and now exist for most EU agricultural products. They are the basic instruments of the common agricultural market in as far as they eliminate the obstacles to the intra-Union trade of agricultural products and maintain a common customs barrier with respect to third countries.

3.   D

See the Treaty objectives of the CAP above.

4.   A

Three main principles, defined in 1962, characterise the common agricultural market and thus the COMs:
*   **a unified market**: this denotes the free movement of agricultural products within the area of the Member States; for the organisation of the unified market, common means and mechanisms should be used throughout the EU;
*   **Community preference**: this means that EU agricultural products are given preference and a price advantage over imported products; also, the protection of the internal market from products imported from third countries at low prices and from considerable fluctuations in the world market;
*   **financial solidarity**: all expenses and spending which result from the application of the CAP are borne by the Community budget.
(*ScadPlus*)

5.   B

The EAGGF was set up in 1962.

6.   C

The CAP is financed from the European Agricultural Guidance and Guarantee Fund (EAGGF), which accounts for a substantial part of the Community budget. The EAGGF was set up in 1962 and separated into two sections in 1964:
*   the Guidance Section, one of the structural funds, which contributes to structural reforms in agriculture and the development of rural areas (e.g. investing in new equipment and technology);
*   the Guarantee Section, which funds expenditure concerning the common organisation of the markets (e.g. to buy or store surplus and to encourage agricultural exports).

The Guarantee Section is by far the more important one and is classified as compulsory expenditure within the Community budget. The Guidance Section is one of the structural funds aimed at promoting regional development and reducing disparities between areas in Europe.
(*ScadPlus*)

7.   C

SAPARD was established by Council Regulation 1268/1999 in June 1999, on the basis of a Commission proposal as part of the Agenda 2000 programme for increased pre-accession assistance in the period 2000 - 2006. The aim of SAPARD is to help the 10 beneficiary countries of Central and Eastern Europe deal with the problems of the structural adjustment in their agricultural sectors and rural areas, as well as in the implementation of the acquis communautaire concerning the CAP and related legislation. It is designed to address priorities identified in the Accession Partnerships.

As a result of the first wave of enlargement the Copenhagen European Council decided in December 2002 to increase EU assistance to Romania by 20% (over 2003 levels) in 2004, 30% in 2005 and 40% in 2006. The total volume of pre-accession assistance available to Romania is substantial (around €700 million per year from PHARE, ISPA and SAPARD). This represents a very important financial resource for Romania, equal to around 1.4% of GDP, 4.4% of consolidated budget revenues, or 36% of investment expenditure from the national budget. Bulgaria's allocation from SAPARD for 2000 was €53 million, €54.1 million for 2001 and €55.6 million for 2002. The allocation for 2003 was €56.5 million and the indicative allocation for 2004 was €68.0 million.

8.   D

In short, the key elements of the 2003 CAP reform can be divided into four categories:
* the Single Farm Payment (decoupling);
* horizontal measures (cross compliance, modulation, financial discipline);
* Rural Development Policy;
* market measures.

For a fuller account of the reform see the official website of DG AGRI. Also, certain elements of the reform are referred to in greater detail in the answers below.

9.   B

In order to finance the additional rural development measures, direct payments for bigger farms will be reduced ("modulation"). As regards the distribution of the funds generated through modulation, one percentage point will remain in the Member States where the money is raised. The amounts corresponding to the remaining percentage points will be allocated among Member States according to:
* criteria of agricultural area;
* agricultural employment; and
* GDP per capita in purchasing power.

As a bottom line, every Member State will receive at least 80% of its modulation funds in return.

10.   A

Cross-compliance requirements are closely linked to the decoupled income support system introduced by Council regulation (EC) No 1782/2003 of 29 September 2003. While decoupling will leave the actual amounts paid to farmers unchanged, it will significantly increase the effectiveness of the income aid. Therefore, it became necessary to make the single farm payment conditional upon cross-compliance with environmental, food safety, animal health and welfare criteria, as well as the maintenance of the farm in good agricultural and environmental condition.

11.   B

Each Member State is to set up an integrated administration and control system (IACS) comprising:
* A computerised data base;
* An identification system for agricultural parcels;
* A system for the identification and registration of payment entitlements;

- Aid applications;
- An integrated control system;
- A single system to record the identity of each farmer who submits an aid application.

IACS will enable farmers' payment applications to be checked. Each year, farmers are to submit an application for direct payments and Member States are to carry out the requisite checks. In the event of non-compliance with the rules, the aid granted may be reduced or cancelled. The Commission will be kept informed of, and monitor, the application of IACS.

(*ScadPlus*)

12.   B

ECCP stands for the European climate change programme that was launched in March 2000. ECCP sets out plans for how the EU will meet its commitments stemming from the Kyoto Protocol for reducing greenhouse gas emissions by 8% by 2012.

13.   C

Since Agenda 2000, the Common Agricultural Policy has two pillars: the market and income policy ("first pillar"), and the sustainable development of rural areas ("second pillar"). The 2003 CAP reform brings greater quality to environmental integration, with new or amended measures to promote the protection of the farmed environment in both pillars.

Concerning market and income policy, cross-compliance is the core instrument. The CAP 2003 reform also involves decoupling most direct payments from production. From 2005 (2007 at the latest), a single payment scheme is established based on historical reference amounts. This will mean reducing many of the incentives for intensive production that have been associated with increased environmental risks. The second package of reform (2004) of market regimes for Mediterranean sectors has confirmed the change of direction taken by the CAP in 2003. For the sectors concerned (olive oil, cotton, tobacco and hops), a significant part of the current production-linked payments will be transferred to the decoupled single payment scheme starting in 2006.

As regards the rural development policy, compliance with minimum environmental standards is a condition for eligibility for support under several different rural development measures, such as assistance for investments in agricultural holdings, setting-up of young farmers, and improving the processing and marketing of agricultural products. Moreover, only environmental commitments above the reference level of Good Farming Practice (GFP) may qualify for agri-environment payments. The support to less-favoured areas also require the respect of the codes of GFP.

(*Commission DG AGRI*)

14.   A

The March 2005 Mombasa meeting was to add fresh impetus to the Doha Round which was about to collapse after the Cancún meeting. The EU used the meeting to reiterate its firm commitment to the development goals of the round and presented a package of proposals to that effect. The EU called for

- an immediate start to negotiations on special and differential treatment in Geneva. It pushed for agreement on giving some additional flexibility in the WTO rules where needed by Least Developed Countries (LDCs) and other poor countries in justifiable need. The EU has called for the package of special and differential treatment measures prepared for Cancun to be adopted with as few changes as possible;
- Developed Countries to increase the level of trade related assistance that they currently provide for developing countries, particularly in building trading capacity and infrastructure. In Kenya, the EU called for the G8 Summit and the UN Review of the Millennium Goals to firmly endorse, and act as a catalyst in, this process;
- The EU called for all developed countries to develop their own versions of the Everything But Arms tariff and quota free trading scheme currently applied by the EU to all LDCs;
- immediate and concrete moves to make the various rules of origin systems more flexible. The EU committed to simplifying its own rules of origin system to assist development goals as a matter of priority. The EU called for this process also to be reinvigorated at the WTO level.

(*Commission*)

15.   A

According to the results of a Eurobarometer poll, 66% of European Union citizens believe that granting more funds for the protection and development of the overall rural economy and for direct support to farmers is a good thing. In the first survey of its type to be carried out in the 25 EU Member States, a clear majority have said that they support recent changes in the Common Agricultural Policy and would like to see the way in which it supports EU farmers continue to evolve further along these lines.
(*Commission DG AGRI*)

16.   D

All domestic support measures considered to distort production and trade (with some exceptions) fall into the amber box, which is defined in Article 6 of the Agriculture Agreement as all domestic supports except those in the blue and green boxes. These include measures to support prices, or subsidies directly related to production quantities. These supports are subject to limits: "de minimis" minimal supports are allowed (5% of agricultural production for developed countries, 10% for developing countries); the 30 WTO members that had larger subsidies than the de minimis levels at the beginning of the post-Uruguay Round reform period are committed to reducing these subsidies.
(*WTO*)

17.   A

According to Article 37 of the EC Treaty, matters with agriculture aspects fall under the consultation procedure.

18.   C

Germany is the largest producer and collector of cow's milk in the EU (2123.7 thousand tonnes collected in November 2004, followed by the second largest producer France with 1894.7 thousand tonnes collected).
(*Eurostat*)

19.   A

Agricultural production employs around 8% of EU25 workforce. (*Commission's research paper –"Plants for the Future"*)

20.   A

TAC: Total Allowable Catch. The Council, within the framework of the Common Fisheries Policy, fixes TACs on a yearly basis by species and determines quotas allocating the respective TACs between the Member States.

21.   D

Over 40% of the EU budget goes on the CAP and a total of EUR 49.7 billion has been allocated to the CAP under the EU budget for 2005.

22.   B

Regulation (EC) No 178/2002 provides the legal basis for the establishment of the European Food Safety Authority (EFSA). The primary responsibility of the Authority will be to provide independent scientific advice on all matters with a direct or indirect impact on food safety. EFSA is not empowered to make laws.

23.   A

The ISPA (instrument for structural policies for pre-accession) was established by Council Regulation (EC) No 1267/1999 (17) and covers the period 2000-2006. Its aims are similar to the Cohesion Fund, which funds major infrastructure projects in the field of transport and environment in Greece, Spain, Ireland, Portugal and all new Member States that joined the EU in 2004. With an annual budget of EUR 1040 million for 2000-2006, ISPA funds up to 85% of the cost of environmental infrastructure projects (focusing on investments aimed at bringing up to EU standard legislation on drinking water supplies, treatment of waste water, solid waste management and air pollution). It is also invested into improving transport infrastructure. (*Commission DG AGRI – EU Agriculture and Enlargement*)

24.   C

Common market organisation (CMO): a uniform set of regulations for each agricultural sector across the EU, set up to manage agricultural markets. They are designed to control agricultural output and stabilise markets, providing farmers with a steady income and consumers with secure food supplies. The CMOs make up the "first pillar" of the CAP. Various measures may be used to fulfil the objectives of the CMOs. These include:

- market support, including buying up surplus production, providing storage aid, or managing supply;
- direct payments to farmers;
- trade measures and border protection, including customs duties, tariff rate quotas (TRQs) and export refunds. (*Commission DG AGRI – Enlargement and Agriculture – Glossary*)

25.   B

Compensatory allowances are payments to farmers in naturally less favoured areas (LFAs) aiming to ensure continued agricultural land use and thereby contribute to the maintenance of a viable rural community; to maintain countryside; and to maintain and promote sustainable farming systems which take account of environmental protection requirements. Also paid in areas with environmental restrictions, to ensure environmental requirements and to safeguard farming in areas with environmental restrictions. (*Commission DG AGRI – Enlargement and Agriculture – Glossary*)

26.   B

The abbreviation FADN stands for the Farm Accountancy Data Network. Based on the agricultural accountancy offices in each EU Member State,

FADN provides data on the income and economy of agricultural holdings.

27.   A

Reflecting the Salzburg conference conclusions (November 2003) and the strategic orientations of the Lisbon and Göteborg European Councils emphasising the economic, environmental, and social elements of sustainability, the following three major objectives for regional development policy have been set in the Communication on the Financial Perspectives for the period 2007–2013:

- increasing the competitiveness of the agricultural sector through support for restructuring;
- enhancing the environment and countryside through support for land management (including rural development actions related to Natura 2000 sites);
- enhancing the quality of life in rural areas and promoting diversification of economic activities through measures targeting the farm sector and other rural actors.

   In summary, the importance of the EU dimension of rural development policy lies in:

- accompanying and complementing further CAP reform and ensuring coherence with the instruments and the policies of the first pillar;
- contributing to other EU policy priorities such as sustainable management of natural resources, innovation and competitiveness in rural areas, and economic and social cohesion.

(*Commission's Proposal for a Council Regulation on support for rural development by the European Agricultural Fund for Rural Development (EAFRD) – COM(2004)490 final*)

28.   D

Semi-subsistence farms produce for their own consumption, but also market part of their production. To help to turn them into commercially viable units, and to contribute additional income support while the farm is upgrading, a specific measure of maximum EUR 1000 a year per semi-subsistence farm is offered under the relevant CAP schemes.

29.   A

Protected designation of origin (PDO): term used to describe foodstuffs that are produced, processed and prepared in a given geographical area using recognised know-how.
(*Commission DG AGRI – Enlargement and Agriculture – Glossary*)

30.   C

In May 2002, the Commission presented a first series of proposals to reform the Common Fisheries Policy (CFP). The Council of Fisheries Ministers agreed on the first package of reform measures in December 2002.

The decisions taken impact on several areas of the CFP. The main changes can be summarised as follows:

- **Long-term approach**: until now measures concerning fishing opportunities and related measures have been taken annually. They have often resulted in fluctuations which not only have prevented fishermen from planning ahead but have also failed to conserve fish stocks. Under the new CFP, long-term objectives for attaining and/or maintaining safe levels of adult fish in EU stocks will be set as well as the measures needed to reach these levels.
- **A new policy for the fleets**: the reform has responded to the challenge posed by the chronic overcapacity of the EU fleet by providing two sets of measures:

- A simpler fleet policy that puts responsibility for matching fishing capacity to fishing possibilities with the Member States;
- A phasing out of public aid to private investors to help them renew or modernise fishing vessels, while keeping aid to improve security and working conditions on board.

- **Better application of the rules**: The diversity of national control systems and sanctions for rule breakers undermines the effectiveness of enforcement. This is why measures will be taken to develop co-operation among the various authorities concerned and to strengthen the uniformity of control and sanctions throughout the EU. Commission inspectors' powers to ensure the equity and effectiveness of EU enforcement have been extended. These measures will help establish the level-playing field that fishermen have been calling for.
- **Stakeholders' involvement**: stakeholders, particularly fishermen, need to take a greater part in the CFP management process. It is important that fishermen and scientists share their expertise. Regional advisory councils (RACs) will be created to enable them to work together to identify ways of achieving sustainable fisheries in the areas of interest to the RAC concerned. As fisheries affect a number of parties beyond the fisheries sector, fishermen and scientists will be joined by other stakeholders.

(*Commission DG FISH*)

EMPLOYMENT, SOCIAL AFFAIRS AND EQUAL OPPORTUNITIES

ANSWERS

Question No	A	B	C	D
1.			X	
2.	X			
3.	X			
4.	X			
5.			X	
6.	X			
7.			X	
8.		X		
9.				X
10.	X			
11.				X
12.				X
13.				X
14.	X			
15.			X	
16.			X	
17.				X
18.	X			

Question No	A	B	C	D
19.			X	
20.				X
21.	X			
22.	X			
23.			X	
24.	X			
25.			X	
26.			X	
27.			X	
28.	X			
29.	X			
30.		X		
31.	X			
32.	X			
33.		X		
34.				X
35.		X		

1.   C

Further to the Amsterdam Treaty, Article 136 of the EC Treaty provides that the Community and the Member States must promote employment, as well as improved living and working conditions, proper social protection, dialogue between management and labour, the development of human resources with a view to lasting high employment and the combating of exclusion.

2.   A

Article 126(2) of the EC Treaty provides that "Member States, having regard to national practices related to the responsibilities of management and labour, shall regard promoting employment as a matter of common concern and shall coordinate their action in this respect within the Council, in accordance with the provisions of Article 128."

3.   A

The Luxembourg European Council of November 1997 examined best national practices in fighting unemployment and laid the foundation for future Community action in the field of employment. The so-called Luxembourg process involves the coordination of Member States' employment policies at EU level on a yearly basis. This annual cycle is called the

European Employment Strategy (EES) or Luxembourg Process, based on the commitment of the Member States to establish a set of common objectives and targets and was built around several components:

- **Employment Guidelines**: following a proposal from the Commission, the Council agree every year on a series of guidelines setting out common priorities for Member States' employment policies;
- **National Action Plans**: every Member State must draw up an annual National Action Plan which describes how these guidelines are put into practice nationally;
- **Joint Employment Report**: The Commission and the Council jointly examine each National Action Plan and present a Joint Employment Report. The Commission presents a new proposal to revise the Employment Guidelines accordingly for the following year;
- **Recommendations**: The Council may decide, by qualified majority, to issue country-specific Recommendations upon a proposal by the Commission.

In this way, the Luxembourg process delivers a rolling programme of yearly planning, monitoring, examination and re-adjustment. This new governance mechanism has the objective to promote policy learning through the exchange of good practice. One of the main features of the EES are the mechanisms for joint monitoring and surveillance, including peer review and benchmarking on the basis of common indicators. The Luxembourg process is also called the open method of coordination.

(*ScadPlus*) (see also European Employment Strategy and open method of coordination)

4.   A

The "Cardiff Process", named after the Cardiff Summit of 1998, which embodies the hope that liberalization of product and financial markets can stimulate the structural changes and dynamism required to create knowledge-based economies in the various European countries, while simultaneously deepening European integration. (*Internationale Politik und Gesellschaft Online*)

5.   C

The European Employment Pact, adopted at the Cologne Summit of June 1999, is based on three pillars: the Luxembourg employment strategy (Employment Guidelines and National Action Plans), the Cardiff Process for structural reform of product, service and capital markets, and a new Macroeconomic Dialogue, which envisages a policy mix to foster growth and employment while safeguarding price stability.

6.   A

Technically, the Employment chapter of the Amsterdam Treaty set out the legal base of the European Employment Strategy (EES) (see also "Luxembourg Process" and open method of coordination).

7.   C

The first Employment Policy Guidelines were adopted in December 1997, before the Amsterdam Treaty entered into force. (The Amsterdam Treaty was signed on 2 October 1997 and became effective on 1 May 1999.)

8.   B

In light of the new provisions introduced by the Amsterdam Treaty, the Commission proposed an initial series of guidelines for 1998, which were adopted by the European Council in December 1997.

These guidelines rest on four pillars:
- developing entrepreneurship;
- improving employability;
- encouraging adaptability of businesses and their employees;
- strengthening the policies for equal opportunities.

9. D

The open method of coordination is based on five key principles: subsidiarity, convergence, management by objectives, country surveillance and an integrated approach.

10. A

The 2004 Employment Guidelines remained unchanged compared to the 2003 Employment Guidelines.

11. D

According to Article 128(2) of the EC Treaty, the Employment Committee has an advisory status to promote coordination between Member States on employment and labour market policies. The Committee monitors the employment situation and employment policies in the Member States and the Community and formulates opinions at the request of either the Council or the Commission or on its own initiative. Also, the Committee contributes to the preparation by the Council of the Employment Policy Guidelines. Each Member State and the Commission appoint two members of the Committee.

The Employment Committee was created by a Council Decision dated 24 January 2000.

12. D

The "European Works Council Directive" (Council Directive 94/45/EC on the establishment of a European Works Council or a procedure in Community-scale undertakings and Community-scale groups of undertakings for the purposes of informing and consulting employees) aims at improving the right to information and to consultation of employees in the so-called Community-scale undertakings (i.e. any undertaking with at least 1000 employees within the Member States and at least 150 employees in each of at least two Member States) and their affiliates. The Directive imposes an obligation on the central management to initiate negotiations for the establishment of a European Works Council or an

information and consultation procedure on its own initiative or at the written request of at least 100 employees or their representatives in at least two undertakings or establishments in at least two different Member States.

13. D

One of the most disputed features of the Commission's proposal is the new category of on-call time, the so-called "inactive" part of on-call time, when the worker, although available for work at his/her place of employment, does not carry out his/her duties. According to the proposal, inactive on-call time will not be counted as working time, unless otherwise provided by national law or collective agreement. ETUC, amongst others, argue that "the proposal is in clear contradiction with the fundamental objectives of the Directive and with other existing Community legislation, and has disproportionate effects. There is a real danger that the introduction of a definition of the "inactive part of working time" will have a disastrous effect on working time arrangements in many more sectors and jobs than only healthcare."

14. A

Article 128 of the EC Treaty provides that the European Council must each year consider the employment situation in the Community and adopt conclusions, on the basis of a joint annual report by the Council and the Commission.

15. C

The 1991 Agreement on Social Policy which was concluded among the social partners and annexed to the Maastricht Treaty, imposes an obligation on the Commission to promote social dialogue between the parties and to consult with them when taking Community decisions, including some areas for mandatory consultation of the social partners.

16.   C

The Treaty of Nice, which came into force in February 2003, provided for the establishment of the Social Protection Committee. Under Article 144 of the EC Treaty, the Employment Committee has an advisory status to promote cooperation on social protection policies between the Member States and with the Commission. The Committee monitors the social situation and the development of social protection policies in the Member States and the Community, and promotes exchanges of information, experience and good practice between Member States and with the Commission. Further, the Committee prepares reports, formulates opinions or undertakes other work within its fields of competence, at the request of either the Council or the Commission or on its own initiative.

17.   D

The Nice European Council in December 2000 invited the Commission to present annually from the Stockholm Summit onwards a Scoreboard outlining the progress made in implementing the Social Policy Agenda. In February 2001, the European Commission has adopted the first Scoreboard on implementation of the Social Policy Agenda. The Scoreboard reports on the concrete steps already taken in those areas of employment and social affairs aimed at economic and social renewal. As it follows, the third scoreboard was adopted in February 2003 (*Communication from the Commission –Scoreboard on Implementing the Social Policy Agenda – COM(2003) 57 final) (Commission DG EMPL)*

18.   A

Originally set up by the Treaty of Rome, the ESF is the longest established Structural Fund which, for over 40 years has invested, in partnership with the Member States, in programmes to develop people's skills and their potential for work
For further information, see:
http://europa.eu.int/comm/dgs/employment_social/index_en.htm

19.   C

In June 1999 the Cologne Summit decided that the citizens' "fundamental rights at Union level should be consolidated in a Charter and thereby made more evident".

20.   D

EQUAL is part of the European Union's strategy for more and better jobs and for ensuring that no-one is denied access to them. Funded by the European Social Fund, this initiative is testing since 2001 new ways of tackling discrimination and inequality experienced by those in work and those looking for a job.

EQUAL co-finances activities in all EU Member States. The EU contribution to EQUAL of 3.274 billion EUR is matched by national funding. EQUAL differs from the European Social Fund mainstream programmes in its function as a laboratory (principle of innovation) and in its emphasis on active co-operation between Member States. Two calls for proposals for EQUAL projects in the Member States have taken place so far, the first one in 2001, the second one in 2004. Responsibility for the implementation of the Community Initiative programmes in the Member States lies with the national authorities. (*Commission DG EMPL*)

21.   A

Informal social summits have been held on the eve of the annual spring European Council meeting on economic and social issues in Stockholm in March 2001 and in Barcelona in March 2002. The decision to formalise the arrangement is a result of a call from the social partners that they had made in a joint contribution to the Laeken European Council in December 2001, initiating a concertation committee on growth and employment to be established. The tripartite social summit for growth and employment was formally established by a Council Decision of 6 March 2003. The summit is held annually, on the eve of the annual spring economic and social Council. The objective of this summit is to strengthen contacts between the social partners and the European institutions in the areas of econ-

omic and social policies and to "send a strong political signal about the importance of tripartite concertation in boosting the involvement of the social partners in the pursuit of the Lisbon objectives", that is, the EU employment targets and objectives set at the March 2000 Lisbon Council.
(*Eironline*)

22.   A

In 1985 Commission President Jacques Delors invited the social partners in the Chateau de Val Duchesse (Belgium) to pave the way of the European Social Dialogue. Article 139 of the EC Treaty imposes a task on the Commission to encourage and facilitate consultation with the social partners on the future development of Community action and on the content of any proposals on the European Union's social policy, which is essentially concerned with the labour market.

23.   C

(See more in Communication from the Commission on Partnership for change in an enlarged Europe –Enhancing the contribution of European social dialogue (*COM(2004) 557 final*).

Agreements implemented in accordance with Article 139(2): minimum standards

Agreements implemented by Council decision and monitored by the Commission have included the following examples:
*   Framework agreement on part-time work, 1997;
*   Framework agreement on fixed-term work, 1999;
*   European agreement on the organisation of working time of seafarers, 1998;
*   European agreement on the organisation of working time of mobile workers in civil aviation, 2000;
*   European agreement on certain aspects of the working conditions of mobile workers assigned to interoperable cross-border services, 2004.
Autonomous agreements implemented by the procedures and practices specific to management

and labour and the Member States and implemented and monitored by the social partners have included the following examples:
*   Framework agreement on telework, 2002;
*   Framework agreement on work-related stress, 2004;
*   Agreement on the European licence for drivers carrying out a cross-border interoperability service, 2004.

24.   A

In December 2000, the Nice Summit approved the European Social Agenda, which defines specific priorities for action around six strategic guidelines in all social policy areas:
*   more and better jobs;
*   anticipating and capitalising on change in the working environment by creating a new balance between flexibility and security;
*   fighting poverty and all forms of exclusion and discrimination in order to promote social integration;
*   modernising social protection;
*   promoting gender equality;
*   strengthening the social policy aspects of enlargement and the European Union's external relations.

25.   C

The Lisbon Strategy, launched in 2000 at the Lisbon Summit, aims to make the EU "the most competitive and dynamic knowledge-based economy in the world, capable of sustainable economic growth with more and better jobs and greater social cohesion" by 2010.
   As regards job creation, the overall target was to increase the employment rate to 70% of the total EU population by 2010, with an intermediate target of 67% by 2005. Also, a subsidiary target was to raise the percentage of women employed to 60% and older workers to 50% until 2010.
   See also answer no. 27.

26.   C

The European Council held in Brussels in March 2004 invited the Commission to establish a High Level Group headed by Mr Wim Kok to carry out an independent review to contribute to the mid-term review of the Lisbon Strategy. Its report was expected to identify measures which together form a consistent strategy for the European economies to achieve the Lisbon objectives and targets. In November 2004, the High Level Group presented its report: "Facing the Challenge – The Lisbon Strategy for Growth and Employment".

27.   C

According to the Presidency Conclusions, "five years after the launch of the Lisbon Strategy, the results are mixed. Alongside undeniable progress, there are shortcomings and obvious delays." Therefore, the European Council believes that "it is essential to re-launch the Lisbon Strategy without delay and re-focus priorities on growth and employment. Europe must renew the basis of its competitiveness, increase its growth potential and its productivity and strengthen social cohesion, placing the main emphasis on knowledge, inno-vation and the optimisation of human capital." (*see more: Presidency Conclusions – Brussels, 22 and 23 March 2005*)

28.   A

Enlargement has raised the EU population by 20%, to more than 450 million people, but only increased its GDP by 4.5%.
(*Eurostat*)

29.   A

Commission Communication "European Initiative for Growth – Investing in Networks and Knowledge for Growth and Jobs" was adopted in 2003 by the Brussels European Council.

30.   B

The report prepared by the "Employment Task Force" identifies four areas for action:
* increasing adaptability of workers and enter-prises;
* attracting more people to the labour market;
* more effective investment in human capital;
* a better governance for employment.

31.   A

ENEA pilot projects on mobility of elderly people are intended to test the feasibility and usefulness of the establishment of European exchange pro-grammes for the elderly through specialised organ-isations tasked with developing, among other things, resources for mobility and changes to infra-structure. At the end of the pilot projects the Commission will assess the feasibility and useful-ness of establishing such programmes on the basis of the knowledge, know-how and experiences gen-erated. The programme was launched in May 2003 and finished at the end of 2004.
(*Age and Mobility*)

32.   A

In 2003 the overall unemployment rate for women in the EU25 rose slightly (to 10.0%). The EU25 unemployment rate was 9.1% in August 2003 and 9.0% in August 2004.
(*Eurostat*)

33.   B

Council Decision 2000/750/EC of 27 November 2000 on the "Community Action Programme to Combat Discrimination 2001-2006" does not deal with gender equality.
Article 1 of the above Decision provides:
"This Decision establishes a Community action programme, hereinafter referred to as "the pro-gramme" to promote measures to combat direct or

indirect discrimination based on racial or ethnic origin, religion or belief, disability, age or sexual orientation, for the period from 1 January 2001 to 31 December 2006."

34.   D

The Mutual Information System on Social Protection (MISSOC) was established in 1990 to promote a continuous exchange of information on social protection among the EU Member States. MISSOC has become the central information source on social protection legislation in all Member States of the European Union and countries of the European Economic Area.
(*Commission DG EMPL*)

35.   B

DELSA - Directorate for Employment, Labour and Social Affairs within the OECD. DELSA and DG EMPL hold regular meetings twice per year. The meetings are generally devoted to discuss current economic, employment and social policy issues, and to exchange views on the scope of further co-operation in the main areas of employment, migration, responses to ageing, social inclusion and pensions. DG EMPL regularly participates in the OECD meetings on Employment, Labour and Social Affairs. Moreover, the Commission and DELSA jointly organise seminars.
(*Commission DG EMPL*)

INTERNAL MARKET

ANSWERS

Question No	A	B	C	D
1.				X
2.		X		
3.	X			
4.	X			
5.				X
6.			X	
7.				X
8.		X		
9.	X			
10.				X
11.			X	
12.	X			
13.			X	
14.		X		
15.			X	
16.	X			
17.				X
18.	X			
19.				X
20.	X			

Question No	A	B	C	D
21.			X	
22.				X
23.		X		
24.				X
25.			X	
26.				X
27.	X			
28.				X
29.	X			
30.		X		
31.			X	
32.	X			
33.			X	
34.		X		
35.		X		
36.	X			
37.		X		
38.			X	
39.				X
40.			X	

1.   D

The Treaty of Rome establishing the European Economic Community (which was colloquially known as the "Common Market") affirmed in its preamble that signatory States were "determined to lay the foundations of an ever closer union among the peoples of Europe". The Member States agreed to dismantle all tariff barriers over a 12-year transitional period. In view of the economic success that freer commercial exchanges brought about, the transition term was shortened and in July 1968 all tariffs among the EEC States were abrogated. At the same time, a common tariff was established for all products coming from third countries.

2.   B

The Single European Act (SEA) signed on 18 February 1986 intends to amend the three founding treaties of the European Communities and to link the rather loosely-knit "European Political Cooperation" (EPC) to the Community's institutional framework. Article 8A introduces the notion of an "internal market", replacing the well-established one of a "common market" in Article 2 of the EEC Treaty. The SEA only purports to realize under a new flag the objectives which had already been set out in the founding treaties of 1951-57, by setting a definite date for the completion of the internal market on 31 December 1992 at the latest and by streamlining the decision-making process, that is by opening the field of harmonization to majority decisions in the Council (Article 100A). (*European Journal of International Law*)

3.   A

The customs union was achieved in 1 July 1968, when all customs duties and restrictions among the six founding Member States of the Community were abolished and the Common Customs Tariff, an external tariff which applies to third country goods, was introduced.

4.   A

The mutual recognition principle was laid down by the Court of Justice in the Cassis de Dijon judgment in 1979. It implies that a Member State may not in principle prohibit the sale in its territory of a product lawfully produced and marketed in another Member State even if the product is produced according to technical or quality requirements which differ from those imposed on its domestic products. Where a product "suitably and satisfactorily" fulfils the legitimate objective of a Member State's own rules (public safety, protection of the consumer or the environment, etc.), the importing country cannot justify prohibiting its sale in its territory by claiming that the way it fulfils the objective is different from that imposed on domestic products. Also, the mutual recognition principle implies that Member States, when drawing up commercial or technical rules liable to affect the free movement of goods, may not take an exclusively national viewpoint and take account only of requirements confined to domestic products. The proper functioning of the common market demands that each Member State also give consideration to the legitimate requirements of the other Member States.
(*Communication from the Commission concerning the consequences of the judgment given by the Court of Justice on 20 February 1979 in case 120/78 'Cassis de Dijon'*)

5.   D

Briefly, criminal proceedings in Belgium were brought against a trader who acquired a consignment of Scotch whisky in free circulation in France, and imported it into Belgium without being in possession of a certificate of origin from the UK customs authorities. This was in violation of the Belgian customs requirements, the UK at the time not being part of the customs union. Dassonville prepared its own certificate of origin and was prosecuted for forgery. The Court of Justice held that "all trading rules enacted by Member States which are capable of hindering directly or indirectly, actually or potentially, intra-Community trade are to be considered as measures having equivalent effect to quantitative restrictions".
(*Case 8/74 Procureur du Roi v Dassonville*)

6.   C

In the Cassis de Dijon judgement, the Court of Justice laid down the concept of *mandatory requirements* as a non-exhaustive list of protected interests in the framework of Article 28 of the EC Treaty. In contrast, Article 30, as a derogation to the general principle, has to be applied in a restrictive manner and establishes an exhaustive list of grounds for derogation. These mandatory requirements relate in particular "to the effectiveness of fiscal supervision, the protection of public health (also in Article 30), the fairness of commercial transactions and to the defence of the consumer." Furthermore, the improvement of working conditions, cultural activities (e.g. cinema going and theatre going), the variety of media and the protection of the environment may count as mandatory requirements.

- **Fairness of commercial transactions and consumer protection:** Measures may be justified on the grounds of consumer protection but, in what might be termed the "golden rule", the fundamental principle is that the sale of a product should not be prohibited when the consumer can be sufficiently protected by adequate labelling requirements.
- **Improvement of working conditions:** While health and safety at work fall under the heading of public health in Article 30, the improvement of working conditions constitutes "a mandatory requirement" even in the absence of any health consideration. The Court of Justice stated that the prohibition on night baking was a legitimate economic and social policy decision in a manifestly sensitive sector.
- **Cultural activities:** The protection of culture constitutes a "mandatory requirement" capable of justifying restrictions on imports or exports.
- **Protection of the environment:** In Case 302/86 the Court confirmed that the protection of the environment constitutes a "mandatory requirement" under Article 30. The case concerned the requirement of Danish law that beer and soft drinks be sold in reusable containers and be made subject to a deposit; the Court held that this was justified on environmental grounds to ensure that containers were in fact reused. It was therefore proportionate to the aim of protecting the environment. However the Court distinguished this from the requirement that only containers conforming to types approved by the Danish authorities could be used, although each producer was entitled to sell no more than 3,000 hectolitres of beer or soft beverages per year in unapproved containers. The Court stressed the expense which this measure imposed on foreign producers, since they would have to use special containers for their sales to Denmark. It found that this specific measure was disproportionate and thus not justified.

(*Guide to the concept and practical application of Articles 28–30 EC, DG Internal Market, Agnete Philipson*)

7.   D

An important judgement concerning the scope of application of Article 28 of the EC Treaty is the Keck and Mithouard case in relation to rules on "selling arrangements" (in that case a rule against selling goods below their purchase price). The judgement has been clarified by subsequent case law. It is now clear that the rules on "selling arrangements" relate to matters extrinsic to the goods themselves such as when, where, by whom and at what price goods may be sold. From the judgement one can conclude that rules on "selling arrangements" indistinctly applicable to domestic and imported goods fall outside the scope of application of Article 28. Rules on selling arrangements include, apart from rules against selling goods below their purchase price, restrictions on advertising, mandatory shop closing hours, and the limitation of the sale of certain goods to specific stores. (*source as for no. 6*)

8.   B

As set out in the Maastricht Treaty, any national of a Member State is a citizen of the Union. The aim of European citizenship is to strengthen and consolidate European identity by greater involvement of the citizens in the Community integration process. Thanks to the single market, citizens enjoy a series of general rights in various areas such as the free movement of goods and services, consumer protection and public health, equal opportunities and treatment, access to jobs and social protection. There are four categories of specific provisions and rights attached to citizenship of the European Union:

- freedom of movement and residence throughout the Union;
- the right to vote and stand as a candidate in municipal elections and in elections to the European Parliament in the state where he/she resides;
- protection by the diplomatic and consular authorities of any Member State where the State of which the person is a national is not represented in a non-member country;
- the right to petition the European Parliament and apply to the Ombudsman.

Although the exercise of these rights is dependent on European citizenship and is subject to certain limitations laid down by the Treaties or secondary legislation, the right to apply to the Ombudsman or to petition the European Parliament is open to all natural or legal persons residing in the Member States of the Union. Likewise, any person residing in the European Union has fundamental rights.

(*ScadPlus*)

9.   A

The Commission's 1985 White Paper, "Completing the Internal Market" focused the attention of Member States on the formal and informal barriers to intra-EU trade, the removal of which would create the environment for the development of European industries capable of competing in global markets. The 1987 Single European Act established a legislative programme of some 300 directives designed to remove these barriers, which were classified under three headings in the White Paper:

- Physical Barriers, associated with frontier inspections;
- Technical Barriers, causing legal and regulatory obstacles;
- Fiscal Barriers, epitomised by differences in indirect taxes and excise duties.

The White Paper defined a deadline for achieving a Single European Market by 31 December 1992. After adjustments, the Single European Market programme comprised 282 directives designed to create:

- a New Community Standards Policy;

- a Common Market for Services;
- Conditions for Industrial Co-operation;
- a Single Public Procurement Market;
- Plant and Animal Health Controls.

The directives are either horizontal (industry independent) or vertical (industry specific) in nature. Examples of the former include the removal of border controls and the harmonisation of indirect taxation, and of the latter, mutual recognition in the pharmaceuticals industry.

10.   D

A research programme, Research on the Cost of Non-Europe (resulting in what was known as the Cecchini Report), was launched in 1986 and completed in 1988. It analysed the costs of European market fragmentation and, thus, the potential benefits from their removal. First, the title of the research implied the need for a more unified Europe. Then the findings of the research showed that the removal of economic barriers would provide a base for political and social convergence.

11.   C

The removal of technical barriers to trade is a precondition for the completion of the internal market. Since the adoption of the "new approach" to technical harmonisation and standardisation in 1985, the harmonisation of European industrial standards in the 16 areas covered by European technical legislation has become an essential instrument for the achievement of this objective. The main goal is to help establish a European policy on quality in cooperation with national and international standardisation bodies to enable businesses to manufacture and sell their products throughout the Community with the aid of a system for the mutual recognition of trade marks and manufacturing processes.

Technical specifications which meet these essential requirements are drawn up on the basis of the Council Resolution of 7 May 1985 setting out a new approach to technical harmonisation and to standardisation and Directive 83/189/EEC. This provides for an information procedure covering progress on standardisation, as well as a mechanism whereby the Commission can empower the national standardisation bodies (CEN, CENELEC, ETSI) to draw up those standards. The effect of this is to impose a "standstill" on all national work falling within the scope of the European mandate.

These standards are voluntary; manufacturers therefore remain free to offer, on the Community market, products meeting other standards or not meeting any, provided that they satisfy the procedures for assessing conformity laid down by the Directive in question. Products manufactured in accordance with the standards, for their part, are presumed to conform to the essential requirements.

Products meeting the essential requirements laid down by the Directive(s) in question may be recognized by the CE marking that they bear.

12.   A

The Single Market Action Plan presented by the Commission in June 1997 (before the Amsterdam European Council met) outlines details of the priority actions required to improve the functioning of the Single Market by 1 January 1999. The Action Plan sets out four strategic targets:

- making the rules more effective;
- dealing with key market distortions;
- removing obstacles to market integration; and
- delivering a Single Market for the benefit of all citizens.

Specific actions were to be implemented under a three phase timetable, with application in the very short term of urgent actions, rapid adoption of a number of proposals and attaining maximum possible agreement on remaining measures by 1 January 1999.

13.   C

The European Commission's "Internal Market Strategy 2003-2006" is a ten-point plan to make the Internal Market work better and it builds on the new jobs and economic wealth it has already created since Europe's frontiers were dismantled at the end of 1992.

On the one hand, the Strategy outlines the significant benefits that a properly functioning Internal Market can bring. On the other hand, it also point out that the Internal Market is not yet functioning

optimally in a number of ways. There is a need for a new impetus to overcome the remaining obstacles and to allow the Internal Market to deliver its full potential in terms of competitiveness, growth and employment.

The 10 priorities set out in the Strategy are as follows:

- facilitating the free movement of goods;
- integrating services market;
- ensuring high quality network industries;
- reducing the impact of tax obstacles;
- expanding procurement opportunities;
- improving conditions for business;
- meeting the demographic challenge;
- simplifying the regulatory environment;
- enforcing the rules;
- providing more and better information.

For a fuller account of the Strategy, see COM(2003) 238.

14.   B

The Agreement on the European Economic Area (EEA Agreement) entered into force on 1 January 1994. It presently applies between Iceland, Liechtenstein and Norway on the one side and the 25 Member States of the European Union on the other, forming together the 28 EEA States. The European Community is also a contracting party to the Agreement.

The aim of the EEA Agreement is to guarantee the free movement of goods, persons, services and capital, as well as equal conditions of competition and non-discrimination against individuals in all 28 EEA States. By removing barriers to trade and by opening new opportunities for some 455 million Europeans, the EEA Agreement stimulates economic growth and adds to the international competitiveness of the EEA States.

According to Article 28 of the EEA Agreement, freedom of movement for workers shall be secured among EEA States. Such freedom of movement entails the abolition of any discrimination based on nationality between workers of these States as regards employment, remuneration and other conditions of work and employment. Moreover, this freedom entails the right to accept offers of employment actually made, to move freely within the territory of EEA States for this purpose, to stay on the territory of an EEA State for the purpose of employment in accordance with the provisions governing

the employment of nationals of that State, and to remain on the territory of an EEA State after having been employed there. These rights are subject to limitations justified on grounds of public policy, public security or public health, and they do not apply to such employment in the public service which involves exercise of public authority.
(*EFTA Surveillance Authority*)

The movement of persons between Switzerland and the European Union (EU) is at present governed by the transitional provisions of the bilateral Agreement on the Free Movement of Persons between Switzerland and the EU, which has been in force since 1 June 2002.

Since 1 June 2004, Swiss nationals have been granted the same treatment in the 15 previous EU countries as EU nationals with regard to entry and residence provisions and access to the labour market. Swiss nationals no longer require work permits. EU employers may now give Swiss applicants a job immediately and without any permit procedure. On 25 September 2005, the Swiss voted in favour of Switzerland extending its Agreement on the Free Movement of Persons to the 10 new Member States.

15.   C

The transitional arrangements are set out in the Accession Treaties of the Czech Republic, Estonia, Cyprus, Latvia, Lithuania, Hungary, Malta, Poland, Slovenia and Slovakia to the European Union – although the Treaty with Cyprus contains no restrictions on free movement of workers and with regard to Malta, there is only the possibility of invoking a safeguard clause. It is important to note that the transitional arrangements *only* apply to access to the labour market by workers.
(*Commission: Free movement of workers to and from the new Member States - how will it work in practice?*)

16.   A

17.   D

Regulation (EEC) No 1612/68 on freedom of movement for workers within the Community provides

in its Article 10(1) that "[t]he following shall, irrespective of their nationality, have the right to install themselves with a worker who is a national of one Member State and who is employed in the territory of another Member State: (a) his spouse and their descendants who are under the age of 21 years or are dependants; (b) dependent relatives in the ascending line of the worker and his spouse."

18.   A

Regulation (EEC) No 1612/68 on freedom of movement for workers within the Community provides in its Article 11 that "[w]here a national of a Member State is pursuing an activity as an employed or self-employed person in the territory of another Member State, his spouse and those of the children who are under the age of 21 years or dependent on him shall have the right to take up any activity as an employed person throughout the territory of that same State, even if they are not nationals of any Member State. "

19.   D

Regulation 1408/71 and implementing Regulation 574/72 offer practical solutions to most of the cross-border problems that may arise in the field of social security.

These Regulations do not harmonise but co-ordinate the social security schemes of EU Member States, i.e. they do not replace the different national social security systems by a single European scheme. Therefore, Member States are free to determine the details of their own social security systems, including which benefits shall be provided, the conditions of eligibility and the value of these benefits, as long as they adhere to the basic principle of equality of treatment and non-discrimination.
(*DG Employment*)

20.   A

The rights of EU citizens to establish themselves or to provide services anywhere in the EU are fundamental principles of European Community law.

Regulations which only recognise professional qualifications of a particular jurisdiction present obstacles to these fundamental freedoms. These obstacles are overcome by rules guaranteeing the mutual recognition of professional qualifications between Member States.

These rules are mainly the following:

- Sectoral directives which provide for automatic recognition of professional qualifications and which are mainly in the health sector (doctors, nurses, dentists, midwives, veterinary surgeons, pharmacists and architects);
- Three "general system" Directives which apply to all the professions which are regulated from the point of view of qualifications;
- Two Directives applying to lawyers, one of which concerns the provision of services and the other establishment under the title of country of origin;
- Two "transitory" Directives concerning activities in the fields of commerce and the distribution of toxic substances.

(*DG MARKT*)

21.   C

Article 1 of the Council Directive 93/96/EEC of 29 October 1993 on the right of residence for students provides that "[i]n order to lay down conditions to facilitate the exercise of the right of residence and with a view to guaranteeing access to vocational training in a non-discriminatory manner for a national of a Member State who has been accepted to attend a vocational training course in another Member State, the Member States shall recognize the right of residence for any student who is a national of a Member State and who does not enjoy that right under other provisions of Community law, and for the student's spouse and their dependent children, where the student assures the relevant national authority, by means of a declaration or by such alternative means as the student may choose that are at least equivalent, that he has sufficient resources to avoid becoming a burden on the social assistance system of the host Member State during their period of residence, provided that the student is enrolled in a recognized educational establishment for the principal purpose of following a vocational training course there and that he is covered by sickness insurance in respect of all risks in the host Member State."

22.   D

In *Rudy Grzelczyk vs Centre public d'aide sociale d'Ottignies-Louvain-la-Neuve* (Case C-184/99) the Court of Justice held that a Member State may take the view that a student who has recourse to social assistance no longer fulfils the conditions of his right of residence (see Article 1 of the Council Directive 93/96/EEC of 29 October 1993 on the right of residence for students) or may take measures, within the limits imposed by Community law, either to withdraw his residence permit or not to renew it. "Nevertheless, in no case may such measures become the automatic consequence of a student who is a national of another Member State having recourse to the host Member State's social assistance system."

Article 13(3) of the Directive 2004/58/EC of the European Parliament and of the Council of 29 April 2004 on the right of citizens of the Union and their family members to move and reside freely within the territory of the Member States outlines that "[a]n expulsion measure shall not be the automatic consequence of a Union citizen's or his or her family member's recourse to the social assistance system of the host Member State." Recital 16 of the Directive emphasises that as long as the beneficiaries of the right of residence do not become an unreasonable burden on the social assistance system of the host Member State they should not be expelled. Therefore, an expulsion measure should not be the automatic consequence of recourse to the social assistance system. The host Member State should examine whether it is a case of temporary difficulties and take into account the duration of residence, the personal circumstances and the amount of aid granted in order to consider whether the beneficiary has become an unreasonable burden on its social assistance system and to proceed to his expulsion. In no case should an expulsion measure be adopted against workers, self-employed persons or job-seekers as defined by the Court of Justice save on grounds of public policy or public security.

23.   B

Under the Regulation on the Statute for a European company (2157/2001, entered into force on 8 October 2004), a company may be set up within the territory of the Community in the form of a public limited-liability company, known by the Latin name "Societas Europaea" (SE). The SE will make it possible to operate at Community level while being subject to Community legislation directly applicable in all Member States. The statute will enable a public limited-liability company with a registered office and head office within the Community to transform itself into an SE without going into liquidation. The SE will be entered in a register in the Member State in which it has its registered office. Every registered SE will be published in the Official Journal of the European Communities. The SE will have to take the form of a company with share capital. In order to ensure that such companies are of reasonable size, a minimum amount of capital is set at not less than EUR 120,000.

The SE may be set up in one of four ways:
* by the merger of two or more existing public limited companies from at least two different EU Member States;
* by the formation of a holding company promoted by public or private limited companies from at least two different Member States;
* by the formation of a subsidiary of companies from at least two different Member States;
* by the transformation of a public limited company which has, for at least two years, had a subsidiary in another Member State.

(*http://www.europarl.eu.int/factsheets/3_4_2_en.htm*)

24.   D

A Community facility providing medium-term financial assistance may be granted to one or more Member States experiencing difficulties in their balance of payments on current or capital account. Only those Member States that have not adopted the euro may benefit from this facility. To this end, the Commission is empowered, on behalf of the European Community, to contract loans on the capital markets or with financial institutions.

If Member States which have not adopted the euro call upon sources of financing outside the Community which are subject to economic policy conditions, they must first consult the Commission and the other Member States in order to examine the possibilities available under the Community medium-term financial assistance facility. Such consultations will be held within the Economic and Financial Committee.

The facility may be implemented by the Council on the initiative of either the Commission (pursuant to Article 119 of the EC Treaty), in agreement with the Member State concerned, or a Member State experiencing difficulties.

After examining the situation in the Member State seeking assistance, the Council decides:
* whether to grant a loan or appropriate financing facility, its amount and its average duration;
* the economic policy conditions attached to the medium-term financial assistance with a view to re-establishing a sustainable balance of payments situation;
* the techniques for disbursing the loan or financing facility, the release or drawings of which are, as a rule, by successive instalments;

In cases where restrictions on capital movements are introduced or reintroduced (Article 120 of the EC Treaty) during the period of the financial assistance, the conditions and arrangements governing financial assistance are re-examined.

At regular intervals, the Commission, in conjunction with the Economic and Financial Committee, verifies that the economic policy of the Member State receiving assistance accords with the commitments laid down in the adjustment programme or any other conditions. The Member State makes all the necessary information available to the Commission. The release of further instalments depends on the findings of such verification.

Loans granted as medium-term financial assistance may be granted as consolidation of short-term monetary support made available by the European Central Bank (ECB) under the very short-term financing facility.

The borrowing and lending operations are carried out in euros. They use the same value date and must not involve the Community in the transformation of maturities, in any exchange or interest-rate risk or in any other commercial risk.

At the request of the beneficiary Member State, loans may carry the option of early repayment. At the request of the debtor Member State and where circumstances permit an improvement in the interest rate on the loans, the Commission may refinance all or some of its initial borrowings or restructure the corresponding financial conditions. These operations may not have the effect of extending the average duration of the borrowing concerned or increasing the amount of capital outstanding. The costs incurred in concluding and carrying out each operation are borne by the beneficiary Member State. The Economic and Financial Committee must be kept informed of these operations.

The Council decisions on this matter are taken by qualified majority on a proposal from the Commission made after consulting the Economic and Financial Committee. The ECB makes the necessary arrangements for the administration of the loans.
(*ScadPlus*)

For a fuller account of the facility, see Council Regulation (EC) No 332/2002 of 18 February 2002 establishing a facility providing medium-term financial assistance for Member States' balances of payments.

25.   C

The EFTA Surveillance Authority is responsible for ensuring that capital moves freely between the EFTA States, and between those States and the EU Member States. The Authority monitors restrictions to the free movement of capital arising in the EFTA States. The European Commission, in particular via its Directorate General for Economic and Financial Affairs, supervises restrictions originating in the EU Member States.

The fourth fundamental freedom of the EEA Agreement is the free movement of capital. This freedom is governed by Articles 40 to 45 of the EEA Agreement and by Directive 88/361/EEC, which is listed in Annex XII to the EEA Agreement. The purpose of those provisions is to allow cross-border investment by residents in the European Economic Area, without discrimination based on nationality, the place of residence or the place where the capital is invested. Moreover, restrictions on such operations may only be permitted if justified by objective reasons.

The operations in capital covered by the EEA Agreement comprise, for example, the acquisition of securities in companies established in the European Economic Area, whether they are listed or not on a stock exchange, or the acquisition of real estate in the territory of the EEA States. Directive

88/361/EEC gives a non-exhaustive list of operations covered by the free movement of capital.

The EFTA Court has confirmed the importance of the free movement of capital within the European Economic Area in Case E-1/00 of 14 July 2000.
(*EFTA Surveillance Authority*)

26.   D

Article 60(1) of the EC Treaty provides for Community sanctions against third countries, in the context of the Common Foreign and Security Policy of the European Union mentioned in Article 301. The European Union lacking legal personality, the establishment of a link between both articles was necessary so as to allow the European Community to adopt such restrictions and for these to be compatible with the freedom.

These restrictions may cover by definition all types of capital movements and payments. In practice, they usually materialise in the shape of freezing of bank accounts and other financial assets of specific natural and legal persons or a ban on foreign direct investments in the country involved. Such restrictions are sometimes adopted in response to United Nations sanctions (Security Council Resolutions), although this does not form a necessary condition. Financial sanctions are defined and implemented through the adoption by the Council of regulations that benefit from direct applicability in the legal order of Member States. Recent examples of financial sanctions adopted by the Community are the freeze of funds and the ban on investments in relation to the Federal Republic of Yugoslavia and the flight ban and the freeze of funds and other financial resources in respect of the Taliban in Afghanistan.
(*Restrictions on Foreign Ownership: European Community and International Framework by Jean-Pierre Raes of the European Commission - February 2003*)

27.   A

The Action Plan was a five year plan, commenced in 1999, containing a set of 42 legislative measures. It included, on the wholesale side, common rules for integrated securities and derivatives, raising capital on an EU-wide basis and comparable financial reporting through accountancy rules. On the retail side, the emphasis was on information and transparency, redress procedures, charges for cross-border transactions and safeguards for e-commerce. The majority of the measures on the wholesale side have now been implemented.

Banking: The Basel Capital Accord (Basel I) set rules on what level of capital internationally active banks are required to hold. The accord is overseen by banking representatives from the G10 countries, sitting as the Basel Committee, which launched a review of the accord in 1999. At the same time, the Commission commenced a review of the EU's capital adequacy directives in order to incorporate the new rules into European law. The Basel Committee endorsed Basel II in June 2004 and a proposal from the Commission on a new Consolidated Banking Directive and Capital Adequacy Directive was adopted in July 2004.

Clearing and Settlement: this deals with the procedural arrangements on how securities are actually transferred from one owner to another. These require harmonisation as they currently differ greatly throughout the member states and in April 2004 the Commission issued a communication proposing a framework directive.

Payment Services: the aim in this field is to create a single European payment area which eliminates obstacles to cross-border payment in all forms – bank transfer, e-payments, credit cards etc. Charges are a difficulty as is fraud. In July 2003, the Cross-border Payments Regulation established the principle that charges for bank transfers should be the same cross-border as domestically. In October 2004 the Commission published a Fraud Prevention Action Plan, a 3 year plan to fight fraud affecting non-cash payments.
(*EurActiv*)

28.   D

In October 2004 the Commission published a new *Fraud Prevention Action Plan* (FPAP) to fight payment fraud between 2004 and 2007. It aims to increase confidence in non-cash payments – for example those made by credit card and bank transfer – thus encouraging cross-border purchases and boosting e-commerce. The new FPAP builds on its predecessor for 2001-2003 and will complement the Directive on payment services – which the

Commission will propose in 2005 – in underpinning a Single Payment Area in the EU with the ultimate aim of making cross-border payments as convenient, quick and secure as domestic ones.

Priorities in the new FPAP are the security of payment products and systems, co-operation between public authorities and the private sector, the integration of new Member States in the EU fraud prevention framework and closer ties with non-EU countries. It points to emerging threats and urges the rapid EU-wide completion of the changeover to more secure chip cards.

From 2001-2003, under the first FPAP, the growth of payment fraud slowed down, but prevention must be reinforced to maintain momentum against criminal activities such as use of counterfeit cards in cash machines, on-line fraud, data hacking and identity theft.

Action under the new FPAP will include:

- the EU's Fraud Prevention Expert Group (FPEG) will be streamlined by identifying experts in each sector and/or country as contact points and advocates for its work;
- a new FPEG sub-group on user issues will involve the retail sector and consumer associations more closely;
- even closer cooperation between the Commission and national authorities to assist the payments industry in making payments more secure;
- a Commission study on cardholder verification methods;
- the Commission will clarify EU data protection law related to fraud prevention, to allow more effective cross-border information exchanges, and if necessary, the Commission will propose new legislation;
- the Commission will encourage best practice: for example, in some Member States, specialised central law enforcement units have been set up against payment fraud;
- the Commission will organise, with the payment industry, Europol and other stakeholders, training for specialised law enforcement officers;
- the Commission will organise a second conference for senior police officers, magistrates and prosecutors, to raise awareness of payment fraud and its impact;
- work will continue on the Commission's initiative – supported by 94% of respondents in a consultation – to encourage the payment

industry to set up a single phone number in the EU for reporting lost and stolen cards;

- the Commission will assess the merits of establishing an EU single contact point on identity theft, for citizens and businesses;

- the Commission will promote the creation of a database, for public authorities and the private sector, of original and counterfeit identity documents.

(*Commission*)

29.   A

The Green Paper is a consultative paper and contains no concrete initiatives. A more final position will be taken in November 2005, when the Commission expects to come forward with its final policy programme in the area of financial services for the following four years.

30.   B

UCITS are undertakings whose sole object is the collective investment in transferable securities of capital raised from the public and the units of which are, at the request of the holders, repurchased or redeemed out of the undertakings' assets.

UCITS must be authorised by the Member State in which they are situated. The authorisation is valid for all Member States.

There are obligations concerning the investment policies of UCITS, e.g. at least 90% of the investments of a unit trust must consist of transferable securities listed on a stock exchange or on another regulated market, or of recently issued transferable securities.

There is a requirement to publish a prospectus, regular reports, and information on the sale price of units.

There are special provisions applicable to UCITS which market their units in Member States other than those in which they are situated, e.g. a UCITS which markets its units in another Member State must comply with the laws in force in that State.

Directive 88/220/EEC amends Directive 85/611/EEC and introduces special arrangements for certain investments by UCITS.

Directive 95/26/EC imposes the same obligation of professional secrecy on the authorities respon-

sible for authorising and supervising UCITS and the undertakings that take part in those activities and the same possibilities for exchanging information as those granted to the authorities responsible for authorising and supervising credit institutions, investment firms and insurance undertakings.

Directive 2001/107/EEC introduces harmonised rules on market access and conditions for conducting business, together with prudential requirements on management companies. It sets up a "European passport" system equivalent to that which already exists for other financial service providers (such as banks, investment firms and insurance companies), whereby a financial company authorised to provide its services in one Member State may do so throughout the single market without having to apply for a new authorisation. The Directive also introduces a simplified prospectus to improve information for investors. Lastly, it clarifies certain aspects of Directive 85/611/EEC, in particular those relating to collective portfolio management such as:

- the activities which may form part of managing unit trusts/common funds and investment companies;

- the conditions under which a management company may be authorised to delegate to third parties specific functions which form part of collective portfolio management.

Directive 2001/108/EC widens the scope of Directive 85/611/EEC to include collective investment undertakings which invest in financial instruments other than transferable securities, such as money market instruments, bank deposits, options and standardised financial-futures contracts, and units of other collective investment undertakings. Geared to the "product" (units in the investment undertaking), it widens the range of financial assets in which collective investment undertakings covered by the single authorisation may invest. It clarifies certain aspects of Directive 85/611/EEC, in particular by introducing a clear definition of transferable securities (which includes shares and other securities equivalent to shares, bonds and other debt securities, and any other negotiable securities which carry the right to acquire any such transferable securities by subscription or exchange). Lastly, the Directive introduces more flexible risk-spreading rules in order to facilitate replication of selected stock indices.

Directive 2004/39/EC amends this Directive so that certain provisions relating to the markets in financial instruments apply to certain services provided by management companies (exemptions,

initial capital endowments, organisational requirements or conduct of business obligations when providing investment services to clients).
(*ScadPlus*)

31.   C

The attempts to harmonise numerous state legislations have frequently faced inextricable difficulties
so that it may be tempting to establish a specific
regime dedicated to cross-border commercial operations which could in particular cover contract law.
The so-called "26th regime" is an idea of a voluntary code of pan-European laws governing financial products such as insurance and mortgages.
Companies could choose this legal form of
Esperanto for doing business. The Commission is
still in the process of carrying out a wide-scope feasibility study on the possible application of a "26th
regime".

32.   A

The European Commission launched on 1 February
2001 an out-of-court complaints network for
financial services to help businesses and consumers
resolve disputes in the Internal Market rapidly and
efficiently by avoiding, where possible, lengthy and
expensive legal action. This network, called FIN-
NET, has been designed particularly to facilitate the
out-of-court resolution of consumer disputes when
the service provider is established in an EU
Member State other than that where the consumer
lives. The network brings together more than 35
different national schemes that either cover
financial services in particular (e.g. banking and
insurance ombudsmen schemes) or handle consumer disputes in general (e.g. consumer complaint
boards). Both on- and off-line services are covered.
(*Commission*)

For further information, see:
*http://europa.eu.int/comm/internal_market/finservices-
retail/finnet/index_en.htm*

33.   C

The CESAME Group's tasks are to *advise and assist*

the Commission in the integration of EU securities clearing and settlement systems. The advent of the expert
group follows the publication in April 2004 of the
Commission's consultative Communication on
securities clearing and settlement (IP/04/551). The
Communication includes an action plan outlining
the various initiatives necessary to achieve an integrated, safe and efficient clearing and settlement
environment for securities trading in the EU, based
on a level playing field for the different providers
of services.

The Group is chaired by the Commission. It is
composed of around 20 high level representatives
of various mainly private bodies involved in clearing and settlement, along with four observers from
public authorities.

The Group is to advise on market-led initiatives
to bring down barriers to integration, on the coordination of action between the public and the private
sectors and on the practicalities for the removal of
barriers for which the private sector has sole or joint
responsibility. The Group has to ensure wide dissemination of all necessary information on the state
of reform and to contribute to building awareness
of the importance of the project for the success of
the EU's financial markets and for attaining the
overall economic objectives incorporated in the
Lisbon agenda.
(*Commission*)

34.   B

The Lamfalussy Report, i.e. the Final Report of the
Committee of Wise Men on the Regulation of
European Securities Markets, was published on 15
February 2001 and adopted by the European
Council in Stockholm on 23 March 2001. It presents
a diagnosis of the following issues and problems.
Firstly, the introduction of the single currency is
creating pressure for common standards of
financial regulation, especially with regard to securities markets. Also, compared to the United States,
European capital markets appear to be too small,
insufficiently competitive and excessively frag-
mented. Furthermore, progress towards a single
market in financial services is hindered by the existence of different national systems of financial legislation and by slow and rigid European Community
procedures.

At the core of these concerns lie the difficulties of
implementing reforms through national regulators

who, given their inherent risk aversion reinforced by their accountability to national policy makers, have a tendency to exploit any ambiguities in EU Directives in favour of national exchanges and constituencies. The issue is whether the new proposals meet the challenge of overcoming inertia.

The Report proposes a four-level regulatory approach. Level 1 refers to EU framework legislation and involves the EU Commission, Council and Parliament. Level 2 refers to EU implementation and involves in addition to the EU Commission a European Securities Committee (ESC) and a European Securities Regulators Committee (ESRC), both yet to be created. Level 3 refers to national implementation and co-operation and involves the ESRC and the Member States. Level 4 refers to enforcement and involves the Commission and the Member States. The Report states that the proposed ESC would be set up following the regulatory "comitology" procedure suggested for implementing powers conferred on the Commission. It would be composed of high-ranking officials – State Secretaries in the Finance Ministries of the Member States or their personal representatives – and would be chaired by the European Commissioner responsible for the Internal Market in Financial Services. The ESRC would be set up as an independent advisory group to the Commission (outside the comitology process) and would be composed of national securities regulators.
(*Centre for European Policy Studies*)

35.   B

The Electronic Commerce Directive (2000/31/EC) provides that each Member State must ensure that the information society services provided by a service provider established on its territory comply with the national provisions applicable in the Member State in question which fall within the coordinated field. Member States may not, for reasons falling within the coordinated field, restrict the freedom to provide information society services from another Member State ("Internal Market clause").

However, the Directive makes it possible, in certain limited circumstances, for the Member States to impose additional national rules on on-line services:

• First, the annex to the Directive contains a number of derogations from the Internal Market clause. These derogations reproduce a number of the provisions laid down in the Directives on insurance, advertising in the case of UCITS and the issue of electronic money by institutions not in possession of a European passport.

• Second, there are a number of other general derogations that could be particularly relevant to financial services. They relate to the freedom of the parties to choose the law applicable to their contract, the contractual obligations set out in contracts concluded with consumers, etc.

• Third, Article 3(4), (5) and (6) of the Directive allows Member States to take measures such as sanctions or injunctions that may restrict the provision of on-line services from other Member States. These measures are subject to strict conditions.

The relevant provisions of the Directive read as follows:

"4. Member States may take measures to derogate from paragraph 2 in respect of a given information society service if the following conditions are fulfilled:

(a)   the measures shall be:

(i)   necessary for one of the following reasons:
– public policy, in particular the prevention, investigation, detection and prosecution of criminal offences, including the protection of minors and the fight against any incitement to hatred on grounds of race, sex, religion or nationality, and violations of human dignity concerning individual persons,
– the protection of public health,
– public security, including the safeguarding of national security and defence,
– the protection of consumers, including investors;

(ii)   taken against a given information society service which prejudices the objectives referred to in point (i) or which presents a serious and grave risk of prejudice to those objectives;

(iii)   proportionate to those objectives;

(b)   before taking the measures in question and without prejudice to court proceedings, including preliminary proceedings and acts carried out in the framework of a criminal investigation, the Member State has:
– asked the Member State referred to in

paragraph 1 to take measures and the latter did not take such measures, or they were inadequate,

– notified the Commission and the Member State referred to in paragraph 1 of its intention to take such measures.

5. Member States may, in the case of urgency, derogate from the conditions stipulated in paragraph 4(b). Where this is the case, the measures shall be notified in the shortest possible time to the Commission and to the Member State referred to in paragraph 1, indicating the reasons for which the Member State considers that there is urgency.

6. Without prejudice to the Member State's possibility of proceeding with the measures in question, the Commission shall examine the compatibility of the notified measures with Community law in the shortest possible time; where it comes to the conclusion that the measure is incompatible with Community law, the Commission shall ask the Member State in question to refrain from taking any proposed measures or urgently to put an end to the measures in question."

36.   A

CEN's mission is to promote voluntary technical harmonisation in Europe in conjunction with worldwide bodies and its partners in Europe. Harmonisation diminishes trade barriers, promotes safety, allows interoperability of products, systems and services, and promotes common technical understanding. In Europe, CEN works in partnership with CENELEC – the European Committee for Electrotechnical Standardisation and ETSI – the European Telecommunications Standards Institute.

37.   B

The European Telecommunications Standards Institute (ETSI) is a non-profit making organisation whose mission is to produce telecommunications standards. Based in Sophia Antipolis (France), ETSI unites 875 members from 54 countries inside and outside Europe, and represents administrations, network operators, manufacturers, service providers, research bodies and users.

38.   C

CENELEC, the European Committee for Electrotechnical Standardization, was created in 1973 as a result of the merger of two previous European organizations: CENELCOM and CENEL. Nowadays, CENELEC is a non-profit technical organization set up under Belgian law and composed of the National Electrotechnical Committees of 28 European countries. In addition, 8 National Committees from Eastern Europe and the Balkans are participating in CENELEC work with an Affiliate status.

CENELEC members have been working together in the interests of European harmonization since the 1950s, creating both standards requested by the market and harmonized standards in support of European legislation and which have helped to shape the European Internal Market. CENELEC works with 15,000 technical experts from 28 European countries. Its work directly increases market potential, encourages technological development and guarantees the safety and health of consumers and workers.

CENELEC's mission is to prepare voluntary electrotechnical standards that help develop the Single European Market/European Economic Area for electrical and electronic goods and services removing barriers to trade, creating new markets and cutting compliance costs.
(*CENELEC*)

39.   D

Since its presentation in January 2004, the Commission's proposal for a Directive on Services in the Internal Market has come under fire from trade unions, socialist parties and some national governments (such as France, later Germany, Belgium, Austria and Sweden). The critics of the draft proposal feared that opening up the market for services would lead to a big influx of service providers from new central and eastern European member states, who would offer their services at much lower prices.

On 3 March 2005 Internal Market Commissioner Charlie McCreevy announced that the Commission would seriously amend the services proposal after the first reading in the Parliament. The "country of origin" provision, which is one of the main controversial issues of the proposal, will be reviewed to make sure that the new directive would not undermine higher wage and safety standards. Also, the health-care services sector would be excluded from the revamped proposal. (The "country of origin" principle means that when a service provider wants to provide his services into another Member State without a permanent presence there, he has, in principle, to comply only with the administrative and legal requirements of his country of establishment. This means that Member States may not restrict incoming cross-border services from a provider established in another Member States by applying its own administrative and legal regime in addition to the requirements the service provider is already subject to in his Member State of establishment. For example, if a service provider has an authorisation in his Member State of establishment, he does not need to have a new authorisation in another Member State. However, this principle is subject to a limited number of important derogations in the proposed Directive.

(*EurActiv, Commission*).

40.   C

On 26 May 2005 the European Parliament approved the proposed Third Directive on the prevention of the use of the financial system for the purposes of money laundering or terrorist financing. The Directive was adopted by the ECOFIN Council of 7 June in Luxembourg.

The *Third Anti-Money Laundering Directive* builds on existing EU legislation and incorporates into EU law the June 2003 revision of the Forty Recommendations of the Financial Action Task Force (FATF), the international standard setter in the fight against money laundering and terrorist financing.

The Directive is applicable to the financial sector as well as lawyers, notaries, accountants, real estate agents, casinos, trust and company service providers. Its scope also encompasses all providers of goods, when payments are made in cash in excess of EUR15 000. Those subject to the Directive need to:

- Identify and verify the identity of their customer and of its beneficial owner, and to monitor their business relationship with the customer;

- Report suspicions of money laundering or terrorist financing to the public authorities – usually, the national financial intelligence unit; and

- Take supporting measures, such as ensuring a proper training of the personnel and the establishment of appropriate internal preventive policies and procedures.

The Directive introduces additional requirements and safeguards for situations of higher risk (e.g. trading with correspondent banks situated outside the EU).

(*Commission*)

For further information see:

http://europa.eu.int/comm/internal_market/company/financial-crime/index_en.htm

REGIONAL POLICY
ANSWERS

Question No	A	B	C	D
1.	X			
2.			X	
3.		X		
4.			X	
5.			X	
6.			X	
7.				X
8.		X		
9.		X		
10.	X			
11.				X
12.	X			
13.				X
14.				X
15.		X		
16.			X	
17.	X			
18.		X		
19.			X	
20.	X			

Question No	A	B	C	D
21.		X		
22.				X
23.				X
24.				X
25.		X		
26.		X		
27.		X		
28.	X			
29.			X	
30.				X
31.		X		
32.				X
33.	X			
34.		X		
35.		X		
36.			X	
37.	X			
38.				X
39.			X	
40.			X	

1. A

Danuta Hübner (born in 1948), former Minister for European Affairs and former member of the Convention on the future of Europe, is of Polish nationality.

2. C

Article 158 of the EC Treaty provides:

"In order to promote its overall harmonious development, the Community shall develop and pursue its actions leading to the strengthening of its economic and social cohesion.

In particular, the Community shall aim at reduc-ing disparities between the levels of development of the various regions and the backwardness of the least favoured regions or islands, including rural areas."

3. B

Article 2 of Regulation 1164/94 provides that a Member State is eligible for Cohesion Funds if it has a per capita gross national product (GNP), measured in purchasing power parities, of less than 90% of the Community average, and has a programme leading to the fulfilment of the conditions of economic convergence as set out in Article 104c of the EC Treaty (avoidance of excessive government deficits).

4.   C

Four Member States – Spain, Greece, Portugal and Ireland – were eligible under the Cohesion Fund from 1 January 2000. The Commission's mid-term review of 2003 deemed Ireland as ineligible under the Cohesion Fund as of 1 January 2004 due to its GNP average of 101%.

5.   C

Following the enlargement in 2004, all new Member States became eligible under the Cohesion Fund.

6.   C

Based on the above answers, in 2005 the ten new Member States plus Portugal, Spain and Greece are eligible.

7.   D

Cohesion Fund support is conditional. The funding granted to a Member State may be suspended if the country fails to comply with its convergence programme for economic and monetary union (stability and growth pact) running e.g. an excessive public deficit (more than 3% of GDP for Spain, Portugal and Greece, this threshold is being negotiated separately for each of the ten new Member States according to their own public deficit at the moment of the accession). Until the deficit has been brought back under control, no new projects might be approved.

Environment projects helping to achieve the objectives of the EC treaty and in particular projects in line with the priorities conferred on Community Environmental policy by the relevant Environment and Sustainable Development action plans are eligible under the Cohesion Fund. The Fund gives priority to drinking-water supply, treatment of wastewater and disposal of solid waste. Reforestation, erosion control and nature conservation measures are also eligible. The other main priority relates to transport infrastructure projects establishing or developing transport infrastructure as identified in the Trans-European Transport Network (TEN) guidelines. There has to be a due funding balance between transport infrastructure projects and environment projects.
(*DG Regio*)

8.   B

The total rate of the EU assistance cannot exceed 85% of public or equivalent expenditure and depends on the type of operation to be carried out. For projects which generate revenue, the support is calculated taking into account the forecast revenue. The polluter-pays principle (the body that causes pollution should pay for it) has an impact on the amount of support granted. For projects to be carried out over a period of less than two years or where Community assistance is less than EUR 50 million, an initial commitment of 80% of assistance may be made when the Commission adopts the decision to grant Community assistance. The combined assistance of the Fund and other Community aid for a project shall not exceed 90% of the total expenditure relating to that project. Exceptionally, the Commission may finance 100% of the total cost of preliminary studies and technical support measures – in view of the limited budget available for such levels of support this is restricted to EU wide technical assistance. The Member States are responsible for implementing the projects in line with the Commission Decision, managing the funds, meeting the timetable, complying with the financing plan and, in the first instance, ensuring financial control. The Commission makes regular checks and all projects are subject to regular monitoring.

9.   B

According to DG Regio, the following amounts were allocated for the period 2004-2006 (million euros):

Czech Republic	936.05
Estonia	309.03
Cyprus	53.94
Latvia	515.43
Lithuania	608.17
Hungary	1,112.67
Malta	21.94

Poland	4,178.60
Slovenia	188.71
Slovakia	570.50

10.   A

According to the Commission proposal for the reform of the Cohesion Fund, the following changes are planned to be implemented as of 2006:

- simpler programming, greater flexibility, less administrative burden and a renewed Cohesion Fund;
- the number of Objectives limited from 7 to 3, the number of funds involved from 6 to 3;
- programming simplified: one step in programming instead of two – Community Support Framework and the Programme Complement are abolished;
- greater flexibility for authorities involved in the financial management of funds;
- eligibility rules to be defined at Member States level – except a limited number of exemptions – and an existing regulation on this issue abolished;
- proportionality provides less obligations for administrations concerning programmes with a Community share of less than one third of the total;
- the renewed Cohesion Fund is now part of multi-annual programmes instead of being decided project by project.

11.   D

Additionality is one of the Structural Funds' four principles which were strengthened by the revised regulations adopted in July 1993. It means that Community assistance complements the contributions of the Member States rather than reducing them. Except for special reasons, the Member States must maintain public spending on each Objective at no less than the level reached in the preceding period.

12.   A

A coastal area is normally defined as a strip of land

and sea, the width of which depends on the nature of the environment and of human activity related to aquatic resources. Taking into account these two factors, the size of these areas may extend beyond the sea coast to stretch far inland.

13.   D

Community initiatives are aid or action programmes set up to complement Structural Fund operations in specific problem areas. Community initiatives are drawn up by the Commission and coordinated and implemented under national control. They absorb 5.35% of the budget of the Structural Funds. Each Initiative is financed by only one Fund.

14.   D

Community initiatives are as follows:
- **Interreg III**: it promotes cross-border, transnational and interregional cooperation, i.e. the creation of partnerships across borders to encourage the balanced development of multi-regional areas (financed by the ERDF)
- **Urban II**: it concentrates its support on innovative strategies to regenerate cities and declining urban areas (financed by the ERDF)
- **Leader+**: it aims to bring together those active in rural societies and economies to look at new local strategies for sustainable development (financed by the EAGGF Guidance Section)
- **Equal**: it seeks to eliminate the factors leading to inequalities and discrimination in the labour market (financed by the ESF).

15.   B

According to the so-called "comitology", i.e. the implementation of Community legislation by the Commission, the following Committees assist the Commission in the implementation of the Structural Funds:
- Committee on the Development and Conversion of Regions;

- Committee pursuant to Article 147 of the Treaty;
- Committee on Agricultural Structures and Rural Development;
- Committee on Structures for Fisheries and Aquaculture.

16. C

Compensatory allowances are a form of aid intended for farmers that is designed to compensate for the handicap of difficult physical and climatic conditions. These allowances are specifically targeted at the mountain and Arctic areas.

17. A

Since 1994, the FIFG (Financial Instrument for Fisheries Guidance) has grouped together the Community instruments for fisheries. It is applied in all coastal regions, its main task being to increase the competitiveness of the structures and develop viable business enterprises in the fishing industry while striving to maintain the balance between fishing capacities and available resources.

18. B

Rural development is closely linked to the common agricultural policy and measures to support employment. In order to make it fully coherent, the reform of the common agricultural policy in 1999 under Agenda 2000 was accompanied by the strengthening of rural development measures, which were arranged in a single regulation. This instrument establishes an integrated policy of sustainable rural development which ensures greater coherence between rural development and the prices, and promotes all aspects of rural development by encouraging all the local players to become involved. Rural development has thus become the second pillar of the agricultural policy. With its links to agricultural activities and conversion, it is concerned in particular with:
- modernisation of farms;
- safety and quality of food products;
- fair and stable incomes for farmers;

- environmental challenges;
- supplementary or alternative job-creating activities, in a bid to halt the drift from the country and to strengthen the economic and social fabric of rural areas;
- improvement of living and working conditions, and promotion of equal opportunities. (*DG Regio*)

19. C

SAPARD (Support for Pre-accession Measures for Agriculture and Rural Development) aims to assist the candidate countries and prepare them for participation in the common agricultural policy and internal market on the basis of a wide range of adjustment measures relating to agricultural structures and rural development. These measures are part of the pre-accession strategy in the framework of Accession Partnerships formed between the Commission and the candidate countries. After accession, the Structural Funds and the Cohesion Fund take over, depending on the capacity of the individual beneficiary countries to use the Community grants effectively.

20. A

The nomenclature of territorial units for statistics (NUTS) was created by the European Office for Statistics (Eurostat) in order to create a single and coherent structure of territorial distribution. It has been used in the Community legislation pertaining to the Structural Funds since 1988.

21. B

The Regulation on the European Agricultural Guidance and Guarantee Fund defines mountain areas as follows:
- Areas in which altitude gives rise to very difficult climatic conditions, the effect of which is substantially to shorten the growing season. (The minimum altitude is between 600 and 1000 m, depending on the Member State involved and the number of days on

which the temperature does not fall below freezing).

- Areas at a lower altitude in which the slopes are so steep (as a rule greater than 20%) that the use of machinery is not possible or the use of very expensive special equipment is required.
- Areas which are characterised by both altitude and slopes and in which the combination of the two handicaps gives rise to a handicap equivalent to the two preceding handicaps taken separately.
- Areas north of the 62nd parallel (Finland and Sweden) and certain adjacent areas are treated as mountain areas.

22.   D

The European Social Fund (ESF) is the main financial tool through which the European Union translates its strategic employment policy aims into action. Set up by the Treaty of Rome, it is the longest established Structural Fund which, for over 40 years, has invested, in partnership with the Member States, in programmes to develop people's skills and their potential for work. It provides financial assistance for vocational training, retraining and job-creation schemes. Focus is on the new goals of improving the functioning of the labour markets and helping to reintegrate unemployed people into working life. Further action deals with equal opportunities, helping workers adapt to industrial change and changes in production systems.

23.   D

The European Regional Development Fund (ERDF) is intended to help reduce imbalances between regions of the Community. The Fund was set up in 1975 in order to reduce the gap between the levels of development of the various regions and the extent to which the least-favoured regions and islands (including rural areas) are lagging behind. The ERDF contributes to the harmonious, balanced and sustainable development of economic activity, to a high degree of competitiveness, to high levels of employment and protection of the environment, and to equality between women and men, all in the context of Objective 1. In terms of financial

resources, the ERDF is by far the largest of the EU's Structural Funds.

24.   D

More than two thirds of the appropriations of the Structural Funds (more than EUR 135 billion) are allocated to helping areas lagging behind in their development ("Objective 1") where the gross domestic product (GDP) is below 75% of the Community average.

25.   B

Objective 2 of the Structural Funds aims to revitalise all areas facing structural difficulties, whether industrial, rural, urban or dependent on fisheries. Though situated in regions whose development level is close to the Community average, such areas are faced with different types of socio-economic difficulties that are often the source of high unemployment.
   These include:
- the evolution of industrial or service sectors;
- a decline in traditional activities in rural areas;
- a crisis situation in urban areas;
- difficulties affecting fisheries activity.
(*DG Regio*)

26.   B

27.   B

The FIFG's priorities are:
- renewal of the fleet and modernisation of fishing vessels, adjustment of fishing activity to fish stocks, and socio-economic measures;
- assistance for small-scale coastal fishing, protection of fish stocks in sea coast areas, fishing port equipment, and fish farming;
- processing and marketing of products, etc.

28.   A

In order to exploit the full potential of the single market, the Community is contributing towards the development of trans-European networks (Articles 129b-129d of the EC Treaty), that is cross-frontier infrastructures in the field of transport, energy, tele-communications and the environment. Measures taken must promote the interoperability of national networks and access to them. In 1994 the European Council decided to provide support for 14 priority transport projects and 10 energy projects.
(*DG Regio*)

29.   C

Under Article 161 of the EC Treaty, the Council is to act unanimously, on a proposal from the Commission and after obtaining the assent of the European Parliament and consulting the Economic and Social Committee and the Committee of the Regions, to determine the following matters relating to both the Structural Funds and the Cohesion Fund:
• the tasks, priority objectives and organisation of the Funds;
• the general rules applicable to them;
• the provisions necessary to ensure their effectiveness and the coordination of the Funds with one another and with the other existing financial instruments.

The decision-making procedure was changed by the Treaty of Nice, therefore as of 1 January 2007, the Council will act by a qualified majority in matters relating to the Structural Funds and the Cohesion Fund. This means that Council will still have to adopt the financial perspectives for the next programming period (2007-13) unanimously.
(*ScadPlus*)

30.   D

See answer above.

31.   B

32.   D

The Edinburgh European Council held in December 1992 decided to increase the appropriations earmarked for structural operations in 1994-99 by a further 40%.

33.   A

Interreg III (2000-2006) is made up of 3 strands and has a total budget of €4.875 billion (1999 prices). These are as follows:
Strand A: Cross-border cooperation between adjacent regions aims to develop cross-border social and economic centres through common development strategies.
Strand B: Transnational cooperation involving national, regional and local authorities aims to promote better integration within the Union through the formation of large groups of European regions.
Strand C: Interregional cooperation aims to improve the effectiveness of regional development policies and instruments through large-scale information exchange and sharing of experience (networks).

34.   B

The objective of ESPON (European Spatial Planning Observation Network) is to improve the knowledge of spatial development trends at EU level that affect the development of the Union, to encourage the harmonious development of the entire Community, as laid down in Article 158 of the EC Treaty, and to clarify the concept of territorial cohesion referred to in Article 16 of the EC Treaty. In particular, ESPON seeks to study the spatial dimension of economic and social cohesion policy and other EU policies with a view of ensuring better co-ordination of decisions which have an impact on spatial planning.

35.   B

To enable itself to respond in a rapid, efficient and flexible manner to urgent situations, the Community has established a Solidarity Fund. This will intervene mainly in cases of major natural disasters with serious repercussions on living conditions, the natural environment or the economy in one or more regions of a Member State or a country applying for accession. The budget of the Solidarity Fund is one billion euros per year.

A natural disaster is considered as "major" if:

* In the case of a State, it results in damage estimated either at over EUR 3 billion (2002 prices), or at more than 0.6% of its gross national income.
* By way of exception, the Fund may be mobilised for extraordinary regional disasters resulting in damage lower than this threshold, affecting the major part of its population, with serious and lasting repercussions on living conditions and the economic stability of the region. In this context, particular attention is paid to remote and isolated regions, for example the outermost and island regions.

In these specific cases, the annual amount available is limited to no more than 7.5% of the annual amount allocated to the Solidarity Fund (i.e. 75 M). (*ScadPlus*)

36.   C

For a detailed list of eligible regions and country-specific data, please refer to:
http://europa.eu.int/comm/regional_policy/objective1/regions_en.htm

37.   A

Financing of programmes by the Structural Funds:

	ERDF	ESF	EAGGF	FIFG
Objective 1	X	X	X	X
Outside Objective 1 Regions			X	X
Objective 2	X	X		
Objective 3		X		
Interreg III	X			
Urban II	X			
Leader +			X	
Equal		X		

(*DG Regio*)

38.   D

See answer above.

39.   C

40.   C

In financial terms, the European Commission proposes a budget for 2007-2013 equivalent to 0.41% of the Gross Domestic Product (GDP) of the Union of 27, or 336.3 billion for that period. The Commission is basing its proposals on the socio-economic situation of the Union and the study of the impact of the regional policy, the other European policies and national policies.
(*ScadPlus*)

COMPETITION POLICY
ANSWERS

Question No	A	B	C	D
1.	X			
2.			X	
3.			X	
4.		X		
5.			X	
6.		X		
7.			X	
8.				X
9.		X		
10.	X			
11.			X	
12.			X	
13.				X
14.		X		
15.	X			

Question No	A	B	C	D
16.		X		
17.	X			
18.			X	
19.			X	
20.				X
21.	X			
22.				X
23.		X		
24.				X
25.		X		
26.	X			
27.			X	
28.	X			
29.			X	
30.		X		

1.   A

Commission Notice on the definition of the relevant market for the purposes of Community competition law contains the definition of the relevant product market: "a relevant product market comprises all those products and/or services which are regarded as interchangeable or substitutable by the consumer, by reason of the products' characteristics, their prices and their intended use." These substitute products are the most immediate competitive constraints on the behaviour of the undertaking supplying the product in question. In order to establish which products are the closest substitutes to be in the relevant product market, a conceptual framework known as the hypothetical monopolist test is usually employed (see next answer).

2.   C

The assessment of demand substitution entails a determination of the range of products which are viewed as substitutes by the consumer. One way of making this determination can be viewed, as a thought experiment, postulating a hypothetical small but significant non-transitory increase in prices (SSNIP) and evaluating the likely reactions of customers to that increase. The exercise of market definition focuses on prices for operational and practical purposes, and more precisely on demand substitution arising from small, permanent changes in relative prices. This concept can provide clear indications as to the evidence that is relevant to define markets. Conceptually, this approach implies that starting from the type of products that the undertakings involved sell and the area in which they sell them, additional products and areas will be included into or excluded from the market definition depending on whether competition from these other products and areas affect or restrain sufficiently the pricing of the parties' products in the short term.

The question to be answered is whether the parties' customers would switch to readily available substitutes or to suppliers located elsewhere in response to an hypothetical small (in the range 5%-10%), permanent relative price increase in the products and areas being considered. If substitution would be enough to make the price increase unprofitable because of the resulting loss of sales, additional substitutes and areas are included in the relevant market. This would be done until the set of products and geographic areas is such that small, permanent increases in relative prices would be profitable.

A practical example of this test can be provided by its application to a merger of, for instance, soft drink bottlers. An issue to examine in such a case would be to decide whether different flavours of soft drinks belong to the same market. In practice, the question to address would be if consumers of flavour A would switch to other flavours when confronted with a permanent price increase of 5% to 10% for flavour A. If a sufficient number of consumers would switch to, say, flavour B, to such an extent that the price increase for flavour A would not be profitable due to the resulting loss of sales, then the market would comprise at least flavours A and B. The process would have to be extended in addition to other available flavours until a set of products is identified for which a price rise would not induce a sufficient substitution in demand.

(*Commission Notice on the definition of the relevant market for the purposes of Community competition law*)

The *Nestlé/Perrier case* was an early example of the use of SSNIP test. In this case, the Commission initially considered that there might be two relevant product markets: in high mineralised still water and low mineralised still water. In contrast, Nestlé considered the relevant market to include all soft drinks, including water and colas. A price correlation analysis showed that all of the water brands were highly correlated with one another regardless of whether they were sparkling or still. Further, the correlations between the water brands and the soft drink brands were much weaker. This evidence suggested that the market should include both still and sparkling waters but should exclude soft drinks. The correlation analysis provided firm objective evidence (which was accepted by the Commission) for a relevant product market consisting of all bottled water.
(*Lexecon*)

3.   C

Commission Notice on the definition of the relevant market for the purposes of Community competition law outlines that firms are subject to three main sources of competitive constraints: demand substitutability, supply substitutability and potential competition. The third source of competitive constraint, potential competition, is not taken into account when defining markets, since the conditions under which potential competition will actually represent an effective competitive constraint depend on the analysis of specific factors and circumstances related to the conditions of entry. If required, this analysis is only carried out at a subsequent stage, in general once the position of the companies involved in the relevant market has already been ascertained, and such position is indicative of concerns from a competition point of view.

4.   B

The Irish national competition authority is the Competition Authority that was set up in 1991. The DOJ operates in the USA, the OFT operates in the United Kingdom and the Competition Bureau operates in Canada.

5.   C

Article 81(1) of the EC Treaty prohibits agreements, concerted practices, and decisions of undertakings which may affect trade between Member States and which have as their object or effect the prevention, restriction, or distortion of competition. Article 81(2) of the EC Treaty provides that "[a]ny agreements or decisions prohibited pursuant to this Article shall be automatically void."

6.   B

Article 81(3) of the EC Treaty sets out an exception rule, which provides a defence to undertakings against a finding of an infringement of Article 81(1). Agreements, decisions of associations of undertakings and concerted practices caught by Article 81(1) which satisfy the *four cumulative conditions* of Article

81(3) are valid and enforceable, no prior decision to that effect being required. Article 81(3) can be applied in individual cases or to categories of agreements and concerted practices by way of block exemption regulation.

Article 81(3) provides that the prohibition contained in Article 81(1) may be declared inapplicable in case of agreements which contribute to

- improving the production or distribution of goods or to promoting technical or economic progress; while
- allowing consumers a fair share of the resulting benefits; and
- which do not impose restrictions which are not indispensable to the attainment of these objectives; and
- do not afford such undertakings the possibility of eliminating competition in respect of a substantial part of the products concerned.

On the basis of the Community Courts' case law, one may come to the conclusion that there is no anticompetitive conduct which is excluded, out of hand, from the possibility of being exempted if the conditions set out in Article 81(3) are met. In *Matra-Hachette v Commission* (T-17/93) the Court of First Instance outlined that "in principle, no anti-competitive practice can exist which, whatever the extent of its affect on the given market, cannot be exempted, provided that all of the conditions laid down in Article [81(3)] are satisfied ..."

(For a fuller account of the application of the four conditions of Article 81(3) see *Guidelines on the application of Article 81(3) of the Treaty, 2004/C 101/08*)

7.   C

Council Regulation (EC) No 1/2003 of 16 December 2002 on the implementation of the rules on competition laid down in Articles 81 and 82 of the Treaty ("Regulation") provides in its Article 7 that where the Commission finds that there is an infringement of Article 81 or of Article 82 of the EC Treaty, it may require the undertakings and associations of undertakings concerned to bring such infringement to an end. For this purpose, it may impose on them any behavioural or structural remedies which are proportionate to the infringement committed and necessary to bring the infringement effectively to an end. Structural remedies can only be imposed either where there is no equally effective behavioural remedy or where any equally effective behavioural

remedy would be more burdensome for the undertaking concerned than the structural remedy.

In cases of urgency due to the risk of serious and irreparable damage to competition, the Commission may, on the basis of a prima facie finding of infringement, order interim measures (Article 8 of the Regulation).

Further, Article 9 of the Regulation provides that where the Commission intends to adopt a decision requiring that an infringement be brought to an end and the undertakings concerned offer commitments to meet the concerns expressed to them by the Commission in its preliminary assessment, the Commission may make those commitments binding on the undertakings.   Such a decision may be adopted for a specified period and must conclude that there are no longer grounds for action by the Commission.   It is important to note that Article 9 decisions are silent on whether there was or still is a breach of law.   Therefore, if a customer or a competitor seek private enforcement in national courts, there is a need to prove the illegality of the challenged behaviour (i.e. the violation by the defendant of Article 81 or of 82 of the EC Treaty) to obtain compensation for the resulting damages.

8.   D

It is a stated objective of the Council Regulation (EC) No 1/2003 of 16 December 2002 on the implementation of the rules on competition laid down in Articles 81 and 82 of the Treaty ("Regulation") to ensure compliance with the principles of legal certainty and the uniform application of EC competition rules so as to avoid conflicting decisions.   According to Article 16 of the Regulation, when national competition authorities and courts rule on agreements, decisions or practices under Article 81 or Article 82 of the EC Treaty which are already the subject of a Commission decision, they cannot take decisions running counter to the decision adopted by the Commission.   Also, the courts must also avoid giving decisions which would conflict with a decision contemplated by the Commission in proceedings it has initiated.   To that effect, the national court may assess whether it is necessary to stay its proceedings.

9.   B

The Advisory Committee is composed of representatives and experts appointed by the Member States. It is consulted by the Commission in antitrust and merger cases where such a consultation is envisaged. Council Regulation (EC) No 1/2003 of 16 December 2002 on the implementation of the rules on competition laid down in Articles 81 and 82 of the Treaty ("Regulation") provides that the Commission must consult the Advisory Committee prior to taking any important decision (i.e. cease and desist from decisions, interim measures, commitments, finding of inapplicability, imposing fines or periodic penalty payments). Similarly, Council Regulation (EC) No 139/2004 of 20 January 2004 on the control of concentrations between undertakings imposes an obligation on the Commission to consult the Advisory Committee before taking any important decision (i.e. when declaring a concentration compatible or incompatible with the common market, obligations and conditions, dissolving the concentration, interim measures, revoking the decision, imposing fines or periodic penalty payments).

10.   A

Council Regulation (EC) No 1/2003 of 16 December 2002 on the implementation of the rules on competition laid down in Articles 81 and 82 of the Treaty ("Regulation") provides in its Article 27(4) that where the Commission intends to adopt "a decision pursuant to Article 9 or Article 10 [i.e. commitments or inapplicability], it shall publish a concise summary of the case and the main content of the commitments or of the proposed course of action. Interested third parties may submit their observations within a time limit which is fixed by the Commission in its publication and which may not be less than one month. Publication shall have regard to the legitimate interest of undertakings in the protection of their business secrets." The purpose of this market test is to provide the Commission with an opportunity to become aware of the views of those that are potentially affected by the adoption of measures against anticompetitive behaviour.

11.   C

Commission notice on immunity from fines and reduction of fines in cartel cases (2002/C 45/03) outlines that the Commission may grant immunity from fines where it is unaware of a cartel and the disclosing party is the first to disclose evidence. To obtain total immunity, the party must contact the Commission and provide it with all relevant information and evidence in its possession, generally including a description of the activity, the suspected geographical scope, the number and identity of participants and the size of the market affected, together with relevant documents. A party may make a hypothetical approach to the Commission to determine whether it qualifies for immunity. Unless the Commission confirms that the undertaking does not qualify, it will be given a maximum of five working days to make full disclosure of all information and evidence in its possession. The system provides for first-come, first-served: the Commission will not consider another application for immunity until it has taken a position on a prior application. After verifying the evidence, the Commission will provide a written conditional immunity from fines. A final decision is not made until the Commission renders its decision at the end of the administrative process. Under the new policy, parties that cooperate fully in cartel investigations and immediately terminate their involvement in unlawful activity may apply for a reduction in fines to reflect the level of contribution of the company to the Commission's investigation of the extent of the infringement. This may be a provision of direct, written and contemporaneous evidence that either strengthens the Commission's case or adds further detail.
(*William J Baer and Tim Frazer of Arnold & Porter – Competition Leniency*). For a fuller account of the leniency programme, see Commission notice on immunity from fines and reduction of fines in cartel cases 2002/C 45/03.

12.   C

The EC Merger Regulation (Council Regulation (EC) No 139/2004 of 20 January 2004 on the control of concentrations between undertakings) applies from 1 May 2004, the date of the last enlargement of the EU.
    The ECMR is part of a reform package aiming to improve the transparency and predictability of the

decision-making process and to give a predominant role to economic analysis. The package consists of

- the EC Merger Regulation (ECMR);
- guidelines on the assessment of horizontal mergers;
- best practice guidelines on the conduct of EC merger control proceedings;
- a series of non-legislative measures to improve the decision-making process (e.g. appointing a chief competition economist for the first time, appointing peer review panels for all in-depth merger investigations, allowing companies to review the content of the Commission's files at early stages of the review process, setting up "state-of-play" meetings between interested parties at key stages of the review process).

13.   D

The ECMR (see answer 12) was created to provide a one-stop shop where companies can request clearance for their mergers and acquisitions in the whole of the EU. This is hugely appreciated by companies as it reduces costs, bureaucracy and legal uncertainty – all inherent to the multiple filings that they would need to comply with to absent the Merger Regulation.

Further, to resolve the problem of the multiple filings, of which there are still plenty, the Council has agreed that companies will be able to ask to benefit from the one-stop shop if they have to notify in three or more Member States. Where none of the competent Member States object to the referral within 15 working days of receiving the submission, the merger benefits from the one-stop-shop, and it will be examined by the Commission. (*Commission*)

14.   B

The previous regulation was based on the concept of dominance: a merger must be blocked if it creates a dominant position, and therefore would likely result in higher prices, less choice and innovation. This concept has been interpreted by the Commission and the European Courts along the years as applying also to situations of "joint dominance" or duopolies (*Kali und Salz/MdK* and *Gencor/Lonrho*) as well as to situations of "collective dominance" or oligopolies

(*Airtours/First Choice*). The test has now been adapted to make clear that all anti-competitive mergers resulting in higher prices, less choice or innovation are covered. This is achieved by the new test, which states that a merger must be blocked if it would "significantly impede effective competition" (SIEC test). Dominance, in its different forms, will remain the main scenario. But the test will also now clearly encompass anticompetitive effects in oligopolistic markets where the merged company would not be strictly dominant in the usual sense of the word (i.e. much bigger than the rest). The central question is whether sufficient competition remains after the merger to provide consumers with sufficient choice. (*Commission*)

15.   A

As a general rule, the first sub-paragraph of Article 4(1) of the ECMR provides that all concentrations with a Community dimension (see Article 1 of the ECMR) must be notified to the Commission prior to their implementation and following the conclusion of the agreement, the announcement of the public bid, or the acquisition of a controlling interest.

Further, the second sub-paragraph of Article 4(1) of the ECMR provides that notification is also possible where the undertakings concerned satisfy the Commission of their intention to enter into an agreement for a proposed concentration and demonstrate to the Commission that their plan for that proposed concentration is sufficiently concrete, for example on the basis of an agreement in principle, a memorandum of understanding, or a letter of intent signed by all undertakings concerned, or, in the case of a public bid, where they have publicly announced an intention to make such a bid, provided that the intended agreement or bid would result in a concentration with a Community dimension. The implementation of concentrations should be suspended until a final decision of the Commission has been taken. However, it should be possible to derogate from this suspension at the request of the undertakings concerned, where appropriate. When deciding whether or not to grant derogation, the Commission takes account of all pertinent factors, such as the nature and gravity of damage to the undertakings concerned or to third parties, and the threat to competition posed by the concentration. In the interest of legal certainty, the validity of transactions must nevertheless be protected as much as necessary.

16.   B

The ECMR aims to ensure that the process of reorganisation does not result in lasting damage to competition and, therefore, includes provisions governing those concentrations which may significantly impede effective competition in the common market or in a substantial part of it. Article 1(2) of the ECMR establishes the principle that a concentration with a Community dimension which would significantly impede effective competition in the common market or in a substantial part of it, in particular as a result of the creation or strengthening of a dominant position, is to be declared incompatible with the common market.

Article 6(1)c provides that where "the Commission finds that the concentration notified falls within the scope of this Regulation and raises serious doubts as to its compatibility with the common market, it shall decide to initiate proceedings." (For a fuller account of the powers of decision of the Commission, see Article 8 of the ECMR.)

17.   A

According to Article 7(1) of the ECMR, a concentration with a Community dimension may not be implemented either before its notification or until it has been declared compatible with the common market. However, the Commission may, on reasoned request, grant derogation from this obligation. In deciding on such a request, the Commission takes into account inter alia the effects of the suspension on one or more undertakings concerned by the concentration or on a third party and the threat to competition posed by the concentration. Such a derogation may be made subject to conditions and obligations in order to ensure conditions of effective competition. Undertakings are free to apply for derogation at any time, be it before notification or after the transaction.

18.   C

In order for a concentration to be properly appraised, the Commission is entitled to request all necessary information and to conduct all necessary inspections throughout the Community. To that end, and with a view to protecting competition effectively, the

Commission has the right to interview any persons who may be in possession of useful information and to record the statements made. According to Article 11 of the ECMR, the Commission may, by simple request or by decision, require the persons acquiring control of one or more undertakings, as well as undertakings and associations of undertakings, to provide all necessary information (Article 11 letter). The Commission must state the legal basis and the purpose of the request, specify what information is required and fix the time limit within which the information is to be provided, as well as the penalties for supplying incorrect or misleading information. Further, at the request of the Commission, the governments and competent authorities of the Member States must also provide the Commission with all necessary information to carry out the duties assigned to it by this Regulation.

19.   C

The *Guidelines on the assessment of horizontal mergers under the Council Regulation on the control of concentrations between undertakings* (2004/C 31/03) (the Guidelines) refers to "well established case law" under which very large market shares – 50% or more – may in themselves be evidence of the existence of a dominant market position. For instance, in *Endemol v Commission* (T-221/95) the Court of First Instance concluded that "[a]ccording to settled case-law, a particularly high market share may in itself be evidence of the existence of a dominant position, in particular where, as here, the other operators on the market hold only much smaller shares".

Similarly, in *Gencor v. Commission* (T-102/96) the CFI argued that "although the importance of the market shares may vary from one market to another, the view may legitimately be taken that very large market shares are in themselves, save in exceptional circumstances, evidence of the existence of a dominant position. An undertaking which has a very large market share and holds it for some time, by means of the volume of production and the scale of the supply which it stands for – without those having much smaller market shares being able rapidly to meet the demand from those who would like to break away from the undertaking which has the largest market share – is in a position of strength which makes it an unavoidable trading partner and which, already because of this, secures for it, at the very least during relatively long periods, that freedom of action which is the special feature of a dominant position (Hoffmann-La Roche, paragraph 41)."

Further, the Commission points out that a merger involving a firm whose market share will remain below 50% after the merger may also raise competition concerns in view of other factors such as the strength and number of competitors, the presence of capacity constraints or the extent to which the products of the merging parties are close substitutes. The Commission has, therefore, in several cases considered mergers resulting in firms holding market shares between 40% and 50%, and in some cases below 40%, to lead to the creation or the strengthening of a dominant position (point 17 of the Guidelines).

20.   D

The Herfindahl-Hirschman Index (HHI) is a commonly accepted measure of market concentration. It is calculated by the squaring the market share of each firm competing in a market, and then adding together the resulting numbers. The HHI number can range from close to zero to 10,000.

The closer a market is to being a monopoly, the higher the market's concentration (and the lower its competition). If, for example, there were only one firm in an industry, that firm would have 100% market share, and the HHI would equal 10,000 (i.e. squares of 100), indicating a monopoly. Or, if there were thousands of firms competing, each would have nearly 0% market share, and the HHI would be close to zero, indicating nearly perfect competition. (*Investopedia*)

21.   A

The *Guidelines on the assessment of horizontal mergers under the Council Regulation on the control of concentrations between undertakings* (2004/C 31/03) (the Guidelines) concludes that there are two main ways in which horizontal mergers may significantly impede effective competition, in particular by creating or strengthening a dominant position:
*   First, by eliminating important competitive constraints on one or more firms, which consequently would have increased market power, without resorting to coordinated behaviour **(non-coordinated effects).**

*   Second, by changing the nature of competition in such a way that firms that previously were not coordinating their behaviour, are now significantly more likely to coordinate and raise prices or otherwise harm effective competition. A merger may also make coordination easier, more stable or more effective for firms which were coordinating prior to the merger **(coordinated effects)**.

A merger that is capable of eliminating important competitive constraints on one or more firms without resorting to coordinated behaviour is considered to trigger unilateral effects which is termed as non-coordinated effects in the Guidelines. The substantive test set out under the EMCR (see SIEC test) has been designed to make it possible to review the effects of concentrations in oligopolistic market structures also where coordination, or "collective dominance" is less likely.

22.   D

In its judgement in *Airtours v Commission* (T-342/99), the Court of First Instance concluded that three conditions are necessary for a finding of collective dominance:
*   First, each member of the dominant oligopoly must have the ability to know how the other members are behaving in order to monitor whether or not they are adopting the common policy. As the Commission specifically acknowledges, it is not enough for each member of the dominant oligopoly to be aware that interdependent market conduct is profitable for all of them but each member must also have a means of knowing whether the other operators are adopting the same strategy and whether they are maintaining it. There must, therefore, be sufficient market transparency for all members of the dominant oligopoly to be aware, sufficiently precisely and quickly, of the way in which the other members' market conduct is evolving.
*   Second, the situation of tacit coordination must be sustainable over time, that is to say, there must be an incentive not to depart from the common policy on the market. As the Commission observes, it is only if all the members of the dominant oligopoly maintain the parallel conduct that all can benefit. The notion of retaliation in respect of conduct deviating

from the common policy is thus inherent in this condition. In this instance, the parties concur that, for a situation of collective dominance to be viable, there must be adequate deterrents to ensure that there is a long-term incentive in not departing from the common policy, which means that each member of the dominant oligopoly must be aware that highly competitive action on its part designed to increase its market share would provoke identical action by the others, so that it would derive no benefit from its initiative (see, to that effect, *Gencor v Commission*, paragraph 276).

- Third, to prove the existence of a collective dominant position to the requisite legal standard, the Commission must also establish that the foreseeable reaction of current and future competitors, as well as of consumers, would not jeopardise the results expected from the common policy.

23.   B

The *Guidelines on the assessment of horizontal mergers under the Council Regulation on the control of concentrations between undertakings* (2004/C 31/03) (the Guidelines) concludes that efficiencies must

- benefit consumers;
- be a direct consequence of the notified merger and cannot be achieved to a similar extent by less anticompetitive alternatives (i.e. merger specific); and
- be verifiable such that the Commission can be reasonably certain that the efficiencies are likely to materialise and be substantial enough to counteract a merger's potential harm to consumers.

Although not stated in the Guidelines, it is understood that the criterion of merger-specificity does not imply that it should be demonstrated that the efficiencies could not be achieved by other means than a merger.

24.   D

The *Guidelines on the assessment of horizontal mergers under the Council Regulation on the control of concentrations between undertakings* (2004/C 31/03) (the Guidelines) outlines the "failing firm defence" in its

points 89 and 90. "The Commission may decide that an otherwise problematic merger is nevertheless compatible with the common market if one of the merging parties is a failing firm. The basic requirement is that the deterioration of the competitive structure that follows the merger cannot be said to be caused by the merger. This will arise where the competitive structure of the market would deteriorate to at least the same extent in the absence of the merger." The Commission considers the following three criteria to be especially relevant for the application of a "failing firm defence":

- the allegedly failing firm would in the near future be forced out of the market because of financial difficulties if not taken over by another undertaking;
- there is no less anti-competitive alternative purchase than the notified merger; and
- in the absence of a merger, the assets of the failing firm would inevitably exit the market.

25.   B

Under the Community's competition policy, a dominant position is such that a firm or group of firms would be in a position to behave to an appreciable extent independently of its competitors, customers and ultimately of its consumers. Such a position would usually arise when a firm or group of firms would account for a large share of the supply in any given market, provided that other factors analysed in the assessment (such as entry barriers, capacity of reaction of customers, etc.) point in the same direction.
(*Commission Notice on the definition of the relevant market for the purposes of Community competition law*)

26.   A

State aid is a form of state intervention used to promote a certain economic activity. State aid implies that certain economic sectors, regions or activities are treated more favourably than others. State aid thus distorts competition because it discriminates between companies that receive assistance and others that do not. Therefore, it presents a threat to the running of the Internal Market. The authors of the EC Treaty recognised this risk and set up a system which, while it is centred on the principle that

State aid is incompatible with the common market, nevertheless accepts that the granting of such aid can be justified in exceptional circumstances.

27.   C

Article 87(1) of the EC Treaty provides that "[s]ave as otherwise provided in this Treaty, any aid granted by a Member State or through State resources in any form whatsoever which distorts or threatens to distort competition by favouring certain undertakings or the production of certain goods shall, insofar as it affects trade between Member States, be incompatible with the common market."

As it follows, State aid in the sense of Article 87(1) of the EC Treaty has four characteristics:
- it is granted by the State or through State resources;
- it favours certain undertakings or production of certain goods;
- it distorts or threatens to distort competition;
- it affects trade between Member States.

As regards the third characteristic, to which the question referred, it is important to outline that almost all selective aid will have potential to distort competition, regardless of the scale of potential distortion or market share of the aid recipient. Therefore, it is not necessary for an aid to cause serious and irreparable damage for it to be declared incompatible with the common market.

28.   A

Article 87(1) of the EC Treaty contains a general ban on State aid, but Article 87(2) allows for certain aid categories that the Treaty declares compatible:
- Social aid granted to individual consumers;
- Aid to make good damage by natural disasters or exceptional occurrences;
- Aid to certain areas of Germany affected by the division of Germany.

It must be noted that, in practice, Article 87(2) categories seldom arise.

29.   C

In July 2003 the Court of Justice ruled in a landmark case, *Altmark Trans*, (which concerned the provision of a public service bus service in Germany) that state payment of compensation to undertakings for performance of a public service obligation could fall outside the concept of State aid, but only under very strict conditions:
- The undertaking must have an actual public service obligation, which is clearly defined.
- The basis of compensation must be established in advance in an objective and transparent manner, to avoid it conferring an economic advantage which would favour the recipient undertaking over competitors.
- The compensation cannot exceed what is necessary to cover all or part of the costs incurred in the discharge of the public service obligation, taking into account relevant receipts and a reasonable profit for discharging the obligation.
- Where an undertaking has not been chosen by competitive tender, the level of compensation must be determined by an analysis of the costs which a typical undertaking, well run and able to adequately discharge the same function, would have incurred in discharging those obligations, taking into account a reasonable profit for discharging the obligations.

If the stringent conditions above were not satisfied, there would be State aid.
(*DTI – The State Aid Guide – November 2004*)

30.   B

The "new" Member States spend more than the old ones in state subsidies to businesses as a percentage of their gross domestic product (GDP), but this is likely to be corrected as they overcome problems specific to their economies prior to accession. In absolute amounts, however, they granted an annual average of €6 billion in the four years 2000-2003 compared with €34 billion for the EU15 in 2002, the latest EU State Aid Scoreboard reveals. EU25 data will be published in the autumn 2005 update of the Scoreboard.

The three largest economies of the new Member States were the most generous in absolute terms. Poland granted the biggest amount (average of €2.4 billion a year), followed by the Czech Republic (€1.9 billion) and Hungary (€0.6 billion). The overall level of State aid in the EU10 increased from €4 billion in 2000 to just under €8 billion in 2003. But this is linked to the difficult transition from centrally planned to market economies and the specific problems in a few sectors, such as the crisis in the Czech banking sector (which cost the state €2.4 billion in 2002) and the restructuring of the Polish coal sector (€3.9 billion in 2003). The doubling in aid also reflects a special tax relief in Cyprus for international businesses and the restructuring of the Maltese shipbuilding and ship repair sector. All of the above measures are either being phased out under transitional arrangements or limited in time.

On average, State aid in the new Member States amounted to 1.42% of GDP over the period 2000-

2003. This is significantly higher than the EU15 average of 0.4% in 2002, with Malta (3.9 %), Cyprus (2.9 %) and the Czech Republic on the high end and the Baltic States (Estonia, Lithuania and Latvia) with around 0.2% well below the EU15 average. But if the specific difficulties or adjustments were excluded, the average would drop to 0.67% of GDP.
(*Commission*)

The State Aid Scoreboard can be consulted on the Commission's Competition website:
http://europa.eu.int/comm/competition/state_aid/scoreboard/

ENVIRONMENT POLICY

ANSWERS

Question No	A	B	C	D
1.			X	
2.			X	
3.	X			
4.				X
5.			X	
6.				X
7.				X
8.		X		
9.		X		
10.		X		
11.	X			
12.	X			
13.				X
14.	X			
15.		X		
16.	X			
17.				X
18.			X	
19.			X	
20.		X		

Question No	A	B	C	D
21.			X	
22.				X
23.			X	
24.		X		
25.				X
26.	X			
27.	X			
28.				X
29.			X	
30.				X
31.		X		
32.	X			
33.		X		
34.	X			
35.			X	
36.				X
37.		X		
38.	X			
39.			X	
40.				X

1.   C

Even though environment had been present since the Treaty of Rome, due to the renumbering of the Articles carried out by the Amsterdam Treaty – which enshrines the principle of sustainable development as one of the European Community's aims and makes a high degree of environmental protection one of its absolute priorities under Articles 130r–130t – the legal basis of this policy today is set out in Articles 174-176 of the EC Treaty.

2.   C

Environmental action by the Community began in July 1972 at the Paris Summit with five successive action programmes, based on a vertical and sectoral approach to ecological problems. During this period, the Community adopted some 200 pieces of legislation, chiefly concerned with limiting pollution by introducing minimum standards, notably for waste management, water pollution and air pollution.
(*ScadPlus*)

3.   A

The Commission in its 1998 Communication confirmed the aim of integrating the environment into European Union policies, which was reproduced by the Vienna European Council of 11 and 12 December 1998. The Community institutions were thereon obliged to take account of environmental considerations in all their other policies. Since then, this obligation was taken into account in various Community acts, particularly in the fields of employment, energy, agriculture, development cooperation, single market, industry, fisheries, economic policy and transport.
(*ScadPlus*)

4.   D

Commissioner Stavros Dimas is of Greek nationality.

5.   C

"Development that meets the needs of the present without compromising the ability of future generations to meet their own needs" – the concept of sustainable development was first used prominently in the 1987 Report of the World Commission on Environment and Development (the Brundtland Commission) and at the subsequent UN Earth Summit in Rio de Janeiro in 1992. Sustainable Development is a sound approach to policy making as it looks at the long term and at interlinkages between different developments and policy actions.

6.   D

The European Pollutant Emission Register (EPER) is a web-based register, which enables the public to view data on emissions of key pollutants from large industrial point sources in the European Union. It is hosted by the European Environment Agency (EEA). The main objective of EPER is to fulfil the public's right to know about the releases of pollutants in their neighbourhood, but it also gives people emissions data on a national or European scale. The European Pollutant Emission Register was established by decision based on Article 15(3) of Council Directive 96/61/EC concerning integrated pollution prevention and control (IPPC). The overall purpose of the IPPC Directive is to reduce pollution by industry by controlling emissions from larger facilities.
(*EEA*)

7.   D

The sixth environment action programme for the period 2001–2010 (6EAP) gives a new sense of purpose and direction to the Community's environmental policy. It clearly sets out the objectives for the next decade and determines the actions that will need to be taken within a 5–10 year period if those goals are to be achieved.

8.   B

The programme puts forward a series of actions to tackle persistent environmental problems in four priority areas:

- climate change;
- · nature and biodiversity;
- environment, health and quality of life;
- natural resources and waste.

9.   B

The Convention on access to information, public participation in decision making and access to justice in environmental matters is known as the Aarhus Convention after the Danish city where it was adopted in June 1998. It seeks to strengthen the role of members of the public and environmental organisations in protecting and improving the environment for the benefit of future generations.

10.   B

The Commission adopted Strategic Objectives for the period 2005-2009 on 26 January 2005. The aim is to deliver Prosperity, Solidarity and Security for all Europeans. Environment Policy has been included in the Solidarity Priority with the objective "to sustain and reinforce Europe's commitment to solidarity and social justice, to strengthen the cohesion of the enlarged Union and environmental protection. Key elements of this programme include using cohesion policies to promote competitiveness and growth, while reducing economic disparities. Solidarity must extend to future generations through continued EU leadership on environmental protection including climate change and sustainable management of natural resources...". For the first time, the Commission has proposed a joint programme of strategic objectives in partnership with the European Parliament and Council.
(*DG Environment*)

11.   A

Clean Air for Europe (CAFE) is a programme of tech-

nical analysis and policy development designed to lead to the adoption of a thematic strategy on air pollution under the Sixth Environmental Action Programme by the end of 2005. The major elements of the CAFE programme, are outlined in the Communication on CAFE. Its aim is to develop a long-term, strategic and integrated policy advice to protect against significant negative effects of air pollution on human health and the environment.

12.   A

TREMOVE is a policy assessment model, designed to study the effects of different transport and environment policies on the emissions of the transport sector. The model estimates for policies such as road pricing, public transport pricing, emission standards, subsidies for cleaner cars etc. the transport demand, modal shifts, vehicle stock and renewal decisions as well as the emissions of air pollutants and the welfare level.
(*DG Environment*)

13.   D

Manufacturers or importers of a product may apply for an eco-label to the competent body in the Member State in which they manufacture or first market the product or import it from a third country. This body decides whether to award a label after assessing the product in accordance with the principles in the regulation and the specific criteria for individual product groups. The Commission defines the product groups and specific criteria in close cooperation with a special committee of Member State representatives. Before taking a decision it consults representatives of the main interest groups from industry, trade, consumer and environmental organisations. It publishes the product groups and criteria, a list of products awarded the eco-label and the names and addresses of the competent national bodies in the Official Journal.

14.   A

On 29 October 2003, the Commission adopted a proposal for a new EU regulatory framework for chemicals. The proposed new system is called REACH (Registration, Evaluation and Authorisation of CHemicals).

15.   B

At the UN Conference on Climate Change in Kyoto in December 1997 the EU Member States agreed to reduce their greenhouse gas emissions (mainly carbon dioxide, CO_2; also methane CH and chlorofluorocarbons, CFCs) by 8% by between 2008 and 2012. The Kyoto Protocol allows for the use of various flexible instruments: international emissions trading, joint implementation and clean development mechanism.

16.   A

The Seveso accident happened in 1976 at a chemical plant manufacturing pesticides and herbicides. A dense vapour cloud containing tetrachlorodibenzoparadioxin (TCDD) was released from a reactor, used for the production of trichlorofenol. Commonly known as dioxin, this was a poisonous and carcinogenic by-product of an uncontrolled exothermic reaction. Although no immediate fatalities were reported, kilogramme quantities of the substance lethal to man even in microgramme doses were widely dispersed which resulted in an immediate contamination of some ten square miles of land and vegetation. More than 600 people had to be evacuated from their homes and as many as 2,000 were treated for dioxin poisoning. In 1982, Council Directive 82/501/EEC on the major-accident hazards of certain industrial activities – so-called Seveso Directive – was adopted. On 9 December 1996, Council Directive 96/82/EC on the control of major-accident hazards – so-called Seveso II Directive - was adopted. Member States had up to two years to bring into force the national laws, regulations and administrative provisions to comply with the Directive.
(*DG Environment*)

17.   D

The EU's objectives in the field of civil protection are:

- to support and supplement efforts at national, regional and local level with regard to disaster prevention, the preparedness of those responsible for civil protection and intervention in the event of disaster;
- to contribute to the information of the public in view of increasing the level of self-protection of the European citizens;
- to establish a framework for effective and rapid cooperation between national civil protection services when mutual assistance is needed;
- to enhance the coherence of actions undertaken at international level in the field of civil protection especially in the context of cooperation with the candidate Central and Eastern European countries in view of enlargement and with the partners in the Mediterranean region.

(*DG Environment*)

18.   C

The Emission Trading Scheme (ETS) is a cornerstone in the fight against climate change. It is the first international trading system for CO_2 emissions in the world. It covers some 12,000 installations representing close to half of Europe's emissions of CO_2. The aim is to help EU Member States achieve compliance with their commitments under the Kyoto Protocol. Emission trading does not imply new environmental targets, but allows for cheaper compliance with existing targets under the Kyoto Protocol. Letting participating companies buy or sell emission allowances means that the targets can be achieved at least cost.

19.   C

The European Commission has been the driving force in the development of the Regional Environmental Reconstruction Programme (known as REReP). This programme seeks to provide a framework in which environmental actions can be pursued at a regional level in the Balkans. Aiming to bring about the necessary reforms for sustainable environmental protection it currently focuses on four principal themes: institution building; civil society; support to existing regional mechanisms;

and reducing environmental health threat. The initiative was developed under the Stability Pact for South Eastern Europe that was shaped by the countries of the region themselves – including Albania, Bosnia and Herzegovina, Bulgaria, Croatia, FYR Macedonia, Romania, Serbia and Montenegro and Kosovo (currently under UN interim administration).

20.   B

LIFE, the Financial Instrument for the Environment, introduced in 1992, is one of the spearheads of the European Union's environmental policy. It is open to all EU Member States, some candidate countries (currently Romania) and some third   countries bordering the Mediterranean and the Baltic Sea. It co-finances projects in three areas:

LIFE Nature works to conserve natural habitats and the wild fauna and flora of European Union interest, according to the Birds and Habitats directives, thus supporting implementation of the European Union's nature conservation policy and the Natura 2000 Network.

LIFE-Environment aims to implement Community policy and legislation on the environment in the European Union and candidate countries. This approach enables demonstration and development of new methods for the protection and the enhancement of the environment.

LIFE-Third Countries concerns technical assistance activities for promoting sustainable development in third countries. This component of the programme supports the development of environmental management capacities, both for administrative partners outside the Union and for companies and NGOs in those countries.

21.   C

The DABLAS Task Force was set up in November 2001 with the aim of providing a platform for co-operation for the protection of water and water-related ecosystems in the Danube and Black Sea Region. This was in response to an EC Communication adopted in 2001, which highlighted priority actions required to improve the environmental situation in the region. The DABLAS Task Force comprises a number of representatives from the coun-

tries in the region, the International Commission for the Protection of the River Danube (ICPDR), the Black Sea Commission, International Financing Institutions (IFIs), the EC, interested EU Member States, bilateral donors and other regional/international organisations with relevant functions. Civil Society is also involved in the various tasks carried out by the Task Force, according to their respective experience and expertise.

22.   D

Human biomonitoring (HBM) is an effective tool to assess human exposure to environmental pollutants and potential health effects of such pollutants and an essential element in a strategy aiming to integrate health and environment. Biomarker data are considered more relevant for risk assessment than are extrapolations from chemical concentrations in soil, water, air or food. Monitoring the quality of environmental media (air, food, water and soil) has a long tradition in European countries and there is ample legislation dealing with how and where to monitor and what levels should not be exceeded.

(*DG Environment*)

23.   C

The Thessaloniki European Council (19-20 June 2003) agreed to launch an initiative aimed at promoting the integration of environment into external relations through the creation of an informal network of environment experts within foreign ministries, the so-called Green Diplomacy Network. This was one of the elements included in the strategy on environmental integration in external policies adopted by the Barcelona General Affairs Council in March 2002.

24.   B

The Short and Medium-term Priority Environmental Action Programme (SMAP) is a framework programme of action for the protection of the Mediterranean environment, within the context of the Euro-Mediterranean Partnership. It was adopted unanimously by the Euro-Mediterranean Ministerial Conference on the Environment, held in Helsinki on 28 November 1997. The SMAP is the common basis for environmental purposes (as regards both policy orientation and funding) in the Mediterranean region.

25.   D

Community policy on waste management involves three complementary strategies:
- eliminating waste at source by improving product design;
- encouraging the recycling and re-use of waste;
- reducing pollution caused by waste incineration.

26.   A

The Convention on Biological Diversity (CBD) was signed by the Community and all the Member States at the United Nations Conference on Environment and Development in Rio de Janeiro from 3 to 14 June 1992. The CBD is designed to conserve biological diversity, ensure the sustainable use of this diversity and share the benefits generated by the use of genetic resources, in particular through appropriate access to genetic resources and appropriate transfer of relevant technologies, taking into account all rights over those resources and technologies, and through adequate funding.

27.   A

The European Union Network for the Implementation and Enforcement of Environmental Law (IMPEL) is an informal network of the environmental authorities of the Member States, acceding and candidate countries of the European Union and Norway. The network is commonly known as the IMPEL Network. The European Commission is also a member of IMPEL and shares the chairmanship of meetings.

28.   D

The precautionary principle should be informed by three specific principles:
- Implementation of the principle should be based on the fullest possible scientific evaluation. As far as possible this evaluation should determine the degree of scientific uncertainty at each stage.
- Any decision to act or not to act pursuant to the precautionary principle must be preceded by a risk evaluation and an evaluation of the potential consequences of inaction.
- Once the results of the scientific evaluation and/or the risk evaluation are available, all the interested parties must be given the opportunity to study the various options available, while ensuring the greatest possible transparency.

Besides these specific principles, the general principles of good risk management remain applicable when the precautionary principle is invoked. These are the following five principles:
- proportionality between the measures taken and the chosen level of protection;
- non-discrimination in application of the measures;
- consistency of the measures with similar measures already taken in similar situations or using similar approaches;
- examination of the benefits and costs of action or lack of action;
- review of the measures in the light of scientific developments;
- burden of proof.

(*ScadPlus*)

29.   C

The Convention on the Control of Transboundary Movements of Hazardous Wastes and Their Disposal (the Basel Convention) entered into force in 1992. A central goal of the Basel Convention is to protect human health and the environment by minimising hazardous waste production whenever possible through environmentally sound management. The convention requires that the production of hazardous wastes be managed using an integrated life-cycle approach, which involves strict controls from its generation to storage, transport, treatment, reuse, recycling, recovery and final disposal.

30.   D

Euroairnet is the European air quality monitoring network. Its main goal is to establish a network with sufficient spatial coverage, representativeness and quality to provide the basic data as soon as possible, with a time delay no longer than six months, to fulfil the information requirement of the European Environment Agency (EEA). Euroairnet comprises a selection from already existing stations in the countries. Data from Euroairnet are reported to Airbase, the European air quality database. Euroairnet and Airbase are managed by the European Topic Centre on Air Quality and climate change under contract to the EEA.
(*EEA*)
    For further information, see:
http://glossary.eea.eu.int/EEAGlossary/

31.   B

Eurovignette is a fixed annual charge for heavy vehicles calculated in accordance with the damage caused to the environment and road infrastructure, necessary for using the roads in EU countries that do not levy tolls on motorways.

32.   A

Directive 2002/49/EC of the European Parliament and of the Council relating to the assessment and management of environmental noise defines it as an unwanted or harmful outdoor sound created by human activities, including noise emitted by means of transport, road traffic, rail traffic, air traffic, and from sites of industrial activity such as those defined in Annex I to Council Directive 96/61/EC of 24 September 1996 concerning integrated pollution prevention and control.
(*EEA*)

33.   B

The Energy Charter Treaty provides the broadest multilateral framework of rules in existence under international law governing energy cooperation. As the trend towards globalisation continues, it is likely that the strategic value of these rules will increasingly be appreciated by governments, in the context of their efforts to build a legal foundation for global energy security, based on the principles of open, competitive markets and sustainable development. The Energy Charter Treaty and the Energy Charter Protocol on Energy Efficiency and Related Environmental Aspects were signed in December 1994 and entered into legal force in April 1998. To date the Treaty has been signed or acceded to by fifty-one states plus the European Communities (the total number of its Signatories is therefore fifty-two).

34.   A

The Habitat Agenda was adopted by 171 governments at Habitat II (UN Conference on Human Settlements), Istanbul 1996. The Agenda provides a practical roadmap to an urbanising world, setting out approaches and strategies towards the achievement of sustainable development of the world's urban areas.
(*EEA*)

35.   C

36.   D

The Landsat program is the longest running enterprise for acquisition of imagery of Earth from space. The first Landsat satellite was launched in 1972; the most recent, Landsat 7, was launched on 15 April 1999. The instruments on the Landsat satellites have acquired millions of images. These are archived in the United States and at Landsat receiving stations around the world and are a unique resource for global change research and applications in agriculture, geology, forestry, regional planning, education and national security.

37.   B

The major accident reporting system (MARS) is used by both EU and OECD member countries to report industrial accidents in the MARS standard format and to exchange accidents information on this basis. It is a distributed information network, consisting of local databases on a MS-Windows platform in each Member State of the European Union and a central UNIX-based analysis system at the European Commission's Joint Research Centre in Ispra that allows complex text retrieval and pattern analysis.
(*EEA*)

38.   A

The European Union is seeking to ensure biodiversity by conserving natural habitats and wild fauna and flora in the territory of the Member States. An ecological network of special protected areas, known as "Natura 2000", is being set up for this purpose. The network is given coherence by other activities involving monitoring and surveillance, reintroduction of native species, introduction of non-native species, research and education.
(*ScadPlus*)

39.   C

The INSPIRE initiative will make available relevant, harmonised and quality geographic information for the purpose of formulation, implementation, monitoring and evaluation of Community environmental policy-making and for the citizen. Furthermore, by establishing from the onset cross-sectoral co-ordination mechanisms, INSPIRE will provide access to compatible information across sectors such as environment, transport and agriculture. It will also help the integration of environmental considerations in other sectors and supporting the new approach to more coherent policy-making advocated by the EU sustainable development strategy.
(*DG Environment*)

40.   D

The purpose of Directive 2002/96/EC on waste electrical and electronic equipment (WEEE) is, as a first priority, the prevention of waste electrical and electronic equipment (WEEE), and in addition, the reuse, recycling and other forms of recovery of such wastes so as to reduce the disposal of waste. It also seeks to improve the environmental performance of all operators involved in the life cycle of electrical and electronic equipment, e.g. producers, distributors and consumers and in particular those operators directly involved in the treatment of waste electrical and electronic equipment.
(*EEA*)

RESEARCH, CULTURE
AND EDUCATION POLICY
ANSWERS

Question No	A	B	C	D
1.		X		
2.			X	
3.			X	
4.			X	
5.				X
6.		X		
7.			X	
8.	X			
9.		X		
10.				X

Question No	A	B	C	D
11.	X			
12.	X			
13.	X			
14.	X			
15.		X		
16.			X	
17.				X
18.	X			
19.			X	
20.			X	

1.   B

Article 165(1) of the EC Treaty provides that "[t]he Community and the Member States shall coordinate their research and technological development activities so as to ensure that national policies and Community policy are mutually consistent." Article 165(2) of the EC Treaty outlines that "[i]n close cooperation with the Member State, the Commission may take any useful initiative to promote the coordination referred to in paragraph 1."

2.   C

Today the EU devotes only 1.96% of its GDP to research and development, compared to 2.59% for the United States, 3.12% for Japan and 2.9% for Korea. The gap between the US and EU is currently about €130 billion a year, 80% of which can be attributed to the difference in private sector spending in research and development.
(*Communication from the Commission "Building the era of knowledge for growth" - COM(2005) 118 final*)

3.   C

The Barcelona European Council in March 2002 concluded that "[i]n order to close the gap between the EU and its major competitors, there must be a significant boost of the overall R&D and innovation effort in the Union, with a particular emphasis on frontier technologies." Along these lines, the European Council agreed that overall spending on R&D and innovation in the Union should be increased with the aim of approaching 3% of GDP by 2010. Two-thirds of this new investment should come from the private sector.

4.   C

The 2003 Commission Communication on *"Investing in research: an action plan for Europe"* concludes that in order to reach the Barcelona objective (see answer 3), research investment in Europe should grow at an average rate of 8% every year, shared between a 6% growth rate for public expenditure and a 9% yearly growth rate for private investment. To achieve this, the Commission set out four set of actions as follows:

- A first set of actions aims at supporting the steps taken by European countries and stakeholders, ensuring that they are mutually consistent and that they form an effective mix of policy measures. This includes a process of co-ordination with and between Member States and acceding countries. It also entails creating a number of "European technology platforms", which will bring together the main stakeholders – research organisations, industry, regulators, user groups, etc. – around key technologies, in order to devise and implement a common strategy for the development, the deployment and the use of these technologies in Europe.

- The second set of actions aims at improving considerably public support to research and technological innovation. In order to invest in research in Europe, enterprises need to find here abundant and excellent teams of researchers, a strong public research well articulated with industry, and effective public financial support, including through fiscal measures. The Action Plan focuses on actions to improve the career of researchers, to bring public research and industry closer together, and to develop and exploit fully the potential of European and national public financial instruments. For example, the Action Plan asks public authorities to eliminate by 2005 the current rules and practices, attached to many public funding schemes, which prevent trans-European cooperation and technology transfer and thus reduce considerably the research and innovation opportunities available to the beneficiaries.

- A third set of actions addresses the necessary increase in the levels of public funding for research. Given the current economic downturn, it is all the more important to ensure that budgetary policies favour investments that will lead to higher sustainable growth in the future, among which research is a strong priority. Actions focus on encouraging and monitoring the redirection of public budgets, and on making full use of the possibilities for public support to industry offered by State aid rules and public procurement rules. For example, the Action Plan proposes to clarify and improve awareness of the types of public support that public authorities can use with no distortion to competition.

- Lastly, a fourth set of actions aims at improving the environment of research and technological innovation in Europe: intellectual property protection, regulation of product markets and related standards, competition rules, financial markets, the fiscal environment, and the treatment of research in companies' management and reporting practices. For example, the Action Plan sets the objective that every student in science, engineering and business should receive at least a basic training on intellectual property and technology transfer.

5.   D

The 2004 Commission Communication on "Science and technology, the key to Europe's future – Guidelines for future European Union policy to support research" sets out six major objectives as follows:

- creating European centres of excellence through collaboration between laboratories;
- launching European technological initiatives
- Stimulating the creativity of basic research through competition between teams at European level;
- making Europe more attractive to the best researchers;
- developing research infrastructures of European interest;
- improving the coordination of national research programmes.

(For a fuller account of the above six objectives, see *Communication from the Commission – Science and technology, the key to Europe's future* (COM(2004) 353)

6.   B

Further information on the European Research Area can be collected from:
http://europa.eu.int/comm/research/era/index_en.html

7. C

The 6th Framework Programme has been adopted for the period 2002 to 2006.

8. A

Within the remit of the 6th Framework Programme, the purpose of "networks of excellence" is to strengthen and develop Community scientific and technological excellence by means of the integration, at European level, of research capacities currently existing or emerging at both national and regional level. Each network will also aim at advancing knowledge in a particular area by assembling a critical mass of expertise. They will foster cooperation between capacities of excellence in universities, research centres, enterprises, including SMEs, and science and technology organisations. The activities concerned will be generally targeted towards long-term, multidisciplinary objectives, rather than predefined results in terms of products, processes or services.

A "network of excellence" will be implemented by a joint programme of activities involving some or, where appropriate, all of the research capacities and activities of the participants in the relevant area to attain a critical mass of expertise and European added value. A joint programme of activities could aim at the creation of a self-standing virtual centre of excellence that may result in developing the necessary means for achieving a durable integration of the research capacities.
(*Decision No. 1513/2002/EC*)

9. B

The Community Research and Development Information System (CORDIS) is an internet information system containing information on past and ongoing projects, current calls for proposals, partner search facilities, an electronic proposal submission system (EPSS) and many more features.
For further information, see:
http://www.cordis.lu

10. D

The European Research Advisory Board (EURAB) is an independent high-level advisory committee created by the Commission to provide advice on the design and implementation of EU research policy. EURAB is made up of 45 top experts from EU countries and beyond. Its members are nominated in a personal capacity and come from a wide range of academic and industrial backgrounds, as well as representing other societal interests.
For further information, see:
http://europa.eu.int/comm/research/eurab/index_en.html

11. A

In the context of the Commission's 2003 Action Plan for reaching the Barcelona objective, and recognising that primary competence for policy in this area lies with Member States, the Spring European Council of 2003 called for the Open Method of Coordination (OMC) to be used in support of research and development policy-making.

OMC is the soft governance tool, agreed between Member States in Lisbon, to ensure satisfactory progress in policy areas which are primarily of Member State competence. OMC involves:

• fixing guidelines for the Union combined with specific timetables for achieving the goals which they set in the short, medium and long terms;

• establishing, where appropriate, quantitative and qualitative indicators and benchmarks against the best in the world and tailored to the needs of different Member States and sectors as a means of comparing best practice;

• translating these European guidelines into national and regional policies by setting specific targets and adopting measures, taking into account national and regional differences;

• periodic monitoring, evaluation and peer review organised as mutual learning processes.
(*Commission*)

12. A

In its 2005 Communication titled *"Building the ERA of knowledge for growth"* the Commission is proposing a new Research Framework Programme with four objectives:

- **To gain leadership in key scientific and technology areas** by supporting cooperation between universities, industry, research centres and public authorities across the European Union as well as with the rest of the world: With more than half of the total 7th Framework Programme budget, this programme will cover the whole range of research activities performed in trans-national cooperation, from collaborative projects and networks to the coordination of national research programmes. Within each thematic area, flexible use will be made of all actions and funding schemes in a way that best serves to achieve the theme's objectives. The organisation of all themes in one programme will facilitate joint approaches across themes to answer challenges of common interest, thus also encouraging multidisciplinarity. The catalytic effect of Community funding on other public research spending will be reinforced through scaled up ERANET actions that will boost research in given areas through joined up national programmes. International cooperation between the EU and third countries is an important dimension of this action: depending on the themes addressed, specific actions will be undertaken with countries or groups of countries outside the EU, where there is mutual interest in doing so.

- **To stimulate the creativity and excellence of European research** through the funding of "frontier research" carried out by individual teams competing at European level: In order to introduce a new dynamic in research by putting a premium on excellence through competition and attracting the best brains, a European Research Council will be created to fund investigator-driven projects in all scientific and technological fields, including engineering, socio-economic sciences and the humanities. Projects will be selected through peer review on the sole basis of scientific excellence. The European Research Council will act in full autonomy, under the governance of an assembly of eminent scientists working across disciplines appointed by the Commission on the advice of the scientific community. Setting up the European Research Council within the European Community Framework provides the best guarantee for its autonomy.

- **To develop and strengthen the human potential** of European research through support to training, mobility and the development of European research careers: This programme will reinforce the existing "Marie Curie" actions of support to researchers, better focusing on key aspects of skills and career development, increasing mobility between university and industry, and strengthening links with national systems.

- **To enhance research and innovation capacity** throughout Europe: Ensuring optimal use and development of research infrastructures; supporting regional research-driven clusters; unleashing the full research potential existing in the EU's convergence regions and outermost regions; supporting research for the benefit of SMEs; bringing science and society closer together; and developing and coordinating an international science and technology co-operation policy. Through their combined impact, these programmes will allow for the emergence and reinforcement of European poles of excellence in various fields.

For a fuller account of the 7th Research Framework Programme see the above Communication the Commission's Proposal for a Decision of the European Parliament and of the Council establishing a Competitiveness and Innovation Framework Programme (2007-2013).

13.   A

Article 151(1) of the EC Treaty provides that "[t]he Community shall contribute to the flowering of the cultures of the Member States, while respecting their national and regional diversity and at the same time bringing the common cultural heritage to the fore." According to Article 151(2) of the EC Treaty, "[a]ction by the Community shall be aimed at encouraging cooperation between Member States and, if necessary, supporting and supplementing their action in the following areas:

- improvement of the knowledge and dissemination of the culture and history of the European peoples;

- conservation and safeguarding of cultural heritage of European significance;

- non-commercial cultural exchanges;
- artistic and literary creation, including in the audiovisual sector."

14.   A

The Culture 2000 programme is a single programming and financing instrument for Community measures in the field of culture for the period from 1 January 2000 to 31 December 2006. The Culture 2000 programme enhances the cultural area common to Europeans by promoting cooperation between creative artists, cultural operators and the cultural institutions of the Member States. The programme therefore furthers the promotion of creativity, the transnational dissemination of culture, the movement of creators, other cultural operators and professionals and their works. Culture 2000 emphasises the role of culture as an economic factor and as a factor in social integration and citizenship. The Culture 2000 programme furthers a linkage with measures implemented under other Community policies which have cultural implications.

The programme's objectives are achieved by the following actions:

- Specific innovative and/or experimental actions involving operators from at least three participating countries. These actions aim mainly to encourage the emergence and spread of new forms of cultural expression, improve access to culture, in particular for young people and the underprivileged, and promote live broadcasting of cultural events using the new technologies of the information society.
- Integrated actions covered by structured, multiannual cultural cooperation agreements. These agreements are between cultural operators from at least five participating countries and their aim is to create, within a period of up to three years, structured cultural actions which help to achieve an objective of cultural interest which has been set in advance. The cooperation agreements relate either to enhancing a cultural field or to integrating several cultural sectors.
- Special cultural events with a European and/or international dimension. These events must be substantial in scale and scope and must help to increase the sense of

belonging to the same community (such as the "European Capital of Culture" initiative).

The funding for the implementation of the Culture 2000 programme for the period 2000-2006 is set at EUR 236.5 million. The annual appropriations will be authorised by the budgetary authority within the limit set by the financial perspective. This budget is broken down as follows:

- a maximum of 45% for specific innovative and/or experimental actions;
- a minimum of 35% for integrated actions;
- 10% for special cultural events;
- 10% for other expenditure.

The Commission is responsible for implementing the Culture 2000 programme, assisted by an advisory committee. Member States may use Commission financial assistance to open cultural contact points (CCPS) on a voluntary basis. These are responsible for promoting the programme, facilitating access to it and encouraging participation, and also for providing an efficient link with the various institutions providing aid to the cultural sector in the Member States.

Operators from 30 European countries are currently participating in the "Culture 2000" Programme: the 25 Member States of the European Union – Austria, Belgium, Cyprus, Czech Republic, Denmark, Estonia, Finland, France, Germany, Greece, Hungary, Ireland, Italy, Latvia, Lithuania, Luxembourg, Malta, Netherlands, Poland, Portugal, Slovakia, Slovenia, Spain, Sweden, United Kingdom – the three countries of the European Economic Area (EEA – Iceland, Liechtenstein, Norway) and the candidate countries (Bulgaria and Romania).

By 31 December 2005 at the latest, the Commission will present to the European Parliament and the Council a detailed assessment of the results obtained by the "Culture 2000" Programme. This will allow Parliament and the Council to consider the proposal for a new framework programme, announced for 2004 and planned to start in 2007. (*ScadPlus*)

15.   B

The European Cities of Culture had been chosen until 2004 on an intergovernmental basis. The Member States unanimously selected cities worthy of hosting the event, and the European

Commission awarded a grant each year to the city selected.

Decision 1419/1999/EC, adopted in 1999, changed the procedure for selecting the cities from 2005 onwards. Henceforth, the European Capital of Culture is decided each year by the Council on a Commission recommendation, which takes into account the view of a jury comprising seven prominent independent members, each of them experts in the culture sector. The selection is based on criteria laid down in the above Decision.

The ten Member States that joined the Union in 2004 were not included in the 1999 Decision, as the names of the countries and their accession dates had not yet been decided at that time. Accordingly, the text approved by the European Parliament on 22 February 2005 makes up for this by providing, from 2009 onwards, for two "European Capitals of Culture" per year. The chronological order adopted had already been discussed with the Member States concerned.

Order for the submission of candidate cities for the "European Capital of Culture"

2005	Ireland	Cork
2006	Greece	Patras
2007	Luxembourg	Luxembourg + Sibiu (Romania)
2008	UK	Liverpool + Stavanger (Norway)
2009	Austria	Lithuania
2010	Germany	Hungary
2011	Finland	Estonia
2012	Portugal	Slovenia
2013	France	Slovakia
2014	Sweden	Latvia
2015	Belgium	Czech Republic
2016	Spain	Poland
2017	Denmark	Cyprus
2018	Netherlands	Malta
2019	Italy	

16.   C

The Erasmus Mundus programme is a co-operation and mobility programme in the field of higher education. It aims to enhance quality in European higher education and to promote intercultural understanding through co-operation with third countries.

The programme is intended to strengthen European co-operation and international links in higher education by supporting high-quality European Masters Courses, by enabling students and visiting scholars from around the world to engage in postgraduate study at European universities, as well as by encouraging the outgoing mobility of European students and scholars towards third countries.

The Erasmus Mundus programme comprises four concrete actions:

- **ACTION 1** – Erasmus Mundus Masters Courses: they constitute the central component around which Erasmus Mundus is built. They are high-quality integrated courses at masters level offered by a consortium of at least three universities in at least three different European countries. The courses must be "integrated" to be selected under Erasmus Mundus, which means that they must foresee a study period in at least two of the three universities and that it must lead to the award of a recognised double, multiple or joint diploma.

- **ACTION 2** – Erasmus Mundus scholarships: in order to give the Erasmus Mundus Masters Courses selected under Action 1 a strong external projection, a scholarship scheme for third-country graduate students and scholars from the whole world is linked to them. This scholarship scheme addresses highly qualified individuals who come to Europe to follow the Erasmus Mundus Masters Courses or to work for them.

- **ACTION 3** – Partnerships: in order to encourage European universities to open themselves up to the world and to reinforce their worldwide presence, Erasmus Mundus Masters Courses selected under Action 1 also have the possibility of establishing partnerships with third-country higher education institutions. These partnerships allow for outgoing mobility of graduate EU students and scholars involved in the Erasmus Mundus Masters Courses.

- **ACTION 4** – Enhancing attractiveness: Erasmus Mundus also supports projects aimed at enhancing the attractiveness of and the interest in European higher education. It supports activities that improve the profile, the visibility and the accessibility of European higher education as well as issues crucial to the internationalisation of higher education, such as the mutual recognition of qualifications with third countries.

In concrete terms, Erasmus Mundus will support about 100 Erasmus Mundus Masters Courses of outstanding academic quality. It will provide grants for some 5,000 graduate students from third countries to follow these Masters Courses, and for more than 4,000 EU graduate students involved in these courses to study in third countries. The programme will also offer teaching or research scholarships in Europe for over 1,000 incoming third-country academics and for a similar number of outgoing EU scholars. Last but not least, Erasmus Mundus will support about 100 partnerships between Erasmus Mundus Masters Courses and higher education institutions in third countries.

Higher education institutions coming from the 25 European Union Member States and the EEA/EFTA countries (European Economic Area / European Free Trade Association) are eligible for offering Erasmus Mundus Masters Courses jointly, under Action 1. Action 1 is also open to current European Union candidate countries, but official participation of these countries in the programme has not yet been formalised.

(*Commission*)

17.   D

Grundtvig is aimed at enhancing the European dimension of lifelong learning. It supports a wide range of activities designed to promote innovation and the improved availability, accessibility and quality of educational provision for adults, by means of European co-operation.

The Grundtvig action addresses a great variety of educational providers, but the final beneficiaries are adults who, at whatever stage of their lives, wish to learn in order to:

- increase their capacity to play a full and active role in society and develop their inter-cultural awareness;
- improve their employability by aquiring or updating their general skills;
- enhance their capacity to access or re-enter formal education schemes.

This learning can be accomplished within the

framework of formal or non-formal or by means of autonomous learning.

(*Commission*)

18.   A

The Bologna Declaration of 19 June 1999 involves six actions relating to:

- a system of academic grades which are easy to read and compare, including the introduction of the diploma supplement (designed to improve international "transparency" and facilitate academic and professional recognition of qualifications);
- a system essentially based on two cycles: a first cycle geared to the employment market and lasting at least three years and a second cycle (Master) conditional upon the completion of the first cycle;
- a system of accumulation and transfer of credits (of the ECTS type already used successfully under Socrates-Erasmus);
- mobility of students, teachers and researchers;
- cooperation with regard to quality assurance;
- the European dimension of higher education.

The aim of the process is to make the higher education systems in Europe converge towards a more transparent system which whereby the different national systems would use a common framework based on three cycles – Degree/Bachelor, Master and Doctorate.

(*Commission*)

For further information, see:
http://europa.eu.int/comm/education/policies/educ/bologna/bologna_en.html

19.   C

Within the meaning of Article 151 of the EC Treaty the European Union is obliged to operate its cultural activities and programmes on the subsidiarity principle, i.e. the European Union's actions can only be as a complement to the activities of the Member States. Subsidiarity means that in areas that "are not exclusively within its competence" (such as for example culture) the EU can only take action "only if and in so far as the objectives of the proposed action cannot be sufficiently achieved by the Member States and can therefore, by reason of the scale or effects of the proposed action, be better achieved by the Community." Therefore, directives and regulations cannot be passed when regulating on cultural matters.

(On 10 May 2005 the European Parliament adopted the report by Gyula Hegyi MEP broadly approving the proposal, subject to a number of compromise amendments in order to avoid a second reading on film heritage and the competitiveness of related industrial activities. The final text of the Recommendation was still to be published in the Official Journal by the manuscript closing date.)

20.   C

The European Commission adopted ambitious proposals on 14 July 2004 for the next generation of EU programmes in education, training, culture, youth and the audiovisual sector. The aim is to have the new programmes approved by the Council of Ministers and the European Parliament before the end of 2005. They will run from 2007 to 2013.

The four programmes proposed are:

- **An Integrated Action Programme in Lifelong Learning**, focusing on school education (Comenius), higher education (Erasmus), vocational training (Leonardo da Vinci) and adult education (Grundtvig), completed by transversal measures and a new programme (Jean Monnet) focusing on European integration. The proposed budget is €13.62 billion and the aims of the programme are:

– *Comenius*: To involve at least 5% of EU school pupils in joint educational activities.

– *Erasmus*: To provide EU study abroad opportunities for a total of 3 million university students by 2011.

– *Leonardo da Vinci*: To increase training placements in enterprises and training centres in another EU country to 150,000 in 2013.

– *Grundtvig*: To help 25,000 adult education students benefit from studying abroad in 2013.

- **Youth in Action**, which aims to develop a sense of personal responsibility, initiative, concern for others, citizenship and active involvement at local, national and European level among young people. The programme will also help to improve support systems for youth activities. The proposed budget is €915 million.

- **Culture 2007**, taking over from the current Culture 2000 programme and extending it, with a proposed budget of €408 million, through three objectives considered to offer strong European added value:

– Transnational mobility for everyone working in the cultural sector in the EU.

– The transnational circulation of works of art and cultural/artistic products.

– Intercultural dialogue.

- **MEDIA 2007**, following on from the current MEDIA Plus and MEDIA Training programmes with a proposed budget of €1.055 billion, with the principal aims of:

– Preserving and promoting Europe's cultural diversity and cinematic/audiovisual heritage, ensuring public access to this heritage and encouraging dialogue between cultures.

– Increasing the circulation of European films and other audiovisual productions, both inside and outside the EU.

– Strengthening the commercial performance of the European audiovisual sector in an open and competitive market context. (*Commission*)

INDUSTRY, INFORMATION TECHNOLOGY, TRANSPORT, ENERGY POLICY

ANSWERS

Question No	A	B	C	D
1.			X	
2.				X
3.		X		
4.	X			
5.			X	
6.			X	
7.		X		
8.				X
9.			X	
10.	X			

Question No	A	B	C	D
11.			X	
12.				X
13.		X		
14.	X			
15.				X
16.			X	
17.	X			
18.				X
19.		X		
20.		X		

1.   C

The Multiannual Programme for Enterprise and Entrepreneurship – Council Decision (2000/ 819/ EC) of 20 December 2000 on a multiannual programme for enterprise and entrepreneurship, and in particular for small and medium-sized enterprises (SMEs) (2001-2005) – is a framework plan of activities which aim at
- enhancing the growth and competitiveness of business in a knowledge-based internationalised economy;
- promoting entrepreneurship;
- simplifying and improving the administrative and regulatory framework for business so that research, innovation and business creation in particular can flourish;
- improving the financial environment for business, especially SMEs;
- giving business easier access to Community support services, programmes and networks and improving the coordination of these facilities.

It is also an instrument for implementing the 10 Action Lines of the European Charter for Small Enterprise.
(*Commission*)

2.   D

The European Investment Fund (EIF) was founded in 1994 as a joint venture between three shareholder groups: European Investment Bank, European Commission and European financial institutions. Its main task was to provide financial institutions with infrastructure and SME guarantees. The EIF began its involvement in venture capital in 1997, as part of the European Commission's "Growth and Employment" initiative. Its venture capital instruments consist of equity investments in venture capital funds that support SMEs, particularly those that are in their early stages of development and those that are technology-oriented. To support its remit, the EIF has significant means available for investment, with a current portfolio of in excess of € 2.5 billion invested in 184 venture capital funds.

3.   B

In June 2000, the EIB launched its "Innovation 2000 Initiative" to further the March 2000 Lisbon European Council's guidelines for developing a knowledge-based society driven by innovation. The "Innovation 2000 Initiative" groups together the EIB's actions to promote information networks, human capital formation and intangible corporate investment.

Under this initiative, EIB financing will be channelled into the following five areas:

- **Human capital formation**: by financing the provision of schools, colleges and universities with computing equipment and lending in support of IT training centres;
- **Research and development**: by co-financing public or private-sector research programmes, corporate investment in R&D, research infrastructure, centres of excellence and measures enabling SMEs to obtain access to research programmes;
- **Information and communications technology networks**: by financing trans-European broadband and multimedia networks and physical or virtual infrastructure providing local access to such networks, especially in the Union's less advanced regions. The EIB will focus its lending in this field on innovative technology projects such as ADSL, XDSL and UMTS;
- **Diffusion of innovation**: by financing "online healthcare" services and the use of information technologies to bring Europe's citizens closer to local authorities and public services; by helping to equip companies, especially SMEs, with advanced information technologies;
- **Development of SMEs and entrepreneurship**: by strengthening venture capital support for the development of innovative SMEs, fostering science parks and company incubators and launching new products tailored to the business needs of very small enterprises.

Support for these areas of EIB activity will be provided under a dedicated lending programme of EUR 12 to 15 billion over the next three years. More than simply an increase in the Bank's lending volume, this will represent a qualitative reorientation of the EIB's traditional operations towards sectors with high technological value added having a positive impact on the economy. To this end, the EIB will both broaden the range of its financial instruments and reach out to new partners and customers, especially to take account of the extension of its financing operations to include intangible investment.
(*CORDIS*)

4.   A

PAXIS is managed by the Commission's Enterprise Directorate-General under the 6th Framework Programme, "Research & Innovation Programme". PAXIS promotes the setting-up and development of innovative companies across Europe – a driving force for employment and economic growth.

The PAXIS programme has two major objectives:

- to boost the transfer of local and regional excellence in innovation;
- to have an instrument for co-operation and the exchange of tacit knowledge and learning among local innovation stakeholders, profiting from each other's experience.

PAXIS was launched in 1999 with three working areas: Thematic Networks, Projects and Accompanying Measures.
(*PAXIS*)

5.   C

The "European TrendChart on Innovation" is a major operation of the European Commission (DG Enterprise). The TrendChart offers its services primarily to innovation policy makers and scheme managers in Europe. Advised by a Group of Senior Officers (GSO) from the Member States, it includes three major building blocks:

- the survey of innovation policy to collect and analyse information on innovation policy measures in Europe;
- the European Innovation Scoreboard delivering aggregate statistical data to compare and analyse national innovation performances;
- the Innovation policy reviews offering platforms for innovation policy makers and scheme managers to assess the effectiveness of schemes and to identify "good practice" in the framework of a series of benchmarking workshops.

(*TrendChart*)

6.   C

The Commission proposed a Competitiveness and Innovation Framework Programme (CIP) with a budget of €4.213 billion for the period 2007 – 2013. The CIP will support actions that develop the capacity of enterprise and industry to innovate. It will boost the use of Information and Communication Technology (ICT), environmental technologies and efficient and renewable energy sources. The CIP provides a comprehensive response to the call of the Lisbon mid-term review for simpler, more visible and more targeted EU action.

Whilst building on tried and tested programmes, CIP also includes many new elements such as:
- a risk capital instrument for High Growth and Innovative Companies (GIF2);
- "securitisation" of banks' SME loan portfolios;
- enhanced role for innovation and business support networks;
- demonstrators of technological and organisational solutions to European ICT-services;
- a twinning programme for policy makers.

In its three specific programmes the CIP combines concrete actions which will promote:
- Start up and growth of SMEs: the **"Entrepreneurship and Innovation Programme"** with a budget of 2.631 billion including up to €520 million to promote eco-innovation, will facilitate access to finance and support investment in innovation activities. It will provide SMEs with information and advice on single market opportunities and Community matters and assist Member States in introducing a better regulatory and administrative environment for business and innovation. It will also further develop strategies for industrial and service sectors and monitor their progress.
- Information and communication technologies: the **"ICT Policy Support Programme"**, with a budget of €802 million, will contribute to competitiveness, growth and jobs through stimulating a wider adoption and more efficient take up of ICT. In particular, it will support operational demonstrations of technological and organisational solutions to ICT-based services at EU level in particular addressing interoperability, identity management and security challenges.
- 12% share of renewable energy by 2010 and reduce energy consumption: the **"Intelligent**

Energy-Europe Programme" with a budget of €780 million will support energy efficiency, new and renewable energy sources, and technological solutions to reduce greenhouse gas emissions caused by the transport sector.
(*Commission*)

7.   B

See the "Entrepreneurship and Innovation Programme" within the framework of CIP (answer 6).

8.   D

IDABC is a Community programme managed by the European Commission's Enterprise and Industry Directorate General, and stands for *Interoperable Delivery of European eGovernment Services to public Administrations, Business and Citizens*. It uses the opportunities offered by information and communication technologies to encourage and support the delivery of cross-border public sector services to citizens and enterprises in Europe, to improve efficiency and collaboration between European public administrations and to contribute to making Europe an attractive place to live, work and invest.

To achieve its objectives, IDABC issues recommendations, develops solutions and provides services that enable national and European administrations to communicate electronically and offer modern public services to businesses and citizens in Europe. The programme also provides financing to projects that address European policy requirements and improve cooperation between administrations across Europe.

National public sector policy-makers are represented in the IDABC programme's management committee and in many expert groups. This makes of the programme a unique forum for the coordination of national e-government policies.

By using state-of-the-art information and communication technologies, developing common solutions and services and providing a platform for the exchange of good practice between public administrations, IDABC contributes to the eEurope objective of modernising the European public sector.
(*Commission*)

9.   C

The Barcelona European Council called on the Commission to draw up an eEurope action plan focusing on "the widespread availability and use of broadband networks throughout the Union by 2005 and the development of Internet protocol IPv6 and the security of networks and information, eGovernment, eLearning, eHealth and eBusiness". The eEurope 2005 Action Plan was launched at the Seville European Council in June 2002 and endorsed by the Council of Ministers in the eEurope Resolution of January 2003. It aims to develop modern public services and a dynamic environment for e-business through widespread availability of broadband access at competitive prices and a secure information infrastructure.

The eEurope Action Plan is based on two groups of actions which reinforce each other. On the one hand, it aims to stimulate services, applications and content, covering both online public services and e-business; on the other hand it addresses the underlying broadband infrastructure and security matters. (For a fuller account of eEurope 2005 Action Plan see Commission Communication "eEurope 2005: An information society for all" – COM(2002) 263 final)

10.   A

The European Commission's view of the challenges that need to be addressed in a European Information Society strategy up to 2010 are set out in a Commission Communication on "Challenges for Europe's Information Society beyond 2005: Starting point for a new EU strategy", adopted on 19 November 2004.

This communication highlights the need to step up research and investment in information and communication technologies (ICT), and to promote their take-up throughout the economy. ICT should be more closely tailored to citizens' needs and expectations, to enable them to participate more readily in socially fulfilling and culturally creative virtual communities. The Commission communication identifies a number of challenges that will remain relevant for Europe's future Information Society policy, such as electronic inclusion and citizenship, content and services, public services, skills and work, ICT as a key industry sector, interoper-

ability, trust and dependability and ICT for business processes.

Issues for an Information Society policy beyond 2005:

*   content and services;
*   eInclusion and citizenship;
*   public services;
*   skills and work;
*   ICT as a key industrial sector;
*   interoperability;
*   trust and dependability;
*   exploitation of ICT by business.

The policies known as "eInclusion" aim at ensuring equal access to and the availability of ICT services for all, at an affordable cost. The importance of such polices increases as ICT permeate society. Citizenship is about the participation of all in society, but it faces new challenges with the increasing use of ICT in everyday life. New and complex technologies create the risk that some sectors of society will be unable to deal with them. eInclusion should be tackled at national, regional and local level. (Commission Communication on "Challenges for Europe's Information Society beyond 2005: Starting point for a new EU strategy" – COM(2004) 757 final)

11.   C

The study, executed under the Commission's eEurope 2005 programme, focuses on the online availability and sophistication of 20 public services (12 for citizens, 8 for businesses). The survey examined 14,000 web sites in 28 countries, the 25 EU Member States plus Norway, Iceland and Switzerland. Sweden is the most advanced country for online public services; Austria is a close second. The method used defined an index of sophistication of services ranging from simple online information to fully interactive services including online payments and, where appropriate, online service delivery. This index increased at each measurement and has now reached 65%.

The ten new EU Member States still score largely in the lower half of the ranking. However, their development of e-Government services is now at the level of EU15 two years ago, so they are progressing fast. Estonia is already situated in the upper part of the ranking.

The study has been carried out since 2001 in the former 15 EU Member States and Norway, Iceland

and Switzerland. Countries with the biggest advance in the past year are Iceland (+20%), Germany (+15%, Italy (+13%), the UK (+13%) and Belgium (+9%).

The study suggests that growth in online sophistication (such as full interactivity of services) will level off in the coming years. Further progress will require greater connection between civil services' front and back offices, increased collaboration and cultural and process change.

Improved delivery of public services forms a key element of the wider economic strategy to modernise the EU economy. The relaunched Lisbon strategy will aim to encourage a clear, stable and competitive environment for electronic communications and digital services; increase research and innovation in information and communication technology, and promote an Information Society dedicated to inclusion and quality of life.
(*Commission, Capgemini*)

12.   D

The Modinis programme provides financial support for the implementation of the eEurope 2005 Action Plan. In this context it sets four generic objectives:

- **Action 1 - Monitoring and comparison of performance:**
    data collection and analysis on the basis of the benchmarking indicators as defined in the Council resolution of 18 February 2003 on the implementation of the eEurope 2005 action plan;
- **Action 2 - Dissemination of good practices:**
    – studies to identify good practices, at national, regional and local level, contributing to successful implementation of the eEurope 2005 action plan,
    – support for targeted conferences, seminars or workshops in support of the objectives of the eEurope 2005 action plan in order to promote cooperation;
- **Action 3 - Analysis and strategic discussion:**
    – support the work of social and economic experts,
    – support for the eEurope Steering Group (called now the eEurope Advisory Group) to provide a strategic overview of implementation of the eEurope 2005 action plan;

- **Action 4 – Improvement of network and information security:**
    preparation for the establishment of the European Network and Information Security Network by financing surveys, studies, workshops on subjects such as security mechanisms and their interoperability, network reliability and protection, advanced cryptography, privacy and security in wireless communications.
(*Commission*)

13.   B

In its White Paper *European Transport Policy for 2010: time to decide*, the Commission proposed to take measures which should make the market shares of the modes of transport return, by 2010, to their 1998 levels. This will prepare the ground for a shift of balance from 2010 onwards.

One measure to achieve this objective is the establishment of the **Marco Polo Programme** with its adoption on 22 July 2003. The Programme's objective is to reduce road congestion and to improve the environmental performance of the freight transport system within the Community and to enhance intermodality, thereby contributing to an efficient and sustainable transport system. To achieve this objective, the Programme supports actions in the freight transport, logistics and other relevant markets. These actions should contribute to maintain the distribution of freight between the various modes of transport at 1998 levels by helping to shift the expected aggregate increase in international road freight traffic of 12 billion tkm per year to short sea shipping, rail and inland waterways or to a combination of modes of transport in which road journeys are as short as possible.

All segments of the international freight transport market are within the scope of the Programme.

The Programme runs from 2003 to 2006 with a budget of €100 million for the EU25. Countries such as Norway, Iceland and Liechtenstein have joined the programme. Each additional fully participating country will contribute to the available budget.

Marco Polo II (2007-2013)

On 15th July 2004 the Commission presented a proposal COM (2004) 478 to establish a second, significantly expanded "Marco Polo" programme from 2007 onwards. Marco Polo II includes new actions such as motorways of the sea and traffic avoidance measures. The programme, which has a budget of €740 million for 2007-2013, has been extended to countries bordering the EU. The Commission estimates that every €1 in grants to Marco Polo will generate at least €6 in social and environmental benefits.

The final form of Marco Polo II will depend on the outcome of the negotiations with the European Parliament and the Council.
(*Commission*)

14.   A

Following the recommendations of 2003 from the Van Miert high-level group on the TEN-T, the Commission compiled a new list of 30 priority projects to be launched before 2010. The total cost is estimated at EUR 225 billion. The list takes full account of the recent enlargement and will establish more sustainable mobility plans by concentrating investment on rail and water transport. The 30 priority projects are defined as being in the interests of the Community so as to speed up the completion of the border crossing sections.

They are:
- rail axis Berlin-Verona/Milan-Bologna-Naples-Messina;
- high-speed train Paris-Brussels/Brussels-Cologne-Amsterdam-London;
- high-speed rail axis of south-west Europe;
- high-speed rail axis East (including Paris-Strasbourg-Luxembourg);
- conventional rail/combined transport (or Betuwe line 2007);
- rail axis Lyon-Trieste-Divaca/Koper-Ljubljana-Budapest-Ukrainian border;
- motorway axis Igoumenitsa/Patra-Athens-Sofia-Budapest;
- multimodal axis Portugal-Spain-rest of Europe;
- rail axis Cork-Dublin-Belfast-Stanraer (2001);
- Malpensa airport in Milan (completed in 2001);
- the Øresund Link (completed in 2000);
- rail/road axis Nordic triangle;
- road axis Ireland/United Kingdom/Benelux (2010);
- rail link West Coast Main Line (2007);
- Galileo global navigation and positioning satellite system (2008);

- rail freight axis across the Pyrenees Sine/Algeciras-Madrid-Paris;
- rail axis Paris-Stuttgart-Vienna-Bratislava;
- inland waterway axis Rhein/Meuse-Main-Danube;
- interoperability of the Iberian Peninsula high-speed rail network;
- rail axis between Germany and Denmark (Fehmarn Belt);
- "motorways of the sea": Baltic Sea, Atlantic Arc, south-east Europe, and western Mediterranean;
- rail axis Athens-Sofia-Budapest-Vienna-Prague-Nürnberg/Dresden;
- rail axis Gdansk-Warsaw-Brno/Bratislava-Vienna;
- rail axis Lyon/Geneva-Basel-Duisburg-Rotterdam/Antwerp;
- motorway axis Gdansk-Brno/Bratislava-Vienna;
- rail/road axis Ireland/UK/continental Europe;
- Rail Baltica railway axis Warsaw-Kaunas-Riga-Tallinn;
- Eurocaprail on the Bruxelles-Luxembourg-Strasbourg rail axis;
- rail axis on the Ionian Sea/Adriatic intermodal corridor
- inland waterway link Seine-Escaut.
(*ScadPlus*)

15.   D

The Single European Sky (SES) initiative originated with the European Commission in 1999 when there was general dissatisfaction with the levels of delay experienced by airlines and passengers. A High Level Group (HLG) was established by the European Commission to investigate and report on the underlying issues. The general thrust of the HLG's recommendations were accepted by the Member States and this resulted in 4 legislative measures which came into effect in April 2004:
- Regulation (EC) No 549/2004 of the European Parliament and of the Council of 10 March 2004 laying down the framework for the creation of the single European sky (the framework Regulation);
- Regulation (EC) No 550/2004 of the European Parliament and of the Council of 10 March 2004 on the provision of air navigation

services in the single European sky (the service provision Regulation);

- Regulation (EC) No 551/2004 of the European Parliament and of the Council of 10 March 2004 on the organisation and use of the airspace in the single European sky (the airspace Regulation);
- Regulation (EC) No 552/2004 of the European Parliament and of the Council of 10 March 2004 on the interoperability of the European Air Traffic Management network (the interoperability Regulation).

The objectives of the legislation are to improve and reinforce safety, to restructure European airspace as a function of air traffic flow, rather than according to national borders, to create additional capacity and to increase the overall efficiency of the air traffic management system (ATM). This can be achieved by a more effective and integrated air traffic management architecture and by ensuring that this architecture is based on demand driven service provision. The legislation will enhance crossboarder co-ordination, remove administrative and organisational bottlenecks in the area of decision-making and enhance enforcement in ATM.
(*Commission*)

16.   C

Galileo will be Europe's own global navigation satellite system, providing a highly accurate, guaranteed global positioning service under civilian control.

For further information, see:
http://www.esa.int

17.   A

At the meeting of the European Council in Dublin in June 1990, the Prime Minister of the Netherlands suggested that cooperation in the energy sector could stimulate economic recovery in eastern Europe and the then Soviet Union and ensure security of supply to the Community. Invited by the Council to study how best to implement this cooperation in 1991, the Commission proposed the concept of a *European Energy Charter*. Negotiations on this Charter were launched in Brussels in July 1991 and culminated with the signature of a

Concluding Document in The Hague on 17 December 1991.

The 51 signatories of the European Energy Charter undertook to pursue the objectives and principles of the Charter and to implement their cooperation in the framework of a legally binding Basic Agreement – later called the *Energy Charter Treaty* – designed to promote east-west industrial cooperation by providing legal safeguards in areas such as investment, transit and trade. The Energy Charter Treaty and Energy Charter Protocol on energy efficiency and related environmental aspects were signed on 17 December 1994 in Lisbon by all signatories of the 1991 Charter except for the United States and Canada. The European Communities and their Member States are signatories of the Treaty and Protocol.

The Energy Charter Treaty and the Energy Charter Protocol on energy efficiency and related environmental aspects are approved by this Decision on behalf of the European Coal and Steel Community (ECSC), the European Community (EC) and the European Atomic Energy Community (Euratom).
(*ScadPlus*)

18.   D

"Intelligent Energy – Europe" (EIE) is the Community's support programme for non-technological actions in the field of energy, precisely in the field of energy efficiency and renewable energy sources. The duration of the programme is from 2003 to 2006.

The programme was adopted by the European Parliament and the Council on 26 June 2003 and entered into force on 4 August 2003.

Intelligent Energy – Europe (EIE) is intended to support the European Union's policies in the field of energy as laid down in the Green Paper on Security of Energy Supply, the White Paper on Transport and other related Community legislation (including the Directives on renewable electricity, energy performance of buildings and biofuels). Its aim is to support sustainable development in the energy context, making a balanced contribution to achieving the general objectives of security of energy supply, competitiveness, and environmental protection (Art. 1 of the programme Decision).

The programme is structured in four fields

- **SAVE** – improvement of energy efficiency

and rational use of energy, in particular in the building and industry sectors.

- **ALTENER** – promotion of new and renewable energy sources for centralised and decentralised production of electricity and heat and their integration into the local environment and the energy systems
- **STEER** – support for initiatives relating to all energy aspects of transport, the diversification of fuels, such as through new developing and renewable energy sources, and the promotion of renewable fuels (biofuels) and energy efficiency in transport
- **COOPENER** – support for initiatives relating to the promotion of renewable energy sources and energy efficiency in the developing countries, in particular in the framework of the Community cooperation with developing countries in Africa, Asia, Latin America and the Pacific.

(*Commission*)

19.   B

See answer above.

20.   B

Directive 2001/77/EC of the European Parliament and of the Council of 27 September 2001 on the promotion of electricity from renewable energy sources in the internal electricity market follows up the White Paper on renewable sources of energy (RES). This confirmed a target of 12% of gross inland energy consumption from renewables for the Community as a whole by 2010, of which electricity would represent 22.1%.

EUROPEAN MONETARY UNION
EUROPEAN SINGLE CURRENCY
ANSWERS

Question No	A	B	C	D
1.	X			
2.	X			
3.			X	
4.			X	
5.				X
6.		X		
7.				X
8.	X			
9.		X		
10.				X

Question No	A	B	C	D
11.	X			
12.			X	
13.	X			
14.			X	
15.				X
16.				X
17.		X		
18.	X			
19.	X			
20.			X	

1.   A

The European exchange rate mechanism (ERM) was a system introduced in March 1979, as part of the European Monetary System (EMS), to reduce exchange-rate variability and achieve monetary stability in the Communities, in preparation for Economic and Monetary Union and the introduction of a single currency, the euro, which took place in January 1999.

The ERM is based on the concept of fixed currency exchange rate margins, but with exchange rates variable with those margins. Before the introduction of the euro, exchange rates were based on the ECU, the European unit of account, whose value was determined as a weighted average of the participating currencies.

A grid of bilateral rates was calculated on the basis of these central rates expressed in ECUs, and currency fluctuations had to be contained within a margin of 2.25% either side of the bilateral rates (with the exception of the Italian lira, which was allowed a margin of 6%). Determined intervention and loan arrangements protected the participating currencies from greater exchange rates fluctuations.

Unlike the Werner Plan, it did not propose a new body to co-ordinate economic policy, but rather that these functions could be carried out within the existing institutional framework.

The three stages for the development of EMU were:

- **Stage One:** Increased co-operation between central banks with relation to monetary policy, removal of obstacles to financial integration, monitoring of national economic policies, co-ordination of budgetary policy;
- **Stage Two:** Preparatory stage for the final phase of EMU, establishment of the ESCB and progressive transfer of monetary policy to European institutions, narrowing of margins of fluctuation within exchange rate mechanism;
- **Stage Three:** Fixing of exchange rates between national currencies and their replacement by a single European currency; responsibility for monetary policy would be transferred to the ESCB.

Most of the ideas set out in the Delors report later formed the basis for the EMU provisions agreed in the Maastricht Treaty.
(*Commission*)

2.   A

The establishment of the internal market brought a new stimulus to the idea of a single currency, and the 1988 Hanover European Council concluded that "in adopting the Single Act, the Member States of the Community confirmed the objective of progressive realisation of economic and monetary union."

A committee was set up under the chairmanship of Commission President Jacques Delors with "the task of studying and proposing concrete steps leading towards this union."

The 1989 Delors Report set out a plan to introduce the European Monetary Union (EMU) over three stages, including an institutional framework to allow policy to be decided and executed at the Community level in economic areas of direct relevance for the functioning of EMU.

It included the creation of a monetary institution, namely a European System of Central Banks (ESCB), which would become responsible for formulating and implementing monetary policy as well as managing external exchange rate policy.

3.   C

The first paragraph of Article 2 of the Maastricht Treaty provides that (emphasis added) "[t]he Union shall set itself the following objectives):

-   to promote economic and social progress and a high level of employment and to achieve balanced and sustainable development, in particular through the creation of an area without internal frontiers, through the strengthening of economic and social cohesion and through the *establishment of economic and monetary union, ultimately including a single currency* in accordance with the provisions of this Treaty."

4.   C

On the basis of the Delors Report, the European Council held in Madrid in June 1989 decided that the first stage of the realisation of EMU should begin on 1 July 1990. On this date, in principle, all restrictions on the movement of capital between Member States were abolished.

5.   D

Article 116(1) of the EC Treaty provides that the "[s]econd stage for achieving economic and monetary union shall begin on 1 January 1994." Stage Two of EMU provided for, inter alia, the establishment of the European Monetary Institute (EMI), the prohibition of financing of the public sector by the central banks, the prohibition of privileged access to financial institutions by the public sector and the avoidance of excessive government deficits.

6.   B

The European Monetary Institute (EMI) was a temporary institution established at the start of Stage II of Economic and Monetary Union (EMU) on 1 January 1994. The two main tasks of the EMI were to strengthen central bank cooperation and monetary policy coordination and to make the preparations required for the establishment of the European System of Central Banks (ESCB), for the conduct of the single monetary policy and for the creation of a single currency in Stage Three. It went into liquidation following the establishment of the ECB on 1 June 1998.
(*ECB*)

7.   D

8.   A

Article 121 of the EC Treaty establishes that the integration in Phase III of EMU (i.e. adoption of the euro) depends on the fulfilment of nominal and legal convergence criteria.

The nominal convergence criteria are as follows.
* **Inflation**: the average rate of inflation must be inferior or equal to 1.5% points based on the average of three Member States that have the best behaviour in price matters.
* **Types of interest**: the countries that attempt

to accede to the euro will have to have an average rate of nominal interest in the long term inferior or equal to 2 points on the long term average rate of the three Member States of lowest inflation.
* **Public deficit**: the public deficit will not be able to exceed 3% of Gross Domestic Product (GDP) at market prices.
* **Public debt**: the aspiring countries must adjust their public debt so that it will not be superior to 60% of their GDP. If this is not the case, exceptions can be made with countries that have diminishing debt and are achieving a rhythm that will bring them close to the established percentage.
* **Exchange rates**: the different currencies of the countries that adopt the euro will have to remain during a minimum period of 2 years within the normal fluctuation bands of the EMS, before their "examination".

The legal convergence criteria require the national legislations and of the bylaws of the central banks of the Member States to be adjusted, so that they are compatible with the Statute of the ESCB. These include matters such as the independence of the national central banks and the integration of these banks in the ESCB.

9.   B

Article 121 of the EC Treaty provides that the Council is responsible for setting the date for passage to Stage III of EMU. The 1995 Madrid European Council decided that Stage III of EMU would begin on 1 January 1999. It gave the single currency a name, euro, and after consultation with the Commission and the European Monetary Institute, adopted the scenario for its introduction. The 1998 Brussels European Council decided that eleven countries, Germany, Belgium, Spain, France, Ireland, Italy, Luxembourg, Austria, Netherlands, Portugal and Finland, would proceed to Stage III of EMU. Finally, Stage III began on 1 January 1999 with the above 11 Member States and Greece joined them two years later, i.e. on 1 January 2001.

10.   D

ERM II provides the framework for exchange rate

policy cooperation between the euro area and EU Member States not participating in the euro area. ERM II is based on the 16 June 1997 Amsterdam Resolution of the European Council on the establishment of an exchange-rate mechanism (ERM) in Stage III of EMU. ERM II replaced the European Monetary System (EMS) as from 1 January 1999. Membership of the mechanism is voluntary. Nevertheless, Member States with a derogation are expected to join the mechanism. The ERM II mechanism is based on stable but adjustable central rates to the euro for the participating currencies, with standard fluctuation bands being +/-15% around the central rate. Exchange rate policy co-operation may be further strengthened, as is presently the case with Denmark, which has an agreed fluctuation band of +/- 2.25%.

The "new" Member States that joined the EU on 1 May 2004 will join ERM II as their preparations for adopting the euro advance. On 27 June 2004 the Estonian kroon, the Lithuanian lita and the Slovenian tolar joined ERM II. The currencies of Cyprus, Latvia and Malta joined ERM II on 3 May 2005.

11.   A

12.   C

13.   A

Article 106(1) of the EC Treaty provides that "[t]he ECB shall have the exclusive right to authorise the issue of banknotes within the Community. The ECB and the national central banks may issue such notes. The banknotes issued by the ECB and the national central banks shall be the only such notes to have the status of legal tender within the Community."

Article 106(2) of the EC Treaty allows Member States to issue euro coins subject to approval by the ECB of the volume of the issue.

14.   C

On 1 January 2002, euro notes and coins were introduced in the 12 Euro-zone Member States and the notes and coins of the national currencies were withdrawn over the following two months.

15.   D

The euro banknote series comprises *seven different values* (denominations): €5, €10, €20, €50, €100, €200 and €500.

Each euro banknote shows a European architectural style: a classical, a Romanesque, a Gothic, a Renaissance, a baroque and rococo, one from the age of iron and glass, and one modern 20th century architecture. On the front, the banknotes show windows and gateways. They symbolise the European spirit of openness and cooperation. The 12 stars of the European Union represent the dynamism and harmony of contemporary Europe. The bridges on the back symbolise communication between the people of Europe and between Europe and the rest of the world. The other design elements are: the name of the currency (euro) in both the Latin and the Greek alphabets; the initials of the European Central Bank in five linguistic variants – BCE, ECB, EZB, EKT and EKP – covering the then 11 official languages of the European Union (EU); the symbol © indicating copyright protection; and the flag of the European Union.

The euro banknotes were designed by Mr Robert Kalina of the Austrian central bank (Oesterreichische Nationalbank). He won the Europe-wide design competition held in 1996.
(*ECB*)

16.   D

The Stability and Growth Pact (SGP) is the concrete EU answer to concerns on the continuation of budgetary discipline in Economic and Monetary Union (EMU). Adopted in 1997, the SGP strengthened the Treaty provisions on fiscal discipline in EMU foreseen by Articles 99 and 104, and the full provisions took effect when the euro was launched on 1 January 1999.

The principal concern of the SGP was enforcing

fiscal discipline as a permanent feature of EMU. Safeguarding sound government finances as a means to strengthening the conditions for price stability and for strong and sustainable growth conducive to employment creation. However, it was also recognised that the loss of the exchange rate instrument in EMU would imply a greater role for automatic fiscal stabilisers at national level to help economies adjust to asymmetric shocks, and would make it "necessary to ensure that national budgetary policies support stability oriented monetary policies". This is the rationale behind the core commitment of the SGP, i.e. to set the "[...] medium-term objective of budgetary positions close to balance or in surplus" which "[...] will allow all Member States to deal with normal cyclical fluctuations while keeping the government deficit within the reference value of 3% of GDP".

Formally, the SGP consists of three elements as follows:

- **A political commitment** by all parties involved in the SGP (Commission, Member States, Council) to the full and timely implementation of the budget surveillance process. These are contained in a Resolution agreed by the Amsterdam European Council of 17 June 1997. This political commitment ensures that effective peer pressure is exerted on a Member State failing to live up to its commitments.
- **Preventive elements** which through regular surveillance aim at preventing budget deficits going above the 3% reference value. To this end, Council Regulation 1466/97 reinforces the multilateral surveillance of budget positions and the co-ordination of economic policies. It foresees the submission by all Member States of stability and convergence programmes, which are examined by the Council. The Regulation foresees also the possibility to trigger the early warning mechanism in the event a significance slippage in the budgetary position of a Member State is identified.
- **Dissuasive elements** which in the event of the 3% reference value being breached, require Member States to take immediate corrective action and, if necessary, allow for the imposition of sanctions. These elements are contained in Council Regulation 1467/97 on speeding up and clarifying the implementation of the excessive deficit procedure.

Besides these legal bases, the Code of Conduct

on the content and format of the stability and convergence programmes, endorsed by the ECOFIN Council on 10 July 2001, incorporates the essential elements of Council Regulation 1466/97 into guidelines to assist the Member States in drawing up their programmes. It also aims at facilitating the examination of the programmes by the Commission, the Economic and Financial Committee and the Council.
(*Commission*)

17.   B

Article 104 of the EC Treaty obliges the Member States to avoid excessive budgetary deficits. In particular Member States must comply with budgetary discipline by respecting two criteria: a deficit to GDP ratio and a debt to GDP ratio not exceeding a reference value of respectively 3% and 60%, as defined in the Protocol on the Excessive Deficit Procedure (EDP) annexed to the Treaty.

Article 104 sets out in detail the EDP to be followed at Community level to identify and counter such excessive deficits, including the possibility of financial sanctions. To make this a more effective deterrent, the Stability and Growth Pact (SGP) clarified and speeded up the excessive deficit procedure, in particular with the Council Regulation 1467/97.

The EDP sets out schedules and deadlines for the Council, following reports from and on the basis of opinions by the Commission and the Economic and Financial Committee, to reach a decision that an excessive deficit exists. Such a decision is taken within three months of the reporting deadlines for government finances of 1 March and 1 September each year established by Council in the Council Regulation 3605/93. A government deficit exceeding the reference value of 3% of GDP is considered exceptional and temporary and not subject to sanctions when:

- it results from an unusual event outside the control of the Member State concerned and has a major impact on the financial position of the general government;
- it results from a severe economic downturn (if there is an annual fall of real GDP of at least 2%).

When it decides that an excessive deficit does exist, the Council makes recommendations to the Member State concerned and establishes a deadline

of four months for effective corrective action to be taken. In the absence of special circumstances, such action is that which ensures completion of the correction of the excessive deficit in the year following its identification. If, after a progressive notice procedure, the Member State fails to comply with the Council's decisions, the Council normally decides to impose sanctions, at the latest, ten months after reporting of the data indicating an excessive deficit exists.
(*Commission*)

For a fuller account of the measures that the Council may contemplate to apply in an Excessive Deficit Procedure, see Article 104 of the EC Treaty.

18.   A

See table opposite.

19.   A

The euro overnight index average (EONIA) is a measure of the effective interest rate prevailing in the euro interbank overnight market. It is calculated as a weighted average of the interest rates on unsecured overnight lending transactions denominated in euro, as reported by a panel of contributing banks.
(*ECB*)

20.   C

ECU had the ISO 4217 currency code XEU and euro has the currency code EUR.

Excessive Deficit Procedures:

Country	Date of the Commission report Article 104(3)	Last update
Year 2005		
Netherlands	28 April 2004	18 May 2005
Greece	19 May 2004	6 April 2005
Hungary	12 May 2004	8 March 2005
Year 2004		
Greece	19 May 2004	22 December 2004
Hungary	12 May 2004	22 December 2004
Czech Republic	12 May 2004	22 December 2004
Cyprus	12 May 2004	22 December 2004
Malta	12 May 2004	22 December 2004
Poland	12 May 2004	22 December 2004
Slovakia	12 May 2004	22 December 2004
The Netherlands	28 April 2004	22 December 2004
France	2 April 2003	14 December 2004
Germany	19 November 2002	14 December 2004
Greece	19 May 2004	5 July 2004
Czech Republic	12 May 2004	5 July 2004
Cyprus	12 May 2004	5 July 2004
Hungary	12 May 2004	5 July 2004
Malta	12 May 2004	5 July 2004
Poland	12 May 2004	5 July 2004
Slovakia	12 May 2004	5 July 2004
The Netherlands	28 April 2004	2 June 2004
United Kingdom	28 April 2004	
Year 2003		
France	2 April 2003	25 November 2003
Year 2002		
Germany	19 November 2002	25 November 2003
Portugal	24 September 2002	28 April 2004

(*Source: Commission*)

JUSTICE AND HOME AFFAIRS,
AREA OF FREEDOM, SECURITY AND JUSTICE
ANSWERS

Question No	A	B	C	D
1.		X		
2.			X	
3.			X	
4.	X			
5.			X	
6.		X		
7.				X
8.	X			
9.				X
10.			X	

Question No	A	B	C	D
11.			X	
12.			X	
13.		X		
14.			X	
15.			X	
16.				X
17.	X			
18.	X			
19.				X
20.		X		

1.   B

The Amsterdam Treaty which came into force on 1 May 1999 introduced a new title headed "Visas, asylum, immigration and other policies related to free movement of persons" into the EC Treaty. As a result, the areas of visa, asylum, immigration and other policies related to free movement of persons, like judicial cooperation in civil matters, are transferred from the EU's third pillar to its first pillar, whereas provisions on police and judicial cooperation in criminal matters contained in Title VI of the EU Treaty remain within the EU's third pillar. In addition to these changes in responsibilities, the Amsterdam Treaty also lays down the broad lines of action in the areas currently assigned to the third pillar.

2.   C

Article 34(2) of the EU Treaty provides that "[t]he Council shall take measures and promote cooperation, using the appropriate form and procedures as set out in this title, contributing to the pursuit of the objectives of the Union. To that end, acting unanimously on the initiative of any Member State or of the Commission, the Council may:
(a)   Adopt common positions defining the approach of the Union to a particular matter;
(b)   Adopt framework decisions for the purpose of approximation of the laws and regulations of the Member States. Framework decisions shall be binding upon the Member States as to the result to be achieved but shall leave to the national authorities the choice of form and methods. They shall not entail direct effect;
(c)   Adopt decisions for any other purpose consistent with the objectives of this title, excluding any approximation of the laws and

regulations of the Member States. These decisions shall be binding and shall not entail direct effect; the Council, acting by a qualified majority, shall adopt measures necessary to implement those decisions at the level of the Union;

(d) Establish conventions which it shall recommend to the Member States for adoption in accordance with their respective constitutional requirements. Member States shall begin the procedures applicable within a time limit to be set by the Council."

3.   C

According to Article 34 of the Treaty on European Union, measures implementing conventions must be adopted within the Council by a majority of two thirds of the Contracting Parties.

4.   A

Under Article 34 of the Treaty on European Union the Council acts unanimously in police and judicial cooperation in criminal matters (i.e. Title VI).

5.   C

Article 39 of the Treaty on European Union provides that the Council must consult the European Parliament before adopting a decision, a framework decision or establishing a convention.

6.   B

Article 21 of the EC Treaty provides that every citizen of the Union may write to any of the institutions or bodies of the Union in *one of the official languages* of the Union and have an answer in the same language.

7.   D

Citizenship of the Union may be limited. Article 18(1) of the EC Treaty provides that "[e]very citizen of the Union shall have the right to move and reside freely within the territory of the Member States, subject to the limitations and conditions laid down in this Treaty and by the measures adopted to give it effect." For example, after enlargement of the EU on 1 May 2004, transitional periods set out in the Accession Treaty commenced, limiting the free movement of workers from eight of the new Member States (Cyprus and Malta were exceptions) for a period of 2 + 3 + 2 years.

8.   A

The Tampere agenda adopted in 1999 included actions in a range of areas. In the field of asylum and immigration, it included taking steps to develop a *"Common EU Asylum and Migration Policy"*, including a common asylum system (e.g. common standards for a fair and efficient asylum procedure, common minimum conditions for reception of asylum seekers, and the approximation of rules on the recognition and content of the refugee status); *fair treatment of 3rd country nationals* (e.g. approximation of conditions regulating the entry and residence of 3rd country nationals, fighting racism and xenophobia); *managing migration flows* (e.g. combating trafficking of human beings, combating illegal immigration, promotion of voluntary return to countries of origin, co-operation between border control services); and *partnership with countries of origin* around migration issues.

The Tampere agenda also included actions to create an *"Area of Justice"* in Europe (e.g. mutual recognition of judicial decisions, better access to justice, greater convergence in civil law); *"A Union-wide Fight Against Crime"* (e.g. increasing co-operation against crime) and *"Stronger External Action"* (e.g. making external affairs and justice and home affairs activities consistent with each other).

Arguably, the original ambitions agreed by governments at Tampere in 1999 have been repeatedly compromised by governments themselves when it came to actually taking decisions. This has happened for a number of reasons. Firstly, since 1999, many new governments have come to power who did not necessarily agree with the original approach signed up to by their predecessors. Secondly, since 11 September 2001 the changes in the international environment and domestic political contexts have meant that much greater emphasis has been placed on the "security" aspects than on the "justice" and "freedom" aspects of the Tampere agenda, which has led to steps backwards from the original ambitions.

While nearly all the measures for an asylum and migration policy have been adopted, many of these were only achieved after long and difficult negotiations, and are more restrictive than the original Commission proposals on which they were based.

The Commission published in June 2004 a Communication assessing the Tampere agenda and proposing guidelines for future priorities. They have given a fairly positive assessment of the achievements over the last 5 years, while acknowledging the institutional and legal constraints on action.

(*Social platform*)

9.   D

Article 4(1) of Council Directive 2003/109/EC of 25 November 2003 concerning the status of third-country nationals who are long-term residents states that: (emphasis added) "Member States shall grant long-term resident status to third-country nationals who have resided legally and continuously within its territory for *five years* immediately prior to the submission of the relevant application."

10.   C

A "sponsor" means a third country national residing lawfully in a Member State and applying or whose family members apply for family reunification to be joined with him/her. (Council Directive 2003/86/EC of 22 September 2003 on the right to family reunification.)

11.   C

France, Germany, Belgium, Luxembourg and the Netherlands agreed on 14 June 1985 to sign an agreement on the gradual abolition of checks at the common borders. This became known as the Schengen Agreement, after the name of the town in Luxembourg where it was signed.

The Schengen Convention was signed in June 1990 and came into effect in March 1995. By that time, other EU Member States (Italy, Spain, Portugal and Greece) had joined the initial signatories of this inter-governmental agreement signed outside the EU framework, but later partly transfered into the Community pillar (see next answer).

The Schengen Convention abolished the checks at internal borders of the signatory States and created a single external frontier, where checks for all the Schengen signatories were to be carried out in accordance with a common set of rules.

The Schengen Convention is designed to take into account the interests of all the States that have signed up to it. Accordingly, this freedom of movement without being submitted to checks at internal borders was accompanied by so-called compensatory measures. These measures involve setting a common visa regime, improving coordination between the police, customs and the judiciary and taking additional steps to combat problems such as terrorism and organised crime.

The harmonised EU external border controls are defined in Article 6 of the Schengen Convention. They are further specified in the common manual on external borders, a set of operational instructions on the conditions for entering the territory of the signatories States and detailed procedures and rules for carrying out checks. A complex information system known as the Schengen information system (SIS) was set up to exchange data on certain categories of people and lost or stolen goods.

(*Commission*)

12.   C

In the framework of the "communitarisation" of the Schengen acquis, title IV of the EC Treaty lists all fields in the area of freedom, security and justice, which fall within the first pillar, i.e. where the community method is applied. Judicial cooperation in criminal matters is not one of such fields.

13.   B

Article 1 of Council Regulation (EC) No 1683/95 of 29

May 1995 laying down a uniform format for visas provides that visas issued by the Member States must be produced in the form of a uniform format (sticker), in conformity with the specifications set out in the Annex attached to the Regulation.

14.   C

Europol has no executive powers. It is a support service for the law enforcement agencies of the EU Member States. This means that Europol officials are not entitled to investigate Member States or to arrest suspects. However, in providing support, Europol with its tools – fast information exchange, sophisticated intelligence analysis, expertise and training – can contribute to the executive measures carried out by the relevant national authorities.

15.   C

Eurojust is a European Union body established in 2002 and functions as a permanent network of judicial authorities. It aims to enhance the effectiveness of the competent authorities within Member States when they are dealing with the investigation and prosecution of serious cross-border and organised crime.

16.   D

ARGO is an action programme for administrative cooperation at European Union level in the fields of asylum, visas, immigration and external borders, replacing in part the Odysseus programme. The ARGO programme covers the period from 1 January 2002 to 31 December 2006. It aims to promote cooperation between national administrations responsible for implementing Community rules and to ensure that proper account is taken of the Community dimension in their actions; to promote the uniform application of Community law; and to encourage transparency of actions taken by the national authorities and to improve the overall efficiency of national administrations in their tasks.

17.   A

With effect from 1 September 2003, the Dublin II Regulation provides the legal basis for establishing the criteria and mechanism for determining the State responsible for examining an asylum application in one of the Member States of the EU (excluding Denmark but also including Iceland and Norway) by a third country national. However, from that date, the Dublin Convention remains in force between Denmark and other Member States of the EU (as well as Iceland and Norway).

The Regulation applies to the following countries: Austria, Belgium, France, Greece, Germany, Finland, Iceland, Ireland, Italy, Luxembourg, the Netherlands, Norway, Portugal, Spain, Sweden and the United Kingdom.

18.   A

Council Framework Decision 2002/584/JHA of 13 June 2002 on the European arrest warrant and the surrender procedures between Member States applies throughout the European Union and there is no mention of the death penalty as it has been abolished in all Member States.

19.   D

AGIS is a framework programme replacing the Grotius, Oisin, Stop, Hippocrates and Falcone programmes. It runs from 2003 till 2007. Its purpose is to help legal practitioners, law enforcement officials and representatives of victim assistance services from the EU Member States and Candidate Countries to set up Europe-wide networks, exchange information and best practices. It also aims at encouraging member states to step-up cooperation with the applicant countries and other third countries. AGIS will support transnational projects for a maximum duration of two years. Each year, the European Commission launches a work programme and a call for proposal.

20. B

In June 2004, the Commission presented a Communication taking stock of the implementation of the Tampere agenda and setting future guidelines for a new justice and home affairs agenda for the years to come. Following Council discussions in July and October 2004, the Dutch Presidency produced a new programme for justice and home affairs for the years 2005 - 2010, to be known as the **"Hague Programme"**.

On 10 May 2005 the Commission produced a roadmap implementing the Hague Programme which identifies ten specific priority areas for 2005 - 2010 as follows:

- **Fundamental rights and citizenship**: creating fully-fledged policies to ensure the full development of policies monitoring and promoting respect for fundamental rights for all people and of policies enhancing citizenship.
- **The fight against terrorism**: working toward a global response to focus on different aspects of prevention, preparedness and response in order to further enhance, and where necessary complement, Member States capabilities to fight terrorism, in relevant areas such as recruitment, financing, risk analysis, protection of critical infrastructures and consequence management.
- **A common asylum area**: establish an effective harmonised procedure in accordance with the Union's values and humanitarian tradition in order to work towards the establishment of a common asylum area.
- **Migration management**: defining a balanced approach to migration management by developing a common immigration policy which addresses legal migration at Union level, while further strengthening the fight against illegal migration, smuggling and trafficking in human beings, in particular women and children.
- **Integration**: maximising the positive impact of migration on society and economy through developing supportive measures to help Member States and deliver better policies on integration so as to maximise the positive impact of migration on our society and economy and to prevent isolation and social exclusion of immigrant communities. This will contribute to understanding and dialogue between religions and cultures, based on the fundamental values of the Union.
- **Internal borders, external borders and visas**: developing an integrated management of external borders for a safer Union including the development of a common visa policy, while ensuring the free movement of persons (people-to-people).
- **Privacy and security in sharing information**: striking the right balance between privacy and security in the sharing of information among law enforcement and judicial authorities, by supporting and encouraging a constructive dialogue between all parties concerned to identify balanced solutions, while fully respecting fundamental rights of privacy and data protection, as well as the principle of availability of information as laid down in the Hague Programme.
- **Organised crime**: developing a strategic concept on tackling organised crime at EU level. Make full use of and further develop Europol and Eurojust.
- **Civil and criminal justice**: guaranteeing an effective European area of justice for all and the enforcement of judgments. Approximation will be pursued, in particular through the adoption of rules ensuring a high degree of protection of persons, with a view to building mutual trust and strengthening mutual recognition, which remains the cornerstone of judicial cooperation. Improve the EU substantive contract law.
- **Freedom, Security and Justice**: sharing responsibility and solidarity is meant to give practical meaning to notions of shared responsibility and solidarity between Member States by providing adequate financial resources that can meet the objectives of Freedom, Security and Justice in the most efficient way.

EXTERNAL RELATIONS
SECURITY, DEFENCE, EXTERNAL TRADE AND DEVELOPMENT
ANSWERS

Question No	A	B	C	D
1.				X
2.	X			
3.				X
4.	X			
5.		X		
6.			X	
7.		X		
8.	X			
9.				X
10.	X			
11.		X		
12.			X	
13.				X
14.				X
15.		X		
16.		X		
17.			X	
18.			X	
19.	X			
20.	X			
21.		X		
22.			X	
23.		X		
24.				X
25.				X
26.	X			
27.	X			
28.		X		
29.	X			
30.			X	
31.			X	
32.				X
33.			X	
34.				X

Question No	A	B	C	D
35.				X
36.			X	
37.	X			
38.	X			
39.				X
40.			X	
41.	X			
42.			X	
43.		X		
44.		X		
45.		X		
46.	X			
47.			X	
48.		X		
49.				X
50.				X
51.	X			
52.	X			
53.		X		
54.	X			
55.		X		
56.		X		
57.			X	
58.			X	
59.	X			
60.			X	
61.				X
62.		X		
63.	X			
64.				X
65.			X	
66.			X	
67.				X
68.		X		

Question No	A	B	C	D
69.	X			
70.	X			
71.	X			
72.				X
73.		X		
74.			X	
75.	X			
76.		X		
77.		X		
78.	X			
79.		X		
80.			X	
81.		X		
82.				X
83.				X
84.			X	
85.	X			
86.				X
87.	X			
88.		X		
89.		X		
90.	X			
91.			X	
92.			X	
93.				X
94.		X		
95.			X	
96.		X		
97.				X
98.			X	
99.	X			
100.	X			

1.   D

Benita Ferrero-Waldner (born on 5 September 1948) is Austrian.

2.   A

The European Neighbourhood Policy (ENP) is distinct from the issue of potential membership. It offers a privileged relationship with neighbours, which will build on mutual commitment to common values mainly within the fields of the rule of law, good governance, the respect for human rights, including minority rights, the promotion of good neighbourly relations, and the principles of market economy and sustainable development. The level of ambition of the EU's relationships with its neighbours will take into account the extent to which these values are effectively shared.

3.   D

Regarding the countries involved in the European Neighbourhood Policy, a Commission Strategy Paper confirms that "[t]he method proposed is, together with partner countries, to define a set of priorities, whose fulfilment will bring them closer to the European Union. These priorities will be incorporated in jointly agreed Action Plans, covering a number of key areas for specific action: political dialogue and reform; trade and measures preparing partners for gradually obtaining a stake in the EU's Internal Market; justice and home affairs; energy, transport, information society, environment and research innovation; social policy and people-to-people contacts."

For further information, see:

http://europa.eu.int/comm/world/enp/pdf/strategy/Strateg y_Paper_EN.pdf

4.   A

The report "Wider Europe – Neighbourhood: A New Framework for Relations with our Eastern and Southern Neighbours" was prepared by Pasqualina Napoletano on behalf of the European Parliament's Committee on Foreign Affairs, Human Rights, Common Security and Defence Policy. The committee adopted the resolution at its meetings of 6-7 October and 3-4 November 2003.

Those given as alternative answers are all members of the above Committee.

5.   B

Southern Mediterranean countries are: Algeria, Egypt, Israel, Jordan, Lebanon, Libya, Morocco, Palestinian Authority, Syria, Tunisia.

6.   C

Western Newly Independent States (WNIS): Ukraine, Moldova, Belarus.

7.   B

Countries involved in the ENP are: Israel, Algeria, Egypt, Libya, Morocco, Tunisia, Jordan, Lebanon, Palestinian Territories, Syria, Belarus, Moldova, Ukraine, Armenia, Georgia and Azerbaijan. In the case of the Russian Federation, there is a special strategic relationship.

8.   A

As regards financial assistance, from 2007 onwards a European Neighbourhood and Partnership Instrument (ENPI) will replace the current TACIS and MEDA programmes in the ENP partner countries and Russia. Drawing on substantially increased funds, it will support the Neighbourhood Policy and its Action Plans, as well as the EU's strategic partnership with Russia. It will furthermore have a specific and innovative component catering for the needs of cross-border cooperation at the EU's external borders. Until 2006, the Commission is substantially enhancing the coordination of existing instruments for cross-border cooperation in so-called "Neighbourhood Programmes".

(Commission ENP)

9.   D

Every year, the European Union provides over 7 billion euros in external assistance to more than 150 countries and territories in order to meet the daily challenge of improving lives worldwide by building long-term partnerships.
(*http://europa.eu.int/comm/world/*)

10.   A

EuropeAid Co-operation Office's mission is to implement the external aid instruments of the European Commission which are funded by the European Community budget and the European Development Fund. The Office is responsible for all phases of the project cycle (identification and appraisal of projects and programmes, preparation of financing decisions, implementation and monitoring, evaluation of projects and programmes) that are necessary to ensure the achievement of the objectives of the programmes established by the Directorates-General for External Relations and Development and approved by the Commission. It does not deal with pre-accession aid programmes (Phare, Ispa and Sapard), humanitarian activities, macro-financial assistance, the Common Foreign and Security Policy (CFSP) or the Rapid Reaction Facility.
(*EuropeAid*)

11.   B

The Agadir Agreement is a Free Trade Agreement between Jordan, Egypt, Tunisia and Morocco. This agreement is a crucial step towards the creation of a Euro-Mediterranean free trade area by 2010. The Commission has been one of the main political supporters of this initiative since the Agadir Declaration was signed in May 2001 and it is also supporting it with a €4 million programme funded under MEDA.

12.   C

Since 1991 the European Union has committed, through various assistance programmes, €6.8 billion to the Western Balkans. In 2000 aid to the region was

streamlined through a new programme called CARDS (Community Assistance for Reconstruction, Development and Stabilisation) adopted with the Council Regulation (EC) No 2666/2000 of 5 December 2000. The programme's wider objective is to support the participation of the countries of the Western Balkans (Albania, Bosnia and Herzegovina, Croatia, Serbia, Montenegro and the former Yugoslav Republic of Macedonia) in the Stabilisation and Association Process.
(*CARDS*)

13.   D

Regulation No. 99/2000 (adopted in January 2000) opened a phase of co-operation between the European Union and the partner countries of Eastern Europe and Central Asia for the period from 2000 to 2006. Its aim is to provide assistance totalling Euro 3,138 million to focus on certain key areas of activity in the region, namely:

- support for institutional, legal and administrative reform;
- support for the private sector and assistance for economic development;
- support for addressing the social consequences of transition;
- development of infrastructure networks;
- nuclear safety;
- promotion of environmental protection and management of natural resources;
- development of the rural economy.

(*TACIS*)

14.   D

The EU's proximity policy towards the Mediterranean region is governed by the global and comprehensive Euro-Mediterranean Partnership launched at the 1995 Barcelona Conference between the European Union and its 12 Mediterranean Partners. This is called the Barcelona Process.

Main objectives of the Barcelona Declaration are:

- to establish a **common Euro-Mediterranean area** of peace and stability based on fundamental principles including respect for human rights and democracy (political and security partnership).
- to create an **area of shared prosperity** through

the progressive establishment of a free-trade area between the EU and its Partners and among the Mediterranean Partners themselves, accompanied by substantial EU financial support for economic transition in the Partners and for the social and economic consequences of this reform process (economic and financial partnership).

• to develop **human resources**, promote understanding between cultures and rapprochement of the peoples in the Euro-Mediterranean region as well as to develop free and flourishing civil societies (social, cultural and human partnership).

15.   B

Maghreb: Morocco, Algeria, Tunisia.
Mashrek: Egypt, Israel, Jordan, the Palestinian Authority, Lebanon, Syria.

16.   B

17.   C

In order to facilitate the discussion of topics of common interest, the countries of Latin America created a forum for political consultation called the Rio Group. Established in 1986 with an initial membership of six, it now comprises all of Latin America as well as representatives from the Caribbean countries. It is administered by a rotating and temporary secretariat. The EU-Rio Group is a key forum for political dialogue and one of the main platforms through which EU-Latin American relations are enhanced, and the direction of the relationship discussed. The most recent EU-Rio Group Summit was held in Greece in 2003, these meetings are one of the main instruments for the fortification of this relationship.
(*DG Relex*)

18.   C

Created in 1991, "El Mercado del Sur" (Mercosur, Southern trade-zone) is a dynamic process of regional integration between Argentina, Brazil, Paraguay and Uruguay. The European Union has supported Mercosur from the outset and has provided technical and institutional support for the organisation's structures.

19.   A

The EU has supported the process of Andean regional integration since the Cartagena Agreement established the Andean Community (originally named Andean Pact – Bolivia, Colombia, Ecuador, Peru and Venezuela) in 1969. Regular political dialogue between the EU and the Andean region is conducted on the basis of the Rome declaration of 1996. Among the priority topics of this political dialogue are regional integration, democracy and human rights, as well as the fight against drugs. A first Framework Agreement on Cooperation was concluded in 1983. It was replaced by a second agreement in 1993. Specific areas of co-operation include social infrastructure and services.
(*DG Relex*)

20.   A

Since neither Mexico nor Chile belong to any regional grouping, they have developed strong bilateral links with the EU. Economic and Political Association Agreements, were signed with Mexico in 1997 and with Chile in 2002.

21.   B

22.   C

The EU policy against drugs is reflected in and inspired by five principles of international drug policy adopted at the United Nations General Assembly Special Session on Drugs of June 1998. These principles are: shared responsibility, emphasis on multilateralism, balanced approach, development mainstreaming and respect for human rights.

23. B

The Kimberley Process is a unique initiative by government authorities, the international diamond industry and NGOs to stem the flow of 'conflict diamonds' – rough diamonds which are used by rebel movements to finance wars against legitimate governments, and which have contributed to fuelling devastating conflicts in a number of countries in Africa. The Kimberley Process began in May 2000 in Kimberley (South Africa) as an informal attempt by interested governments, NGOs and industry groups to come up with a practical way of ensuring that illicit diamonds cannot enter the legitimate diamond trade.
(*DG Relex*)

24. D

25. D

According to the Road Map of 2002:
"The following is a performance-based and goal-driven road map, with clear phases, timelines, target dates, and benchmarks aiming at progress through reciprocal steps by the two parties in the political, security, economic, humanitarian and institution-building fields, under the auspices of the Quartet. The destination is a final and comprehensive settlement of the Israel-Palestinian conflict by 2005, as presented in President Bush's speech of June 24, and welcomed by the EU, Russia and the UN in the 15 July and 17 September Quartet Ministerial statements."

26. A

The Convention on the Prohibition of the Use, Stockpiling, Production and Transfer of Anti-Personnel Mines and on Their Destruction, typically referred to as the "Ottawa Convention" or "Mine Ban Treaty," seeks to end the use of anti-personnel landmines (APLs) worldwide. It was opened for signature on 3 December 1997, and it entered into force on 1 March 1999. By 1 January 2005, 144 states had become party to the accord, and another eight countries had signed but not ratified it.

27. A

The WTO was established in 1995 as a result of the Uruguay Round of multilateral trade negotiations (1986-1994). It is an international organisation that sets global rules of trade between nations. The core of the WTO system, referred to as the multilateral trading system, are the WTO agreements which lay down the legal ground rules for international trade as well as the market-opening commitments taken up by its Members. These agreements are negotiated and signed by all Members of the WTO, and ratified in their parliaments. The EU is one of the key players in the WTO based on the common trade policy, where the European Commission negotiates on behalf of the Union's 25 Member States.

28. B

Currently, the WTO Members are engaged in a broad round of multilateral trade negotiations called "the Doha Development Agenda" (DDA). In July 2004, Members agreed on a Framework Agreement that sets a clear agenda for the formulation of a new set of trade rules by the end of the DDA and decided that the next WTO Ministerial will be held in Hong Kong in December 2005.
The Doha Development Agenda includes:
*   further trade liberalisation and new rule-making, underpinned by commitments to strengthen substantially assistance to developing countries;
*   help developing countries implement the existing WTO agreements;
*   interpret the TRIPS (Trade Related Aspects of Intellectual Property Rights) Agreement in a manner that ensures Members' rights under TRIPS to take actions to protect public health.

29. A

The WTO Agreement on Trade-Related Aspects of Intellectual Property Rights (TRIPs) is an international treaty which sets down minimum standards for most forms of intellectual property regulation within all member countries of the WTO.

Specifically, TRIPs deals with copyright and related rights (i.e. rights of performers, producers of sound recordings and broadcasting organisations); geographical indications (including appellations of origin); industrial designs; integrated circuit layout-designs; patents (including the protection of new varieties of plants); trademarks; and undisclosed or confidential information (including trade secrets and test data). TRIPs also specifies enforcement procedures, remedies, and dispute resolution procedures.

The obligations under TRIPs apply equally to all member states, however developing countries are allowed a longer period in which to implement the applicable changes to their national laws.
(*Wikipedia*)

30.   C

The Cotonou Agreement is a treaty which sets out the relationship between the European Union and the African, Caribbean and Pacific governments (the "ACP countries") of the signatories on foreign aid, trade, investment, human rights and governance. The agreement was established in June 2000 in Benin, succeeding the Lomé Convention which did not address human rights and governance issues. There are 77 signatories and the agreement came into force on 1 April 2003.

The Agreement provides for replacing the unilateral trade preferences that the EU accorded to the ACP countries under the Lomé convention with Economic Partnership Agreements involving reciprocal obligations. Not only will the EU provide free access to its markets for ACP exports, but ACP countries will also have to provide free access to their own markets for EU exports. In addition to reciprocity, a second principle of the Cotonou Agreement is that of differentiation, whereby ACP least-developed countries (LDCs) are to be treated differently from ACP non-LDCs.

For further information, see:
http://europa.eu.int/comm/development/body/cotonou/agreement_en.htm

31.   C

The Economic Community of West African States (ECOWAS) is a regional group of fifteen countries, founded on May 28, 1975 when 15 West African countries signed the Treaty of Lagos. Its mission is to promote economic integration.

It was founded to achieve "collective self-sufficiency" for the member states by means of economic and monetary union creating a single large trading bloc. The very slow progress towards this aim meant that the treaty was revised towards a looser collaboration. The ECOWAS Secretariat and the Fund for Cooperation, Compensation and Development are its two main institutions to implement policies.

Member states of ECOWAS are Benin, Burkina Faso, Cape Verde, Côte d'Ivoire, The Gambia, Ghana, Guinea, Guinea Bissau, Liberia, Mali, Niger, Nigeria, Senegal, Sierra Leone, and Togo. Mauritania left the organisation in 2002.

32.   D

The Lomé Convention, signed in 1975, sets out the principles and objectives of the Union (at the time Community) cooperation with ACP (see answer 30) countries. Its main characteristics were: the partnership principle, the contractual nature of the relationship, and the combination of aid, trade and political aspects, together with its long-term perspective (5 years for Lomé I, II, and III, and ten for Lomé IV).

For further information, see:
http://europa.eu.int/comm/development/body/cotonou/lome_history_en.htm

33.   C

The ACP-EC Cooperation dates back to the birth of the European Treaty of Rome in 1957, which expressed solidarity with the colonies and overseas countries and territories and a commitment to contribute to their prosperity.

The first association of ACP (see answer 30) and EC Member States (1963-69) Yaoundé I, was drawn up in the Cameroonian capital. Yaoundé II (1969-75), also signed in the Cameroonian capital, pledged the lion's share of financial support to French-speaking Africa to build infrastructure in the wake of decolonisation. But the Yaoundé accords importantly sowed the seeds for the new generation of Lomé accords.

34.   D

Regarding EU-ACP relations, the stabilisation of export receipts on agricultural products (STABEX) gave funds to make up for losses to the ACP countries on a large number of agricultural products: cocoa, coffee, groundnuts, tea and others, as a result of crop failures and price falls. SYSMIN was also an innovation of the '70s: a country heavily dependent on a particular mineral and suffering export losses could access SYSMIN loans which were designed to lessen a country's dependency on mining.

35.   D

Part Four of the EC Treaty created "the association of the overseas countries and territories" (OCTs), meaning the association dates back to 1957. The objectives of this association were laid down in Articles 131 - 135 of the Treaty of Rome, now Articles 182 - 188 of the EC Treaty. The purpose of this association, according to Article 182, is "to promote the economic and social development of the countries and territories and to establish close economic relations between them and the Community as a whole". Other relevant provisions of the Treaty are Article 3(1s), Article 299 and Annex 2.

There are 21 OCTs. These include 12 British possessions; 6 French overseas territories and territorial communities; Aruba and Netherlands Antilles (part of the Kingdom of the Netherlands) and the autonomous Danish territory of Greenland.

Concerning the relationship between the above countries and territories and the European Union, please refer to answer 38.

For further information, see:
http://europa.eu.int/comm/development/oct/index_en.htm

36.   C

The Commonwealth of Independent States (CIS) is a confederation or alliance consisting of 12 of the 15 former Soviet Republics: Azerbaijan, Armenia, Belarus, Kazakhstan, Kyrgyzstan, Moldova, Russia,

Tajikistan, Turkmenistan, Uzbekistan, Ukraine and Georgia. The exceptions are the three Baltic states, Estonia, Latvia, and Lithuania. Its creation signalled the dissolution of the Soviet Union. Its member states have since signed a large number of documents concerning integration and cooperation on matters of economics, defence and foreign policy.

37.   A

The Hungarian city of Visegrád was first mentioned in 1009 as a county town and chief town of archdeaconry. King Charles I of Hungary made Visegrád the capital of Hungary where he hosted a two-month congress of kings of Poland, Hungary and Bohemia in 1335.

In 1991, the leading politicians of Hungary, Czechoslovakia and Poland met here to form a political cooperation between these countries, hence the name of the Visegrád group.

38.   A

(see summary table at the end of answer)

Islands
1. **Åland Islands**: The Åland Islands form an autonomous and demilitarised province of Finland. Åland's special relationship with the EU is regulated by Protocol 2 to the Finnish Act of Accession. Regulation 82/97/EC stipulates that the Åland Islands are part of the customs territory of the European Union. The euro is the currency in the Åland Islands.
2. **Azores**: The Azores are part of Portugal and entered the EU when Portugal and Spain became members in 1986. As such, the Azores are part of the customs territory of the EU, and the euro is their currency. The Azores have no separate agreements with the EU, but as one of the "remote regions," they benefit from special Community support. The POSEIMA program was established to this end to benefit the Azores and Madeira.
3. **Canary Islands**: The Canary Islands are part of the territory of Spain and, as such, part of the territory of the European Union. The euro is the official currency. Initially, the Canary Islands were specifically excluded from the customs territory of the EU (Article 1(2) of Protocol 2 to the Spanish and

Portuguese accession agreement). However, Regulation 1911/91/EEC changed that status and included the Canary Islands in the EU's customs territory from 1 July 1991, introducing a gradual application of the common customs tariff (CCT) from that date until its full application in 2000. The Canary Islands are excluded from the EU VAT in Article 3 (3) of the EU's Sixth Council Directive on the common system of VAT (77/388/EEC, as amended). As with the Azores, the Canary Islands benefit from the EU's efforts to support the outermost regions, as stated in Article 299(2) of the Amsterdam Treaty. To this end, the EU's POSEICAN programme was established.

4. **Channel Islands**: The Channel Islands (Alderney, Guernsey, Herm, Jersey and Sark) are self-governing Crown dependencies with their own legislative assemblies, systems of local administration and law and their own courts. The British government is responsible for their defence and international relations, including relations with the European Union. Protocol 3 to the UK act of accession applies EU customs rules to the Channel Islands, and Article 3 of the Customs Code (EU Regulation 2913/92/EEC, as amended) includes the Channel Islands as part of the EU's customs territory. The islands are excluded from the provisions of the EC Treaty, apart from those ensuring the proper functioning of free trade with the European Union (Article 25(c) of the UK Act of Accession). EU VAT requirements do not apply in the Channel Islands. Both the UK and the Channel Islands issue notes and coinage.

5. **Faeroe Islands**: The Faeroes (or Faroes), part of the Kingdom of Denmark, have been a self-governing overseas administrative division of Denmark since 1948. The currency is the Danish krone. Unlike Denmark, the Faeroe Islands are not part of the European Union. Article 299(6a) of the EC Treaty states that "this Treaty shall not apply to the Faeroe Islands." In 1974, the Faeroese Parliament decided by a unanimous vote not to apply for EU membership. Instead, a trade agreement was concluded between the Faeroe Islands and the EU. Article 3(1) of the EU's Customs Code, as amended, specifically excludes the Faeroe Islands from the customs territory of the European Union.

6. **French Overseas Departments**: The French Overseas Departments are part of France and part of the customs territory. The euro is their currency. The provisions of EU treaties apply to these departments and, because of their remoteness, they also benefit from special EU assistance under Article 299(2) of the EC Treaty. The POSEIDOM program was established

by Council Decision 89/687EEC to achieve these objectives.

7. **French Overseas Territorial Communities**: Saint Pierre-et-Miquelon and Mayotte are not part of the EU and are excluded from the customs territory in Article 3(1) of the EU's Customs Code, as amended. Council Decision 1999/95/EC stipulates that in both of these overseas territorial communities the currency is the euro.

8. **Greenland**: Greenland is the world's largest island with more than 80 percent of its area covered by ice. Greenland, like the Faeroe Islands, is part of the Kingdom of Denmark. All three areas have in common: the Danish Royal Family, the Constitution, foreign policy, defence, the judicial system and the currency. Greenland does exercise a certain amount of autonomy through "home rule," approved by the Danish legislature and effective in 1979. Greenland entered the EU in 1973 as part of Denmark; however a 1982 referendum on EU membership was narrowly defeated and Greenland left the Community. The Treaty of withdrawal (of 13 March 1984) or "Greenland Treaty" came into force on 1 February 1985 and granted Greenland the status of an Overseas Country and Territory (OCT). One of the most important applications of the OCT status for Greenland is the non-reciprocal trade regime, the most generous granted to any Community partner. Greenland is ensured of unlimited duty-free access to the EU market for its fisheries products. The Danish krone is used in Greenland. Greenland is not part of the customs territory of the EU, as spelled out in Article 3(1) of the EU's Customs Code, as amended.

9. **Isle of Man**: The Isle of Man holds neither membership nor associate membership of the European Union, but forms part of the customs territory of the Union, allowing it to trade freely with EU members. Citizens of the Isle of Man (Manxmen) are defined as also being European Union citizens; however Protocol Three in the treaty of accession of the United Kingdom stipulates that "Manx people shall not benefit from provisions relating to the free movement of persons and services". This means that a special endorsement is placed in their passports preventing them from freely living or working in other EU states. Travel to the Isle of Man is regulated by the local government laws. Visitors from countries who require a UK visa may also require a special Man visa, obtainable from a British Embassy. All non-Manx, including UK citizens, are required to obtain a work permit to take up employment on the Island.
(*Wikipedia*)

The Isle of Man neither contributes nor receives

funds from the European Union, thus guaranteeing the island's fiscal independence. Any proposal to change Protocol 3 would require the unanimous approval of all Member States of the EU, including the UK. The Isle of Man does impose a Value Added Tax (VAT) as though it were part of the EU, but it is administered through its own Office of Customs and Excise.

10. **Madeira**: While part of Portugal, Madeira does enjoy partial autonomy. The Madeira Islands entered the EU as part of Portugal in 1986. There is no separate agreement. As such, Madeira is part of the customs territory of the EU and uses the euro as its currency. Article 299(2) of the EC Treaty states that the Treaty applies to the Madeira Islands and it provides for the same supportive measures applicable to other remote Community regions. Madeira, like the Azores, benefits from the provisions of the POSEIMA programme.

Principalities

1. **Andorra**: The Principality of Andorra bases its relations with the European Union on an Agreement between the European Economic Community and the Principality of Andorra in the form of an exchange of letters, signed in June 1990 and effective on 1 July, 1991. Article 2 of this agreement establishes a customs union between the EU and Andorra for the bulk of non-agricultural goods. Andorra uses euro banknotes and coins. Andorra has neither its own currency nor a monetary issuing authority.

2. **Liechtenstein**: In 1923, Liechtenstein formed a customs union with its most important partner, Switzerland. The customs union remains in force today. The Swiss franc is the currency used in Liechtenstein. Liechtenstein is a member both of the European Free Trade Association and of the European Economic Area (EEA). It is the EEA that defines Liechtenstein's relations with the EU. (*EurUnion*)

3. **Monaco**: The Principality of Monaco is part of the customs territory of the European Union, a relationship defined by the Customs Convention between France and Monaco, signed on 18 May 1963. The euro is the official currency in Monaco. Council Decision 1999/96/EC entitles Monaco to use the euro as its official currency and to grant legal tender status to euro banknotes and coins. Value Added Tax (VAT) applies in Monaco.

Dependencies

1. **Ceuta and Melilla**: These Spanish enclaves on Morocco's Mediterranean coast gained limited autonomy in 1994. Ceuta is part of the Spanish province of Cadiz and Melilla is part of the Spanish province of Malaga. While both Ceuta and Melilla have been part of the European Union since Spain became a member in 1986, each exercises local autonomy. Ceuta and Melilla are not part of the EU's customs territory (see Article 3 of EU Regulation 2913/92/EEC, as amended). Both are duty-free, VAT-free ports. The euro is the currency used in Ceuta and Melilla.

2. **Gibraltar**: It is a UK dependency, which has been in British possession since 1704. Historically, Gibraltar has been an object of contention between Britain and Spain. Following a 1984 agreement between Britain and Spain, the border, which Spain had closed in 1969, was fully reopened. Gibraltar entered the European Union in 1973 as a dependent territory in Europe, but was excluded, at the request of the government of Gibraltar, from the common external tariff, the common agricultural policy and value added tax. Gibraltar is not part of the EU's customs territory, according to Article 3(1) of the Customs Code, as amended. Article 28 of the UK's Act of Accession exempts Gibraltar from the application of EU laws relating to agricultural policy and the harmonisation of turnover taxes (VAT). Gibraltar's customs revenue is not part of the revenue of the Community. Although part of the Community, Gibraltar is not subject to the full application of EU law and policy. It is effectively treated as a third country as far as trade is concerned. Exports of goods of local (Gibraltar) origin to the Community benefit from the EU's Generalised System of Preferences (GSP). The monetary unit is the Gibraltar pound, on a par with Sterling. The legal tender is Gibraltar government notes and coins, though Bank of England notes and coins are equally accepted.

San Marino, Holy See, Kaliningrad

1. **San Marino**: The basis of the EU's relationship with San Marino is the Agreement on Cooperation and Customs Union between the European Economic Community and the Republic of San Marino, which was signed in 1991 and entered into force on April 1, 2002, following ratification by all parties. Council Decision 2002/45/EC approves the Agreement and its accompanying Protocol. Among other provisions, this Agreement establishes a customs union between the European Community and the Republic of San Marino for products covered by Chapters 1 to 97 of the Common Customs Tariff, except products that fell within the scope of the ECSC Treaty. A Monetary Agreement between the Italian

Republic, on behalf of the European Community, and the Republic of San Marino, authorises San Marino to use euro notes and coins as the official currency, and it permits a limited minting of euro coins, but not the notes.

2. **Vatican City (The Holy See)**: Vatican City, or the Holy See, is located in Rome, Italy, but is an independent state. The Holy See has diplomatic relations with the European Union. The euro is the official currency in the Vatican and is subject to the conditions laid out in the Monetary Agreement between the Italian Republic, on behalf of the European Community, and the Vatican City State and, on its behalf, the Holy See. This agreement allows the Vatican to issue a limited number of euro coins, but does not authorise the issuing of euro notes.

3. **Kaliningrad**: It is a political subdivision (oblast) of Russia, separated from Russia by Lithuania to its north and east, Poland to its south and the Baltic Sea to its west. The European Union introduced the necessary legislation establishing from 1 July 2003 a Facilitated Transit Document (FTD) scheme that applies to the transit of Russian citizens only between Kaliningrad and other parts of Russia by land. The FTD is valid for direct transit by land from a single third country to the same third country within a limited period of time and is issued free of charge or at a very low cost.

Others

Sovereign bases on Cyprus: Article 299(6b) of the EC treaty defines the status of the UK sovereign base areas on Cyprus. While they were formerly totally outside the scope of EC law, their legal situation has been modified since the accession of Cyprus to the European Union. The EC Treaty now stipulates that "[t]his Treaty shall not apply to the United Kingdom Sovereign Base Areas of Akrotiri and Dhekelia in Cyprus except to the extent necessary to ensure the implementation of the arrangements set out in the Protocol on the Sovereign Base Areas of the United Kingdom of Great Britain and Northern Ireland in Cyprus (...) and in accordance with the terms of that Protocol." However, Xylotimbou and Ormidhia are Cypriot enclaves within the Dhekelia base, and are therefore part of the EU.

Büsingen am Hochrhein: The German enclave town of Büsingen am Hochrhein is in customs union with Switzerland. The euro is legal tender, although the Swiss franc is preferred. Büsingen is excluded from the EU VAT area.

Island of Heligoland: Heligoland is part of the EU, but is excluded from the EU VAT area and customs union.

Mount Athos: Mount Athos in Greece is outside EU VAT area.

Campione d'Italia: The enclave town of Campione d'Italia is part of Italy, but is in customs union with Switzerland. The Swiss franc is legal tender, but the euro is accepted. This town is excluded from EU fiscal VAT area.

Livigno commune: Livigno is excluded from EU VAT area. The euro is legal tender.

	EU Member	NOT EU Member
In the customs area	Azores	Åland Islands
	Canary Islands	Channel Islands
	French Overseas Departments	Andorra
	Madeira	Lichtenstein
	Büsingen am Hochrhein	Monaco
	Mount Athos	San Marino
	Livigno commune	Isle of Man
NOT in customs area	Ceuta and Melilla	Faeroe Islands
	Gibraltar	Saint Pierre-et-Miquelon
	Island of Heligoland	Mayotte
	Campione d'Italia	Greenland
		Vatican City (Holy See)

Country / Area	EU Membership	Customs area	Currency	EU VAT
Åland Islands	–	Euro	Euro	–
Azores	X	X	Euro	X
Canary Islands	X	X	Euro	X
Channel Islands	–	X	Pound	–
Faeroe Islands	–	–	Krone	–
French Overseas Departments	X	X	Euro	X
Saint Pierre-et-Miquelon and Mayotte	–	–	Euro	–
Greenland	(since 1982)	–	Krone	–
Isle of Man	–	X	Pound	X
Madeira	X	X	Euro	X
Andorra	–	X	Euro	–
Liechtenstein	(only EFTA)	X (EEA)	Franc	–
Monaco	–	X	X	X
Ceuta and Melilla	X	–	Euro	–
Gibraltar	X	–	Pound	–
San Marino	–	X	X	–
Vatican City (Holy See)	–	–	Euro	–
Büsingen am Hochrhein	X	X (EEA)	Euro	–
Island of Heligoland	X	–	Euro	–
Mount Athos	X	X	Euro	–
Campione d'Italia	X	–	Franc (Euro)	–
Livigno commune	X	X	Euro	–
Sovereign bases on Cyprus	(limited)	(limited)	Pound	–

39.   D

See answer 38.

40.   C

See answer 38.

41.   A

See answer 38.

42.   C

See answer 38.

43.   B

See answer 38.

44.   B

See answer 38.

45.   B

See answer 38.

46.   A

See answer 38.

47.   C

See answer 38.

48.   B

See answer 38.

49.   D

See answer 38.

50.   D

See answer 38.

51.   A

See answer 38.

52.   A

See answer 38.

53.   B

The Maastricht Treaty introduced the three-pillar structure. The CFSP pillar was built on the foun-

dation of European Political Cooperation (EPC), but brought it under a treaty and extended it.

54.   A

After the failure of two attempts to establish a European defence policy in the 1950s and 1960s, the Pléven plan and the Fouchet plan respectively, the gradual transfer method proved to be more effective. This took the form of European Political Cooperation (EPC), launched informally in 1970.

55.   B

Title V of the EU Treaty replaced the EPC with an intergovernmental pillar in the Community structure. Article 11 sets out its five main principles:
*   to safeguard the common values and fundamental interests of the Union;
*   to strengthen the security of the Union;
*   to preserve peace and strengthen international security;
*   to promote international cooperation;
*   to develop democracy and the rule of law, including human rights.

56.   B

The CFSP is also mentioned in Article 2 of the common provisions of the EU Treaty, which provides that one of the Union's objectives is "to assert its identity on the international scene, in particular through the implementation of a common foreign and security policy including the progressive framing of a common defence policy, which might lead to a common defence […]".

57.   C

The Maastricht Treaty provides the CFSP with the following key instruments:
*   **Common positions:** these require the Member States to implement national policies that comply with the position defined by the Union on a particular issue, e.g. fight against the illicit

traffic in diamonds as a contribution to prevention and settlement of conflicts (2001/758/PESC) in countries such as Liberia, Sierra Leone and Angola.

- **Joint actions:** these are operational actions by the Member States under the auspices of the CFSP. One example is the support for the Palestinian Authority in its efforts to counter terrorist activities emanating from its territories (2000/298/PESC).

58.   C

The Commission, the European Parliament and the Court of Justice play a less important role in the CFSP. The Commission's role includes the right to submit legislative proposals and budget execution. It therefore has a certain degree of influence over the formulation and coordination of this "inter-pillar policy". The European Parliament may put questions and recommendations to the Council and it holds an extensive annual debate on the implementation of the CFSP. It is now possible to adopt measures by a qualified majority vote, with the dual safeguards of constructive abstention and the possibility of referring a decision to the European Council if a Member State resorts to a veto (known as the "emergency brake").

59.   A

Article 23, as amended by the Amsterdam Treaty, stipulates that decisions shall be taken by the Council acting unanimously. In seeking to overcome the constraints that produced the rule of unanimity, the Treaty introduced the instrument of *constructive abstention* (Article 23(1) of the EU Treaty) as a means towards more flexibility. Thus when a Member State abstains from a vote, it shall not be obliged to apply the decision but shall accept that the decision commits the Union.

60.   C

The Treaty of Nice introduced in the EU Treaty the Political and Security Committee set up by a Council decision in January 2001. It is authorised by the

European Council to exercise political control and strategic direction of a crisis management operation.

Article 25 of the EU Treaty provides:

"[...] a Political and Security Committee shall monitor the international situation in the areas covered by the common foreign and security policy and contribute to the definition of policies by delivering opinions to the Council at the request of the Council or on its own initiative. It shall also monitor the implementation of agreed policies, without prejudice to the responsibility of the Presidency and the Commission.

Within the scope of this Title, this Committee shall exercise, under the responsibility of the Council, political control and strategic direction of crisis management operations.

The Council may authorise the Committee, for the purpose and for the duration of a crisis management operation, as determined by the Council, to take the relevant decisions concerning the political control and strategic direction of the operation, without prejudice to Article 47."

61.   D

Under Article 17(4), the Amsterdam Treaty incorporated into the EU Treaty the so-called Petersberg tasks: humanitarian and rescue tasks, peace-keeping tasks and tasks of combat forces in crisis management, including peace-making. They became part of the CFSP and the common defence policy. All of the Union Member States may participate in these tasks.

62.   B

The Amsterdam Treaty created the formal possibility of a certain number of Member States establishing enhanced cooperation between themselves on matters covered by the Treaties, using the institutions and procedures of the European Union.

Although these provisions had never been used, the European Council considered it necessary to revise them with a view to making them less restrictive in the context of the enlargement of the Union to 27 Member States. Enhanced cooperation was not included in the original mandate of the Intergovernmental Conference (IGC) but was formally included by the Feira European Council of 20 June 2000.

The Treaty of Nice facilitates the establishment of

enhanced cooperation: the right of veto which the Member States enjoyed over the establishment of enhanced cooperation has disappeared (except in the field of foreign policy), the number of Member States required for launching the procedure has changed from the majority to the fixed number of eight Member States, and its scope has been extended to the CFSP. The general provisions applicable to enhanced cooperation have been grouped together in Title VII of the EU Treaty. The provisions on triggering the procedure and on the future participation of other Member States vary across the three pillars. (*ScadPlus*)

63.   A

Since the entry into force of the Amsterdam Treaty, the Secretary-General of the Council has fulfilled the role of High Representative of the CFSP. He is responsible for assisting the Council in CFSP-related matters by contributing to the formulation, preparation, and implementation of decisions. At the request of the presidency, he acts on behalf of the Council in conducting political dialogue with third parties and endeavours to improve the visibility and consistency of the CFSP. The Constitutional Treaty would change this situation by the creation of the Foreign Minister who would at the same time be the Commission's Vice-president. *Please also refer to other answers in this section and the one on the Constitutional Treaty.*

64.   D

The European Union Police Mission was established in the former Yugoslav Republic of Macedonia (FYROM), in line with the objectives of the Ohrid Framework Agreement of 2001 and in close partnership with the country's authorities. The Mission, code-named EUPOL PROXIMA, was launched on 15 December 2003. The EU police experts are monitoring, mentoring and advising the country's police thus helping to fight organised crime as well as promoting European policing standards.

65.   C

The European Defence Agency was established by a

Joint Action of the Council of Ministers on 12 July 2004 "to support the Member States in their effort to improve European defence capabilities in the field of crisis management and to sustain the ESDP as it stands now and develops in the future".

The Agency has four main functions related to:
1.   defence capabilities development;
2.   armaments co-operation;
3.   the European defence technological and industrial base and defence equipment market;
4.   research and technology.

66.   C

As provided in the Helsinki report, the European Union Military Committee (EUMC), "established within the Council", is composed of the Chiefs of Defence (CHODs) represented by their military representatives (Milreps). The EUMC meets at the level of CHODs as and when necessary. This Committee gives military advice and makes recommendations to the Political and Security Committee (PSC), as well as providing military direction to the European Union Military Staff (EUMS). The Chairman of the EUMC (CEUMC) attends meetings of the Council when decisions with defence implications are to be taken.

67.   D

The Council decided on 21 February 2005 to launch an integrated rule-of-law mission for Iraq –"EUJUST LEX". The mission falls under the scope of the European Security and Defence Policy (ESDP). The mission consists of integrated training in the fields of management and criminal investigation, to be given to a representative group of senior officials and executive staff, mainly from the judiciary, the police and the prison service.

68.   B

69.   A

Article 17 of the Amsterdam Treaty states that the CFSP covers all questions relating to the security of the Union, including the progressive outlining of a common defence policy, which might lead to a common defence if the European Council so decides. This article introduced a transfer of competences from the Western European Union (WEU) to the EU. Since then, almost all of the Petersberg tasks have been incorporated into new structures of the Union, as have subsidiary bodies of the WEU such as the Satellite Centre and the Institute for Security Studies, which have been operational since January 2002. (*ScadPlus*)

70.   A

EU Special Representatives are:
1. **Michael Sahlin:** EU Special Representative in the *Former Yugoslav Republic of Macedonia* (FYROM) since 12 July 2004. His mandate is to establish and maintain close contact with the government of FYROM and with the parties involved in the political process and to offer the EU's advice and facilitation in the political process.
2. **Marc Otte:** EU Special Representative for the *Middle East peace process* since 14 July 2003. The mandate of the Special Representative is based on the EU's policy objectives regarding the Middle East peace process, which include a two-State solution with Israel and a democratic, viable, peaceful and sovereign Palestinian State living side-by-side within secure and recognised borders enjoying normal relations with their neighbours in accordance with UN Security Council Resolutions 242, 338, 1397 and 1402 and the principles of the Madrid conference.
3. **Heikki Talvitie:** EU Special Representative for the *South Caucasus* since 7 July 2003. The EUSR will contribute to the implementation of the EU's policy objectives, which include assisting the countries of the South Caucasus in carrying out political and economic reforms, preventing and assisting in the resolution of conflicts, promoting the return of refugees and internally displaced persons, engaging constructively with key national actors neighbouring the region, supporting intra-regional co-operation and ensuring co-ordination, consistency and effectiveness of the EU's action in the South Caucasus.
4. **Francesc Vendrell:** EU Special Representative in *Afghanistan* since 25 June 2002. His mandate is to contribute, through close liaison with and support for the Special Representative of the Secretary-General of the United Nations, Mr Brahmini, to achieving the implementation of the Union's policy in Afghanistan.

5. **Lord Ashdown:** EU Special Representative in *Bosnia and Herzegovina* since 11 March 2002. He shall maintain an overview of the whole range of activities in the field of the Rule of Law and in that context provide advice to the Secretary-General - High Representative and the Commission as necessary.
6. **Erhard Busek:** EU Special Representative since 19 December 2001. His task is to carry out the tasks defined in the *Stability Pact for South Eastern Europe* of 10 June 1999 to help the countries concerned develop a joint strategy for ensuring the stability and growth of the region.
7. **Aldo Ajello:** EU Special Envoy for the *African Great Lakes Region* since 25 March 1996. Mr Ajello works closely with the UN and African Union and with the prominent African figures who are assisting the international community's efforts. He maintains constant contact with the Governments of the countries in the region. Through its Special Envoy the Union is able – in extremely difficult circumstances – to make its voice heard and make known its desire to contribute to solving the crises in the region.
(*Council Foreign Policy*)

71.   A

See answer 70.

72.   D

The generalised system of preferences offers manufactured products and certain agricultural products exported by developing countries tariff reductions or duty-free access to the Community market. It is therefore an autonomous tariff instrument that is complementary to the multilateral liberalisation of the GATT and, since 1995, the WTO.

73.   B

The Western European Union (WEU) today is almost non-existent due to the circumstances described in answer 69. However, officially it still consists of 28 countries with four different statuses: Member States, Associate Members, Observers and Associate Partners. All EU countries are full Member States except Denmark, Ireland Austria, Finland and

Sweden, which have observer status. The six Associate Members are the Czech Republic, Hungary, Iceland, Norway, Poland and Turkey, and there are seven Associate Partners: Bulgaria, Estonia, Latvia, Lithuania, Romania, Slovakia and Slovenia.

For further information, see: *http://www.weu.int*

74.   C

See answer above.

75.   A

The European Union Satellite Centre (EUSC) is an Agency of the Council of the European Union dedicated to the exploitation and production of information derived primarily from the analysis of earth observation space imagery in support of Union decision-making in the field of "second pillar", the Common Foreign and Security Policy (CFSP). The establishment of the EUSC is considered by the Union as an essential asset for the strengthening of CFSP especially in the crisis monitoring and conflict prevention function. The Centre has been operational since 1 January 2002, under the political supervision of the Political and Security Committee and the operational direction of the Secretary-General. It is located in Torrejón, close to Madrid, Spain.

76.   B

The Minister for Foreign Affairs is appointed by the European Council acting by qualified majority, with the agreement of the President of the Commission. The European Council may end the Minister's tenure by the same procedure as that through which he or she was appointed.

77.   B

In the Constitutional Treaty, the Union is accorded international legal personality (Article I-7), taking over the rights and obligations of the European Community and the Union in their current form. Discarding the pillar structure in the field of foreign

policy is one of the main novelties of the Constitutional Treaty. The provisions relating to the external action of the Union are grouped together under a single title covering all aspects of that action.

At the institutional level, the Constitution introduces two important innovations. First, it creates the post of Minister for Foreign Affairs (see answer 76). Secondly, the Constitution provides for the creation of a President of the European Council who shall, amongst other things, ensure at his or her level the external representation of the Union on issues concerning the CFSP, without prejudice to the responsibilities of the Minister for Foreign Affairs. Article III-292 of the Constitutional Treaty lays down the detailed objectives of the Union's external action. In the pursuit of these objectives, the Council of Ministers and the Commission, assisted by the Minister for Foreign Affairs, will ensure consistency between the different areas of its external action and between these and its other policies.

(ScadPlus)

78.   A

Areas of foreign policy according to the Constitutional Treaty:
* the common foreign and security policy (CFSP);
* the common security and defence policy;
* the common commercial policy;
* development cooperation policy;
* economic, financial and technical cooperation with third countries;
* humanitarian aid;
* international agreements;
* relations with international organisations;
* implementation of the solidarity clause.

79.   B

Article I-13 of the Constitution clearly accords the Union exclusive competence for the common commercial policy. The common commercial policy is extended to foreign direct investment (Article III-315). However, agreements in the field of transport remain outside the scope of the common commercial policy. The Constitution provides for the common commercial policy to be implemented through European laws.

80.   C

In terms of decision-making, the provisions of the current Article 133 of the EC Treaty are simplified. However, qualified majority voting is not extended to all aspects of the common commercial policy. In fact, the Constitution retains the *principle of parallelism* between internal and external rules established at Nice. According to this principle, decisions relating to the negotiation and conclusion of agreements in the areas of trade in services, commercial aspects of intellectual property and direct foreign investment are subject to unanimity when these agreements contain provisions for which unanimity is required for the adoption of internal rules. The Constitution also provides for unanimity for agreements in the field of trade in cultural and audiovisual services, where there is a risk that they could prejudice the Union's cultural and linguistic diversity. Compared with the present situation, the Constitution adds a further case where unanimity is required: trade in social, education and health services, where agreements risk seriously disturbing the national organisation of these services or prejudicing the Member States' responsibility to deliver them. All trade agreements have to be approved by the Parliament, which must be kept fully informed on the progress of negotiations.
(*ScadPlus*)

81.   B

CFSP expenditure is charged to the general budget of the European Union, with the exception of expenditure arising from operations having military or defence implications.

82.   D

The Court of Justice does not have jurisdiction over the CFSP. However, it does have jurisdiction to rule on proceedings reviewing the legality of restrictive measures adopted by the Council of Ministers against natural or legal persons.

The Court of Justice also has jurisdiction to rule on whether an international agreement, including in the area of the CFSP, is compatible with the provisions of the Constitution, and on the clause which states that the implementation of the CFSP shall not affect the competences related to other policies, and vice versa.
(*ScadPlus*)

83.   D

Article III-329 of the Constitutional Treaty provides:
    "Should a Member State be the object of a terrorist attack or the victim of a natural or man-made disaster, the other Member States shall assist it at the request of its political authorities. To that end, the Member States shall coordinate between themselves in the Council [...]"

84.   C

Article 133 of the EC Treaty allows the European Union to negotiate, conclude and implement trade agreements with other countries of the world. It is therefore at the foundation of the European Common Commercial Policy. It states that:
*   The common commercial policy shall be based on uniform principles.
*   The Commission is the negotiator, responsible for conducting trade negotiations on the basis of "directives for negotiation" given by the Council to guide the Commission in its work and decides ultimately, whether to adopt an accord.
*   The Commission is the enforcer, responsible for ensuring compliance by third countries with international trade accords.
*   The European Parliament gives its assent to international agreements that set up an institutional structure (Article 300). Though Parliament has no explicit powers regarding the conduct of trade policy, the Commission informs Parliament on a regular basis about developments in European trade policy.
*   The Treaty of Nice has extended the coverage of the common trade policy to the fields of trade in services and the commercial aspects of intellectual property.
*   The Council acts by a qualified majority. Agreements on services and intellectual property are decided under the same qualified majority rule as applies to trade in goods. However the principle of "parallelism" applies, see answer 80.

- Shared competencies: Article 133 also makes room for areas where competencies are shared between the EC and member states, namely in the areas relating to trade in cultural and audiovisual services, educational services, and social and human health services. Agreements thus negotiated shall be concluded jointly by the Community and the Member States.

GATT and other WTO agreements have special provisions for developing countries. These include: a significantly lower level of market access commitments (i.e. higher tariffs or less open services commitments) and the possibility to be granted preferential access to developed countries' markets, in derogation from the MFN obligation (in the EU, for example, through use of our Generalised System of Preferences).
(*DG Trade*)

85. A

The agreement creating the Central American Common Market (CACM) was signed in Managua on 13 December 1960. This trade regional grouping comprises Costa Rica, El Salvador, Guatemala, Honduras and Nicaragua. Panama, without being a member, benefits too from the special arrangements.

86. D

The Central European Free Trade Agreement is an economic co-operation agreement that entered into force in March 1993 between the Czech Republic, Hungary, Poland, and Slovakia, which were later joined by Bulgaria, Slovenia, Croatia and Romania. The members' common goal was to have market economies and to secure development, greater welfare for their citizens, human rights, and democracy. All CEFTA member states have signed a Europe Agreement with the EU. Following the integration of several CEFTA countries into the EU in 2004, the remaining members are Bulgaria, Romania and Croatia.

87. A

88. B

Developing countries: this term refers to the low- and middle-income countries in which most people have a lower standard of living with access to fewer goods and services than do most people in high-income countries. There are currently about 125 developing countries with populations over 1 million. As of 2000, 4.9 billion people lived in developing countries. The

89. B

On 26 February 2001 the EU eliminated all duties and quotas for all products originating from the least developed countries (LDCs), with only three transition periods for bananas (2006), sugar (2009) and rice (2009). This initiative, known as Everything But Arms (EBA), is part of the EU policy to enhance market access for developing countries.

90. A

The Quint Agriculture Ministerial Meeting is a gathering of the agriculture ministers of Japan, the US, the EU, Canada and Australia to exchange frank views on various issues concerning agriculture and agricultural polices.

91. C

92. C

It was Decision No 1/95 of the EC-Turkey Association Council of 22 December 1995 on implementing the final phase of the Customs Union that created the customs union.

93. D

Turkey shares a border with Armenia, Azerbaijan, Bulgaria, Georgia, Greece, Iran, Iraq and Syria.

94.   B

The Brussels European Council of 17 December 2004 confirmed the conclusion of accession negotiations with Bulgaria and accordingly looked forward to welcoming it as a member from January 2007.

95.   C

96.   B

The Stabilisation and Association Agreement (SAA) with Croatia was signed on 29 October 2001. An Enlargement Protocol, necessary to take into account the accession of ten New Member States on 1 May 2004, was signed on 21 December 2004. The SAA and its Enlargement Protocol replaced an Interim Agreement on trade and trade-related provisions in force since 1 March 2002 as well as an Enlargement Protocol to the Interim Agreement. Croatia applied for EU membership in February 2003. In April 2004, the European Commission issued a positive opinion ("avis") on this application and recommended the opening of accession negotiations. This recommendation was endorsed by the June 2004 European Council, which decided that Croatia was a candidate country and that the accession process should be launched. The December 2004 European Council requested the Council to agree on a negotiating framework with a view to opening the accession negotiations with Croatia on 17 March 2005 provided that there is full cooperation with ICTY; however, as this did not happen, negotiations were postponed. In the meantime the Association Agreement entered into force on 1 February 2005.

97.   D

98.   C

The European Union Institute for Security Studies (EUISS) was created by a Council Joint Action on 20 July 2001. It has the status of an autonomous agency that comes under the EU's second "pillar" – the Common Foreign and Security Policy.

99.   A

Mr Gijs de Vries was appointed the first EU Counter-terrorism Co-ordinator. His main tasks are to co-ordinate the work of the Council of the EU in combating terrorism, to maintain an overview of all the instruments at the Union's disposal, to closely monitor the implementation of the EU Action Plan on Combating Terrorism, and to secure the visibility of the Union's policies in the fight against terrorism.

100.   A

The Group of Eight (G8) is an informal group of eight of the world's leading industrialised nations: France, Germany, Italy, Japan, the United Kingdom, the United States, Canada and Russia. The EU also participates in its meetings. Its origins lay in the perceived need to create a forum to discuss economic problems such as inflation and unemployment, in the context of the impact of the 1973-74 oil shock. The first summit of national leaders was held in 1975; Canada participated from 1976; the EC from 1977; and Russia's partial involvement began in 1991, with complete involvement (the G-7 becoming the G-8) from 1998. The agenda of G-8 meetings has broadened over the years to the full range of international issues.

MISCELLANEOUS

DECISION MAKING
ANSWERS

Question No	A	B	C	D
1.		X		
2.			X	
3.			X	
4.				X
5.	X			
6.				X
7.			X	
8.		X		
9.	X			
10.			X	
11.		X		
12.				X
13.			X	

Question No	A	B	C	D
14.				X
15.	X			
16.			X	
17.	X			
18.		X		
19.		X		
20.				X
21.			X	
22.		X		
23.				X
24.	X			
25.			X	

1. B

In the codecision procedure, provided for in Article 251 of the EC Treaty, Parliament and the Council share legislative power. The Commission sends its proposal to both institutions. The Council and Parliament read and discuss the Commission's proposal. If the Council and Parliament are unable to reach agreement after the second reading, then a conciliation committee is set up with an equal number of members from both institutions. Commission representatives also attend the committee meetings and contribute to the discussion. Once the committee has reached an agreement, the agreed text is then sent to Parliament and the Council for a third reading, so that they can finally adopt it as law.

The areas covered by the codecision procedure are (non-exhaustive list):

- non-discrimination on the basis of nationality;
- the right to move and reside;
- the free movement of workers;
- social security for migrant workers;
- the right of establishment;
- transport;
- the internal market;
- employment;
- customs co-operation;
- the fight against social exclusion;
- equal opportunities and equal treatment;
- implementing decisions regarding the european Social Fund;
- education;
- vocational training;
- culture;
- health;
- consumer protection;
- trans-European networks;
- implementing decisions regarding the European Regional Development Fund;
- research;
- the environment;
- transparency;
- preventing and combating fraud;
- statistics;
- setting up a data protection advisory body.

2. C

The Commission has a monopoly on the initiative in Community decision-making and drafts proposals for a decision by the two decision-making institutions: the Parliament and the Council. Thus, the legislative process begins with Commission proposals (for regulations or directives) which need to be in line with the Treaties and help to implement them. Normally, the Commission takes guidelines of national authorities into account. Commission proposals must encompass three core objectives:

- identifying European interest;
- organising consultation as widely as necessary;
- respecting the principle of subsidiarity.

Once the Commission has formally sent a proposal for legislation to the Council and the Parliament, the Union's law-making process is dependent on effective cooperation between three institutions – the Council, the Commission and the European Parliament. However, given the Commission's almost exclusive right of initiative, the Parliament and the Council may call on the Commission to initiate legislation. Nevertheless the Commission maintains the right to decide whether or not it considers such legislation appropriate.

(*EUR-lex/Process and players*)

3. C

Article 7(1) of the EU Treaty provides:

"On a reasoned proposal by one third of the Member States, by the European Parliament or by the Commission, the Council, acting by a majority of four fifths of its members after obtaining the assent of the European Parliament, may determine that there is a clear risk of a serious breach by a Member State of principles mentioned in Article 6(1), and address appropriate recommendations to that State. Before making such a determination, the Council shall hear the Member State in question and, acting in accordance with the same procedure, may call on independent persons to submit within a reasonable time limit a report on the situation in the Member State in question.

The Council shall regularly verify that the grounds on which such a determination was made continue to apply."

4. D

Article 23(2) of the EU Treaty provides:

"By derogation from the provisions of paragraph 1, the Council shall act by qualified majority:

– When adopting joint actions, common positions or taking any other decision on the basis of a common strategy,
– When adopting any decision implementing a joint action or a common position,
– When appointing a special representative in accordance with Article 18(5).
(…)"

The Treaty of Nice, repealing the provision that required at least ten Member States to be in favour of the proposal, provides that at least two thirds of the Member States have to support the proposal.

However, according to the second subparagraph of the above article, "if a member of the Council declares that, for important and stated reasons of national policy, it intends to oppose the adoption of a decision to be taken by qualified majority, a vote shall not be taken. The Council may, acting by a qualified majority, request that the matter be referred to the European Council for decision by unanimity."

5.   A

The consultation procedure requires an opinion from the Parliament before the Council can adopt a legislative proposal from the Commission. Neither the Commission nor the Council is obliged to accept the amendments contained in the Parliament's opinion; however, the Parliament may propose any amendment it deems appropriate. Once the opinion has been produced, the Council can adopt the proposal with or without the amendments.

The Treaty requires the compulsory consultation of the Parliament in some fields, the infringement of which may result in the annulment of the act (Article 230 EC Treaty). Such fields are: Common Agricultural Policy (Article 37 EC Treaty), Transport Policy (Article 71 EC Treaty), approximation of legal provisions for directives requiring Council unanimity in the field of internal market (Article 94 EC Treaty), outline program for industrial development (Article 157 EC Treaty).

6.   D

Article 190(4) of the EC Treaty provides:

"The European Parliament shall draw up a proposal for elections by direct universal suffrage in accordance with a uniform procedure in all Member States or in accordance with principles common to all Member States.

The Council shall, acting unanimously after obtaining the assent of the European Parliament, which shall act by a majority of its component members, lay down the appropriate provisions, which it shall recommend to Member States for adoption in accordance with their respective constitutional requirements."

7.   C

Article 135 of the EC Treaty provides that the Council, acting in accordance with the procedure referred to in Article 251 (i.e. codecision procedure), must take measures in order to strengthen customs cooperation between Member States and between the Member States and the Commission, without any specific reference to the majority required. In the case of social security related to the free movement of workers, citizenship of the Union and culture, unanimity is required from the Council.

8.   B

The Single European Act (SEA), signed in Luxembourg and The Hague on February 1986 and entered into force on 1 July 1987, introduced a new procedure that is known as cooperation procedure, governed by Article 252 of the EC Treaty. The cooperation procedure is now limited to certain decisions relating to economic and monetary union.

Procedure:

At a first reading Parliament delivers an opinion on the Commission proposal. The Council, acting by a qualified majority, then adopts a common position and forwards it to Parliament, enclosing all the information required and its reasons for adopting the common position.

Parliament has three months to take a decision: it can adopt, amend or reject the common position. In the latter two instances it must do so by an absolute majority of its Members. If Parliament rejects the proposal the Council can only take a decision at second reading unanimously. Within a period of one month, the Commission reconsiders the proposal on which the Council adopted its common position and forwards the reconsidered proposal to the Council. It has discretion to incorporate or exclude the amendments proposed by Parliament.

Within a period of three months, which can be extended by a maximum of one month, the Council may, acting by a qualified majority, adopt the proposal as reconsidered by the Commission or, acting unanimously, amend the reconsidered proposal or adopt amendments not taken into account by the Commission. As long as the Council has not acted, the Commission may alter or withdraw its proposal at any time.

(*http://www.europarl.eu.int/factsheets/1_4_1_en.htm*)

9   A

Parliament has gradually become the second arm of the budgetary authority.

- Before 1970, budgetary powers were vested in the Council alone; Parliament had only a consultative role. After having adopted the draft budget, the Council forwarded it to Parliament for its opinion. If Parliament's opinion contained proposed modifications, the Council gave the budget a second reading and adopted the final version.
- The Treaties of 22 April 1970 and 22 July 1975 increased Parliament's budgetary powers:
- the 1970 Treaty, which followed on from the introduction of the Community's own resources, gave Parliament the last word on what is known as "non-compulsory expenditure";
- the 1975 Treaty gave it the right to reject the budget as a whole.
- Generally speaking, budgetary decisions have to be taken jointly by Parliament and the Council although Parliament has a decisive role to play: it finally adopts the budget and can also reject it as a whole, and it has the last word on non-compulsory expenditure, which now accounts for a majority of all expenditure (currently approximately 55%).

Compulsory expenditure (CE)

Compulsory expenditure is expenditure necessarily resulting from the Treaties or from acts adopted in accordance with them. As far as this type of expenditure is concerned, Parliament may only propose modifications, on which the Council has the last word. However, as we saw above, if Parliament's proposals would not increase the overall expenditure of any of the Institutions, the Council must act by a

qualified majority in rejecting them, failing which they will be deemed accepted. This arrangement enables Parliament to exert influence even over compulsory expenditure.

Compulsory expenditure, currently approximately 45% of the budget, consists mainly of:
- agricultural price support expenditure (EAGGF-Guarantee Section);
- various items of expenditure connected with structural agricultural policy (EAGGF-Guidance Section) and the common fisheries policy;
- flat-rate refunds to the Member States, in particular of costs incurred in collecting own resources;
- part of development aid expenditure.

Non-compulsory expenditure (NCE)

Parliament has the last word on this type of expenditure, in that it takes the final decision at last reading on the amendments which it adopted previously. However, its powers are restricted by the maximum rate of increase in expenditure. As a result, Parliament cannot add to the draft budget adopted by the Council a volume of non-compulsory expenditure equivalent to more than half this rate. Nonetheless, if the Council has already increased expenditure by more than half the rate, Parliament may still make use of the remaining half.

(*http://www/europarl.eu.int/factsheets/ 1_4_3_en.htm*)

10.   C

The general rule is that the Council confers on the Commission the power to issue measures implementing its instrument. Only in special cases may the Council reserve implementing powers for itself (e.g. Article 202, third indent, of the EC Treaty). When exercising its implementing powers the Commission may neither amend nor supplement the Council instrument. In 1999, the decision-making procedure was redesigned to make for greater simplicity and transparency, and not least greater Parliamentary involvement. The number of decision-making procedures was reduced from five to three: Advisory Committee procedure, Management Committee procedure, Legislation Committee procedure. Parliament was brought into the procedures concerning the adoption of implementing measures with which it had been involved as part of the codecision procedure.

The implementing procedures, given that they are

carried out in Committees, is also known as "Comitology".
(*EUR-lex/ABC*)

11.   B

The Legislative Committee, like the Management Committee, consists of representatives of the Member States and gives its opinion on the Commission's proposed implementing measures by qualified majority.

12.   D

Under the simplified procedure, no Commission proposal is needed to initiate the legislative process.
- This procedure applies to measures within the Commission's own powers (such as approval of State aid).
- The simplified procedure is also used for the adoption of non-mandatory instruments, especially recommendations and opinions issued by the Commission or the Council. The Commission is not restricted to what is expressly provided for in the Treaties, but can also formulate recommendations and deliver opinions where it considers it necessary (EC Article 211, second, indent; Euratom Article 124 subpara. 2). In the ECSC, on the other hand, only the Commission may deliver opinions.

(*Eur-lex/abc/21*)

13.   C

Article 190(5) of the EC Treaty provides:

"The European Parliament, after seeking an opinion from the Commission and with the approval of the Council acting by a qualified majority, shall lay down the regulations and general conditions governing the performance of the duties of its Members. All rules or conditions relating to the taxation of Members or former Members shall require unanimity within the Council."

Therefore both the proposal and the final decision are made by the Parliament itself, with the exception of issues related to taxation.

14.   D

The Council, acting *unanimously* at the request of the Court of Justice and after consulting the European Parliament and the Commission, or at the request of the Commission and after consulting the European Parliament and the Court of Justice, may amend the provisions of the Statute, with the exception of Title I.

15.   A

Codecision procedure, second reading in Parliament:
    Parliament receives the Council common position and has three months to take a decision. It may thus:
- expressly approve the proposal as amended by the common position or take no decision by the deadline; in both cases, the act as amended by the common position is adopted;
- reject the common position by an absolute majority of its Members; the act is not adopted and the procedure ends;
- adopt, by an absolute majority of its Members, amendments to the common position, which are then put to the Commission for its opinion; the matter returns to the Council.

(*http://www.europarl.eu.int/factsheets/1_4_3_en.htm*)

16.   C

If the Council rejects certain amendments or the majority needed for their adoption cannot be obtained, then the President of the Council, acting in consultation with the President of the Parliament, must within six weeks convene a Conciliation Committee consisting of 25-25 representatives from the Council and Parliament to consider the Council's common position in the light of Parliament's proposed amendments. If the Conciliation Committee accepts a joint draft of the legal instrument, the Council and Parliament must confirm its acceptance in a third reading within six weeks.

17.   A

In the case of the Advisory Committee (see answer 10), the Commission representative presents a draft of the measures to be taken, and the Committee gives its opinion on them within a time limit set by the Commission according to the urgency of the matter.

18.   B

19.   B

At first reading, and after conciliation with a Parliament delegation, the Council, acting by a qualified majority, adopts the draft budget and forwards it to Parliament by 5 October at the latest.

Parliament has 45 days to state its position.

*   Within that period, it may adopt the draft or decline to state a position, in both of which cases the budget is deemed finally adopted.
*   It may, on the other hand, call for changes:
    *   either in the form of proposed modifications to compulsory expenditure; these must be adopted by an absolute majority of the votes cast;
    *   or in the form of amendments to non-compulsory expenditure; these must be adopted by a majority of the component Members of Parliament;
    *   thus altered, the draft is then referred back to the Council.

20.   D

In stage four of the budgetary procedure, the Council has 15 days to conduct its second reading. Within that period, it may accept all of Parliament's amendments and proposed modifications, in which case the budget will be deemed adopted.

It may, on the other hand, not accept them, in which case:

*   it takes a final decision on the proposed modifications: if a proposed modification would not increase the overall expenditure of any of the Institutions, the Council must, acting by a qualified majority, expressly reject or alter it, failing which it will be deemed accepted;
*   if the proposed modification would lead to an increase, the Council must, again acting by a qualified majority, expressly accept it, failing which it will be deemed rejected;

*   it may alter the amendments, which are then referred back to Parliament.

(*http://www.europarl.eu.int/factsheets/1_4_3_en.htm*)

21.   C

The Treaty of Brussels of 22 July 1975 gave the European Parliament the right to reject the budget and to grant the Commission a discharge for implementing the budget.

22.   B

Under the provisions of Article 67 of the Treaty of Nice, the Council may, by qualified majority, adopt measures in the field of judicial cooperation in civil matters with cross-border implications, with the exception of aspects relating to family law. The codecision procedure also applies to this article.

23.   D

Concerning the motion of censure on the Commission, Rule 100 of the Rules of Procedure of the European Parliament provides the following:

"Rule 100

Motion of censure on the Commission

1.   A motion of censure on the Commission may be submitted to the President by one tenth of the component Members of Parliament.
2.   The motion shall be called 'motion of censure' and supported by reasons. It shall be forwarded to the Commission.
3.   The President shall announce to Members that a motion of censure has been tabled immediately he receives it.
4.   The debate on censure shall not take place until at least twenty-four hours after the receipt of a motion of censure is announced to Members.
5.   The vote on the motion shall be by roll call and shall not be taken until at least forty-eight hours after the beginning of the debate.
6.   The debate and the vote shall take place, at the latest, during the part-session following the submission of the motion.
7.   The motion of censure shall be adopted if it

secures a two-thirds majority of the votes cast, representing a majority of the component Members of Parliament. The result of the vote shall be notified to the President of the Council and the President of the Commission."

24.   A

Declaration No. 20 adopted when the Treaty of Nice was signed also set out the common position that the Member States are to take for the accession negotiations with Romania and Bulgaria. It provides for 14 votes for Romania and 10 votes for Bulgaria. The total number of votes would thus be 345. Pursuant to Declaration No 21, the qualified majority threshold

after these two countries' accession will therefore have to be 255 votes out of 345 (currently 232 out of 321), i.e. 73.91% (currently 72.3%).

25.   C

Article 214(2) of the EC Treaty stipulates that:
    "The Council, meeting in the composition of Heads of State or Government and acting by a qualified majority, shall nominate the person it intends to appoint as President of the Commission; the nomination shall be approved by the European Parliament."

STAFF REGULATIONS

ANSWERS

Question No	A	B	C	D
1.	X			
2.		X		
3.				X
4.		X		
5.				X
6.				X
7.				X
8.	X			
9.	X			
10.			X	

2.   B

Article 47 of the Staff Regulations provides:
    "Service shall be terminated by:
(a)   resignation;
(b)   compulsory resignation;
(c)   retirement in the interests of the service;
(d)   dismissal for incompetence;
(e)   removal from post;
(f)   retirement; or
(g)   death."
    For further information, see:
http://europa.eu.int/comm/dgs/personnel_administration/statut/tocen100.pdf

1.   A

3.   D

Article 28 of the Staff Regulations provides:

"An official may be appointed only on condition that:

(a) he is a national of one of the Member States of the Communities, unless an exception is authorised by the appointing authority, and enjoys his full rights as a citizen;

(b) he has fulfilled any obligations imposed on him by the laws concerning military service;

(c) he produces the appropriate character references as to his suitability for the performance of his duties;

(d) he has, subject to Article 29(2), passed a competition based on either qualifications or tests, or both qualifications and tests, as provided for in Annex III;

(e) he is physically fit to perform his duties; and

(f) he produces evidence of a thorough knowledge of one of the languages of the Communities and of a satisfactory knowledge of another language of the Communities to the extent necessary for the performance of his duties."

4.   B

Article 11 of the Staff Regulations provides:
"An official shall carry out his duties and conduct himself solely with the interests of the Communities in mind; he shall neither seek nor take instructions from any government, authority, organisation or person outside his institution."

5.   D

For further information, see:
http://www.europa.eu.int/comm/secretariat_general/code/index_en.htm

6.   D

Article 77 of the Staff Regulations provides:
"An official who has completed at least 10 years' service shall be entitled to a retirement pension. He shall, however, be entitled to such pension irrespective of length of service if he is over 63 years, if it has not been possible to reinstate him during a period of

non-active status or in the event of retirement in the interests of the service."

7.   D

According to the Code of Good Administrative Behaviour, "[i]n accordance with Article 21 of the EC Treaty, members of the public who write to the Commission shall receive a reply in the language of their initial letter, provided that it was written in one of the official languages of the European Union.

A reply to a letter addressed to the Commission shall be sent within fifteen working days from the date of receipt of the letter by the responsible Commission department. The reply should identify the person responsible for the matter and state how he or she may be contacted.

If a reply cannot be sent within the deadline mentioned above, and in all cases where the reply requires other work on it, such as interdepartmental consultation or translation, the member of staff responsible should send a holding reply, indicating a date by which the addressee may expect to be sent a reply in the light of this additional work, taking into account the relative urgency and complexity of the matter."

8.   A

The Press and Communication Service is responsible for contacts with the media. However, when requests for information concern technical subjects falling within their specific areas of responsibility, staff may answer them.

9.   A

Article 34 of the Staff Regulations provides:
"Officials shall serve a nine-month probationary period before they can be established. […]"

10.   C

Article 255 of the EC Treaty, implemented through Regulation 1049/2001 of 30 May 2001, grants a right of access to European Parliament, Council and Commission documents to any Union citizen and to any natural or legal person residing, or having its registered office, in a Member State.

ABBREVIATIONS
ANSWERS

Question No	A	B	C	D
1.			X	
2.			X	
3.				X
4.	X			
5.		X		
6.	X			
7.	X			
8.			X	
9.			X	
10.		X		
11.		X		
12.				X
13.		X		
14.				X
15.				X

Question No	A	B	C	D
16.			X	
17.	X			
18.		X		
19.			X	
20.			X	
21.				X
22.		X		
23.		X		
24.			X	
25.	X			
26.		X		
27.				X
28.			X	
29.				X
30.	X			

1.   C

ASEAN: Association of South-East Asian Nations (Brunei, Cambodia, Laos, Malaysia, Myanmar, Philippines, Singapore, Thailand and Vietnam).

2.   C

EMEA: European Medicines Agency is a decentralised body of the European Union with headquarters in London.

Please refer to the section on the EU specialised agencies for further information and see *http://www.emea.eu.int*

3.   D

CORDIS is the European Commission's information service on European Research and Innovation activities.

For further information, see: *http://www.dbl.cordis.lu*

4.   A

CIREA: Centre for Information, Discussion and Exchange on Asylum (within the General Secretariat of the Council)
COGECA: General Committee for Agricultural Cooperation in the EC
(FR: Comité général de la coopération agricole (CE))
RARE: associated networks for European research
INTAS: International Association for the Promotion of Cooperation with Scientists from the new independent States of the former Soviet Union

5.   B

PETRA: action programme for the vocational training of young people and their preparation for adult and working life
SCENT: system for a customs enforcement network
SPRINT: strategic programme for innovation and technology transfer
VALUE: programme for the dissemination and utilisation of research results (FR: valorisation et utilisation pour l'Europe)

6.   A

SAFE: safety actions for Europe – aimed at improving safety, hygiene and health at work, in particular in small and medium-sized enterprises.

7.   A

TIDE: technological initiative for the socioeconomic integration of the disabled and elderly
DECT: digital European cordless telecommunications
DELTA: development of European learning through technological advance
FIDE: International Federation for European Law

8.   C

EURES: European   employment   services
(http://europa.eu.int/eures/)

Eurydice: information network on education in Europe
(http://www.eurydice.org/)
Erasmus: European Community action scheme for the mobility of university students
ERICA: European Research Institute for Consumer Affairs

9.   C

Codest: Committee for the European Development of Science and Technology (FR: Comité de développement européen de la science et de la technologie)
FAST: forecasting and assessment in the field of science and technology
MAST: marine science and technology
NAMSA: NATO Maintenance and Supply Agency

10.   B

ACE: Community actions relating to the environment
CFPE: Community financing projects for the environment
Corine: Coordination of information on the environment in Europe (Community programme)
DIANE: direct information access network for Europe

11.   B

The purpose of Europartenariat is to stimulate the development of less-favoured regions or those suffering from industrial decline or those from rural parts or regions with low population density, by encouraging small and medium-sized businesses from all over the Community and third countries to establish business relationships with their counterparts in these regions. (*DG Enterprise*)

12.   D

FORCE: Community action programme for the development of continuing vocational training.

13.   B

JANUS: Community information system for health and safety at work.

14.   D

Lingua: programme to promote foreign language competence in the European Community.

15.   D

ALFA supports joint co-operation projects between European and Latin American higher education institutions. Its aims are

*   to create or strengthen the links between higher education institutions by enhancing the dialogue between the academic communities of both continents;
*   to create systematic and sustainable mechanisms of co-operation between those involved in higher education in Europe and Latin America, in order to encourage the establishment of mechanisms for mobility between the two continents and at regional level in Latin America.

(*http://europa.eu.int/grants*)

16.   C

NUTS: nomenclature of territorial units for statistics (Eurostat), e.g.: NUTS 1, 2, etc. used in the area of structural funds and regional policy

17.   A

SIMAP: Information system for public procurement
UCLAF: Unit for the Coordination of Fraud Prevention
EURAM: European research on advanced materials
FLAIR: food-linked agro-industrial research

18.   B

FAR: Fisheries and aquaculture research program
FIFG: Financial Instrument for Fisheries Guidance
IBSFC: International Baltic Sea Fishery Commission
INFCE: International nuclear fuel cycle evaluation

19.   C

ALDE: Group of the Alliance of Liberals and Democrats for Europe
UEN: Union for the Europe of the Nations Group
PES: Socialist Group

20.   C

SADCC: Angola, Botswana, Democratic Republic of the Congo, Lesotho, Malawi, Mauritius, Mozambique, Namibia, Seychelles, South Africa, Swaziland, Tanzania, Zambia, Zimbabwe
SAHEL: Burkina Faso, Cape Verde, Chad, Gambia, Guinea-Bissau, Mali, Mauritania, Niger, Senegal
CONTADORA: Colombia, Mexico, Panama, Venezuela

21.   D

COPA: Committee of Agricultural Organisations in the European Community

22.   B

NOW: Community initiative for the promotion of equal opportunities for women in the field of employment and vocational training

23.   B

Comedi: commerce electronic data interchange
Kaleidoscope: programme to support artistic and cultural activities having a European dimension

Konver: Community initiative concerning defence conversion
Recite: regions and cities for Europe

24. C

Hercule: Programme to promote activities in the field of the protection of the Community's financial interests
Daphne: Programme of Community action on preventive measures to fight violence against children, young persons and women
There is no Community programme called Xerxes.

25. A

CARE: Community database on road accidents.

26. B

CENELEC is the European Committee for Electrotechnical Standardisation.

27. D

ERDF: European Regional Development Fund.

28. C

Esprit: European strategic programme for research and development in information technology.

29. D

Eureka: European Research Coordination Agency
Poseidom: programme of options specific to the remote and insular nature of the French overseas departments
Horizon: Community initiative on handicapped persons and certain other disadvantaged groups
Neptune: new European programme for technology utilisation in education

30. A

For a comprehensive list of abbreviations, please refer to:
http://publications.eu.int/code/en/en-5000400.htm

MEMBER STATES
ANSWERS

Question No	A	B	C	D
1.		X		
2.		X		
3.			X	
4.			X	
5.		X		
6.	X			
7.	X			
8.		X		
9.		X		
10.			X	
11.				X
12.				X
13.			X	

Question No	A	B	C	D
14.			X	
15.		X		
16.	X			
17.	X			
18.		X		
19.	X			
20.		X		
21.		X		
22.			X	
23.				X
24.				X
25.				X

1.   B

The European Union's territory is 3,976,372 square km, which is approximately one third of the USA's size.

2.   B

Concerning the European continent, the following countries are bordering the EU Member States:
Albania, Andorra, Belarus, Bulgaria, Croatia, Holy See, Liechtenstein, Macedonia, Monaco, Norway, Romania, Russia, San Marino, Serbia and Montenegro, Switzerland, Turkey, Ukraine.

3.   C

The Czech Republic has a population of approxi-

mately 10,246,178 whereas the EU of 25 has a population of approximately 456,285,839.

4.   C

5.   B

6.   A

EU Member States have the following harbours (only main ones listed):
Antwerp (Belgium), Barcelona (Spain), Bremen (Germany), Copenhagen (Denmark), Gdansk (Poland), Hamburg (Germany), Helsinki (Finland), Las Palmas (Canary Islands, Spain), Le Havre (France), Lisbon (Portugal), London (UK), Marseille (France), Naples (Italy), Peiraiefs or Piraeus (Greece),

Riga (Latvia), Rotterdam (Netherlands), Stockholm (Sweden), Talinn (Estonia).

7.   A

The southernmost part of Greece is very close to Cyprus in terms of longitude, but if we consider their capitals, Nicosia is obviously more to the south than Athens or Valletta (Malta).

8.   B

Ireland: 70,280 sq km
Austria: 83,870 sq km
Portugal: 92,391 sq km
Hungary: 93,030 sq km

9.   B

10.   C

11.   D

Population of these countries are as follows (data of 2004):
Malta: 396,851
Luxembourg: 462,690
Cyprus: 775,927
Estonia: 1,341,664

12.   D

Turkey: 68,893,918
Bulgaria: 7,517,973

13.   C

14.   C

15.   B

The largest EU Member States are:
France: 547,030 sq km (metropolitan area)
Spain: 504,782 sq km
Germany: 357,021 sq km
Poland: 312,685 sq km
Italy: 301,230 sq km
United Kingdom: 244,820 sq km

16.   A

17.   A

23.3% of the exports go to the USA; 7.4% to Switzerland; 6.5% to China; 6.4% to Japan and 5.3% to Russia (Eurostat figures, 2004).

18.   B

Austria, Luxembourg, Hungary, Czech Republic, Slovakia

19.   A

Germany has 9 neighbours, out of which 8 are EU Member States:
Austria, Belgium, Czech Republic, Denmark, France, Luxembourg, Netherlands, Poland, Switzerland

20. **B**

21. **B**

22. **C**

The Danube crosses Germany, Austria, Slovakia and Hungary.

23. **D**

24. **D**

Europa Island is off Southern Africa in the Mozambique Channel, about half way between southern Madagascar and southern Mozambique. Europa island has been a French possession since 1897. It is heavily wooded and the site of a small military base that staffs a weather station.

25. **D**

CONSTITUTIONAL TREATY

ANSWERS

Question No	A	B	C	D
1.	X			
2.	X			
3.				X
4.				X
5.	X			
6.			X	
7.		X		
8.			X	
9.				X
10.		X		
11.			X	
12.	X			
13.		X		
14.	X			
15.			X	
16.				X
17.			X	
18.			X	

Question No	A	B	C	D
19.			X	
20.		X		
21.	X			
22.				X
23.				X
24.			X	
25.	X			
26.	X			
27.	X			
28.			X	
29.				X
30.		X		
31.				X
32.	X			
33.				X
34.			X	
35.		X		
36.	X			

Question No	A	B	C	D
37.			X	
38.	X			
39.		X		
40.	X			
41.	X			
42.				X
43.			X	
44.				X
45.			X	
46.				X
47.				X
48.		X		
49.	X			
50.				X
51.	X			
52.			X	
53.		X		
54.				X
55.	X			
56			X	
57.		X		
58.				X
59.				X
60.				X
61.		X		
62.		X		
63.		X		
64.			X	
65.	X			
66.				X
67.	X			
68.				X

Question No	A	B	C	D
69.	X			
70.				X
71.		X		
72.		X		
73.			X	
74.	X			
75.				X
76.	X			
77.				X
78.				X
79.	X			
80.		X		
81.		X		
82.	X			
83.			X	
84.		X		
85.			X	
86.				X
87.			X	
88.				X
89.	X			
90.		X		
91.	X			
92.			X	
93.			X	
94.			X	
95.		X		
96.				X
97.	X			
98.				X
99.				X
100.		X		

1.   A

The Declaration on the future of the Union was annexed to the Treaty of Nice, agreed politically by the Heads of State or Government at the Nice European Council of December 2000, and it outlined the steps in the process of institutional reform.

2.   A

The Declaration called for the following:

"Following a report to be drawn up for the European Council in Göteborg in June 2001, the European Council, at its meeting in Laeken / Brussels in December 2001, will agree on a declaration containing appropriate initiatives for the continuation of this process.

The process should address, inter alia, the following questions:
- how to establish and monitor a more precise delimitation of powers between the European Union and the Member States, reflecting the principle of subsidiarity;
- the status of the Charter of Fundamental Rights of the European Union, proclaimed in Nice, in accordance with the conclusions of the European Council in Cologne;
- a simplification of the Treaties with a view to making them clearer and better understood without changing their meaning;
- the role of national parliaments in the European architecture."

3.   D

Valéry Giscard d'Estaing (born in 1926), former French president, was the President of the European Convention. Roman Herzog (answer C) was the president of the Convention responsible for drafting the European Union Charter of Fundamental Rights (see answer 4).

4.   D

The European Union Charter of Fundamental Rights was signed and proclaimed by the Presidents of the European Parliament, the Council and the Commission at the European Council meeting in Nice on 7 December 2000. The Charter is the result of a special procedure, which is without precedent in the history of the European Union and may be summarised as follows:
- The Cologne European Council (3-4 June 1999) entrusted the task of drafting the Charter to a Convention.
- The Convention held its constituent meeting in December 1999 (with 62 Members: 15 representatives of the Heads of State and Government, 30 representatives of the national parliaments, 16 representatives of the European Parliament and 1 representative of the Commission) and adopted the draft on 2 October 2000.
- The Biarritz European Council (13-14 October 2000) unanimously approved the

draft and forwarded it to the European Parliament and the Commission.
- The European Parliament gave its agreement on 14 November 2000 and the Commission on 6 December 2000.
- The Presidents of the European Parliament, the Council and the Commission signed and proclaimed the Charter on behalf of their institutions on 7 December 2000 in Nice.

The European Union Charter of Fundamental Rights sets out in a single text, for the first time in the EU's history, the whole range of civil, political, economic and social rights of European citizens and all persons resident in the EU.

For further information, see:
http://www.europarl.eu.int/charter/default_en.htm

5.   A

The Convention met for the first time on 28 February 2002 and completed its work on 18 July 2003, submitting the final draft Treaty establishing a Constitution for Europe to the Italian Presidency.

6.   C

The Convention had all together 105 members and their alternates for the entire duration of its work.

The Convention was composed of a President (Valéry Giscard d'Estaing) and two Vice-Presidents (Giuliano Amato and Jean Luc Dehaene) and:
- 15 representatives of the Heads of State or Government of the Member States (one per Member State);
- 30 representatives of the national parliaments of the Member States (two per Member State);
- 13 representatives of the Heads of State or Government of the candidate countries (one per candidate country);
- 26 representatives of the national parliaments of the candidate countries (two per candidate country: 10 Central and Eastern European countries, Romania, Bulgaria and Turkey);
- 16 representatives of the European Parliament; and
- 2 representatives of the European Commission.

The Economic and Social Committee (three representatives), the Committee of the Regions (six representatives), the social partners (three representatives) and the European Ombudsman were invited to take part as observers.

7.   B

The candidate countries took full part in the discussions without being able to prevent a consensus which might emerge among the Member States. Once the Accession Treaty with the 10 candidate countries had been signed, their observers became full members of the Convention.

The work of the Convention was directed by a Praesidium composed of the Chairman of the Convention, the Vice-Chairmen, two representatives of the European Parliament, two representatives of the Commission, two representatives of the national parliaments and representatives of the Spanish, Danish and Greek governments (the countries holding the Presidency of the European Union during the work of the Convention).

The Convention met at the European Parliament in Brussels once or twice a month in plenary sessions lasting two to three days. The Praesidium held preparatory meetings between the plenary sessions and, during the final phase, met to draft the articles likely to meet with a consensus within the Convention. The Convention was assisted by a Secretariat, which prepared the Convention working documents, drafted discussion papers and summarised the proceedings.
(*ScadPlus*)

8.   C

The Convention set up 11 separate working groups on:
* the role of the principle of subsidiarity;
* the future of the European Charter of Fundamental Rights;
* the legal personality of the Union;
* the role of national parliaments;
* complementary powers;
* economic governance;
* external action;
* defence;

* the simplification of procedures and instruments;
* the area of freedom, security and justice;
* social Europe.

9.   D

The draft Constitutional Treaty is divided into four major parts. Following the Preamble recalling the history and heritage of Europe and its determination to leave its divisions behind, Part I deals with the principles, objectives and institutional provisions governing the new European Union. Part I is Divided into nine Titles and it covers:
* definition and objectives of the Union;
* fundamental rights and citizenship of the Union;
* Union competences;
* the Union's institutions;
* the exercise of Union competence;
* the democratic life of the Union;
* the Union's finances;
* the Union and its immediate environment; and
* membership of the European Union.

Part II of the draft Constitution comprises the European Charter of Fundamental Rights. This Part contains seven Titles, preceded by a Preamble:
* Dignity;
* Freedoms;
* Equality;
* Solidarity;
* Citizens' rights;
* Justice; and
* General provisions.

Part III comprises the provisions governing the policies and functioning of the Union. The internal and external policies of the Union are laid down in this Part, including the provisions on the internal market, on economic and monetary union, on the area of freedom, security and justice, on the common foreign and security policy (CFSP) and on the functioning of the institutions. Part III also contains seven titles:
* Clauses of general application;
* Non-discrimination and citizenship;
* Internal policies and action;
* Association of the overseas countries and territories;
* The Union's external action;
* The functioning of the Union; and

- Common provisions.

Part IV groups together the general and final provisions of the draft constitution, including entry into force, the procedure for revising the Constitution and the repeal of earlier Treaties.

The Convention proposed to annex the following five protocols and three declarations to the Treaty establishing the Constitution:

- Protocol on the role of national parliaments in the European Union;
- Protocol on the application of the principles of subsidiarity and proportionality;
- Protocol on the representation of citizens in the European Parliament and the weighting of votes in the European Council and the Council of Ministers (including the declaration on Romania and Bulgaria);
- Protocol on the Euro Group;
- Protocol amending the Euratom Treaty;
- Declaration on the creation of a European external action service; and

• Declaration in the final act of signature of the Treaty establishing the Constitution.
(*ScadPlus*)

10.   B

See answer 9.

11.   C

See answer 9.

12.   A

On 29 October 2004, the Heads of State or Government of the 25 Member States and the 3 candidate countries signed the Treaty establishing a Constitution for Europe which had been unanimously adopted by them on 18 June of the same year.

13.   B

Lithuania's parliament approved the Constitutional Treaty on 11 November 2004.

14.   A

The Preamble to the draft Constitutional Treaty is preceded by a quotation from Thucydides (between 460 and 455 BC – circa 400 BC, ancient Greek historian and author of the History of the Peloponnesian War): "Our Constitution […] is called a democracy because power is in the hands not of a minority but of the greatest number".

15.   C

Article I-2 of the Constitutional Treaty provides:
"The Union is founded on the values of respect for human dignity, freedom, democracy, equality, the rule of law and respect for human rights, including the rights of persons belonging to minorities. These values are common to the Member States in a society in which pluralism, non-discrimination, tolerance, justice, solidarity and equality between women and men prevail."

16.   D

The Union values play an important role under the procedure for accession set out in Article I-57, as a European State wishing to become a member of the Union must respect these values in order to be considered eligible for admission. Another case when the values play a significant role is when a Member State fails to respect these values, it may lead to the suspension of that Member State's rights deriving from membership of the Union (Article I-58).

17.   C

Article I-5(2) of the Constitutional Treaty provides:
"Pursuant to the principle of sincere cooperation, the Union and the Member States shall, in full

mutual respect, assist each other in carrying out tasks which flow from the Constitution."

18.   C

Giving the EU legal personality (Article I-7) by merging the European Community and the European Union will give the new Union the right to conclude international agreements, in the same way as the European Community can do today, yet without compromising the division of competences between the Union and the Member States.

19.   C

Article I-6 of the Constitutional Treaty provides that "[t]he Constitution and law adopted by the institutions of the Union in exercising competences conferred on it shall have primacy over the law of the Member States." Previously, the most significant case law being the *van Gend en loss* (1963), *Costa v ENEL* (1964) and *Simmenthal* (1978) judgments that established European Community regulations in proceedings as being before that of national courts. To this extent it is possible for national law to be overruled if it is contrary to European law.

20.   B

Article I-3(1) of the Constitutional Treaty provides:
    "The Union's aim is to promote peace, its values and the well-being of its peoples."

21.   A

Article I-9(2) of the Constitutional Treaty provides:
    "The Union shall accede to the European Convention for the Protection of Human Rights and Fundamental Freedoms. Such accession shall not affect the Union's competences as defined in the Constitution."

22.   D

Article I-11 of the Constitutional Treaty provides (emphasis added):
"Fundamental principles
    1. The limits of Union competences are governed by the principle of conferral. The use of Union competences is governed by the principles of subsidiarity and proportionality.
    2. Under the **principle of conferral**, the Union shall act within the limits of the competences conferred upon it by the Member States in the Constitution to attain the objectives set out in the Constitution. Competences not conferred upon the Union in the Constitution remain with the Member States.
    3. Under the **principle of subsidiarity**, in areas which do not fall within its exclusive competence, the Union shall act only if and insofar as the objectives of the proposed action cannot be sufficiently achieved by the Member States, either at central level or at regional and local level, but can rather, by reason of the scale or effects of the proposed action, be better achieved at Union level.
    The institutions of the Union shall apply the principle of subsidiarity as laid down in the Protocol on the application of the principles of subsidiarity and proportionality. National Parliaments shall ensure compliance with that principle in accordance with the procedure set out in that Protocol.
    4. Under the **principle of proportionality**, the content and form of Union action shall not exceed what is necessary to achieve the objectives of the Constitution.
    The institutions of the Union shall apply the principle of proportionality as laid down in the Protocol on the application of the principles of subsidiarity and proportionality."

23.   D

Article I-13 of the Constitutional Treaty provides:
"Areas of exclusive competence
    1. The Union shall have exclusive competence in the following areas:
(a) customs union;
(b) the establishing of the competition rules necessary for the functioning of the internal market;
(c) monetary policy for the Member States whose currency is the euro;

(d) the conservation of marine biological resources under the common fisheries policy;

(e) common commercial policy.

2. The Union shall also have exclusive competence for the conclusion of an international agreement when its conclusion is provided for in a legislative act of the Union or is necessary to enable the Union to exercise its internal competence, or insofar as its conclusion may affect common rules or alter their scope."

Therefore the Constitutional Treaty did not add any new exclusive competence.

24.   C

Shared competencies (Article I-14) are as follows: internal market; social policy, for the aspects defined in Part III; economic, social and territorial cohesion; agriculture and fisheries, excluding the conservation of marine biological resources; environment; consumer protection; transport; trans-European networks; energy; area of freedom, security and justice; common safety concerns in public health matters, for the aspects defined in Part III.

25.   A

Enhanced cooperation (Article I-44) may take place in all non-exclusive areas, i.e. areas of shared competence and of supporting, coordinating or complementary action.

26.   A

Article I-18 of the Constitutional Treaty is entitled "Flexibility clause".

27.   A

Paragraph (1) of the above article provides:

"If action by the Union should prove necessary, within the framework of the policies defined in Part III, to attain one of the objectives set out in the Constitution, and the Constitution has not provided the necessary powers, the Council of Ministers,

acting unanimously on a proposal from the European Commission and after obtaining the consent of the European Parliament, shall adopt the appropriate measures."

28.   C

Before the Constitutional Treaty, the European Parliament had to have an absolute majority on such issues.

29.   D

The Union negotiates a withdrawal agreement with the Member State in question, which sets out the arrangements for its withdrawal and regulates the future relationship between this State and the Union. The Council of Ministers concludes this agreement on the part of the Union, acting by a qualified majority, and after obtaining the consent of the European Parliament. Note that the representative of the withdrawing Member State may not participate in the discussions or in the vote at the Council.

30.   B

Community legal acts will be: law, framework law, regulation, decision, recommendation and opinion. For further information on this issue, please refer to the section on the Court case law and Community legal order.

31.   D

Article I-36 of the Constitutional Treaty provides: "Delegated European regulations

1. European laws and framework laws may delegate to the Commission the power to adopt delegated European regulations to supplement or amend certain non-essential elements of the law or framework law. The objectives, content, scope and duration of the delegation of power shall be explicitly defined in the European laws and framework laws. The essential elements of an area shall be reserved for the European law or framework law

and accordingly shall not be the subject of a delegation of power.

2. European laws and framework laws shall explicitly lay down the conditions to which the delegation is subject; these conditions may be as follows:

(a) the European Parliament or the Council may decide to revoke the delegation;

(b) the delegated European regulation may enter into force only if no objection has been expressed by the European Parliament or the Council within a period set by the European law or framework law.

For the purposes of (a) and (b), the European Parliament shall act by a majority of its component members, and the Council by a qualified majority."

32.   A

Article I-41(6) of the Constitutional Treaty provides:

"European decisions relating to the common foreign and security policy shall be adopted by the European Council and the Council unanimously, except in the cases referred to in Part III. The European Council and the Council shall act on an initiative from a Member State, on a proposal from the Union Minister for Foreign Affairs or on a proposal from that Minister with the Commission's support. European laws and framework laws shall be excluded."

33.   D

Article I-42(1) of the Constitutional Treaty provides:
"The Union shall constitute an area of freedom, security and justice:

(a) by adopting European laws and framework laws intended, where necessary, to approximate laws and regulations of the Member States in the areas referred to in Part III (..)"

34.   C

Article I-43(1) of the Constitutional Treaty provides:
"The Union and its Member States shall act jointly in a spirit of solidarity if a Member State is the object of a terrorist attack or the victim of a natural or manmade disaster. The Union shall mobilise all the

instruments at its disposal, including the military resources made available by the Member States, to:

–   prevent the terrorist threat in the territory of the Member States;

–   protect democratic institutions and the civilian population from any terrorist attack;

–   assist a Member State in its territory, at the request of its political authorities, in the event of a terrorist attack".

35.   B

Article I-45 of the Constitutional Treaty provides:
"The principle of democratic equality.

In all its activities, the Union shall observe the principle of the equality of its citizens, who shall receive equal attention from its institutions, bodies, offices and agencies."

36.   A

Article I-46 of the Constitutional Treaty provides:
"The principle of representative democracy

1. The functioning of the Union shall be founded on representative democracy.

2. Citizens are directly represented at Union level in the European Parliament. Member States are represented in the European Council by their Heads of State or Government and in the Council by their governments, themselves democratically accountable either to their national Parliaments, or to their citizens.

3. Every citizen shall have the right to participate in the democratic life of the Union. Decisions shall be taken as openly and as closely as possible to the citizen.

4. Political parties at European level contribute to forming European political awareness and to expressing the will of citizens of the Union."

37.   C

Article I-47 of the Constitutional Treaty provides:
"The principle of participatory democracy

1. The institutions shall, by appropriate means, give citizens and representative associations the

opportunity to make known and publicly exchange their views in all areas of Union action.

2. The institutions shall maintain an open, transparent and regular dialogue with representative associations and civil society.

3. The Commission shall carry out broad consultations with parties concerned in order to ensure that the Union's actions are coherent and transparent.

4. Not less than one million citizens who are nationals of a significant number of Member States may take the initiative of inviting the Commission, within the framework of its powers, to submit any appropriate proposal on matters where citizens consider that a legal act of the Union is required for the purpose of implementing the Constitution. European laws shall determine the provisions for the procedures and conditions required for such a citizens' initiative, including the minimum number of Member States from which such citizens must come."

38.   A

See answer 37.

39.   B

Second paragraph of Article I-48 of the Constitutional Treaty provides:

"The Tripartite Social Summit for Growth and Employment shall contribute to social dialogue."

40.   A

Article I-50 of the Constitutional Treaty provides: "The European Parliament shall meet in public, as shall the Council when considering and voting on a draft legislative act."

41.   A

Article I-52 of the Constitutional Treaty provides: "Status of churches and non-confessional organisations

1. The Union respects and does not prejudice the status under national law of churches and religious associations or communities in the Member States.

2. The Union equally respects the status under national law of philosophical and non-confessional organisations.

3. Recognising their identity and their specific contribution, the Union shall maintain an open, transparent and regular dialogue with these churches and organisations."

42.   D

The Constitutional Treaty amends the basic institutional structure of the European Union, which currently is made up of five institutions (European Parliament, Council of Ministers, Commission, Court of Justice and Court of Auditors), and four other important bodies (European Economic and Social Committee, Committee of the Regions, European Central Bank and European Investment Bank).

Article I-19 of the Constitutional Treaty provides that the institutional framework comprises: the European Parliament, the European Council, the Council of Ministers, the European Commission and the Court of Justice.

The European Council is therefore recognised as a fully-fledged institution, but the Court of Auditors has been excluded from the basic institutional framework. However, it is mentioned separately in Chapter II of Title IV, the latter being entitled "Other institutions and bodies", as is the European Central Bank (ECB), which is given the status of an institution. This new presentation, in two separate chapters, suggests that alongside the five main institutions (European Parliament, European Council, Council of Ministers, European Commission and Court of Justice) there are two "secondary institutions" (Court of Auditors and European Central Bank).

43.   C

According to Article III-386 and III-390, Members of the two advisory bodies shall be appointed for a period of five years. This is a change to the current situation when the term of office is four years.

44. D

Article III-357 of the Constitutional Treaty provides:

"A panel shall be set up in order to give an opinion on candidates' suitability to perform the duties of Judge and Advocate-General of the Court of Justice and the General Court before the governments of the Member States make the appointments referred to in Articles III-355 and III-356. The panel shall comprise seven persons chosen from among former members of the Court of Justice and the General Court, members of national supreme courts and lawyers of recognised competence, one of whom shall be proposed by the European Parliament. The Council shall adopt a European decision establishing the panel's operating rules and a European decision appointing its members. It shall act on the initiative of the President of the Court of Justice. "

For further and more detailed questions on the Community legal system and the changes in the Court's institutional setup, please refer to the relevant section in the book.

45. C

Second paragraph of Article III-392 of the Constitutional Treaty provides:

"The European Parliament, the Council or the Commission shall, if it considers it necessary, set the [Economic and Social] Committee, for the submission of its opinion, a time-limit which shall not be less than one month from the date on which the chairman receives notification to this effect. Upon expiry of the time-limit, the absence of an opinion shall not prevent further action."

46. D

Article III-396 of the Constitutional Treaty sets out the rules for the "ordinary legislative procedure", currently known as the "codecision procedure".

47. D

The Constitutional Treaty extends the qualified

majority vote to approximately 20 provisions. In many cases, this goes together with the application of the ordinary legislative procedure.

Internal market: questions concerning the freedom of movement for workers, freedom of establishment as regards taking up and pursuing activities as self-employed persons; measures relating to administrative cooperation or to combating tax fraud and tax evasion in the field of indirect taxes may be adopted by qualified majority, after the Council of Ministers has taken a unanimous decision.

Economic and monetary policy: to confer specific tasks upon the European Central Bank (ECB), notably as regards the prudential supervision of credit institutions; certain provisions of the statute of the European System of Central Banks (ESCB) and the ECB may be amended by law, which implies the qualified majority vote.

Cohesion policy: a law shall define the tasks, objectives and organisation of the structural funds, but application of the qualified majority vote will be postponed until 1 January 2007, i.e. the next planning period from 2007 to 2013 will still be adopted on a unanimous basis.

Transport policy: implementation of the common transport policy.

Area of freedom, security and justice: ensuring administrative cooperation between the relevant departments of the Member States and between those departments and the Commission; the Union's policy with regard to border checks; common policy on asylum and temporary protection; measures with a view to developing a common immigration policy (one exception: Member States will retain the right to determine volumes of admission of third country nationals coming from third countries to their territory in order to seek work); judicial cooperation in criminal matters; minimum rules concerning the definition of criminal offences and sanctions; measures to promote crime prevention; the structure, workings, scope of action and tasks of Eurojust; non-operational police cooperation (unanimous vote in case of measures concerning operational cooperation between the authorities referred to in that article); Europol's structure, operation, field of action and tasks.

Culture: incentive actions (excluding any harmonisation of the laws and regulations).

Common foreign and security policy (CFSP): decisions on Union actions or positions, decisions taken on a proposal made by the Minister of External Affairs; decisions implementing a Union action or position; decisions concerning the appointment of a special representative; a "bridge" clause makes it possible to extend the qualified majority vote to other, supplementary cases.

Common defence and security policy: creation of a European Armaments Agency, its statute, seat and operational rules.

Unanimity is kept totally or partly on: non-discrimination and citizenship, taxation, social policy, most decisions concerning common external and Community policy, certain provisions concerning immigration and the conclusion of international trade agreements.

(*ScadPlus*)

48.   B

See answer 47.

49.   A

See Articles III-402 – 412 of the Constitutional Treaty.

50.   D

According to Article I-20 of the Constitutional Treaty:

"The European Parliament shall be composed of representatives of the Union's citizens. They shall not exceed seven hundred and fifty in number. Representation of citizens shall be degressively proportional, with a minimum threshold of six members per Member State. No Member State shall be allocated more than ninety-six seats."

51.   A

Article III-333 of the Constitutional Treaty provides:

"In the course of its duties, the European Parliament may, at the request of a quarter of its component Members, set up a temporary Committee of Inquiry to investigate, without prejudice to the powers conferred by the Constitution on other institutions or bodies, alleged contraventions or maladministration in the implementation of

Union law, except where the alleged facts are being examined before a court and while the case is still subject to legal proceedings.

The temporary Committee of Inquiry shall cease to exist on submission of its report.

A European law of the European Parliament shall lay down the detailed provisions governing the exercise of the right of inquiry. The European Parliament shall act on its own initiative after obtaining the consent of the Council and of the Commission."

52.   C

Article I-21(3) of the Constitutional Treaty provides:

"The European Council shall meet quarterly, convened by its President. When the agenda so requires, the members of the European Council may decide each to be assisted by a minister and, in the case of the President of the Commission, by a member of the Commission. When the situation so requires, the President shall convene a special meeting of the European Council."

53.   B

Article I-22(1) of the Constitutional Treaty provides:

"The European Council shall elect its President, by a qualified majority, for a term of two and a half years, renewable once. In the event of an impediment or serious misconduct, the European Council can end his or her term of office in accordance with the same procedure."

54.   D

Article I-22(2) of the Constitutional Treaty provides:
"The President of the European Council:
(a)   shall chair it and drive forward its work;
(b)   shall ensure the preparation and continuity of the work of the European Council in cooperation with the President of the Commission, and on the basis of the work of the General Affairs Council;
(c)   shall endeavour to facilitate cohesion and consensus within the European Council;
(d)   shall present a report to the European

Parliament after each of the meetings of the European Council.

The President of the European Council shall, at his or her level and in that capacity, ensure the external representation of the Union on issues concerning its common foreign and security policy, without prejudice to the powers of the Union Minister for Foreign Affairs."

55. A

56. C

Article I-25 of the Constitutional Treaty provides:

"1. A qualified majority shall be defined as at least 55% of the members of the Council, comprising at least fifteen of them and representing Member States comprising at least 65% of the population of the Union.

A blocking minority must include at least four Council members, failing which the qualified majority shall be deemed attained.

2. By way of derogation from paragraph 1, when the Council does not act on a proposal from the Commission or from the Union Minister for Foreign Affairs, the qualified majority shall be defined as at least 72% of the members of the Council, representing Member States comprising at least 65% of the population of the Union.

3. Paragraphs 1 and 2 shall apply to the European Council when it is acting by a qualified majority.

4. Within the European Council, its President and the President of the Commission shall not take part in the vote."

57. B

See answer 56.

58. D

Article I-24(7) of the Constitutional Treaty provides:

"The Presidency of Council configurations, other than that of Foreign Affairs, shall be held by Member State representatives in the Council on the basis of equal rotation, in accordance with the conditions established by a European decision of the European Council. The European Council shall act by a qualified majority."

59. D

Article I-26(6) of the Constitutional Treaty provides:

"The first Commission appointed under the provisions of the Constitution shall consist of one national of each Member State, including its President and the Union Minister for Foreign Affairs who shall be one of its Vice-Presidents."

60. D

Article I-26(7) of the Constitutional Treaty provides:

"As from the end of the term of office of the Commission referred to in paragraph 5 [above], the Commission shall consist of a number of members, including its President and the Union Minister for Foreign Affairs, corresponding to two thirds of the number of Member States, unless the European Council, acting unanimously, decides to alter this number."

61. B

See Article I-27 of the Constitutional Treaty. The Union Minister for Foreign Affairs is not appointed by the Commission President, even though he or she is one of the Vice-Presidents of the Commission. See also answer 63 below.

62. B

Article I-28(2) of the Constitutional Treaty provides:

"The Union Minister for Foreign Affairs shall conduct the Union's common foreign and security policy. He or she shall contribute by his or her proposals to the development of that policy, which he or she shall carry out as mandated by the Council.

The same shall apply to the common security and defence policy."

63.   B

Article I-28(1) of the Constitutional Treaty provides:

"The European Council, acting by a qualified majority, with the agreement of the President of the Commission, shall appoint the Union Minister for Foreign Affairs. […]"

64.   C

Article III-296(3) of the Constitutional Treaty provides:

"In fulfilling his or her mandate, the Union Minister for Foreign Affairs shall be assisted by a European External Action Service. This service shall work in cooperation with the diplomatic services of the Member States and shall comprise officials from relevant departments of the General Secretariat of the Council and of the Commission as well as staff seconded from national diplomatic services of the Member States. The organisation and functioning of the European External Action Service shall be established by a European decision of the Council. The Council shall act on a proposal from the Union Minister for Foreign Affairs after consulting the European Parliament and after obtaining the consent of the Commission."

65.   A

The Protocol on the Role of National Parliaments, annexed to the Constitutional Treaty, provides that Commission consultation documents (green and white papers and communications) shall be forwarded directly by the Commission to national Parliaments upon publication. The Commission shall also forward the annual legislative programme as well as any other instrument of legislative planning or policy to national Parliaments, at the same time as to the European Parliament and the Council.

66.   D

Article 2 of the above-mentioned Protocol provides:

"Draft European legislative acts sent to the European Parliament and to the Council shall be forwarded to national Parliaments.

For the purposes of this Protocol, 'draft European legislative acts' shall mean proposals from the Commission, initiatives from a group of Member States, initiatives from the European Parliament, requests from the Court of Justice, recommendations from the European Central Bank and requests from the European Investment Bank for the adoption of a European legislative act. […]"

67.   A

Article IV-444 of the Constitutional Treaty, entitled "Simplified revision procedure", provides:

"1. Where Part III provides for the Council to act by unanimity in a given area or case, the European Council may adopt a European decision authorising the Council to act by a qualified majority in that area or in that case.

This paragraph shall not apply to decisions with military implications or those in the area of defence.

2. Where Part III provides for European laws and framework laws to be adopted by the Council in accordance with a special legislative procedure, the European Council may adopt a European decision allowing for the adoption of such European laws or framework laws in accordance with the ordinary legislative procedure.

3. Any initiative taken by the European Council on the basis of paragraphs 1 or 2 shall be notified to the national Parliaments. If a national Parliament makes known its opposition within six months of the date of such notification, the European decision referred to in paragraphs 1 or 2 shall not be adopted. In the absence of opposition, the European Council may adopt the decision.

For the adoption of the European decisions referred to in paragraphs 1 and 2, the European Council shall act by unanimity after obtaining the consent of the European Parliament, which shall be given by a majority of its component members."

68.   D

Apart from the above-mentioned provisions, Article IV-445 of the Constitutional Treaty, entitled "Simplified revision procedure concerning internal Union policies and action", provides:

"1. The Government of any Member State, the European Parliament or the Commission may submit to the European Council proposals for revising all or part of the provisions of Title III of Part III on the internal policies and action of the Union.

2. The European Council may adopt a European decision amending all or part of the provisions of Title III of Part III. The European Council shall act by unanimity after consulting the European Parliament and the Commission, and the European Central Bank in the case of institutional changes in the monetary area. Such a European decision shall not come into force until it has been approved by the Member States in accordance with their respective constitutional requirements.

3. The European decision referred to in paragraph 2 shall not increase the competences conferred on the Union in this Treaty."

69.   A

70.   D

The second and third paragraphs of Article 4 of the Protocol on the Role of National Parliaments provide:

"Each national Parliament shall have two votes, shared out on the basis of the national Parliamentary system. In the case of a bicameral Parliamentary system, each of the two chambers shall have one vote.

Where reasoned opinions on a draft European legislative act's non-compliance with the principle of subsidiarity represent at least one third of all the votes allocated to the national Parliaments in accordance with the second paragraph, the draft must be reviewed. This threshold shall be a quarter in the case of a draft European legislative act submitted on the basis of Article III–264 of the Constitution on the area of freedom, security and justice."

71.   B

72.   B

With regard to measures needed to combat discrimination, the first paragraph of Article III-124 provides that laws of the Council of Ministers must obtain the prior consent of the European Parliament. The EC Treaty only provides for consultation.

The second paragraph of Article III-124 extends the powers of the Union to the definition of the basic principles on which incentive measures may be adopted.

Second paragraph of Article III-125 extends Union powers to areas previously excluded by the Treaty of Nice, including measures concerning passports, identity cards, residence permits or any other such documents and measures concerning social security or social protection. Laws in this field will be adopted by the Council of Ministers acting unanimously after consulting the European Parliament.

Even though Article III-127 provides that "Member States shall adopt the necessary provisions to secure diplomatic and consular protection of citizens of the Union in third countries", a new legal basis enables the Council to lay down the necessary provisions to *facilitate* diplomatic and consular protection of citizens of the Union. Under the terms of the EC Treaty it is only for the Member States to establish such measures, via traditional agreement-type instruments.

73.   C

The legal basis (Article III-136 of the Constitutional Treaty) facilitating freedom of movement via the coordination of national laws and regulations in the field of social security benefits is extended to cover not only employees but also self-employed workers. Unanimous voting is replaced by qualified majority voting. However, this legal basis cannot be used to adopt provisions applicable to other categories of European citizens (e.g. pensioners or students). Recourse to the flexibility clause – and therefore to unanimous voting in the Council – will remain necessary in these cases.

74.   A

Article III-176 of the Constitutional Treaty provides:

"In the context of the establishment and functioning of the internal market, European laws or framework laws shall establish measures for the creation of European intellectual property rights to provide uniform intellectual property rights protection throughout the Union and for the setting up of centralised, Union-wide authorisation, coordination and supervision arrangements. A European law of the Council shall establish language arrangements for the European intellectual property rights. The Council shall act unanimously after consulting the European Parliament."

75.   D

In Article III-248, promoting cross-border cooperation between researchers has been added.

Article III-250 provides that the Commission shall encourage cooperation between Member States in the field of research and technological cooperation. It has been added that the Commission's action may take the form of initiatives particular to the *open method of coordination* (establishment of guidelines and indicators, organisation of exchange of best practice, periodic monitoring and evaluation). It is also provided that the European Parliament be kept informed.

76.   A

Article III-254 of the Constitutional Treaty provides:

"To promote scientific and technical progress, industrial competitiveness and the implementation of its policies, the Union shall draw up a European space policy. To this end, it may promote joint initiatives, support research and technological development and coordinate the efforts needed for the exploration and exploitation of space.

2. To contribute to attaining the objectives referred to in paragraph 1, European laws or framework laws shall establish the necessary measures, which may take the form of a European space programme.

3. The Union shall establish any appropriate relations with the European Space Agency."

77.   D

See answer 75 above.

78.   D

The Open Method of Coordination is used in the following areas: Article III-213 (social policy in some special fields), Article III-250 (research and development), Article III-278 (public health), Article III-279 (industrial policy).

79.   A

For a comprehensive list of new legal bases, visit: *http://europa.eu.int/scadplus/european_convention/internalpolicies_en.htm* (Note however that references to the draft Constitutional Treaty's article numbers are not correct on this website, due to the renumbering of the final text.)

80.   B

See Articles III-178 to III-184 of the Constitutional Treaty. Regarding qualified majority voting, the second paragraph of Article III-179(4) provides:

"Within the scope of this paragraph, the Council shall act without taking into account the vote of the member of the Council representing the Member State concerned.

A qualified majority shall be defined as at least 55% of the other members of the Council, representing Member States comprising at least 65% of the population of the participating Member States.

A blocking minority must include at least the minimum number of these other Council members representing more than 35% of the population of the participating Member States, plus one member, failing which the qualified majority shall be deemed attained."

81.   B

See Article III-196 of the Constitutional Treaty.

82.   A

Article III-197 of the Constitutional Treaty provides :
"Member States in respect of which the Council has not decided that they fulfil the necessary conditions for the adoption of the euro shall hereinafter be referred to as Member States with a derogation".

83.   C

The first paragraph of Article III-271 of the Constitutional Treaty provides:
"European framework laws may establish minimum rules concerning the definition of criminal offences and sanctions in the areas of particularly serious crime with a cross-border dimension resulting from the nature or impact of such offences or from a special need to combat them on a common basis.

These areas of crime are the following: terrorism, trafficking in human beings and sexual exploitation of women and children, illicit drug trafficking, illicit arms trafficking, money laundering, corruption, counterfeiting of means of payment, computer crime and organised crime.

On the basis of developments in crime, the Council may adopt a European decision identifying other areas of crime that meet the criteria specified in this paragraph. It shall act unanimously after obtaining the consent of the European Parliament."

84.   B

Article III-274(1) of the Constitutional Treaty provides:
"In order to combat crimes affecting the financial interests of the Union, a European law of the Council may establish a European Public Prosecutor's Office from Eurojust. The Council shall act unanimously after obtaining the consent of the European Parliament."

For further questions on the area of freedom, security and justice, please refer to the relevant section of this book.

85.   C

86.   D

The concept of "implied external powers", articulated by Court jurisprudence, now appears in Article III-323(1) of the Constitutional Treaty as follows:
"The Union may conclude an agreement with one or more third countries or international organisations where the Constitution so provides or where the conclusion of an agreement is necessary in order to achieve, within the framework of the Union's policies, one of the objectives referred to in the Constitution, or is provided for in a legally binding Union act or is likely to affect common rules or alter their scope."

87.   C

Article I-40(4) of the Constitutional Treaty provides:
"The common foreign and security policy shall be put into effect by the Union Minister for Foreign Affairs and by the Member States, using national and Union resources."

88.   D

See Article III-293(2) of the Constitutional Treaty provides:
"The Union Minister for Foreign Affairs, for the area of common foreign and security policy, and the Commission, for other areas of external action, may submit joint proposals to the Council."

89.   A

Article III-294(3) of the Constitutional Treaty provides:
"The Union shall conduct the common foreign and security policy by:
(a)   defining the general guidelines;
(b)   adopting European decisions defining:
     (i)   actions to be undertaken by the Union;

(ii)   positions to be taken by the Union;
(iii) arrangements for the implementation of the European decisions referred to in points (i) and (ii);
(c) strengthening systematic cooperation between Member States in the conduct of policy."

90.   B

First paragraph of Article I-59(1) of the Constitutional Treaty provides:

"On the reasoned initiative of one third of the Member States or the reasoned initiative of the European Parliament or on a proposal from the Commission, the Council may adopt a European decision determining that there is a clear risk of a serious breach by a Member State of the values referred to in Article I-2.

The Council shall act by a majority of four fifths of its members after obtaining the consent of the European Parliament."

91.   A

Second paragraph of Article I-59(5) of the Constitutional Treaty provides:

"For the adoption of the European decisions referred to in paragraphs 3 and 4, a qualified majority shall be defined as at least 72% of the members of the Council, representing the participating Member States, comprising at least 65% of the population of these States."

92.   C

Article I-60 of the Constitutional Treaty, entitled "Voluntary withdrawal from the Union", provides:

"1. Any Member State may decide to withdraw from the Union in accordance with its own constitutional requirements.

2. A Member State which decides to withdraw shall notify the European Council of its intention. In the light of the guidelines provided by the European Council, the Union shall negotiate and conclude an agreement with that State, setting out the arrangements for its withdrawal, taking account of the framework for its future relationship

with the Union. That agreement shall be negotiated in accordance with Article III-325(3). It shall be concluded by the Council, acting by a qualified majority, after obtaining the consent of the European Parliament.

3. The Constitution shall cease to apply to the State in question from the date of entry into force of the withdrawal agreement or, failing that, two years after the notification referred to in paragraph 2, unless the European Council, in agreement with the Member State concerned, unanimously decides to extend this period.

4. For the purposes of paragraphs 2 and 3, the member of the European Council or of the Council representing the withdrawing Member State shall not participate in the discussions of the European Council or Council or in European decisions concerning it.

A qualified majority shall be defined as at least 72% of the members of the Council, representing the participating Member States, comprising at least 65% of the population of these States.

5. If a State which has withdrawn from the Union asks to rejoin, its request shall be subject to the procedure referred to in Article I-58. [Conditions of eligibility and procedure for accession to the Union]"

93.   C

The fourth paragraph of Article I-44(3) of the Constitutional Treaty provides:

"A blocking minority must include at least the minimum number of Council members representing more than 35% of the population of the participating Member States, plus one member, failing which the qualified majority shall be deemed attained."

94.   C

Article 1 of the Protocol amending the Treaty establishing the European Atomic Energy Community, annexed to the Constitutional Treaty, provides:

"This Protocol shall amend the Treaty establishing the European Atomic Energy Community (hereinafter referred to as the 'EAEC Treaty') in its version in force at the time of entry into force of the Treaty establishing a Constitution for Europe."

See also the Protocol on the Acts and Treaties which have supplemented or amended the EC

Treaty and the EU Treaty, annexed to the Constitutional Treaty, enumerating the repealed Acts and Treaties.

95.   B

Concerning the Charter of Fundamental Rights, Article II-112(4) of the Constitutional Treaty provides:

"Insofar as this Charter recognises fundamental rights as they result from the constitutional traditions common to the Member States, those rights shall be interpreted in harmony with those traditions."

96.   D

Article II-114 of the Constitutional Treaty, entitled "Prohibition of abuse of rights" provides:

"Nothing in this Charter shall be interpreted as implying any right to engage in any activity or to perform any act aimed at the destruction of any of the rights and freedoms recognised in this Charter or at their limitation to a greater extent than is provided for herein."

97.   A

Article II-65 of the Constitutional Treaty provides:
"Prohibition of slavery and forced labour
1.   No one shall be held in slavery or servitude.
2.   No one shall be required to perform forced or compulsory labour.

3.   Trafficking in human beings is prohibited."

98.   D

Article II-82 of the Constitutional Treaty, entitled "Cultural, religious and linguistic diversity", provides:

"The Union shall respect cultural, religious and linguistic diversity."

99.   D

Article IV-443(1) of the Constitutional Treaty, entitled "Ordinary revision procedure", provides:

"The government of any Member State, the European Parliament or the Commission may submit to the Council proposals for the amendment of this Treaty. These proposals shall be submitted to the European Council by the Council and the national Parliaments shall be notified."

100.   B

The "Declaration on the ratification of the Treaty establishing a Constitution for Europe" provides:

"The Conference notes that if, two years after the signature of the Treaty establishing a Constitution for Europe, four fifths of the Member States have ratified it and one or more Member States have encountered difficulties in proceeding with ratification, the matter will be referred to the European Council."

VERBAL REASONING

ANSWERS

Question No	A	B	C	D
1.	X			
2.				X
3.		X		
4.		X		
5.		X		
6.		X		
7.				X
8.	X			
9.	X			
10.		X		
11.		X		
12.				X
13.			X	
14.			X	
15.		X		
16.				X
17.				X
18.				X
19.			X	
20.				X
21.			X	
22.	X			
23.				X
24.			X	
25.	X			

Question No	A	B	C	D
26.		X		
27.	X			
28.			X	
29.		X		
30.			X	
31.				X
32.		X		
33.	X			
34.		X		
35.	X			
36.			X	
37.	X			
38.			X	
39.			X	
40.				X
41.				X
42.				X
43.		X		
44.	X			
45.			X	
46.		X		
47.				X
48.				X
49.		X		
50.		X		

NUMERICAL REASONING

ANSWERS

Question No	A	B	C	D
1.	X			
2.				X
3.	X			
4.				X
5.		X		
6.		X		
7.			X	
8.			X	
9.		X		
10.		X		
11.	X			
12.		X		
13.			X	
14.				X
15.	X			
16.		X		
17.			X	
18.				X
19.				X
20.			X	
21.		X		
22.	X			
23.			X	
24.			X	
25.		X		

Question No	A	B	C	D
26.				X
27.			X	
28.				X
29.				X
30.				X
31.				X
32.	X			
33.		X		
34.	X			
35.				X
36.		X		
37.				X
38.		X		
39.			X	
40.			X	
41.		X		
42.				X
43.				X
44.	X			
45.			X	
46.		X		
47.	X			
48.		X		
49.				X
50.				X

The symbols used:

Plus or minus	+ –
Multiplication	*
Division	/

1.   A

Henry's current age is X. Judy's current age is 5X.
In two years, Judy's age will be three times that of
Henry's age, or 5X+2 = (X+2)*3
In six years, Judy will be 5X+6 = (X+6)*2
Either of the above equations will give the value of
X, Henry's current age. Therefore:
5X+6 = 2X + 12
5X = 2X + 6
3X = 6
X = 2
Henry is now 2 years old, therefore Judy is 10. In
seven years, Judy will be 17.

2.   D

As the amoebae split into two and double in
volume every 15 seconds, at the point where the jar
is half full, it only takes another 15 seconds to fill up
the jar completely.

3.   A

The number of variations is as follows:
4*3*2*1 = 24

4.   D

The number of colours (five) plus one glove will
make it certain that there are at least two gloves of
the same colour.

5.   B

Considering that everyone has less than 274 dishes,

and no one has the same number of dishes, there
are 274 variations, plus the possibility of someone
not having any dishes at all. However, as it is said
that no one owns an odd number of dishes, that
halves the number and therefore the correct answer
is 137 plus one, i.e. 138.

6.   B

(1250 + 1915 + 450 + 25 + 875 + 3885) / 6 = 8400 / 6
= 1400

7.   C

(88 – 2) * 8 = 688

8.   C

The travel time and the time difference are both
three hours.

9.   B

Five hours of travelling plus one hour time difference added to the 23:00 p.m. means that the man
will arrive at 5.00 a.m. local time.

10.   B

Bangkok time is 6 hours ahead of Paris, therefore 7
hours ahead of London. At 20.00 p.m. in Bangkok it
is 13.00 p.m. in London. If local time upon arrival is
22:00 p.m., that means the trip took 22 – 13 = 9
hours.

11.   A

A man sleeps 7 hours 5 times a week and 9 hours
twice a week. Therefore:

5 * 7 + 2 * 9 = 35 + 18 = 53 (hours slept in 1 week)

53 * 5 = 265

12.   B

A small office will cost 4 times 125 euros per month and 3 small offices 3 * 4 * 125 euros per month. A large office will cost 7 times 117 euros per month and 2 large offices 2 * 7 * 117 euros per month. The monthly totals multiplied by 4 will give the four month rent total. Therefore:
4 * [(3 * 4 * 125) + (2 * 7 * 117)] = 4 * (1500+1638) = 12,552

13.   C

The area of the bathroom to be covered is
8.5 m* 4.5m = 38.25 m^2
Each tile is 40 cm^2 , or 0.04 m^2. Therefore:
38.25 / 0.04 = 956.25.
The correct answer is 957, the next whole number.

14.   D

Divide 18 litres of beer by 0.25 (the volume of each beer bottle) and 9 litres of wine by 0.75 (the volume of each wine bottle), add all the results plus water, as in: 18 / 0.25 + 9 / 0.75 + 23 = 72 + 12 + 23 = 107

15.   A

If the car spent 45 litres of fuel in 9 hours, it spent on average 5 litres per hour (45 / 9), which we know is the consumption at the speed of 100 km/h; so in 9 hours, without stopping, the car would have covered 900 km (9 * 100).

16.   B

Multiply 1000 euros by 7%:
1000 * 0.07 = 70
Add the interest to the deposit and multiply the total by 7% for the 2nd year's interest:
(1000 + 70) * 0.07 = 74.9

Add the 2nd year interest to the 1st year total and multiply by 7% to get the 3rd year's interest :
(1000 + 70 + 74.9) * 0.07 = 80.143
Add the 1st, 2nd and 3rd year interest:
70 + 75 + 80 = 225

17.   C

The man jogs 5 * 4 = 20 days at 9 km/h, and walks 2 days at 6km/h.
His average for the 4 weeks is therefore:
[(20 * 9) + (2 * 6)] / (20 + 2) = 192 / 22 = 8.7

18.   D

3000 m divided by 35 laps (the length of the pool) equals 85.
However, the swimmer will do only 84 turns as he will not turn at the end of the last lap. Therefore:
(3000 / 35) – 1 = 84

19.   D

The easiest way to answer the equation is to calculate the number of fruits that fit in each jar. Based on the proportions given:
blue jar: 1melon, 2 pears, 4 plums;
green jar: 3 melons, 6 pears, 12 plums;
As 3 melons fit in a red jar, it means its volume is the same as that of a green jar. Therefore:
we need 2 jars for the 6 melons (6 / 3 = 2) and 4 jars for the 48 plums (48 / 12 = 4), making the total of 6.

20.   C

Add the ages and divide by the number of people, as in:
(22 + 25 + 30 + 45 + 48) / 5 = 34

21.   B

Add the hours and divide by the number of weeks, as in:

(14 + 16 + 20 + 15 + 25) / 5 = 18

22.   A

Look at the table without calculating any percentages. 30% of whichever is the largest number will be the largest.

23.   C

Country A population = 5,300,000
The unemployed = 5,300,000 * 2% = 106,000
Country D population = 8,999,000
The unemployed = 8,999,000 * 4% = 359,960
The total unemployed = 465,960

24.   C

Just look at the proportions.
Country A: 30.5 : 5.3 (roughly 30/5)
Country B: 93 : 10.2 (roughly 93/10)
Country C: 90 : 10.2 (roughly 90/10)
Country D: 450 : 8.9 (roughly 450/9)
Country E: 200 : 59 (roughly 20/6)
It is plain from the above that by having the biggest territory and one of the lowest number of inhabitants, Country D has the lowest density of population.

25.   B

Add the inflation rates and divide by the number of countries:
(2.8 + 9.1 + 4.9 + 2 + 1.9) / 5 = 4.14

26.   D

Divide the population of Country E by the total of the populations to get the percentage Country E represents in the total. You can calculate in 100s as in: 59 / (5.3 + 10.2 + 10.2 + 9 + 59) = 59 : 93.7 = 0.63 Approximately 63% of the total population lives in country E.

27.   C

The area ratio is 45 : 9, which equals 5:1.

28.   D

A + B + C = 18,000
As drinks sold are expressed in 00s in the chart,
A = 5,000 + 1,000 + 4,200 = **10,200**
B = 3,000 + X + 2,000 = X + 5,000
C= 800 + 1,000 = **1,800**
10,200 +X + 5,000 + 1,800 = 18,000
X = 18,000 – 10,200 - 5,000 - 1,800 = 1,000
Therefore B = 5,000 + 1,000 = **6,000**
Flavour A sold in the largest and flavour C in the smallest quantity.

29.   D

As X is in answer No. 28.

30.   D

As no figures are given for the price of the soft drinks, the question cannot be answered.

31.   D

Use total totals for A and C from answer 28:
C increase in Aug = 1,800 * 20% = 360
C + Aug increase = 1,800 + 360 = 2,160
Add to that the B total in July (unchanged in August): 2,160 + 6,000 = **8,160**

32.   A

Just look at the table. A 50% increase for Company Z, flavour C would add 5 hundreds of litres, making the total of 15 hundreds.
A 10% decrease in flavour A would deduct 5 hundreds of litres, making the total of 45 hundreds.

Therefore the overall quantity sold from all flavours would remain unchanged.

33. B

Bare copper wire income from export:
8,000 * 2 = 16,000 euros
PTFE wire income from export:
1,000 * 10 = 10,000 euros
The total = 26,000 euros.

34. A

As we are looking for proportions, we can use the figures given in 00s:
Total wire produced = 100 + 150 + 30 + 20 = **300**
Total wire exported = 80 + 90 + 10 + 20 = **200**
Production : export = 300 : 200 = 3 : 2

35. D

PTFE wire profit per metre:
10 – 4 = 6 euros;
Exported quantity: 1,000 m; total profit: **6,000** euros
Gold plated wire profit per metre:
20 – 10 = 10 euros;
Exported quantity: 2,000 m; total profit: **20,000**
Total profit: **26,000** euros

36. B

Bare copper wire profit per metre:
2 – 1 = 1 euro
profit margin = 1/2 = **50%**
Tinned copper wire profit per metre:
3 – 2 = 1 euro
profit margin = 1/3 = **33%**
PTFE wire profit per metre: 6 euros, profit margin = 6/10 = **60%**
Gold plated wire profit per metre: 10 euros, profit margin = 10/20 = **50%**
The lowest profit margin is therefore the one for the tinned copper wire.

37. D

The question refers to "Cable & Cable Ltd.", whereas the table relates to "Wire & Wire Ltd".

38. B

In odd years the income is 20 billion euros, in even years it is 22 billion euros. Considering that 2037 is an odd year, the income is likely to be 20 billion euros.

39. C

Considering that production costs amount to 60% of the income, the profit is 40% of the income. The "aircraft industry" includes airplanes and helicopters. Therefore the total profit in 2003 is
(30 + 20) * 0.4 = 20 billion euros (as figures are in billion euros)

40. C

Cars increase: 2 billion euros
Buses increase: –3 billion euros
Airplanes increase: 10 billion euros
Helicopters increase: –2 billion euros

41. B

Cars: gain of 3bn or 6% (3 / 52 = 0.06)
Buses: no gain in income
Trucks: gain of 2bn or 5% (2 / 44 = 0.05)
Boats: gain of 3bn or 25% (3 / 12 = 0.25)
Airplanes: no gain in income
Helicopters: no gain in income

42. D

The question relates to "production", whereas the table only mentions income. Therefore no answer can be given to this question.

43.   D

Fertility rate equals the number of live births per 1000 population, which is highest in country E.

44.   A

Country B is the only country where the deaths per 1000 population exceed the number of live births per 1000 population.

45.   C

The percentage of those 65 years or older is almost the same in every country, yet the population of country E is significantly higher than any other country's. Therefore it is obviously country E that has the highest number of elderly.

46.   B

Company B received 240 million euros for all juices sold in 2004. Pear juice represented a proportion of that, as in:
19 / (19 + 4 + 37) = 19 / 60
240 * (19 / 60) = (240 / 60) * 19 = 76 million euros

47.   A

Company A: 180 + 200 + 220 = **600**
Company B: 225 + 240 + 210 = **675**
Company C: 280 + 225 + 300 = **805**

48.   B

Company A had an income of 200 million euros from selling 46 million juices, or **4.3** euros per juice on average (as in 200 / 46 = 4.3).
Company B had an income of 240 million euros from selling 60 million juices, at **4** euros per juice on average (as in 240 / 60 = 4).
Company C had an income of 225 million euros from selling 58 million juices, at **3.8** euros per juice on average (as in 225 / 58 = 3.8).

49.   D

You need to find the proportion that the income from oranges represents in the total income of 225 million euros. As the price of each pear is three times the price of a grapefruit (or orange), replace the pears' values with grapefruits' values when adding the quantities sold, as in: 27 + 23 + (3 * 8) = 74 (to get a total of price units, rather than product units).
The oranges' income therefore makes up a 23 : 74 share of the three fruits total income, thus: (225 / 74) * 23 = approximately 3 * 23 = 69.

50.   D

46 = (total of juices sold in 2004, in millions)
46 * 10% = 4.6 (the increase in No. of juices sold from 2003)
46 – 4.6 = **41.4** (total juices sold in 2003)
46 + 46 * 20% (the increase for 2005) = **55.2** (total juices sold in 2005)
180 / 41.4 = 4.3 (price per juice in 2003)
200 / 46 = 4.3 (price per juice in 2004)
220 / 55.2 = 3.9 (price per juice in 2005)

MIXED QUESTIONS

MIXED I
ANSWERS

Question No	A	B	C	D
1.				X
2.		X		
3.		X		
4.			X	
5.	X			
6.	X			
7.				X
8.	X			
9.				X
10.				X
11.				X
12.	X			
13.				X
14.			X	
15.			X	
16.		X		
17.		X		
18.	X			
19.			X	
20.		X		
21.		X		
22.	X			
23.			X	
24.			X	
25.		X		

Question No	A	B	C	D
26.	X			
27.	X			
28.			X	
29.			X	
30.		X		
31.				X
32.	X			
33.				X
34.			X	
35.			X	
36.		X		
37.				X
38.			X	
39.		X		
40.			X	
41.				X
42.			X	
43.		X		
44.	X			
45.	X			
46.	X			
47.			X	
48.	X			
49.				X
50.			X	

MIXED II
ANSWERS

Question No	A	B	C	D
1.				X
2.				X
3.	X			
4.	X			
5.			X	
6.		X		
7.		X		
8.		X		
9.			X	
10.			X	
11.			X	
12.	X			
13.				X
14.			X	
15.	X			
16.				X
17.			X	
18.	X			
19.			X	
20.				X
21.			X	
22.	X			
23.				X
24.		X		
25.	X			

Question No	A	B	C	D
26.				X
27.	X			
28.	X			
29.				X
30.	X			
31.	X			
32.	X			
33.		X		
34.				X
35.	X			
36.		X		
37.		X		
38.		X		
39.			X	
40.				X
41.	X			
42.	X			
43.	X			
44.		X		
45.			X	
46.	X			
47.				X
48.		X		
49.				X
50.				X

MIXED III
ANSWERS

Question No	A	B	C	D
1.			X	
2.		X		
3.			X	
4.				X
5.		X		
6.				X
7.		X		
8.	X			
9.		X		
10.			X	
11.			X	
12.				X
13.	X			
14.			X	
15.		X		
16.	X			
17.	X			
18.		X		
19.				X
20.			X	
21.	X			
22.			X	
23.			X	
24.				X
25.				X

Question No	A	B	C	D
26.	X			
27.				X
28.				X
29.		X		
30.				X
31.	X			
32.		X		
33.		X		
34.	X			
35.			X	
36.		X		
37.				X
38.		X		
39.			X	
40.	X			
41.				X
42.			X	
43.	X			
44.	X			
45.		X		
46.				X
47.			X	
48.		X		
49.			X	
50.	X			